AF606032

ETHICS OF WAR AND PEACE IN IRAN AND SHI‘I ISLAM

MOHAMMAD JAFAR AMIR MAHALLATI

Ethics of War and Peace in Iran and Shi'i Islam

UNIVERSITY OF TORONTO PRESS
Toronto Buffalo London

Toronto Buffalo London
www.utppublishing.com
Printed in Canada

ISBN 978-1-4426-2951-6

Printed on acid-free, 100% post-consumer recycled paper with vegetable-based inks.

Library and Archives Canada Cataloguing in Publication

Mahallati, Mohammad Jafar, 1952–, author
Ethics of war and peace in Iran and Shi'i Islam/Mohammad Jafar Amir Mahallati.

Includes bibliographical references and index.
ISBN 978-1-4426-2951-6 (cloth)

1. War – Moral and ethical aspects – Iran. 2. Peace – Moral and ethical aspects – Iran. 3. War – Religious aspects – Islam. 4. Peace – Religious aspects – Islam. 5. Shīʻah – Iran. 6. Shiites – Iran. 7. Jihad. I. Title.

BP192.7.I68M34 2016 297.8'20955 C2016-902989-1

This book has been published with the help of a grant from the Federation for the Humanities and Social Sciences, through the Awards to Scholarly Publications Program, using funds provided by the Social Sciences and Humanities Research Council of Canada.

University of Toronto Press acknowledges the financial assistance to its publishing program of the Canada Council for the Arts and the Ontario Arts Council, an agency of the Government of Ontario.

Canada Council for the Arts
Conseil des Arts du Canada

Funded by the Government of Canada
Financé par le gouvernement du Canada
Canada

To Amirata

With the hope that he builds on his cultural, moral, and peacemaking heritage

Contents

Preface and Acknowledgments

Rules of engagement, ethics of war, and chivalric codes are all attempts to rein in and regulate what is perhaps the most anarchic and illogical of all human activities: war. From the Crusades and jihads to the *miles christianus* (Christian soldier) and the pious *ghāzī* (Muslim warrior), the great religions of the world have certainly played their parts in propagating and mitigating war. This book is a critical overview of the ethics and theology – both actual and ideal – of war and peace and the way these questions are treated in modern Iran and Twelver-Shi'i Islam.

A considerable literature on the ethics of war has been written in Arabic – and more recently in English – often relying on sources related to traditional jurisprudence and law, and often with a readership limited to experts in those fields. There is, however, no well-known analytical work on this topic that is informed by and influencing the wider public opinion on the ethics of war and peace in Persian-speaking societies. This lacuna is particularly critical as Iran's foreign policy approaches a turning point in its relations with the West and with the United States, in particular.

This book explores the wide spectrum of theoretical approaches and practical attitudes concerning the justifications and causes of war (*jus ad bellum*), the conduct of war (*jus in bello*), and after-war conduct (*post bellum*) in Iranian-Shi'i culture. Two recent historical events, above all others, have tested the traditional Muslim theories and theologies of war and peace: the Iran-Iraq War and the violent events in Iraq and Syria, specifically in areas under Daesh (or what is alternatively, and wrongly, called the Islamic State in Iraq and Syria).[1] In effect, a wide-range of Iranian and Shi'i perspectives, traditions, and scholarships concerning war and peace is presently undergoing serious critical review and conceptual reform in Iran.

Most modern literature and research in these areas focus either on particular examples of jurisprudence or on nonreligious political perspectives (e.g., national interest) within the realm of political philosophy. This monolithic and timeless approach neglects the evidence of regional traditions and innovative thinkers by relying solely on a handful of thoughts made popular, not by merit, but by repetition and claiming exclusive authority over certain realms of thought and policymaking. This book aims to avoid just that.

Presently, an increasing amount of theological and philosophical treatises and writings in Iran address questions related to the ethics of war and peace from various angles, including: Qur'ānic exegesis, hadith collections, jurisprudential discourses, historical narratives, theological treatises, philosophical perspectives, Persian epic literature, and chivalric moral codes. These source works, however, are mostly informed by two interrelated and formative elements of the Iranian identity: the glory of the ancient Iranian Empire and the Shi'i world view. This volume navigates such works in search of new perspectives on the ethics of war and peace established by modern Iran and Twelver-Shi'i Islam, and will focus on recovering and exploring the specific Persian literary works, both classical and modern, that have been most influential in the making of the modern Iranian and Shi'i mindset on the subject matter. By examining the sources and traditions, as well as the historical events, that have shaped and moulded the Iranian identity, this study seeks to understand modern Iranian responses – public, academic, and governmental – to war and peace.

This book is intended for the public, academics, and policymakers whose works are informed by the study of the ethics of war and peace, political philosophy, comparative religion, history, and most fittingly, conflict resolution and peacemaking in international relations.

All transliterations in this book for Arabic terms generally follow the standards of the *International Journal of Middle East Studies*, with the exception of proper Persian names or words, which adhere to the standards of *Encyclopaedia Iranica*. I have chosen to adopt Arabic transliteration for proper names and terms when I refer to traditional sources but will use Persian transliteration when I refer to contemporary figures; this explains why I have used both Muhammad and Mohammad for proper names. Arabic and Persian terms appear in italics, except for terms that are very common in English usage. As for diacritical markings, I have marked only long vowels and *ayn* (') and *hamzah* ('), but use no dots. Transliterated Arabic words in the text do not show the silent ending (*h*). The abbreviation b. is used in names for *Ibn*. All dates, unless specified, are in the Common Era (CE), except when referring to the Arabic *hijri* calendar (AH). For encylopedic entries in the appendixes, I have used both the Common Era and corresponding Arabic *hijri* calendars. Whenever citations from primary and secondary sources are accessible both in Persian and another language (e.g., English or Arabic), I have intentionally chosen texts in Persian to point out their availability for Iranian readers.

I have been thinking and working on this book for many years now. My studies in the field, as well as my direct encounter with the effects of war, have proven to me that it is the most ugly and immoral invention in human history. I spent a decade of my life working with the United Nations to contain the devastating Iran-Iraq War, one of the longest in modern history. I had the honour of contributing to ending this war when I served as Iranian ambassador to the United Nations between 1987–9.

The credit for all the above, if any, goes to the spirits of my mother, Saleheh Mojahed, and my late father, Ayatollah Majdeddin Mahallati, the two paragons of peacemaking in Shiraz (Iran) who have inspired me since my early childhood to look at religion and specifically Islam as a divine-human endeavour to moralize love and friendship.

I owe special appreciation to beacons of knowledge and kindness Olga Davidson, Gregory Nagy, and Mohsen Ashtiani for giving me every encouragement, many insights, and invaluable support from the beginning to the end of this scholarly journey. Eric Ormsby was a great supporter of this work from its inception at McGill University, my alma mater.

I am profoundly indebted to the invaluable critical readings, commentaries, and suggestions for improvement of Andre Poupart, Robert Wisnovsky, and most importantly my erudite colleague at Oberlin College Margaret Kamitsuka. The text benefited from the readings and editorial skills of Stuart Sears, Jaclyn Amber Michael, Sam Feigenbaum, Mana Mostatabi, Willis G. Regier, my erudite cousin Hossein Ebneyousef, and above all Carla DeSantis who did the most difficult part of this work, namely, the proofreading, editing, and making the book readable and print-ready.

I am indebted to all the above and many more friends and family members, especially Hossein, Amineh, and Ahmad Mahallati, and my colleagues at Oberlin College, especially David Kamitsuka, A.G. Miller, and Cindy Chapman, without whose spiritual, intellectual, and institutional support this work would have been impossible.

Douglas Hildebrand of University of Toronto Press was very generous with his time and played an essential role in providing invaluable constructive critique of the manuscript. He was very patient in the process of improvements and revisions. I thoroughly enjoyed his insights and working with him, and I owe him deep gratitude.

l also thank both McGill and Harvard Universities for their friendly faculties and libraries that are very rich in Islamic studies and very helpful in providing easy access to bookshelves.

It is heartening that as l was busy searching through piles of ruins and ashes left from past and present wars and violence, I discovered all the above shining gems of humanity. I intended to research the ethics of war, but more than anything else in the process I learned about the ethics and values of love and friendship.

ETHICS OF WAR AND PEACE
IN IRAN AND SHI'I ISLAM

Introduction

The errors I may make as I write can be corrected without harm to anyone, but those that are made by them [warriors] as they act cannot be known except with the ruins of empire.

– Niccolò Machiavelli[1]

By experts in diplomacy and political science, the patterns found in a Persian rug and their relationships to the Iranian political mentality may go entirely unnoticed. To a given student of Persian art and civilization, however, this relationship may not be strange by any means. On 18 June 1998, the US Secretary of State Madeleine Albright officially stated that she was seeking a road map to amity with Iran.[2] A week later, while participating in a panel at Georgetown University, I had the opportunity to respond to her with the following statement: "Madam Secretary, you have asked for a road map, but you already have it at your feet. Please go to the first carpet shop in your neighbourhood, ask to see a traditional Persian rug, look at its patterns of infinitely interwoven branches of flowers, curves, and colours that have conquered the cosmos of the rug, and right there find a perfect road map for imaginative minds and poetic sentiments of many Iranians." For the people of Iran, Persian rug patterns are artistic expressions of the Iranian deep sentiments and world views. The rug is more than the sum of its threads, much the way a French or Italian chef's dish is more than the sum of its ingredients: it represents the nation's generations of cultural mastery, aspirations, the imagery of gardens in paradise, and a cosmology that is full of curves and flexibilities. Geometric and symmetric shapes with sharp angles and the infinite patterns of flower branches, with no beginning and no ending, express the interplay between notions of justice and bounty, the finite and the infinite. It is *Italian*. It is *French*. It is *Persian*.

In the week after my talk, a *New York Times* editorial advocated lifting sanctions on Persian rugs and handicrafts as a prelude to possible US-Iran rapprochement. In less than a year, sanctions were removed, and the master textiles were once again available to American customers.

A decade and a half later, the Persian rug was again prominent, yet unseen, in the meetings between Iran and six Western countries. In Geneva, on 15 October 2013, the new and articulate foreign minister of Iran, Mohammad Javad Zarif, joined European negotiator Catherine Ashton to conduct the first round of talks aimed at reaching a nuclear agreement between the five permanent members of the UN Security Council (Britain, China, France, Russia, the United States, and Germany). The chief negotiators posed for a photo against the backdrop of a large, elaborate Persian rug spanning the floor of the UN hall. The rug's arabesque motif was woven into a deep blue background that suggested a universe of curves and colours. It was a perfect microcosm for that which the United Nations represents.[3] Unnoticed by the media, the intricate rug presented a striking contrast to the tense negotiations. For the Iranian general public, whose historical self-image stands on grounds of art and literature, the rug also symbolically defied hints of international concerns regarding Iran's intentions in pursuing nuclear arms.

Had the interlocutors been conscious of the rug upon which they sat, they would have felt the irony of the situation. As a representative of a country known in history for her ancient civilization, arts, literature, and fine cuisine, the Iranian foreign minister Zarif was now required to reassure his counterparts that his country had no plans to produce weapons of mass destruction. At the same time, he knew that Iran, caught between revolution, ideology, war, sanctions, and a complex web of international pressure, had rarely missed a chance to give conflicting political signals in her official literature, thereby causing confusion across the globe about her intentions in international relations.

The confusion has multiple sources. Iran's civilizational message to a pluralistic but interconnected world is inscribed in calligraphic words on a Persian rug hanging at the UN headquarters in New York.[4] The poem, composed by Sa'di of Shiraz (d. 1292) and scripted onto the rug, states:

بنی آدم اعضای یکدیگرند　که در آفرینش ز یک گوهرند
چو عضوی به درد آورد روزگار　دگر عضوها را نماند قرار
تو کز محنت دیگران بی غمی　نشاید که نامت نهند آدمی

(Of one essence is the human race,
thusly has creation put the base.
One limb impacted is sufficient,

for all others to feel the mace.
The unconcern'd with others' plight,
are but brutes with human face.)[5]

International readers may recognize these lines and appreciate both its eloquence and meaning. But the message is difficult to reconcile with the image of a political system whose closest friends have been North Korea, Libya, and Syria.

The world remembers well that Iran was the only Muslim nation that sympathetically reacted to the lives lost in New York immediately after the 9/11 tragedy. CNN's Joe Klein reported the following: "On the evening of September 11, 2001, about ten thousand Iranian people gathered in Mādar Square, on the north side of Tehran, in a spontaneous candlelight vigil to express sympathy and support for the American People."[6] It is difficult to reconcile the compassionate and sympathetic Iranian public with images of Iranians marching by the hundreds and burning flags on the anniversary of the seizure of the American Embassy in Tehran on 4 November 1979.[7] Peace activists across the globe are inspired by the great humanist Persian poet Jalal al-Din Rumi who advises against judgmental politics: "Beyond our ideas of right-doing and wrong-doing, there is a field, I'll meet you there."[8] But, again, it is difficult for the world to resolve those words with the fact that, for over three decades since the 1979 Revolution, an important part of the Iranian official stance still represents a world view replete with judgmental, highly sentimental, impulsive, and boringly outdated political jargon.

Of course, official inconsistency is universally a part of *realpolitik*. But a country that has been the cradle of an ancient civilization, and whose fine, transcendent, timeless, and perennial thoughts expressed in the words of Rumi, Sa'di, and Hafez keep captivating imaginations worldwide a millennium after the poets' departure, should have been more articulate in her political expressions and communications.

The best result that the conflicting signals coming from Iranian officials and people could have created would have been ambivalence about Iran's intentions in its regional and international politics. Domestic controversies aside, Iran could still have seemed a lesser security threat against Western interests as compared to the Wahhabi al-Qaida and Taliban fundamentalists in Saudi Arabia, Pakistan, Afghanistan, and all sorts of the regional jihadi-salafis or neo-salafis who have formed the terror entity called Daesh (ISIS) not so long ago.[9] Moreover and by real measures, the hazardous potentials of Iran's conventional arms cannot be compared, by any measure, to the monumental risks of Israel's nuclear arsenal. But Iran's image has been marred by the clumsy political literature emerging from President Ahmadinejad's populist government and his outdated, Cold War-style posturing.

Much like the United States, Iran is deeply a religious country. But her version of Islam has historically been esoteric, mystical, rational, and humanistic rather than legalistic. No scholar would dispute that the greater part of Islamic mystic and gnostic literature originated in Persian language. An average Iranian citizen may be surprised and perplexed to know that the poems of Rumi continue to be on the top American bestseller lists. It behooves the observer to ask why, then, Iranian and American politicians seem unable to understand each other. Is it that they are using the wrong language, or is it that they have lost their ability to listen and learn against their mutual prejudgments, misperceptions, and misgivings?

The Entanglement of Sacred History, Revolution, Ideology, and War

Rarely in any religious tradition does history come clean of its use of force under the justification of protecting its values. But as history has progressed, the legitimacy of using force for ideological purposes has become subject to many ethical challenges regarding which values are worth fighting for and to what degree the use of force is legitimate.

The postrevolutionary situation in Iran was complicated. Soon after the 1979 Revolution, Iraq waged a savage war against Iran, deeply affecting a fragile Iranian society still emerging from a regime change. Wars, and specifically defensive war, tend to take the legitimate use of force for granted. At that point, Iran was a culmination of an entangled proselytizing religion, an idealistic revolution, and the pride of a nation now invaded. This combination created a complex matrix of relations between the normative goals of the revolutionary system and the use of force. The religious misconception of the need for sacrifice as a precondition of salvation further complicated the matrix in the Islamic Republic of Iran. As William Frost, a historian notable for his work on the ethics of war in religious cultures, has noted on the interrelationship between the Iran-Iraq War and the revolution in Iran: "The war had succeeded in localizing the Iranian Revolution and the fundamentalist movements today, after financed by Saudi Arabia."[10]

The theology of sacrifice (*self-offering* or *self-giving* as the strongest proof of piety) renders it difficult – and in essence, an irrelevant exercise – in ethically assessing the human toll and material loss. Such ideological desensitization of material, psychological, and social damage, as proven on many occasions in the course of history, has the potential to make a whole nation overlook a large-scale fratricide. As a result, Frost states, Iran had a "spiritual fervor

[that] sustained the war for eight years, but any heritage of Shiite unity paled against a tradition of ethnic rivalries and the ability of Saddam Hussein to sanctify his country's nationalism as a defense of Islam."[11] The prolongation of the Iran-Iraq War kept the revolutionary zeal in Iran alive, and these two factors fuelled each other far beyond the war's natural time-span. For eight long years, it became harder and harder to stop a war that had become, in the view of warriors, an effective litmus test to measure religious and revolutionary fidelity and piety.

Iraq's invasion of Iran in September 1980 revived the image of a tragic war in Karbalā (a city in Iraq), where, in 680, an Umayyad caliph named Yazīd b. Mu'awīya (d. 683) martyred the third Shi'a imam and the grandson of the prophet Muhammad (Husayn b. 'Alī), as well as a small number of his companions and family members. The annual commemoration of this tragedy soon became, and remains to be, an important part of the Shi'i identity and piety. In September 1980, after exactly thirteen centuries, Iranians witnessed an attack on their country that was under the leadership of Imam Husayn's descendant, Ayatollah Khomeini, possessing a genealogy connected to the martyred Imam. Such historic reincarnation of a tragedy, in a society as sensitive to its civilizational and sacred histories as Iran, could easily trigger a theology of war and retaliation nearly impossible to alter. The revival of public urges for revenge against Yazīd's political heirs – which had long lain dormant – were now inevitable.

For Western readers, this may sound strange. Why would Shi'as maintain this grudge for thirteen centuries? Beyond its theological borders, and within the broader Iranian national and cultural identity, the Karbalā catastrophe has become an important source of national political literature. During the Iranian Revolution, the public passion resulting from the mourning festival of 'Āshūrā (tenth of Muharram, the Arabic calendar day when al-Husayn was martyred) was effectively used to topple the previous Iranian regime. An Iranian, therefore, does not need to be deeply religious to be emotionally provoked by hints of the Karbalā incident. Thus, the 1980 invasion prompted all Iranians, religious or not, to exclaim: "Oh no! Not again!"

Seemingly an unresolvable paradox, the Iraqi soldiers who had invaded Iran were predominantly of a Shi'i background, as Iraq is a majority Shi'a country. Iranian soldiers now faced a violent conflict not only with Muslims but specifically with Shi'a Muslims. The puzzle became perfectly complicated when Saddam Hussein, who considered himself a hero of pan-Arabism, coined his invasion of Iran "the Second Qādisīya" (the first being when the Sassanian Empire was defeated by Muslim Arabs in 650). This war of slogans was intended to add insult to injury, as it struck a dissonant chord with Iran's nationalistic pride. Combined, the revolution, the war, the clash of theologies, the reappearance of an old epic battle, the encounter of nationalisms, the profitable arms sales in the region by Western powers, and the United Nations' biased tilt towards Iraq created a perpetual and seemingly unstoppable war machine.

When the war ultimately ended in August 1988, it did not bring with it an immediate nationwide sense of relief. Rather, the nation collectively felt an unbelievable and unexpected shock resulting from an eight-year war that ultimately resulted in no punishment of the invader Saddam Hussein and no remarkable military victory for Iran. The end of war provoked theological and sentimental sets of questions about the relationship between the theology of sacrifice, the fate of justice, the ethics of war and peace, and requirements of faith.

Twenty-five years later, Iran continues to struggle with unsettled war-related issues and unanswered questions, the most recent of which was the nuclear crisis. Iran's endeavour to acquire nuclear technology has the West interpreting the effort as one to acquire nuclear weapons. The result of this ongoing saga was the unprecedented universal economic sanctions suffocating the Iranian economy. While the Iran-Iraq War technically ended in 1988, it still continues in a myriad of other forms for a great number of Iranians.

Perhaps the only positive outcome of the confrontation between Iran and Iraq is that the direct involvement of the Iranian religious elite in war and peace decision making prompted a critical review and reform of the Shi'i's traditional positions on theology, jurisprudence, and the ethics of war and peace.

In other Muslim countries, such as post-Arab Spring Egypt, the entanglement of religion and state politics did not lead to lasting positive results. In Iran, however, the interaction of the two has, for more than three decades, produced a new generation of scholars of religion who have struggled to bridge the gap between the principles of faith and the practicalities of modern life.[12] It is worth noting that the sustainable process of reform within any tradition requires direct social and political engagement between its leaders and believers. The very dynamic process of Iranian-Shi'i scholarly criticism of the ethics of war and peace, as reflected in this book, stands as an important witness to the above.

Goals of the Enquiry and the Binary Source of the Iranian Ethics of War and Peace

For the Western readers of the modern history of the ethics of war and peace, a major question remains as to whether the behaviour and political posture of both modern Iran and Shi'a theology in relation to war and peace have been circumstantial or related to more permanent characteristics of these cultural entities. For Iranians, as well as for Shi'a and Muslim scholars, the additional question is whether a modern experiences of revolution, war, and theocracy have instigated a critical scholarship regarding traditional perspectives on war and peace.

Thirty-five years after the Iraqi invasion of Iran began in September 1980, the only recognized theocracy in the world continues to struggle with war-related moral and policy dilemmas, the most recent of which is the nuclear crisis. The eight-years long and tragic war with Saddam and the unprecedented scale of anti-Shi'a war crimes by Daesh (ISIS), acting in Iran's neighbouring Iraqi and Syrian territories, mark both sides of the Islamic Republic's entanglement with ethics of war in her short history.

The advent of the 1979 Revolution in Iran signalled a turning point in the history of Shi'i political quietism. Close to four decades of ruling over a strategically important country in the Middle East forced the Iranian-Shi'i clerics to shift their focus from scholastic scholarship to policymaking in all fields of day-to-day life, including war and peace. One result was that much of the outdated moral and jurisprudential positions and theologies, stipulated in traditional sources of seminarian studies, received monumental challenges for revision. The war-and-sanction-stricken turbulent history of the Islamic Republic made such revisions in the Shi'i laws and ethics of war more urgent than in many other fields of scholarship. This book is a report about such revisions.

The direct involvement of the Iranian clerics in war and peace management and decision making has subjected traditional theologies and the ethics of war and peace to practical litmus tests. This work explores how the results of the above experiences have instigated theoretical reform processes both within and outside of the Shi'a seminarian circles. The volume provides a critical review of the most significant religious and traditional sources on the ethics of war and peace available in Persian language. Rather than focusing solely on conversations and literature produced by religious scholars, this volume also examines secular and nonjurisprudential literature on the ethics of war and peace that influences and informs large segments of modern Iranian society.

By tying multiple determinants of the ethics of war and peace together with the binary spirit of the Iranian-Shi'i identity and its responses to modernity, this book investigates longer-lasting factors and questions rather than circumstantial ones. Together, these insights will help Western readers and policymakers understand the mindset of the Iranian public, intellectuals, and policymakers on matters related to war and peace.

The overarching thesis of this volume can perhaps be summarized best in the following proposition: a syncretic and civilization-conscious soul in Iran is re-emerging. This volume provides two sets of evidence for its claim: First, modern Iranian intellectuals are shifting gears from ideological conformism to serious critical thinking in the areas of war and peace. As a result, the seminarian jurisprudence in Iran is losing its exclusive claims over normative evaluation of war and peace when other cultural sources such as national epic, mystic, chivalric, and rational philosophic literatures are contributing to the field. Second, the modern Shi'a jurisprudence on the ethics of war and peace is becoming increasingly open to universal wisdom, extrareligious sense of justice, modern philosophy, the etiquettes of chivalry, the politics of forgiveness, theologies of disarmament, and hermeneutics of peace. In other words, an effective practice of *ijtihād* (independent juristic reasoning) is on the rise in modern Shi'i thought on war and peace.

To provide the necessary arguments and evidence for the above thesis, this volume poses a number of questions integral to the understanding of modern Iran and Shi'ism as related to war and peace. For example, what are the most significant ethical norms that inform the Iranian national and collective psyche in the field? What has informed these norms outside strict religious discourse? What are the war-and-peace-related norms specific to Twelver-Shi'a theology as distinct from mainstream Sunni perspectives? What are the nonjurisprudential sources of religious and ethical discourse that influence Iranian views on war and peace? How do traditional Shi'i positions and jurisprudence on war and peace influence the Iranian public, and moreover, how do these positions respond and adjust when faced with the challenges of modernity and national security? How has the Iranian experience with revolution, war, and nuclear issues influenced the Iranian public and seminarian views on war and peace? How do Muslim and Shi'i myths, history, and narratives of war and peace relate to the Iranian-Shi'a normative thinking? And which specific figures and time periods in these histories have provided long-lasting effects? What elements of the Twelver-Shi'a school of law facilitated global conversations with Muslim and non-Muslim faith systems on war and peace? By exploring possible answers to the above, as well as to other questions that may arise, this book aims to facilitate conflict-resolution and peacemaking initiatives beyond the Iranian, Shi'i, and Muslim societies.

My emphasis on Twelver Shi'ism stems from the existence of other schools of Shi'ism, such as Isma'ilis (both Nizārī and Bohra), Zaydīs, and even Alevīs within a broad definition of Shi'ism. Although there are many common factors and perspectives shared between various Shi'i schools, this volume, however, focuses only on Twelver Shi'ism simply because other schools do not exert much influence on the current Iranian mindset. Their ethics, however, substantially sharing many primary sources, deserve independent attention.

Overview of the Content

This volume aims to achieve several goals. First, it provides a critical review of significant Persian language religious and traditional sources on the ethics of war and peace, including nonjurisprudential literature. Second, it reflects on the reform process in the Shi'i's traditional positions on theology and the ethics of war and peace. Third, it endeavours to help Western readers and policymakers understand modern Iran. Finally, it intends to help interfaith and international efforts in peacemaking and conflict resolution to benefit from a greater understanding of cultural nuances beyond the parameters of "liberal peace." The result is a volume that serves several different audiences, including: scholars of Persian language, Iranian studies, humanities, social science, Shi'a studies; and scholars and activists in peacemaking and religious conflict resolution.

Michael Walzer provides two proverbial statements that underscore the broader purposes this volume serves. First he says, "For war is the hardest place: if comprehensive and consistent moral judgments are possible there, they are possible everywhere." Second he asserts, "War strips away our civilized adornments and reveals our nakedness."[13] Accordingly, shedding light on the reformation of Iranian and Shi'i views on war and peace may help reevaluate other annals of life in Iran and Shi'ism.

The book is divided into two parts and nine chapters, excluding introduction and conclusions. Part 1 examines some of the important, nonjuridical Persian language sources that inform and influence the Iranian normative view of war and peace from the country's pre-Islamic period to its present. These sources are not completely independent from Islam or Shi'i influences but are highly connected to the Persian culture (both pre-Islamic and Islamic), language, and identity. Thus, the normative influences of these sources go beyond the Iranian borders and well into all Persianate societies, including Afghanistan, Azerbaijan, Tajikistan, and other Central Asian countries.

Part 2 explores the traditions and reforms in the realm of laws and ethics of war and peace within the seminarian and jurisprudential Twelver-Shi'i (alternatively called Imami Shi'ism) circles in Iran. The influences of such traditions extend beyond the Iranian borders and well into such Shi'i societies as those in Iraq, Azerbaijan, and Lebanon. Together, the two parts of this volume address the normative arguments about war and peace that inform the secular and religious aspects of Persian-Shi'a societies in Iran and beyond.

Chapter 1 provides an overview of the ethics of war and peace in the most important and normatively influential work of epic literature known to the eastern lands of Islam: the *Shahnameh* of Ferdowsi (d. 1020). As one of the greatest sources of Iranian cultural identity for over a millennium, *Shahnameh* (The book of kings) defines normative ideals in the ethics of war and peace within narratives that connect the ancient history of Iran to her mythical eras. What makes the study of ethics of war and peace in *Shahnameh* most relevant to the subject of this volume is its denial of moral authenticity of religious militancy. The *Shahnameh* was well read and considered the normative standard for just monarchs in the royal courts of all three sixteenth-century Muslim empires: the Ottomans, the Safavids, and the Mughals.

Chapter 2 explores, in the light of the interrelationship between ethics and laws of war and peace, the views of a select number of classical Iranian thinkers. The works of these major thinkers, philosophers, mystics, historians, and ethicists remain highly influential in modern Iranian intellectual, philosophical, and political thought. Importantly, to various extents, they still inform part of the Iranian normative and moral identity, specifically in relation to friendship, forgiveness, and the ethos of civic life.

Chapter 3 examines the ethics of war and peace within the Iranian moral system of chivalry. This system, known as *javānmardī* (lit. young manhood, in English; *'ayyarī* in Persian; *futūwwa* in Arabic) deeply influences the Iranian culture and informs codes of behaviour for traditional guilds, professional societies, sports, and specifically Iranian sport clubs called *zurkhaneh*. Standards for *javānmardī* or *futūwwa*, stemming from a fusion of Islamic and pre-Islamic Iranian ethos, have always acted as a moral balancer vis-à-vis strict religious laws. This chapter provides a brief overview of a few real and legendary Iranian-chivalry role models whose legacies are still influential on Iranian ethics of war and peace. The chapter argues that in certain critical instances of their political and intellectual histories, Islamo-Persian institutions acting on ethics of *javānmardī* and *futūwwa* have come close to providing moral solutions and averting excessive hostilities and bloodshed.

Chapter 4, the final chapter in part 1, investigates the views of a select number of influential, contemporary Iranian intellectuals on the ethics of enmity, peace, and nonviolence. The collective views of these intellectuals provide a nonjurisprudential reflection on matters of war and peace and on its philosophical, theological, literary, artistic, and moral aspects. These intellectuals, including scholars, political activists, poets, musicians, and film directors, have produced new discourses and literature of political and moral philosophy that challenge the traditional monopoly of jurisprudence on deciding about the qualities, conditions, and legitimation of war and peace. Through different arguments, these intellectuals continue to remind jurists that valid jurisprudence needs to be based on time-sensitive and solid ethical grounds. Such perspectives, specifically when addressing relationships between faith, the use of force, and nonviolence, hold serious implications for war and peace in theory and practice.

Chapter 5, the first in part 2, studies some of the most significant primary sources and historical narratives that play central roles in forming Twelver-Shi'i views and jurisprudence on war and peace. By examining the details of early Muslim civil wars and their ethics, along with primary Shi'i hadith literature related to war and peace, this chapter explores the reasons for the Shi'i political quietism prevalent in a larger expanse of its history.

Chapter 6 tackles the traditional Shi'i jurisprudence of war and peace through a critical lens. It discusses how centuries of Shi'i political quietism has rendered the Shi'i jurisprudential views on war and peace outdated and somehow irrelevant both to modern international relations and to the extrareligious notion of justice prevalent in early Shi'i theology. The unexpected victory of Iran's 1979 Revolution and, soon after, the outbreak of war with Iraq tested and forced conceptual reforms of many Shi'i views and theories on jihad. This chapter looks specifically at the works of the two highly influential Twelver-Shi'i scholars, Seyyed Hossein Tabātabā'ī and his student Morteẓā Motahharī, on war and peace. It will demonstrate how the semiapologetic views of these scholars on war and peace resulted from a mid-twentieth-century perspectives, a contentious moral matrix composed of historical Shi'i narratives, untested and adopted classical jurisprudence, leftist ideologies, domestic revolution, and forces of modernity. The works of Tabātabā'ī and Motahharī nevertheless provided a fertile intellectual ground for the next generation of Shi'i scholars who launched an effective course of critical jurisprudence on war and peace.

Chapter 7 considers the latest Shi'i critical scholarship on war and peace in Iran and demonstrates how new approaches in these realms effectively transformed modern Shi'i jurisprudence in the related areas of justice at war (*jus ad bellum*), justice in war (*jus in bello*), and justice after war (*post bellum*). Perhaps the most important aspect of this modern jurisprudence is its adaptation to international and interfaith pluralism and human rights, or in short, to exigencies of modernity. This chapter demonstrates how the practice of genuine *ijtihād* (independent juridical reasoning) aimed at transforming the traditional laws of war into a more universally justifiable and objective-based system of ethics is bridging a historic gap between traditional jurisprudence and political philosophy that has continued to exist since the tenth century.

Chapter 8 provides a review of critical modern Shi'i jurisprudence and political philosophy of martyrdom, terrorism, nonviolence, and forgiveness in politics. By comparing these Shi'i views with examples of modern jihadist-salafi theologies, such as those of Daesh, the Taliban, and Boko Haram, that have monumental records of war crimes, this chapter demonstrates how Iranian Shi'i jurists are producing a progressive jurisprudence against the political abuse of martyrdom and for promoting political nonviolence. The chapter shows how the emerging Shi'i *ijtihād* is putting the sanctity of life above martyrdom and justifies martyrdom only as the *last honourable resort* rather than the first in any armed encounter. By developing and promoting the above theologies of forgiveness and nonviolence, the postrevolutionary Iranian scholars seem intent on playing a global role, if not one of leadership, in the delegitimization of suicidal and other sorts of violence.

Chapter 9 discusses how the prolongation of the Iran-Iraq War and the direct involvement of Shi'i jurists in war policymaking led modern religious authorities in Iran to understand the complexities of modern war and peace. Consequently, they are reforming their traditional approaches to the jihad both conceptually and institutionally. This chapter details how Iran's nuclear program, which led to political difficulties in Iran's relations with Western countries, has prompted Twelver-Shi'i jurists both to take clear juristic positions and to issue authoritative edicts (*fatwās*) against the production and the use of weapons of mass destruction (WMDs). Such public positions by contemporary Shi'i authorities seem to bring the ethics and the jurisprudence of war and peace in Twelver Shi'ism to the heart of modern political life and Iran's new civilizational posture.

The volume's conclusions look at some of the significant outcomes of two specific trends of critical treatments and reconstruction of the ethics of war and peace in Iran. The fortunate merge between these intellectual trends hints at the emergence of a cosmopolitanism that is distancing Twelver Shi'ism from minority mentality and theology. It concludes that modern Iranian Shi'ism as an Islamic rationalistic school of law has learned from monumental administrational experiences through revolution and war. As a result, a postrevolutionary Iran seems to be well positioned to act as a sociocultural and political bridge between Muslim and non-Muslim societies.

The volume ends with four appendixes that contain summary translations from the most recent encyclopedic articles on war and peace published in Iran. These articles are published by the *Great Islamic Encyclopedia*, known as the most authoritative encyclopedia on Islam in the Persian language. The first article titled "Jihad" provides a Shi'i overview of the concept of jihad, its epistemological developments, and its use and abuse in Muslim history. The second article titled "Jang" (war; Persian) deals with details of laws and ethics in war (*jus in bello*) according to an Iranian Shi'i perspective. Appendix 3 reflects on Iran's official condemnation of war crimes by Daesh. It provides a prism through which one can compare Shi'i modern scholarly and official positions on war immoralities. Appendix 4 provides the text of the latest authoritative, official manual issued by the Grand Ayatollah Seyyed Alī Sīstānī in Iraq, advising and guiding Shi'i fighters in the battlefields on the etiquette of war conduct. Together, these appendixes provide fresh comparative scholarly and official Shi'i perspectives on the ethics of war and peace.

Some Methodological Considerations

The methodology in this enquiry is primarily inductive, rather than deductive. The theoretical approach, as reflected in various chapters and technical terminologies used in the entire text, is modern. The comparative approach of the book employs, from time to time, nonnormative notions of descriptive ethics, as certain behavioural patterns in wars are considered. The text also deals with categories that correspond to normative teleological ethics, when the consequences of wars are discussed; deontological ethics, when conflicts between certain duties arise; virtue and role ethics, when historical characters are analyzed; and applied ethics, when war is considered as a specific field of human activity. The research is based on a combination of primary and secondary sources.

Given the broad scope of the topic and its varied aspects, choosing only a select group of representative works out of those produced by the many intellectuals in each field was unavoidable. The selections, however, are both character and source driven, based on the specific criteria of the most influential works in each area. The interdisciplinary approach used in this book offers a dimensional alternative to the monolithic approaches, which are all too common in scholarship regarding Islamic countries.

I have dedicated part 1 of the book to nonjuridical reflections on war and peace, primarily because it includes sources connected to pre-Islamic Iranian culture and history. Part 2 is dedicated to juridical discussions, including Shi'i traditions and modern Iranian jurisprudential discourse concerning war and peace. Together, the two parts of the volume reflect on intellectual reforms in ethical thoughts on war and peace outside and inside the Iranian-Shi'i seminarian circles.

My Hope

The great Chinese philosopher Lao-Tzu once said, "I only wished that grown-ups in war were like kids, with no permanent hatred, with utter impatience to resume friendship." The history of the world's civilizations and their relations, however, underscores that, unfortunately, the 'grown-ups' still have a long way to go before reaching a kid's maturity in the realms of peacemaking and the primacy of friendship. However, history is also reflective of many hard and sincere endeavours – on the parts of prophets, philosophers, ethicists, war strategists, artists, poets, and even professional warriors – to contain war tragedies and to find increasingly civilized ways of conflict resolution.

Our world is still engulfed in many wars, some of which, like the current ones in Syria, Iraq, and Palestine/Israel, are ethically worse than caveman or barbaric violence not only because of the scale of human sufferings but also because much of the carnage is justified on account of religion. Under these circumstances, there is an urgent need to explore every intellectual and institutional avenue for peace and nonviolence. It is time to liberate religions from historic abuse. Killing in the name of the Creator has always been one of the most tragic and immoral oxymora of human history. Is there any act more blasphemous than deleting 'mistakes' in God's creativity?

As the seven current wars between Afghanistan and South Sudan (including wars in Yemen, Syria, Iraq, Libya, and Somalia) show many ugly turning points, it is this author's hope that by shedding light on moral grounds and immoral dilemmas related to war and peace, violence and bloodshed may lose religious or any other justifications. The proverbial Qur'ānic phrase *was sulhu khair* (Q. 4:128) denotes the primacy of peace. The resonance of this moral paradigm can be found in thoughts of rare modern politicians and peace activists. Franklin Roosevelt said, "More than just an end to war, we want an end to the beginnings of all wars."[14] Martin Luther King elaborated this aspiration further by saying, "Nonviolence is the answer to the crucial political and moral questions of our time; the need for mankind to overcome oppression and violence without resorting to oppression and violence. Mankind must evolve for all human conflict a method, which rejects revenge, aggression, and retaliation. The foundation of such a method is love."[15] These aspirations best express my better hope as goals for the present volume.

PART I

The Ethics of War and Peace in Iran: Epic Literature, Philosophy, Theology, and Chivalry

Part 1 of this volume looks at some of the important nonjuridical sources of Iranian culture that inform and influence the Iranian normative views of war and peace from the country's pre-Islamic period to its present. These sources are not completely independent from Islam or Twelver-Shi'a perspectives, but are highly connected to the Persian culture, language, and identity in a broader historic and geographical sense. The normative influences of these sources, therefore, go beyond the Iranian proper political borders and well into all Persianate societies, including Azerbaijan, Afghanistan, Tajikistan, and other Central Asian countries.

1 The Ethics of War and Peace in Epic Persian Literature: the *Shahnameh* of Ferdowsi

I believe in the faith of worshiping Mazda
the one who defeats wars and destroys weapons.

– Zoroaster[1]

[2]میاز و مناز و متاز و مرنج   چه تازی بکین و چه نازی به گنج

(Curb your greed, and brag no more,
Forgo all aggression, do not inflict grief
Vain it is to gallop at full speed to settle old scores
Vain it is to gloat over the hoarded treasures [of this transient world]).

– Ferdowsi[3]

On 25 September 2013, newly elected Iranian President Hassan Rouhani, in his first address at the UN General Assembly, focused on the necessity of global peace and emphasized the need for mutual improvement of relations between Iran and Western countries. He tried to alleviate all concerns about the Iranian nuclear program by spending a larger portion of his speech proclaiming Iran's nuclear program had no military purpose and was, in fact, being pursued only for energy. During his address, Rouhani quoted the following line from one of the greatest sources of Iranian cultural identity for over a millennium, namely the *Shahnameh* of Ferdowsi:

بکوشید و خوبی بکار آورید   چو د ید ید سرما بهار آورید

(Be relentless in striving for the cause of good,
Bring the spring, you must, banish the winter, you should.)[4]

In the *Shahnameh* these lines depict a part of the postwar speech delivered by a legendary Iranian role model, King Kaykhosrow, to his victorious army after a battle; he advises them on the ethics of war (*post bellum*). It is significant to note that Rouhani, being a cleric, used epic Persian poetry to address the significance of the ethics of war, instead of referring to a Prophetic hadith that is rich in content on the Islamic laws of war. His choice of referencing epic Persian poetry speaks volumes about how the new generation of Iranian political clergy is becoming conscious that the traditional Iranian ethics of chivalry (*javānmardī*) have more universal appeal than the standard, religious dicta.

The *Shahnameh* defines normative ideals of the ethics of war and peace within narratives that connect the ancient history of Iran to her mythical eras. The author of this epic poem enjoys at least the same status that Homer has in Western literature. I therefore begin the first part of this volume with an overview of the ethics of war and peace in this work of epic literature as an example of one of the most significant nonjurisprudential normative sources that informs the Iranian ethical mindset. In addition, the study of ethics of war and peace in the *Shahnameh* is most relevant to the theme of this volume in its denial of the moral authenticity of religious militancy. Moreover, as post-revolutionary Iran is increasingly posturing towards cosmopolitanism and civilizational syncretism, the *Shahnameh* seems destined to gain more cultural popularity, for its perennial moral philosophy and fine universal language may foster Iranian international and intercultural discourses.

Written by Abu'lqasim Ferdowsi (d. 1020), the *Shahnameh* (The book of kings) has influenced all Eastern Muslim cultures on the ethics of war and peace for more than a millennium. According to Dick Davis, the *Shahnameh* "contributed much toward Iran's perception of the nature of its own continuing reality in the past thousand years ... and as virtually the sole custodian of the narratives of pre-Islamic period ... is popularly seen as the repository of a quintessential 'Iranian-ness.'"[5] It echoes the collective identity of all Persian-speaking people, even beyond Iran, for over a millennium and encompasses the codes of moral conduct, chronicles, and other narrative poems. The *Shahnameh* forms a significant part of the literary genre known as *adab*, that is, the humanist written culture of medieval Persia.

The ethics of war can also be traced in the didactic works of *adab* literature, such as in *Sīyar al-Mulūk* of Nizām al-Mulk (d. 1092), *Qabusnameh* of Keykāvūs b. Iskandar (d. 1085), *Ādāb* (plural of *adab*) *al-Harb wa'l-Shujā'a* of Fakhr Modabbir (d. 1205), Rūdakī (d. 941), and *Rahat al-Sudūr wa Āyat-us-Surūr dar Tārīkh-e Āl-e Saljūq* of Muhammad Ibn Sulaymān Rāwandī (d. ca. 1202). Some other key Arabic authors who have provided significant contributions to the ethics of war include Ibn Muqaffa' (d. 1355), Ibn Qūtayba (d. 1484), al-Māwardī (d. 1085), and al-Qalqashandī (d. 1418). Although the aforementioned sources are important in the study of the ethics of war in Iranian culture, none of these works can parallel the significance of Ferdowsi's *Shahnameh* in terms of acting as an identity maker in modern Iran. This chapter, therefore, only focuses on the work of Ferdowsi.

The *Shahnameh* is the product of an era that is, among other factors, marked by the autonomous rule of the Samanid dynasty (819–1005) in eastern Iran and Tranoxiana. This dynasty has been praised by some modern historians as the foremost of all medieval courts promoting Persian *adab* literature – a major factor in halting the Arabization of Iran after its Islamization. Mohammad 'Alī Eslamī Nadoushan, a historian of medieval literature and an authority on the *Shahnameh* of Ferdowsi, is quoted by Heravī as saying: "As a result of the Samanid policies, a kind of revivalism of the past Persian memories became fashionable and led to a culture of composing various Shahnameh epics, starting with Abu'l Mu'ayyid Balkhī, 'Ammāreh Marvazī, Daqīqī, the Abū Mansūrī Shahnameh and the Shahnameh of Ferdowsi, which brought the genre to its peak."[6]

The Ethics of War and Heroism

As reflected in its first doctrinal principle *'adl* (justice), which is defined as an extrareligious foundation for its moral system, Shi'i Islam has shown a strong inclination towards objective ethics (rational or universal) in its various disciplines. Despite this tendency, it could be found that in epic literature, rather than strictly in religious literature, a Shi'i poet was able to express some of the most ethical and profound views on war. It gave him the ideal platform for exploring the difficult moral dilemmas faced by warriors on the battlefield. Poets revealed the ethics of war through concrete examples of and details about the repercussions of the choices meditated upon by warriors in a way that would have not been possible within the more rigidly defined boundaries of jurisprudence, theology, philosophy, and historiography.

Heroic figures in Shi'i/Iranian history, such as 'Alī b. Abī Tālib and Ya'qūb Layth, as well as demonic figures, such as Yazīd b. Mu'āwīya, al-Hajjāj, and Mahmud Ghaznavi, were moulded in part from these actors' peculiar views of Islam, those of their biographers, and the expectations of readers. Epic literature provides different heroic images based on communal memories and veneration for pre-Islamic heroes, thereby creating a new note of legitimacy and moral authenticity. The veneration process, complementary to folk culture in its conception, becomes fused into one, with Islamic heroes assuming pre-Islamic codes of honour and the pre-Islamic heroes embracing Islamic virtues.

This is why epic poems about Shi'i heroes, such as the *Alinameh* (a collection of epic narratives on Alī Ibn Abī Tālib's heroism, formed shortly after the *Shahnameh* in the eleventh century), have followed the *Shahnameh*'s style to a great extent.

Shahnameh of Ferdowsi, the Paradigm of Persian Epics

The *Shahnameh* is one of the most influential Persian texts, carrying complex and universal codes of ethics for Islamo-Persian civilization. In Muslim history, where orality represents a very important feature of the culture, the epic poetry of the *Shahnameh* successfully penetrated the consciousness of all social strata. Its 60,000 couplets are still frequently read in Persian-speaking societies, as well as in Armenia, Georgia, the North Caucasus, Pakistan, and other countries.

Beginning its narrative in 977 during the Samanid Reign (819–999), the *Shahnameh* addresses three distinct eras: prehistoric (the beginning of the Indo-Iranian mythological history), heroic, and historic (from the Sassanid era to the beginning of the Arab Conquest). Among the sources known to have informed the ethics and narratives of the *Shahnameh* are various works of the Sassanian era, including the *Khudaynameh* (The book of rulers) and the *Andarznameh* (The book of aphorisms), compiled or written by historians and Zoroastrian priests (*mobad*), common sources of Indo-Iranian mythology, and the prose form of the *Shahnameh* by Abu Mansur. Ferdowsi was also influenced by the Qur'ān, Shi'i theology, Islamic historiography, and codes of chivalry (*javānmardī* in Persian; *futūwwah* in Arabic). Needless to say, his views were coloured by his own observations about the politically fragmented world of Islam and the emergence of Islam's golden age.

According to Walter J. Ong, in oral cultures, information storage requires a practical approach and concerns matters familiar to most members of society.[7] However, with relation to the practices of expansionist wars familiar to the peoples and societies of Ferdowsi's era, particularly in Central Asia, the *Shahnameh* defies Ong's theory by rejecting both the theology of Mahmud of Ghaznavi and his methods of war, thus surpassing societal standards of the time. While Ferdowsi condemns unjust wars waged in the name of jihad, the Ghaznavi sultan paid lip service to sharī'a as the foundation of his expansionist wars. The latter pursued a policy of Shi'i extermination in the province of Ray (central Iran) culminating near the end of his reign in 1027.[8]

Ferdowsi's work reflects on a mixed range of ethical norms, from pre-Islamic Persian myths and moral ideologies to those of Islam. He was well acquainted with the medieval court system, for in his early years he had been at the Samanid court. Yet, most of his great epic was written at the time of Mahmud Ghaznavi (d. 1030). Mahmud was fervently anti-Shi'i and considered followers of this school of thought to be little better than disbelievers (*kāfirs*); Ferdowsi, on the other hand, had a strong Shi'i sympathy, but his work's influence on Persian culture and identity is not a function of this doctrinal sympathy; rather, it is based on the rationalist and universalist moral appeal that extended beyond religious and sectarian boarders. This is precisely why the *Shahnameh* had a vast influence on the Ottoman Turks who followed the Hanafi school of Islamic law.

The present chapter takes a hermeneutical approach focused on the ethics of war as reflected in Ferdowsi's *Shahnameh.* Persian-speaking medieval societies were conscious of the kinds of parameters within the ethics of war on which modern scholarship and international law has subsequently elaborated. Specific lines from the *Shahnameh* bring us to the conclusion that Ferdowsi's poetic discourse offers notions germane to the concepts of the ethics of war and peace presently used in peacemaking and conflict resolution.

To understand one of the foundational factors that informed Ferdowsi's ethics of war, it is necessary to point out that, according to Ann Lambton, the predominantly sharī'a-based political philosophy of the Islamic classical periods was replaced by the justice-centred theory of the medieval periods. This substitute theory, which was followed by many writers of *adab* literature and highly influenced by Sassanian and Greek political theory, de-emphasized the necessity of sharī'a knowledge for the ruler. Instead, the medieval theory focused on the sense of justice as the most important quality.[9] Justice was no longer the implementation of sharī'a but rather a general and universal sense of moderation in all affairs.[10]

War, Peace, and the Lack of Absolute Heroism in the *Shahnameh*

The *Shahnameh* by nature does not promote a pacifist view of life and is rather inclined to accept war as a reality of human history. Without war, there are few measures with which to test heroism. Yet, the underpinning political theory of the *Shahnameh*, like many works of medieval *adab* literature, is based on the expansion of justice in the world, as a means of both encouraging moderation in all realms of life and of maintaining the structure of a stable society.[11] In contrast to the traditional Islamic theory of war (*harb*), which justifies territorial expansion to extend the rule of sharī'a, it is the preservation and expansion of universal justice, rather than the right religion, that becomes the prime foundation for Ferdowsi's theory of just war. This is by no means to say that the *Shahnameh* presents a consistent and continuous ethical world. Its material is reflective of different eras and narrative sources, and is therefore impressed by various normative systems. But at the same time, the lack of ethical homogeneity prevents the emergence of a moral absolutism; this, in effect, helps make the epic work more accessible to the public.

The *Shahnameh* opens with an account of creation, explaining how man and civilization came to be. War is introduced as a consequence of the division of the world among the three sons of Fereydun, who had once ruled the world with divine support or charisma (*farr*). He divides the world among his sons: Salm, Tur, and Iraj. Salm receives the Western lands, Tur inherits China and the Central Asian Turkish lands, and Iraj becomes the ruler of Iran.[12] But instead of bringing peace, the tripartite division leads to fratricide. Iraj, the intended ruler of Iran, who is depicted as a man of peace, is killed by his two brothers. This vile deed begins a cycle of revenge occupying much of the earlier sections of the *Shahnameh*.[13] In relating these conflicts, Ferdowsi describes not only heroism in war but also its inhumanity, waste, and horror. In the fluid moral construct of the *Shahnameh,* war itself is never idealized and aggression never rewarded. It is justice and human dignity that remain the ultimate ideals.

There are various heroes and antiheroes in different episodes of the *Shahnameh.* First and foremost stands Rostam from the Persian province of Zabolestan. He is a great warrior who serves, in the words of Julie Meisami, "sovereigns who are often wealthy, arrogant and foolish … perhaps an allusion to contemporary conditions under the later Samanids."[14] Other heroes include Sohrab, Rostam's son, Esfandiyar, Tus, and others. However, none are presented in the *Shahnameh* as faultless, and each has his own specific moral shortcomings. The enemy has its share of good characteristics, such as Piran Veyseh, who finds himself a counsellor to a tyrant. He is caught in a situation where his sense of loyalty and inclination towards reason clash. Aghriras, a brother of Afrasiyab (who was the king of Turan and the chief enemy of Iran), is praised as a peacemaker. This position, however, ends up costing him his life, as he takes a firm stance in the protection of prisoners of war.[15] Piran's brother Pilsam, who is a Turkish general, is presented as a respectful person with good virtues. He tries, for example, to save the life of the Iranian prince Siyavash, his wife Farangis, and their son Kaykhosrow.

Although the *Shahnameh*, as mentioned by Abbas Amanat, provides an "ethno-territorial" source (*Iranzamin*) for Persian identity,[16] many of the warriors on both sides of the conflict are close relatives. This is well formulated by Dick Davis, who says, "We quickly see that notions of an Iranian identity, as they are embodied in the *Shahnameh*, are complicated, and often apparently self-contradictory, and that they strongly resist attempts to essentialize the concept."[17] Rostam, the main hero, is a descendent on his mother's side of Zahhak, a demonic king. Kaykhosrow, one of the most respected, and in the words of Davis, one of the most "paradigmatically perfect"[18] Iranian kings of the *Shahnameh,* is the maternal grandson of Iran's chief enemy, Afrasiyab.[19] As is the case with the aforementioned characters, Ferdowsi refrains from depicting moral and immoral absolutes among his heroes or mapping good and evil within political boundaries. He brings close kin into confrontation, making his epic resemble real life more closely. However, to Ferdowsi, authentic history was a tale of morality in which evil faces good, very often within the same individual.[20] While the ethics of war and peace for Kaykhosrow are different from those of Kaykavus (a Persian monarch who belongs to the same mythical era of the *Shahnameh* and who acts on a lower moral plane, as seen below), these differences appear even more conspicuously between mythical personas living in different eras. However, these broad character variations do not distract Ferdowsi's attention from a critical view of the ethics of war according to a consistent moral perspective.

Heroism in the classical sense is more about how to win a war than how to win peace. Most peace initiatives in the *Shahnameh* fail, and kings are well advised to build powerful armies that are considered as essential foundations of their honour and independence:[21]

[22] در بی نیازی به شمشیر جوی   به کشور شود شاه را آبروی

(It by the sword that one may attain independence,
And so is the way, for kings, to acquire honour.)[23]

Elsewhere in the epic work, and possibly under the influence of Prophetic hadiths such as, "Heaven is under the shadows of swords" (*al-jannatu tahta zilal as-suyuf),* the *Shahnameh* reemphasizes the importance of military might for economic sustenance:

[24] جهانجوی را نان به جنگ اندراست   وگر نه سرش زیر سنگ اندراست

(The atheling's bread is in battling,
Or else under a stone, his head may lie.)

The above line may leave the reader with the impression of two notions of jihad. While the main focus here is courage or valour (*daliri*)[25] as a serious requirement for kingship, war in the *Shahnameh* is more than an important aspect of life: it is also an arena allowing the manifestation of heroic virtues, but never a goal by itself, as the political wisdom of the founder of the Sassanian dynasty will attest to below. War must remain a last resort if a peaceful resolution of a dispute would not be accessible:

زجنگ آشتی بی گمان بهتر   است نگه کن که گاوت به چرم اندر است

(Peace, no doubt, is better than war,
Beware when your cow is still within its skin.)[26]

Just Cause of War

The *Shahnameh* enumerates two legitimate and just causes for war: defending land and dignity (defensive war) and penal or corrective justice (punishing a person or a state for a committed crime or aggression).[27] Most other causes are condemned, even if pursued by a fellow Iranian.[28] Wrath and vengefulness are certainly unjustified motives for war and are ranked among the ten most serious demons, or cardinal vices, upon which the minister Bozorgmehr expounds to Anushirvan (Nushinravan):

ده اند اهرمن هم به نیروی شیر   که آرند جان و خرد را بزیر
بدو گفت کسری که ده دیو چیست   کز ایشان خرد را بباید گریست
چنین داد پاسخ که آز و نیاز   دو دیوند با زور و گردن فراز
دگرخشم و رشک است وننگ است و کین   چو نمام و دو روی ونا پاک دین
[29] دهم آنکه از کس ندارد سپاس   به نیکی و هم نیست یزدان شناس

(The demons are ten, and with the strength of a lion
They knock down one's soul and wisdom.
Khosrow said to him, "What are these ten demons because of whom one need weep for wisdom?"
He [Bozorgmehr] answered thus: "Avarice and greed are two potent and wilful demons,
Also wrath, envy, indignity, and vengefulness
Like the gossipmonger, hypocrite, and heretic.
The tenth is one who is neither grateful for kind deeds of anyone, nor recognizes God.")

Rage and vengefulness are demonic, but paradoxically often they are also the main impetus for heroic action. Therefore, for Ferdowsi, self-containment against anger is a difficult and esoteric struggle. Often times, in various *Shahnameh* narratives, the above paradox may sound personal and refer to conflicts between individuals, leaving a barely discernible distinction between legitimate reasons for war and personal conflicts that catalyse wars. There is no evidence that an illegitimate cause of conflict for an ordinary person or a hero could be legitimate for a state, which explains why both the individual and the state must always remain conscious of the cause and, therefore, the legitimacy of their battles. Leaders typically announce their reasons for war, whether justified or not, before initiating hostilities. Kaykhosrow, for example, declares the main cause for his campaign against Afrasiyab as follows:

منم داغ دل پور آن بیگناه سیاوش که شد کشته بر دست شاه
بدین دشت از ایران بکین آمدم نه از بهر گاه و نگین آمدم [30]

(I am the grief-stricken offspring of that innocent
Siyavash who was killed at the hands of the Shah.
To this plain from Iran I have come for revenge,
Not for the sake of status or possession.)

Kaykhosrow, the paradigmatic and just hero of the *Shahnameh*, delivers a full list of grievances against Afrasiyab, including the murder of Aghriras, Afrasiyab's own brother. Kaykhosrow's father, Siyavash, and others define this as legitimate grounds for war as punitive justice. He nevertheless prays before God that if he is wrong in this judgment, he should not be granted victory over the enemy. Such ideal and perfectionist ethics of war defeat any sense of triumphalism that in Ferdowsi's time, and even in our own, sounds fantastic. In terms of morality, it is striking that right at the threshold of war, Kaykhosrow is ready to think of the possibility that he might be wrong in his judgment about his enemy:[31]

بیامد بیکسو ز پشت سپاه به پیش جهاندار شد داد خواه
که ای برتر از دانش پارسا جهاندار و بر پادشا پا دشا
اگر نیستم من ستم یافته چن آهن بکوره ا ندرون تافته
نخواهم که پیروز باشم بجنگ نه بر دادگر بر کنم جای تنگ
بگفت این و بر خاک مالید روی جهان پر شد از ناله زار اوی [32]

(From behind his army, he [Kaykhosrow] moved to the side, seeking justice
before God.
"Oh! You who are higher even than what an ascetic comprehends! Master
of the world, and king of all!
If I am not really transgressed against,
As iron molten in a kiln,
Then I do not want to be triumphant in war,

Nor to confine the just."
He uttered these words and grazed his head on the earth,
And the world became full of his weeping lamentation.)

The most frequently asserted but rare actual cause of war in medieval Muslim cultures (and in non-Muslim culture, as demonstrated by the Crusades) was the unbelief or heresy (*kufr*) of the enemies, a notion directly related to the priest-army or the church-state relations. During both the Sassanian and the Islamic eras, religious support for the instigation of military advances was of paramount importance. The enemy was accused of "untruth" (*dorugh*) in the Sassanian era and of "infidelity" (*kufr*) in the Islamic period.[33] Distancing himself from these religious justifications for war, Ferdowsi defines infidelity, in the words of Manuchehr, entirely differently from the narrowly defined conceptual disbelief suggested by orthodox jurists.

هر آنکس که در هفت کشور زمین   بگردد ز راه و بتابد ز دین
نماینده ی رنج، درویش را   زبون داشتن مردم خویش را
بر افراختن سر به بیشی و گنج   به رنجور مردم نماینده رنج
[34] همه سر بسر نزد من کافرند   از آهر من بد کنش بترند

(Each person who, in the seven quarters of the earth,
Strays from the path and turns away from faith,
Whoever inflicts suffering upon the poor
and imposes servitude upon his own people,
Whoever stands arrogant for excesses and treasure,
Whoever makes downtrodden people additionally suffer,
All are infidels before me,
And are worse than the evil-doing Ahriman.)

Here, disbelief encompasses universal notions of arrogance, oppression against the weak, and greed, which together undermine divine justice. It is not surprising to find Ferdowsi's concept of justice universal, objective, and independent from the often arbitrary and limited definitions provided by the mainstream Muslim Ash'arī theology.[35] By broadening the definition of infidelity based on a universal sense of justice, Ferdowsi's ethics of war, at the theoretical level, parallels modern discourses in the realm of just-war theories.

In the couplets below, a king advises his subordinate military commander (Gudarz) to be conscious that in the initiation and the conduct of war, justice (*dād*)[36] must be the prime concern. To emphasize his point, the king reminds his commander of the ephemeral nature of mundane life, and hence the need for the centrality of justice in human conduct. Here, while God's name is mentioned as *dādgar* (just), his ultimate attribute is benevolence (*nikidahesh*). The following piece reflects on the essence of Ferdowsi's just-war theory:

به گودرز فرمود پس شهریار   که رفتی کمر بسته کارزار،
نگر تا نیازی به بیداد دست   نگردانی ایوان آبادپست
به کردار بد هیچ مگشای چنگ   براندیش از دوده و نام و ننگ
کسی کو نبندد به جنگت میان   چنان کن که از تو نیابد زیان
که نپسندد از ما بدی دادگر   سپنج ست گیتی و ما بر گذر
[37] به هر کار با هر کسی داد کن   ز یزدان نیکی دهش یاد کن۷۳

(The king then said to Gudarz,
"Once you have prepared for war,
Be watchful not to commit injustice.
Do not bring a developed settlement to ruin,
Never aim resort to misconduct.
Contemplate your ancestry, reputation, and honour.
The person who does not intend to fight with you
Make sure that he does not come to harm,
For the Just One is not pleased with our wrongdoing.
This world is only a few short days, and we are passing.
In every matter with everyone be just.
Remember the bountiful God.)[38]

Ferdowsi condemns excess no matter the status of the perpetrator. In one of the episodes, demons tempt the Iranian king Kaykavus to seize the autonomous northern province of Mazandaran, without a moral justification. Zal (the father of of the main hero in the *Shahnameh*, Rostam) advises the king against this unjust campaign in the following verses:

تو از خون چندین سر نامدا   ز بهر فزونی درختی مکار
[39] که بار و بلندیش نفرین بود   نه آئین شاهان پیشین بود

(Don't, for the sake of covetousness
Plant a tree with the blood of a number of famous men,
For its fruit and growth will be a curse.
Such is not the custom of former kings.)

Here, Ferdowsi again references the necessity of just cause for war. He frequently reminds his heroes that injustice in war stands contrary to the legacy of previous kings. The key term used in this argument is "covetousness" (*fozūnī*), which refers to expansionist wars waged for wealth or glory. Elsewhere, chief paladin Rostam advises his own son, Faramarz, to explore peace through diplomacy and use war as a last resort:

به هر سو که باشد یکی نامجوی   نوندی فرست از پیش پویه پوی
نخستین به نرمی سخنگوی باش   همین راد بر مردم خویش باش
[40] چو کارت به نرمی نگردد نکوی   درشتی کن آنگاه و پس رزم جو

(Wherever there is a fame seeker
Send an emissary to follow him step by step.
First, begin in soft language,
Be upstanding with your own people,
If your task is not resolved with leniency
At that point use rougher language – then seek battle.)

The Sassanian king Anushirvan advises similar war-preventive diplomatic measures:

به هر جایگاهی که جنگ آمدی   ورا رای و هوش و درنگ آمدی
فرستاده ای خواستی راستگو   که رفتی بر دشمن چاره جوی
[41] اگر یافتندی سوی داد را ه   نکردی ستم بر خردمند شاه

(Wherever a war seemed imminent,
He used intelligence and prudence.
He picked a truthful emissary,
Who was dispatched towards the enemy to find an alternative solution.
If they found a way to [the realization of] justice,
Then the king did not transgress against the wise [enemy].)

Ferdowsi pays close attention not only to the suitable characteristics of the war-preventing emissaries but also to the quality and merits of the discourse with the enemy:

[42] تو با دشمن ار خوب گفتی روا است   ز آزادگان خوب گفتن سزا است

(You are in accord with morality if you conduct a good discourse with the enemy,
This is because good speech suits people of liberality.)

The above lines point to the primacy of peace, peaceful resolution of conflict, and meticulous use of soft diplomacy through proper dialogue before turning to war. The key word here is *āzādeh* (singular of *āzādehgān*), which denotes the universal virtue of liberality contrasted with culturally constructed virtues. In one episode, Piran, a prominent Turani (Turkish) general, offers a peace agreement to Rostam, while the latter is on his way to fight the Turanis. Rostam's motive is revenge for the murder of the innocent Persian prince Siyavash by a Turk.[43] Piran asks why armies composed of so many different ethnic groups should face the prospect of destruction for the sake of a blood revenge. He questions the legitimacy of war and hints that the possible casualties (that is, the possible loss of so many soldiers against the loss of one prince) outweigh the initial damage (known in the ethics of war as disproportionality). The conversation begins with Piran's speech:

ز خون سیاوش همه بیگناه   سپاهی کشیده بد ین رزمگاه
مرا آشتی بهتر آید ز جنگبا   ید گرفتن چنین کار تنگ
نگر تا چه بینی تو داناتری   به رزم دلیران تواناتری
ز پیران چو بشنید رستم سخن   نه بر آرزو پاسخ افکند بن
بدو گفت تا من بدین کینه گاه   کمر بسته ام با دلیران شاه
ندیده ستم از تو جز راستی   ز ترکان همه راستی خواستی
[44] پلنگ این شناسد که پیکار و جنگ   نه خوبست و داند همی کوه و سنگ

("For the blood of Siyavash we have brought,
so many innocent troops to the battlefield.
For me, conciliation is better than war,
One must take such a stand firmly.
Be watchful, for you are more knowledgeable,
You are more powerful in battle with valiant fighters."
When Rostam heard these words from Piran,
He did not base his answer on [Piran's] wish.
He said to him, "Since I have come to this revenge battleground,
I have prepared with valiant warriors of the king,
I have not seen anything from you except truthfulness.
From the Turks, you always wanted truthfulness,
Even leopards know that battles and wars
Are not good, as do the rocks and mountains.")

Rostam agrees with Piran to some extent. He nevertheless justifies his insistence on war on the grounds that he is on a mission ordered by the king. This episode, which shows Rostam constrained by a sense of duty against his own conscience, addresses a moral tension between loyalty and justice. This is not the only instance of Ferdowsi hinting at the conflicting values that often mark the tragic side of many wars.

Ferdowsi opposes "haste" and "rage" as two of the most frequent, unjust causes of conflict. He narrates the advice of the Iranian hero Gudarz to his fellow commander Tus and his companion Giv as follows:

چنین گفت با طوس گودرز و گیو   همان نامداران و گردان نیو
که تیزی نه کار سپهبد بود   سپهبد که تندی کند بد بود
جوانی بدینسان ز تخم کیان   بدین فر و این برز و یال و میان
بدادی به تندی و تیزی به باد   زرسب آن سپهدار نوذر نژاد[45]

(Gudarz thus counselled Tus and Giv
Those very notable and courageous paladins:
"Rage should not be the attribute of a chief paladin,
A paladin who behaves in a hot-headed manner is a bad general.
Such a youth, of Kiani descent,
– With such charisma, stature, neck, and torso –
You wasted because of rage and impulsiveness
Zarasb, that commander of Nowzar's lineage.")

Through hasty misjudgment, Tus had previously brought the downfall of Forud, a dissident Iranian hero who was inadvertently attacked and killed as a result of Tus's anger and temper. With punitive justice, as opposed to revenge, seemingly the only legitimate cause of war in the poet's opinion, Ferdowsi introduces reason and control over one's temper as central virtues that can keep war at bay.

Justice in War and after War

In the story of the most significant war of Ferdowsi's ideal king Kaykhosrow, the poet praises Mahmud, perhaps intentionally, to remind him of a high standard of kingship specifically manifested in the ethics of war.[46]

Ardeshir, the founder of the Sassanian dynasty, established for his army an elaborate code of conduct in war. The following is a sample of the codes of conduct in war mentioned in a military campaign manual, as depicted by Ferdowsi, addressing all three realms of justice at war, in war, and after war:

چو لشکرش رفتی بجائی به جنگ   خرد یار کردی و رای و درنگ
فرستاده ای بر گزیدی دبیر   خردمند و با دانش و یاد گیر
پیامی بدادی بآئین و چرب   بدان تا نباشد به بیداد حرب
سپه را بدادی سراسر درم   بدان تا نباشند یک تن دژم
یکی پهلوان خواستی نامجوی   خردمند و بیدار و آرام جوی

دبیری به آئین و با دستگاه　　که دارد ز بیداد لشگر نگاه
وز آن پس یکی مرد بر پشت پیل　　نشستی که رفتی خروشش دو میل
زدی بانگ کای نامداران جنگ　　هر آنکس که دارد دل و نام وننگ
نباید که بر هیچ درویش رنج　　رسد گر بر آنکس بود نام و گنج
بهر منزلی در خورید و دهید　　بر آن زیردستان سپاسی نهید
بچیز کسان کس میازید دست　　هر آنکس که او هست یزدان پرست
به دشمن هر آنکس که بنمود پشت　　شود ز آن سپس روزگارش درشت
بسالار گفتی که سستی مکن　　همان تیزی و پیشدستی مکن
بلشکر چنین گوی کاین خود کیند　　بدین رزمگاه اندرون برچیند
چو پیروز گردی ز بن خون مریز　　که شد دشمن بد کنش در گریز
چو خواهد ز دشمن کسی زینهار　　تو زنهار ده باش و کینه مدار
چو تو پشت دشمن ببینی به چیز　　میاز و مپرداز هم جای نیز
غنیمت بدان بخش کو جنگ جست　　بمردی دل از جان شیرین بشست
هر آنکس که گردد بدستت اسیر　　بدین بارگاه آورش ناگزیر
من از بهر ایشان یکی شارستان　　بر آرم به بومی که بد خارستان
ازین پندها هیچ گونه مگرد　　چو خواهی که مانی تو بی رنج و درد
به پیروزی اندر به یزدان گرای　　که او باشدت بیگمان رهنمای[47]

(Whenever his [Ardeshir's] army would go to a place to fight,
He would resort to wisdom, deliberation, and prudence.
He would select a literate emissary,
Wise, knowledgeable, and smart.
He would give them a message, proper and mellifluous
So that there would not be an unjust war.
He would recompense all in his military
So that no one would feel unsatisfied.
Then he would appoint a fame-seeking commander,
Wise, vigilant, peace seeking,
A secretary both proper and well equipped
Who could keep the troops from transgression;
And after that a man on an elephant
Whose strong voice could be heard for two miles.
He shouted to them,"O fame seekers!
Whoever has heart and reputation and shame
It should not be the case that any poor dervish [i.e., civilian] should be subject
 to suffering or even the famous and the wealthy.
In every stopping place where you eat and are hosted
Give thanks to those servants.
To the property of people do not extend your hand,
All who are worshippers of God.

Whoever turns a back to the enemy
From then on will have a difficult life.
He would say to the commander not to be lax
Nor to be hasty and make preemptive strikes.
You inform the troops about their identity and why they are in the battlefield.
Once you attain victory, stop the bloodshed,
and let the vicious enemy escape.
If anyone among the enemy troops seeks amnesty,
Grant him amnesty and do not be vengeful.
If you see fleeing enemy,
Do not chase it in greed and do not get waylaid.
Apportion the spoils of war among those who sought war,
Giving their sweet lives in a manly fashion.
Everyone who becomes captive at your hands
Compel them to these quarters.
I will build for them a city
On a thorny wasteland.
Do not stray from this counsel in any way
If you wish to remain free of pain and suffering.
In victory turn towards God;
Without a doubt he will guide you.")

The central factors for a just war, as represented above, are reason (*kherad*), moral expediency (*ra'y*), patient contemplation or prudence (*darang*), justice (*dād*), and kindness to the defeated enemy. The sixth line cautions against unjust war. Wisdom, vigilance, and peace seeking are the three central qualities for the military commander, as mentioned in the tenth line. Here, in the most elaborate piece of the *Shahnameh* dealing with the code of conduct in war, far more attention is paid to moral restraints in conflict than to military gains and battle heroism. As portrayed in lines seven and eight, the loudest voice on the battleground speaks more for the human rights of the enemy than for triumphalism. Most importantly, the last line focuses on the ethics of victory and introduces a practical key to avoiding postwar arrogance and violence: turning to and being wary of God.

While Ferdowsi condemns cowardice, he insists that combatants must be fully cognizant of the just cause of war and should confront the enemy face to face without resorting to trickery and deceit. He opposes surprise attacks and ambush, particularly at night. In a letter to his enemy the king of Hamavaran, Rostam similarly admonishes him for his immorality because of his use of tricks to win in battle. Rostam states:

که بر شاه ایران کمین ساختی   به پیوستن اندر بد انداختی
نه مردی بود چاره جستن به رنگ   نرفتن برسم دلاور پلنگ
که در بزم هرگز نسازد کمین   اگر چند باشد دلش پر ز کین [48]

("You tried to ambush the king of Iran
And continually plotted evil.
It is not manly to seek remedy through trickery,
And not even following the etiquette of the courageous leopard
Who in feast never plots ambush
Even if its heart is full of rancour.")

Ferdowsi pays serious attention to the protection of women and children in war. After a war with the Romans, Noushirvan orders the graceful release of captive children:

اسیران رومی که آورده اند   بسی شیر خوار اندر آن برده اند
به توقیع گفت آنچه هستند خرد   ز دست اسیران نباید شمرد
سوی مادرانشان فرستیم باز   به دل شاد و از خواسته بی نیاز [49]

("The Roman captives that they have brought –
Among them are many unweaned babies."
He [the king] decreed: "All the unweaned infants
Shall not be counted among the captives.
We will return them to their mothers,
With light hearts and wanting for nothing.")

The humanitarian treatment of prisoners of war in the *Shahnameh* appears in several important instances. Kaykhosrow, for example, acting against the conventional norms of wars in his time, releases all Turkish prisoners of his war with Piran. He proclaims full protection of these prisoners in the following words:

همه یکسره در پناه منید   وگر چند بد خواه گاه منید [50]

("You are all under my protection,
even though you are ill wishers towards my reign.")

The *Shahnameh's* ethics of victory, which rest in the treatment of defeated enemies, is best represented in the advice King Kaykhosrow gives to his soldiers after Iranian forces seize the Turani capital and defeat their enemy

Afrasiyab. He orders his soldiers to treat the captured city in a just and compassionate manner, showing concern for postwar humanitarian measures:

ز دلها همه کینه بیرون کنید   به مهر اندر این کشور افسون کنید
بکوشید و چربی بکار آورید   چو دیدید سرما بهار آورید
ز خون ریختن دل بباید کشید   سر بیگناهان نباید برید
نه مردی بود خیره آشوفتن   به زیر اندر آورده را کوفتن
زپوشیده رویان بپیچید روی   هر آنکس که پوشیده دارد بکوی
ز چیز کسان سر بپیچید نیز   که دشمن شود دوست از بهر چیز
نیاید جهان آفرین را پسند   که جویند بر بی گزندان گزند
[51] و دیگر که خوانند بیداد و شوم   که ویران کند مهتر آباد بوم[۱۵]

("Cast out all spite from your hearts,
In this country make magic through kindness.
Make effort and bring leniency into effect,
When you see cold, bring spring.
It is not manly to become angry
And beat a downtrodden.
From those who have cast a cloak over themselves avert your gaze
And in homes where women veil themselves.
Avert your gaze from other people's belongings too,
For a friend will turn to an enemy for the sake of possession.
It does not please the Creator of the world
To seek harming peaceful people.
And further, people call injustice and a bad omen
To destroy old towns.")

Kaykhosrow's postwar ethics of magnanimity reaches its apogee, when he advises his army to transform all hatred to mercy and kindness:

[52] به هرجا که کوه است صحرا کنید   به هر جا که صحرا است دریا کنید

("Wherever is a mountain, make it a plain,
Wherever is a desert, turn it to ocean!")

Here, vengefulness (*kīn*) is categorically rejected both in and after war, while *mehr* (love, kindness, compassion), as a key concept in the ancient Iranian world view, is stressed elaborately. Clearly, excessive violence in war is loathed and the innocent (noncombatants) must be spared. A key word used in the above piece is *mardī* (an abbreviated form of *javānmardī/murruwwah* "manliness, or chivalry"),[53] which refers to the codes of moral conduct followed by the Iranian free warriors under the institutions of *javānmardī* and *'ayyārī* in the pre-Islamic and Islamic eras respectively.[54] The moral foundation of these institutions was a universal sense of liberality and justice born within all people. Among the key characteristics of these institutions, the adherents of which were typically composed of stateless groups, was the tenet that in war and peace one remained loyal to principles rather than to specific political systems and figures.[55] Most importantly, a chapter on *javānmardī* in the *Qabusnameh,* an important source of pre-Islamic Persian ethics, places the fair treatment of prisoners of war on a universal ethical plane.[56]

Kaykhosrow is a paradigm of moral kingship in the prehistoric Persian legend. His final advice to his successor Lohrasb in regards to the aftermath of war shows the concept of minimalist war, as seen in epic Persian literature and as depicted by Muslim historiographers, like Abdulmalik al-Tha'alebi: "So asserted Kaykhosrow in his political will to Lohrasb, 'It is incumbent upon any king to remedy the damages of war, and to use all his powers for reconstruction and reform.' 'During war and its aftermath,' Kaykhosrow continues, 'the king must act like a kind surgeon, operating free of charge, dismembering the ruined body-parts, as the last option, closing all open wounds and curing all injuries as fast as possible.'"[57] For Kaykhosrow, such a universal care for humanity entails expanding his ethics of war and threatening his own soldiers to be punished for unnecessary postceasefire violence:

از این پس گر آید ز جایی خروش   ز بیداد و از غارت و جنگ و جوش
ستمکارگان را کنم به دو نیم   کسی کو ندارد ز دادار بیم[58]

(From now on, if a cry is heard,
Caused by injustice and plunder and war and havoc
I will cut transgressors into two pieces,
those who have no fear from the Most Just.)

The *Shahnameh*'s postwar ethics go so far as to regulate the treatment of the corpses of enemies. Virtuous kings and warriors respect the body of slain enemies and sometimes arrange a formal funeral, should the deceased enemy be a nobleman or royalty. When Kaykhosrow slays the king of Mokran, he rejects the suggestion that he sever the head of his vanquished foe:

یکی گفت شاها سرش را بریم   بدو گفت شاه: اندرین ننگریم
سر شهریاران نبرد ز تن   مگر بتر از بچه اهرمن
یکی دخمه سازید و مشک و گلاب   چنان چون بود شاه را جای خواب
برهنه نباید که گردد تنش   بران هم نشان خسته در جوشنش،
بپوشید رویش بدیبای چین   که مرگ بزرگان بود همچنین[59]

(Someone said, “O Shah, let us sever his head,”
The king responded: “We must not consider such an act.
Heads of kings must not be severed, except by worse than the progeny of Evil.
Prepare a grave with musk and rosewater,
Like such as would befit a king’s sleeping place.
His body should not be undressed;
Therein [the tomb] must be laid his injured body in his armor.
Draw over him Chinese silk,
For so must the death of the higher ranks be treated.”)

Significantly, a similar order of a respectful burial of the enemy takes place following Kaykhosrow’s killing of the Turkish commander Piran.[60]

Contradictions and Dramas in War

In his encounter with the question of war as an endeavour to establish justice, Ferdowsi points to a major moral dilemma: a drama wherein two heroes, representing conflicting values, clash. This conflict is exemplified by the tragic episode of the combat between Esfandiyar, an Iranian crown prince, and Rostam. After defeating his enemy Arjasp, Esfandiyar claims the throne, as promised to him by his father Goshtasp. Goshtasp, however, conspires to thwart his son’s throne by ordering him to fetch Rostam to answer for certain alleged offences. Although Rostam agrees to visit the king’s court on honourable terms, Esfandiyar rejects this approach, for his father had insisted on bringing Rostam in a humiliating fashion.

The two most respected heroes in the *Shahnameh*, trapped in a moral dilemma, are bound by circumstance to fight or face dishonour. Seeking advice, Rostam debates the problem with Simorgh, a magical bird that protected his family:

مرا کشتن آسانتر آید ز ننگ   اگر باز مانم به جائی ز جنگ
[61] چنین داد پاسخ کز اسفندیار   اگر سر به خاک آوری نیست عار

(“It would be better that they killed me than brought me disgrace,
When I am stalled from fighting.”
She [Simorgh] answered thus: “If you submit to
Esfandiyar, it is no disgrace.”)

Simorgh reminds Rostam that whoever kills the paladin Esfandiyar will be cursed and remorseful and will suffer the rest of his life. However, the bird guides Rostam during the fatal battle by targeting the only vulnerable spot in

Esfandiyar's body: his eye. Similarly, Esfandiyar pulls out the eye of the Turani king Arjasp and kills him following Arjasp's defeat.

The battle ends with no absolute victor, no hero, and no individual saved from the pain of tragedy. Esfandiyar is killed, but so is Rostam's soul. This battle involves blind obedience to the king, a hero's personal pride, a destiny that settles the accounts of every actor on every side, and enemies who are all related as brothers or cousins. There are good souls on both sides, along with good motives, though much courage spent in vain. It is against this dramatic background that Ferdowsi reminds his readers that they may be subject to the same fate and, with this in mind, warns against hasty judgments about right and wrong in war and peace. He appeals to his audience to consider the middle ground in their judgments. As explained earlier in this chapter, the Sassanian-Greek notion of moderation, or "golden mean," constituted the predominant concept of justice for medieval Muslim political theory. The following advice of Ardeshir to Iranians, which recognizes moderation as the manifestation of wisdom, is therefore foundational in Ferdowsi's political perspective:

[62] میانه گزینی، بمانی به جای   خردمند خواندت پاکیزه رای

(You will prevail if you choose moderation,
the Pure Intellect calls you wise.)

War is not the middle ground of an ideal life, although it remains a permanent feature of life and main driver of classical heroism. Davidson shows how Ferdowsi has his hero Rostam, nearing his final days, speak critically of a life almost entirely spent in war. The following is Rostam's lament song about himself:

که آواره و بد نشان رستم است   که از روز شاد یش بهره کم است
همه جای جنگست میدان اوی   بیابان و کوه است بستان اوی
همه رزم با شیر و با اژدها   ز دیو و بیابان نیابد رها
[63] می و جام و بویا گل و میگسار   نکرده است بخشش ورا کردگار

(O that Rostam is an outcast, and ill fated!
His happy days have amounted to misery.
His sole arena is the battlefield,
His orchard, desert and mountain.
All his battles are with lions and virile dragons,
He has no relief from demon and desert.
The wine, the cup, the scented rose, and the drinking companion,
Are not what the Omnipotent has apportioned to him.)

“Here Rostam sings about himself in the third person,” Davidson contends. “How hard his life is fighting all alone in the wilderness, like an outcast, where the wilderness must serve him as a cultivated garden. He will always be an outsider, that is, a liminal figure.”[64] Davidson notes similarly bitter confessions by other heroes of the *Shahnameh,* including Esfandiyar:

همی گفت بد اختر اسفند یار!   که هرگز نبیند می و میگسار
نبیند جز از شیر و نر اژدها   ز چنگ بلا ها نیابد رها!
نیابد همی زین جهان بهره ای   به دیدار فرخ پری چهره ای!
بیابم ز یزدان همی کام دل   مرا گر دهد چهره ای دلگسل
[65] ببالا چو سرو و چو خورشید روی   فروهشته ازمشک تا پای موی!

(Ill-starred Esfandiyar kept saying
He is never with wine or drinking companions.
He sees nothing but lions and virile dragons,
He finds no escape from the claws of calamity.
He never sees any benefit from this world,
Never sees the sight of blessed fairy faces.
“All the desires of my heart would find satisfaction from God
Were he to give me the face of one who could unseat my heart,
Tall like a cypress and a face like the sun,
With musk-scented hair hanging to her feet.”)

Esfandiyar is a prince who, in the words of Davidson, “potentially embodies the very essence of the body politic” and who, just like Rostam, is “a loner, an outsider, and always will be out of synchronization with society.” “Both heroes,” Davidson maintains, “complain that they are away from ordered society and comfort of a civilized life.”[66] By addressing the humanity of his heroes, as well as their reflections, sentiments, and agonies outside the domain of war, Ferdowsi transfers them from a mythical domain to real life. This is where the full spectrum of their lives appears and where heroes become honest critics of war and of their own lives. It is in this context that Rostam, in stepping out from a war-stricken life, retreats in full consciousness into a solitude where he expresses his own sorrows, indignations, and cravings for civilized life.

Ferdowsi condemns the excesses of war most strongly upon reaching the climax of his work. The chief hero, Rostam, stabs his own son, Sohrab, before realizing his son’s true identity. Ferdowsi cautions his protagonist and, indirectly, his reader against war triumphalism:

همی خواست پیروزی و دستگاه   نبود آگه از بخش خورشید و ماه
[67] که چون رفت خواهد سپهر از سرش   بخواهد ربودن کلاه از سرش

(While he [Rostam] was seeking triumph and status,
He was unaware of sun's and moon's effects on one's destiny
And that as he was going [to the battleground]
The cosmos will steal his hat [honour].)

In this instance, Ferdowsi's condemnation of his own hero is unequivocal, though Rostam seems to have certain justification for his actions. Rostam is defending the Iranian forces against the Turani enemies led by Sohrab. But deep underneath this justification, there is a greed for power that makes a father unable to recognize his beloved son.

[68] نداند همه مردم از رنج آز   یکی دشمنی را ز فرزند باز

(It is the curse of greed that makes human beings
Unable to distinguish an enemy from their own child.)

In the same way, the larger war is a fratricidal conflict that pits three brothers (Iraj, the king of Iran; Salm, the king of the Romans; and Tur, the king of Turan) against each other. The futility of war is summed up by the last words of the Iranian hero Bahram, who loses his life in Turan after leaving his whip in enemy lands and returning to reclaim it to prevent the dishonour of leaving a weapon in the hands of foes. The enemy, however, fatally attacks him before he reaches Iran. With death upon Bahram, his friend Giv swears vengeance and promises to execute his killer. In reaction, Bahram declares the following:

خروشی بر آورد کاندر جهان   که دید این شگفت آشکار و نهان
[69] که گر من کشم یا کسی پیش من   برادر بود کشته یا خویش من

(He let forth a roar: "In the whole world
Who has seen such a paradox, open or hidden?
Whether I kill him or you kill him in my presence
He is like a brother to me or a relative!")

As a final expression of perplexity about the laws of the cosmos, the futility of wars, and the ephemerality of human triumphs over one another, Ferdowsi addresses the universe with the following words:

[70] جهانا شگفتا که کردار تو است   هم از تو شکسته هم از تو درست!

(O universe, how strange is your behaviour!
You are the cause of both the destruction and the creation.)

In the end, the author seems to be sure about only one thing: that kindness is the only important thing and is all that remains in the universal cycle of creation and destruction. Reading between the lines of the following couplets, it becomes clear that war can never achieve a lasting and valuable victory:

همان به که با کینه داد آوریم   به کام اندرون نام یاد آوریم
[71] که نیکی است اندرجهان یادگار   نماند به کس جاودان روزگار

(It is better to tame rancour with justice
And remind ourselves of the significance of good name [honour].
It is only kindness that will remain in the world as memorable,
As life will not last forever for anyone.)

Ferdowsi's powerful and penetrating language has played many different roles since his death. It has been used not only to celebrate war and peace but also to remind rulers about the value of justice and humanity. Next to his organic fusion of pre-Islamic Iranian codes of chivalry and Islamic views of justice, perhaps the most striking aspect of Ferdowsi's work is the masterful use of narrative and poetic metre to propound a consistent ethics for war and peace. Bridging the gap between natural extremes of triumphalist heroism and moral heroism without diminishing the intensity of drama that is a natural part of epic literature is not an easy task. Ferdowsi does well on this ground. He stresses the importance of human dignity, of bringing the "self" under scrutiny, and of recognizing that the "other" or the "enemy" may have great and virtuous men on their sides, too.

Conclusion

Islamic beliefs and local norms, which often lie rooted in pre-Islamic traditions, prove to be mutually dependent factors in shaping attitudes towards the cause and conduct of war and peace in *adab* and medieval Persian epic literature. These attitudes often vary from the legal precepts fixed in books of jurisprudence. A close reading of Persian literature shows that there is no facile celebration of war as an aristocratic pastime. Instead, the literature presents many arguments for avoiding war. When conflict is inevitable, the texts emphasize its horrors, as well as its dramas and contradictions. These writings portray war as fundamentally opposed to the notion of *kherad*, the wisdom that was regarded as the wellspring of a better society. However, much of the literature is the work of scribes, or "people of the pen," who served the "people of the sword." As a result, the texts are full of contradictions reflecting the different outlooks of the authors, their intended audiences, and their patron sponsors. These writers interjected Islamic and Sassanian-Greek notions of war ethics (such as the codes of war and honour in Homer's *Iliad*) among peoples and circumstances that vary as compared to those from the early Muslim world.

For Muslims and non-Muslims living in the modern world, the *Shahnameh* of Ferdowsi is a testament against the inevitable clash of cultures. Its antiwar positions, the elaborate ethics of war it presents, and the emphasis it places on universal wisdom, liberality, and justice, in addition to its portrayal of the indivisibility of humanity at large, all speak to this philosophy. Ferdowsi's political ethics and his view of the ethics of war and peace are well grounded in both reason and revelation. They also reflect a solid and rich tradition that encourages peace activism across all levels of society, while providing plenty of ingredients for the creation of modern antiwar philosophies and ethical theories for peace. Ferdowsi's ethics withstand the test of time: humanitarian concepts and concerns of war ethics as reflected in modern literature hardly present a radical quality departure from moral questions that were raised a millennium ago by Ferdowsi.

Morally timeless, the *Shahnameh* is still widely read by many Muslim, Persian-speaking, and Eastern societies. It informs the moral conscience of many Iranians in their daily encounters with the ups and downs of life. It is a literary thread connecting contemporary Iranian society to elements of ethics and episodic segments of its past, which together inform the present Iranian identity. By bringing the prehistoric and historic, the pre-Islamic and the Islamic eras, and the fragmented Iranian society to a moral dialogue with each other and with other cultures at large, the *Shahnameh* denies the moral authenticity of all militant perspectives that are imposed on people in the name of religion. A clearer picture of this denial in classical Iranian thought requires more elaboration, which will be explored in the next chapter.

2 Iranian Classical Thinkers on War and Peace: A Select View

The one who rules others will never conquer himself.

– Dao De Jing[1]

As for my like, if he slips or blunders
I show grace, for grace bids what is due.

– Nasir al-Dīn Tūsī[2]

The history of Muslim views on war is often based solely on the legal literature of Islam, at the expense of ethical dimensions found in other categories of Islamic literature and discourses. In contrast, this chapter examines a representative selection of Iranian philosophical, theological, and mystical perspectives on war and peace. The classical scholars I have chosen to examine because of their relative significance in the history of Muslim thought are Abū Nasr al-Fārābī (d. 950), a chief philosopher, Nasīr al-Dīn Tūsī (d. 1274), one of the most prominent Shi'i theologians, and Abū 'Alī Miskawayh (d. 1030), a chief ethicist. Two others, Abū Hāmid al-Ghazālī (d. 1111), one of the principal theologians in Muslim history, and Jalāl al-Dīn Rumi Balkhī (d. 1273), the most popular Muslim author on Sufism, are not known for Shi'i inclinations but are nevertheless tremendously influential in Iranian and Shi'i thought. The following discussion explores philosophical, ethical, and theological elements of classical and medieval Iranian literature on war and peace, as well as if and how the aforementioned thinkers have approached these moral questions. The very discipline of "theoretical ethics" (*akhlāq-e nazarī* in Persian) traditionally forms a branch of philosophy in the Islamic curriculum.[3] This chapter will not only mind the epistemological gap related to war and peace but also take a small step in bridging it. In addition, this study provides an overview of the theological backgrounds for the emergence of the new nonjurisprudential theology of war and peace in modern Iran. The chapter is therefore necessary to measure the volume's thesis concerning the return of a syncretic and civilization-concious soul to Iran.

As will be noted below, it seems that I have focused more on classical thinkers such as al-Fārābī and Rumi compared with some others, such as Tūsī or Miskawayh. The reason is simply that I found more material related to war and peace in the works of the former compared with the latter authors. In any case, the significance of each author in his field should not be measured by the extent of the chapter's attention to his contributions; I have simply chosen to focus on the related material that was familiar and available to me.

Relation between Law and Ethics

This book treats ethics as a notion distinct from laws. Within traditional Islamic scholarship, ethics (*akhlāq*) and Islamic law (sharī'a) are separate disciplines, existing distinctly within the Qur'ān itself but not without controversy. Hurgronje defines Islamic jurisprudence (*fiqh*), for example, as a doctrine of ethics and duties.[4]

Even if one distinguishes established laws from commonly accepted moral rules, they still share the same spirit, are driven by the same consensus, and follow the same goals. These similarities have resulted in some coincidences between law and ethics in many cultures, including in Islamic culture. Al-Ghazālī maintains that *fiqh* (jurisprudence) is the ethics of action, whereas *akhlāq* is the ethics of character.[5] According to Izutsu, there are two distinct levels of ethical words in the Qur'ān: "the primary level," or objective language that is "essentially descriptive," and the "secondary-level ethical words," or what he calls metalanguage that is evaluative.[6] He stresses that the pure value words of the second type are rarely scattered in the Qur'ān; "a system of well-developed secondary ethical terms is not to be found in the Qur'ān itself," rather it is the subject matter of a jurisprudence that developed in early Muslim centuries.[7] Izutsu admits the difficulty, if not impossibility, of drawing a clear line between the objective and the metalanguage, because they represent a variation of ethical degrees. Despite this, he stresses that the "difference of degree, when it goes beyond a certain limit, changes into a difference of kind."[8]

Indeed, these intersections have caused contemporary Muslim scholars to try to remove influences of history, geography, and ideology from Islamic law as a way to "purify" it from "nonessential" cultural nuances and make it compatible with modern life. The distinction these scholars try to make in Qur'ānic doctrine falls somewhere between what they consider the eternal moral rules and the ephemeral, culture-bound, and circumstantial legal rulings.

An Iranian scholar of jurisprudence, Mohsen Kadivar, argues that the jurisprudential rule of abrogation (*naskh*), applied to some of the Qur'ānic verses by all schools of Islamic jurisprudence, may extend to cover the entire corpus of the legal injunctions derived from the Medinese Qur'ānic verses. These rules seem to fit only into the historical milieu of nascent Islamic society.[9] At the same time, Kadivar maintains that the Meccan moral rules of the Qur'ān are eternally valid and should be used to codify new positive (*jus positum* or human-made) Islamic laws that are commensurate and relevant to life in the new millennium.[10] His view on the distinction between morality and law closely resembles views expressed in the mid-twelfth century by a Christian monk named Gratian, known to be the first to compile the Christian canon law. Gratian maintained that "morality is divine ordinance, law is human ordinance … Divine ordinances are established by nature, human ordinances by usage."[11]

The proposals by Fazlur Rahman and Sohail Hashmi are less radical than Kadivar's in terms of the latter's extensive use of abrogation rules. Fazlur Rahman looks at ethics as the soul of law. He maintains that the "Qur'ān is not a book of abstract ethics, but neither is it the legal document that Muslim lawyers have made it out to be. It is a book of moral admonitions through and through."[12] In Rahman's view, the "rise and development of Islamic law, as they actually occurred, kept the Muslim's attention focused on details, at the expense of … the general requirements of the Qur'ān."[13] Hashmi suggests that Muslims must "disentangle Islamic ethics from medieval Islamic law" and treat the Qur'ān as "a complete ethical system" in order to produce new rules for Muslim participation in global life.[14] The common thinking between Kadivar, Rahman, and Hashmi suggests that the norms of ethics as the spirit and the foundation of law are eternal, whereas the rules of positive law are ephemeral and constantly subject to change by the vicissitudes of historical and geographical circumstance.

Goodman, a historian of Islamic philosophy and religion, maintains that, similar to biblical Judaism, Qur'ānic Islam does not make a distinction between law and morals. This effectively implies that Islamic laws and morality are less fluid than what the above contenders suggest.[15] For Coulson, sharī'a does contain both; he relays that in certain fields, such as in sexual behaviour, there is clear distinction "between the rule which is enforced by the law as applied by the courts and the rule which finds its sanction only at the Bar of eternity."[16]

In order to accommodate modern life with medieval Islamic law, many theologians have sought to delineate between what is explicit (*muhkam* in Qur'ānic terms) and what is allegorical and/or metaphorical (*mutashābih*). Importantly, much of modern Qu'rānic interpretation is based on the expansive fluid part of the Qur'ān that reinterprets and reintroduces the tradition of Mu'tazilism – wherein law and theology (*kalām*) in their pre-Shāfi'ī modes are not separated. It is important to note, however, that the Mu'tazilites did not see themselves as formulating law.[17] Nevertheless, this debate depends on the criteria and standards used for Qur'ānic analysis.

Whatever is subject to enforcement is law, whereas the basis of morality is choice. In other words, no virtue or moral value can be produced under force; in fact, it can be argued that coercion is very much the antithesis of moral action, as Kantian ethics maintain.[18]

Coulson observed that a British perspective views law as an enforcing instrument of morality.[19] Other perspectives suggest that law provides a minimal order for society.[20] A perfectly legal society, wherein each member observes the law is not necessarily tantamount to a moral society. If in such a society there are absolutely no instances of generosity, forgiveness, liberality, magnanimity, charity, or other moral values and virtues, it may be well functioning and perfectly legal, yet a minimally moral society. From this perspective, ethics hold a position above law. However, the opposite situation is not possible; there cannot be a perfectly moral society that is transgressive and chaotic. Such a society acts at the justice-plus level where people do better than what is required by law. Examples can be found in societies with a substantial number of charity or public-relief organizations and endowments.

The task of differentiating between ethics and law perhaps reflects the axiomatic Aristotelian principle indicating that wherever friendship rules, there is no need for justice.[21] By implication, with intrastate friendship there is no need for war. It is obvious that friendship becomes the rule, not in a perfectly legal society but rather in a perfectly moral one.

Modern Western scholarship engages in many of the same controversies in terms of exploring the relation between ethics and law. Foremost among these arguments is the debate between "formalism" and "content theory." Modern Western formalists, similar to the medieval Muslim *adab* ethicist, propose that morality is a matter of the attitude one takes towards a problem rather than the intrinsic characteristics of the problem itself.[22] In other words, one's morality or ethics reflects one's outlooks and manners.

Having explored the above definitions of and the distinctions between ethics and law, we now turn to a brief review of classical Iranian thought on the ethics of war and peace.

Philosophical Ethics and War

There is controversy among Western scholars about whether medieval Muslim philosophers understood the "just-war" theory within the confines of jihad (as Joel Kraemer suggests) or, conversely, if they considered jihad to fall within a broader just-war category (according to Butterworth).[23] Unlike Butterworth, we will not explore how medieval philosophers tried to explain "dominant opinions"[24] but rather will delve into how these thinkers offered a new set of ideas on social affairs, both in direct ways and by implications. As Butterworth mentions, "Al-Fārābī discussed and questioned just war in several of his writings. Avicenna and Averroes, on the other hand, discussed just war only indirectly and even then in no more than one or two of their writings."[25]

Al-Fārābī, the great Muslim logician, was a major proponent of philosophic ethics in Islamic history. Sympathizing with Shi'i-Mu'tazili theology, and believing in the universality of reason and justice as two faculties inherent in every individual, al-Fārābī did not hesitate to adopt a good part of the Platonic and Aristotelian ethical premises and definitions. He is known as the first Muslim philosopher to have written a commentary on Aristotle's *Nicomachean Ethics*. In his *On Civil Government*, al-Fārābī enumerates various political systems, their foundations, and their moral characters. He explains that the ideal head of state, as in Plato's theory, is a philosopher-king. He does not provide much detail about how his ideal political system works, because in his view, all the methods are well detailed by Islamic law (sharī'a). The "virtuous city" (*al-madīnat al-fādila*) is headed by the philosopher-king, as well as by the joint king-prophet-legist figures in pre-Islamic and Islamic eras, respectively. The virtuous city stands above all other systems.

Al-Fārābī establishes several important points. First, he recognizes the presence of a multiplicity of states.[26] Significantly, this is opposite to the traditional view of Islamic jurists who divide the world into two or sometimes three domains: the abode of peace (*dār al-Islam*), the abode of war (*dār al-harb*), and the abode of treaty (*dār al-'ahd*).[27] Thus, al-Fārābī's recognition of the multiplicity of states removes, at a theoretical level, a major impediment to the development of international Islamic law.[28]

Al-Fārābī also sees no conflict between the sharī'a and natural reason, thus asserting the compatibility of rational philosophy and revelation.[29] In this sense, and by implication, al-Fārābī expands the philosophical notion of justice to include natural justice, which itself belongs to the very foundations of a perfect state's policies of war and peace. In other words, for al-Fārābī the concept of war fits more within the just-war theory as opposed to within a jurisprudential context, as justice becomes universal in the former realm.

According to Walzer, in the *Mabādī ārā' ahl al-madīnat al-fādilah* (The principle of the opinions of the inhabitants of the perfect state), al-Fārābī presupposes the essential solidarity of mankind (considering all men are a part of the same species). This is a factor that facilitates the conception of a universal state. "This demand for world peace," Walzer contends, "goes beyond the ideas of Plato and Aristotle, both of whom were content to aim at peace among Greeks only."[30] Walzer also notes that while both Plato and Aristotle hold that the perfect-state is limited to "city-state," al-Fārābī expands the notion not only to "nation-states, but also to a universal world-state."[31] The universal state, however, does not preclude the possibility of several perfect states. In al-Fārābī's own words, "It is possible that excellent nations and excellent cities exist whose religions differ, although they all have as their goal one and the same felicity and the very same aims."[32]

The ultimate goal for al-Fārābī's ideal city-state is the attainment of "happiness," achieved by replacing intentional and nonintentional evil with intentional and natural good.[33] Notable in this formulation is that al-Fārābī, according to Goodman, adopts Aristotle's view about the natural supremacy of the civilized and "justifies aggressive warfare."[34] In al-Fārābī's own words, "The superior state may conquer nations and cities that do not submit to doing what will give them the happiness man is made to acquire ... the warrior who pursues this purpose is the just warrior."[35]

In his *Book of Aphorisms of the Statesman* (*Fusūl al-madanī*), there are references to eleven types of warfare, including those waged for defence, for acquiring a good the city deserves, for reforming others, for punishment, and for taking back what rightfully belongs to the city. Al-Fārābī also recognizes four kinds of unjust wars (*harb jawr*s) as "bellicose actions undertaken for the sake of the ruler's increasing honor or self-aggrandizement, pure conquest, venting of rage or achieving some other pleasure through victory, and overreaction to an injustice committed by others."[36] Little reference is made to jihad in these formulations.

Although al-Fārābī's argument justifies offensive war, it is important to note that "the argument does not entail, indeed does not allow, mere military self-assertion: it justifies offensive warfare, but only on behalf of civilizing ends."[37] Butterworth notes: "In the Aphorism, by referring to the ruler's or rulers' warring capability in terms derived from the word jihad, he underlines that the only kind of warfare such a ruler or rulers may reasonably resort to is warfare that serves the virtuous city. In the virtuous city, however where the exceptional moral qualities of the ruler or rulers are more clearly stated, he eschews such usage."[38] For al-Fārābī, jihad is as generic as slavery is for Aristotle; it simply takes a just prophet or legist to legitimize it.

Al-Fārābī's work also clearly references the use of force in managing the "ideal city" against the uncivilized minorities who act like "weeds" or "animals." According to him, these types of people deserve to be fully exploited, or, in other words, "if they are like harmful animals, they should be treated in that manner."[39] The application of these rather harsh measures rests on the presence and judgment of a just ruler.

Contrary to the virtuous city-state, al-Fārābī suggests, are other states that range from less than perfect to thoroughly evil. Under the rubric of the ignorant city (*jāhilīyya*) are the city of honour (*kirāma*), the city of necessity (*darūrīyya*), the city of depravity (*khissa*), the city of domination (*taghallub*), the city of meanness (*nadhāla*), and the city of the unbridled masses (*jamā'īyya* or *hurrīyya*). Others include the erring city (*zālla*), the corrupt city (*fāsiqa*), and the transforming city (*mubaddila*). In contrast to the ignorant cities, the main difference between these cities is that the latter group is consciously in error.[40]

The citizens of al-Fārābī's dominant city are driven mainly by a desire to rule over others, both compatriots and aliens, either by force or through trickery and deceit.[41] According to al-Fārābī, among the citizens of this city are those who have a "lust for the use of force" in such a way that "they even refrain to kill their subjects when they are sleeping, not for chivalric concerns, but to wake their victims up and kill them against their resistance just to maximize their joy."[42] Here al-Fārābī delineates three types of inclinations among the users of force: first, those who use force for the very sake of it; second, those who use force for other excessive materialistic gains; and third, those who stop using force once they fulfil their moderate needs.[43] Such a categorization ascribes little ethical value to acquisitive wars. In the same way, modern critiques of just war criticize the moral foundations of colonial wars.

Al-Fārābī rejects the notion that any kind of imperfect state can be reformed by force. In Walzer's words, "He rejects every form of violence and puts his trust rather in education through philosophy."[44]

Towards the end of *On Civil Government*, al-Fārābī considers the matters of war and peace from an important psychological angle that is essential to acknowledge when evaluating the views of his philosopher successors. This angle draws from the Platonic notion of the trichotomy of the soul, a premise accepted unanimously by all Islamic philosophers of ethics. According to this principle, the human soul is made of three essential faculties: namely, the irascible or appetitive (*ghadabīyya*), the concupiscent (*shahawīyya*), and the spirited or rational (*'aqlīyya*). In accordance with Aristotelian ethics, al-Fārābī determines four cardinal virtues that can control and manage all parts of the soul and bring them to moderation. These virtues are temperance, courage, and reason, (corresponding to irascible, concupiscence, and rational faculties), and the fourth is the sum of all virtues (or the most perfect virtue), which is justice.[45] As Fakhry asserts, "The two moral virtues which figure most prominently in al-Fārābī's discussion are friendship (*mahabba*) and justice (*'adāla*)."[46] In fact, al-Fārābī seems to agree with the Aristotelian conviction that one may dispense justice in a society established on friendship. The vices contrary to friendship are animosity and hatred, both of which establish psychological motives for war.[47]

Looking at war from a psychological perspective, al-Fārābī suggests that groups of people, or even the entire population of some city-states, lose their rational faculties in the service of their irascible (wrath and force) and concupiscent senses (animalistic, whimsical, lascivious urges).[48] This again references the power of vices in, for example, anger leading to oppression or war acting as an instrument to attain material joy. These vices reflect a general immoral social trend that, in al-Fārābī's view, is found mostly in nomadic Arab and Turkish tribal societies.[49] Therefore, al-Fārābī concludes, such tendencies are related to the socio-economic lifestyles of those societies, where lust and force are the main driving forces.

It is important to note that al-Fārābī's psychological analysis had a major influence on his followers, as well as on the major ethics philosophers of the Islamic world. For example, other philosophers like al-Ghazālī, Miskawayh, and Tūsī have incorporated al-Fārābī's moral-emotional paradigm.

As indicated by Fakhry, al-Fārābī's view of justice can be divided into foreign and domestic spheres. The concept of domestic justice relates to overall intrasocietal relations, including economic justice in the distribution of goods, services, and honours; this justice of maintenance, then, is primarily protective in all walks of life. Justice in foreign relations is divided into defensive justice and offensive justice, the former of which is meant to ward off aggression, and latter of which drives the pursuit of those things advantageous to the conqueror, in terms of undoing a previous injustice.[50] Such categorizations are reflective of the fact that al-Fārābī combines the Platonic view of justice, an inward, domestic essence (psychic harmony), and the Aristotelian outward, foreign "common justice."[51]

Al-Fārābī's views run counter to those held by the jurists of his time. When it comes to the eradication of "useless" domestic classes, al-Fārābī holds a radical position otherwise absent in his view of external relations. Notably, al-Fārābī's philosopher-king, or the king-prophet, follows an objective justice in full accord with both human objective reason and prophetic revelation. There is no difference in al-Fārābī's opinion of the non-Muslim and the Muslim virtuous ruler and warrior, simply because virtue is universal.[52]

Several specific factors present among the Aristotelian principles of al-Fārābī's philosophical thinking have limiting and mitigating effects on war.

Evil, according to this philosophy, is nonexistent, does not have a positive presence, and thereby cannot be the object of any ideological war.[53] Reason controls anger and violence as features of the irascible soul. Justice controls all excesses. Both reason and justice, according to this philosophy, have objective bases shared among all of mankind. In a world where all nations have a homogeneous concept of reason, irrationality, justice, injustice, aggression, transgression, and evil, there is much less ground for ideological wars than if evil had maintained a positive existence. The combined effects of a positive threat (evil) and subjective reason and justice (voluntarily defined) open the way for authoritarian voluntarism and war.

Al-Fārābī is very conscious of the terms he uses and also of potential for other thinkers to engage in terminological abuses. As Butterworth asserts, in *Al-madina al-fadila,* "Fārābī does not talk about jihad but only of war (*harb*) with no religious goal." Al-Fārābī is therefore "extremely reluctant to declare it ever just to wage war upon others and that he does not rigidly distinguish between the term for war (*harb*) generally and the term for war usually considered to be in defense of Islam [namely] jihad."[54]

In sum, al-Fārābī believes that there are two kinds of wars: evil wars motivated by moral defects and vices, as well as just wars prompted by the need to protect or restore a just status. There is, however, no mention of holy wars or religious offensive wars. The fact that he distinguishes between various perfect states bears witness to his pluralistic view of the political world. Political diversity is not just a temporary, imperfect stage in history.

The Essential Intimacy (*'uns*)

It was Abū 'Alī Ahmad Miskawayh (d. 1030) who inherited al-Fārābī's legacy on ethics and brought philosophic ethics to its peak in his *Tahdhīb al-akhlāq* (Purity of dispositions). Miskawayh, like al-Fārābī and the Brethren of Purity (Ikhwān al-Safā), was of Shi'i inclination.[55] His significant achievement in *Tahdhīb* was the synthesis of pre-Islamic Persian *adab* literature and Indian moral views, which weaves both into a unified structure. Miskawayh does not expand the synthesis to encompass political ethics or philosophy; nevertheless, his views on the essence of friendship and humanity's sociability have important implications for war and peace.

According to Goodman, Miskawayh shares with Ibn 'Adī (d. 974)[56] the notion that one of ethics' chief goals is having control over our natural irascibility, allowing our deeper unity to surface in acts of love and compassion.[57] Notably, he and Ibn 'Adī also share the view that the aim underlying the commands and admonitions of scripture, which are transformed and translated into positive Islamic law, is the refinement of character.[58]

For Miskawayh, following Aristotle's argument, friendship has greater stature than the source of all virtues: justice. Friendship is not merely a virtue; rather, it determines the very humanity of human beings. Miskawayh points out that *insān* (human being, in Arabic) derives from the root word *'uns*, meaning intimacy, or, in the works of Fakhry, "gregariousness."[59] According to Fakhry, "Ibn Miskawayh insists that man's supreme happiness cannot be achieved without the fellowship of friends and associates, for being a 'political animal' by nature, he could not fulfill himself in solitude."[60] In this theoretical scheme, religious law emphasizes that even public worship can foster human fellowship. Miskawayh therefore makes humanity (*al-insānīyya*) the goal of ethics, which can be achieved through the perfection of our identity (*dhāt*) as human beings.[61]

As such, one might infer that Miskawayh's opinion of war and warmongering would be the source of all vices, as it is contrary not only to human beings, but also to humanity at large. He states: "Recklessness and cowardice, like courage, are grounded in the irascible power of the soul when it is over stimulated by anger, or the desire for vengeance. Passionate anger and arrogance are the principal causes of oppression and other social ills, and the essence of arrogance is a false opinion of one's self, as deserving a higher rank than the one it has earned."[62] Only through reason can one control his or her irascible faculty, and therefore his or her arrogance. Yet for Miskawayh, reason is natural and objective, and not subject to legalistic interpretations. As support, he offers a Mu'tazili reading of a familiar oath from the Qur'ān: "And [by] the soul and He who proportioned it. And inspired it [with discernment of] its wickedness and its righteousness."[63]

Miskawayh says, "*Adab* is the content of wisdom and knowledge, tested by experience about the good life and its means of attainment; importantly, without this experience reason is not reason."[64] Culture, Miskawayh argues, makes the man.[65] His interpretation of culture (*adab*) is not external but organic to morals.[66] In other words, the manner in which one carries out an ethical act is at least as important as the outcome of the act. This parallels the standard relation between the means and the ends. Miskawayh believed, however, that the ends could not justify the means. As Goodman asserts, "Unlike Marx, or even Plato in some moods, but like the scriptural ethics of Judaism and Christianity, the Qur'ānic ethics do not countenance breach of its standards in pursuit of its aims."[67] For Miskawayh, it is because *adab* is founded on objective reason that one can have an accurate self-image and, by implication, an image of "others" as equals – all of which helps to avoid war and conflict.

Informed by a Neoplatonic view of Aristotle, Miskawayh's treatment of friendship deepens to the level of political philosophy when he argues that because man is civic by nature, "man's complete human happiness is realized through his friends; and whoever finds his completion through others cannot possibly attain his full happiness in solitude and seclusion." He continues, "The happy man, therefore, is he who wins friends and endeavours to distribute goods generously among them in order that he may attain with them what he cannot attain by himself."[68] Elsewhere, Miskawayh asserts, "This is the nature of human happiness which cannot be achieved without bodily actions, civic conditions, good assistance, and sincere friends."[69]

By situating friendship and benevolence above justice in the moral hierarchy, Miskawayh contributes to a political philosophy that liberates the decision making for war and peace from a juristic monopoly. He asserts, "While the Islamic Law (sharī'a) prescribes universal justice, it does not prescribe benevolence. It only urges people to practice benevolence, and this in particulars, which cannot be specified because they are endless." He concludes, "Law is definitive in [prescribing] universal justice because it is limited and can be specified."[70] In other words, Miskawayh maintains that because benevolence as a justice-plus virtue knows no limits, Islamic law, by definition, is incapable of accessing it, defining its qualities, or codifying rules for it; this is because law deals only with limits.

Miskawayh proposes the idea of foundational friendship as culminating in one significant step that effectively speaks to the Shi'i theory of imam. He points out that the main purpose for all collective, devotional rituals in Islam, such as pilgrimage [*hajj*] and congregational prayers, is to promote fellowship and intimate bonds among members of Muslim society.[71] Viewing devotional rituals as agents for promoting fellowship in society results in a key political philosophy. For Miskawayh, the major function of the imam, who is the legitimate charismatic religio-political leader in a Muslim society, is the maintenance of *'uns* (fellowship or sociability) in that society.[72] This is a novel departure from the conventional Shi'i notion of the imam as the maintainer and promoter of justice in an ideal Islamic society. While justice is the foundation of a legal society, friendship as a justice-plus moral space has far less propensity towards punitive and retributive justice. People in this world live to love and befriend one another, rather than to love in order to live. This perspective suggests that human sociability and intimacy are not a function of survival, but the very goal of a religious life, as well as life in a universal sense. By implication, Miskawayh's perspective provides novel philosophical and theological foundations for peacemaking and conflict-resolution approaches. When justice loses its primacy in favour of friendship and benevolence in a normative system, wars, even just wars, also lose their imperatives.

A direct reference to ethics of war appears in another work of Miskawayh known as *Perennial Wisdom* (*Javidan khirad* in Persian). The book is the collection of wisdom statements from various ancient cultures, including pre-Islamic Iran. Quoting Hushang, a prehistoric figure in ancient Iran introduced by Miskawayh as the second ruler on earth after Noah, Miskawayh writes: "Ignorance at war and being ignorant in it is better than having intellect and deliberately agree to begin it (war)."[73] Apparently referring to expansionist wars that lack moral justification, Miskawayh introduces another telling quotation from Hushang: "A person may not be called thoroughly knowledgeable, meaning fully wise, if he goes to war while he has married a woman and has not consummated his marriage; so is not fully wise a person who has begun a building construction and leaves for war before he finishes the building and settles there; or similarly if one goes to war while having cultivated his farm and leaves before harvesting."[74] Clearly the text gives moral priority to all unfinished professional and family business over war, for hardly any part of society may be caught up in war at a time when no one has unfinished business. The statement provides a strong and very broad moral justification for public avoidance of participating in expansionist wars.

The extent of anticrime posture in this ancient text extends beyond wars. Quoting Azarbad, a pre-Islamic Iranian sage, Miskawayh writes: "Avoid killing animals as much as you can and try to apply moderation in it, for there are severe and numerous blames for it in afterlife. And also avoid its bad omen in this life, because any location where there is less murder and bloodshed, people are more numerous and evil and vice appear less. Conversely, residents of such area are more immune from calamity and austerity, as it is less probable to be subject to miseries, calamities, witchcraft and satanic evil deeds than are other locations."[75] In his philosophical and moral insistence on the primacy of friendship, Miskawayh does not miss a chance in his works to pose against war and bloodshed in human society and beyond.

From a Battle with "Others" to a Battle with the "Self"

Abū Hāmid al-Ghazālī (d. 505), unlike some of the other philosophers discussed in this chapter, was not a Shi'a but rather an Iranian Ash'ari follower of the Shāfi'ī school of law. He attempted to synthesize philosophical ethics with sharī'a law and mysticism. By adopting some Platonic and Aristotelian ethical concepts, he redefined some of the standard notions reintroduced by al-Fārābī and Miskawayh, as discussed previously. Importantly, al-Ghazālī fills the gap created by a major theological rift between the Shi'i, Mu'tazili, and Greek philosophies, as well as by Sunni, Ash'ari, and Shāfi'ī tendencies. For example, al-Ghazālī adopted Aristotle's concept of the rational "mean" in determining the optimum ethical position of a virtue between its two extremes.[76]

However, he applies it to the Qur'ānic notion of the "straight path" (*al-sirāt al-mustaqīm*) in order to identify the concept of "mean" as Islamic. Instead of relying solely on reason as a moral standard like other philosophers, al-Ghazālī asserts the need for both divine guidance and reason.[77]

Al-Ghazālī defines three domains for justice: political, moral, and economic. In agreement with Greek philosophy, he believes justice is a paramount virtue, though in his work *Nasīhat al-mulūk* (*Book of Counsel for Kings*) he prefers an unjust ruler to civil disorder.[78] Justice loses its primacy when social stability is threatened. The source of all vices rests in the worldly pleasures derived from a list of eight main pleasures, as enumerated by the fourth caliph, 'Alī b. Abī Tālib.[79] Among them are "social or political" pleasures, such as the lust for conquest or heightened social position.[80] In this way and by implication, al-Ghazālī condemns many kinds of war pursued outside the expediencies of sharī'a. Hourani indicates that al-Ghazālī does not deviate from the conventional legalistic view that "killing is not evil when it is punishment for crime, or when the victim is to be compensated in the next life."[81] But just like Aristotle, al-Ghazālī condemns all extremes and dedicates a quarter of his main work, *Ihyā' 'Ulūm al-Dīn*, to the pathology of vices. A full chapter of this tome even explores wrath (*al-ghadab*), rancour (*al-intiqām*), and jealousy (*al-hasad*). Al-Ghazālī asserts that the surest moral position is the mean between extremes. However, he adds, while moderate measures of anger (*al-ghadab*) or use of force (*al-'unf*) are a necessity to certain situations, self-control (*al-hilm*), forgiveness (*al-'afw*), clemency (*al-safh*), and soft attitude (*līna*) are further emphasized because of the natural inclination of man towards roughness.[82] According to Ghazālī, however, anger is to be used not against others but, in an esoteric sense, against the self in containing personal lasciviousness (*al-shahwa*). The virtue of self-control (*hilm*), then, must be used to check anger against others.[83] Goodman notes that "*hilm* is a crucial virtue for al-Gazālī as for Miskawayh and Ibn 'Adī because it offers control of anger."[84]

A section of al-Ghazālī's magnum opus, *Ihyā' 'Ulūm al-Dīn* (*The Revival of Religious Sciences*), called "Rub'i muhlikāt" deals with moral pathology and is rich with Prophetic traditions, which convey two important points: first, that there must be no retaliation against the vices of a transgressor; and second, that measures of self-control will be rewarded in the hereafter. A Prophetic tradition shared by the 'Uqbat Ibn 'Āmir and narrated by al-Ghazālī reflects the above points: "I heard from the Prophet, said 'O 'Uqba, shall I inform you of the best morality of both worlds? It is, to rejoin whoever has disconnected from you, to give to who has deprived you, and to forgive who has transgressed against you.'"[85]

From this and from other traditions and Qur'ānic verses referenced by al-Ghazālī, we may conclude that within his moral world view nonconfrontational, nonretaliatory tendencies are very important parts of the Islamic moral structure. It is hardly conceivable that this moral standard suddenly and inconsistently changes its attitudes just once it reaches communities beyond the state's political borders. If war and use of force must be the last resort in an Islamic society, why should this moral code lose its validity beyond borders of Muslim states?

Al-Ghazālī's more detailed views on war appear in the second chapter of his work *Nasīhat al-mulūk* (*Book of Counsel for Kings*), where he discusses the functions of the minister (*vizier*). He specifically mentions that the "worst minister" is the one who encourages his master (the king) to wage war when it is avoidable. He also stresses that once the enemy is defeated in war, the victors must not hasten to kill them, for the enemy subjects were also courageous men. "It is possible to kill the living," al-Ghazālī stresses, "but impossible to bring the dead back to life."[86] He suggests that it is a minister's duty to promptly arrange for freedom, though by ransom, of captive soldiers, effectively affording them hope.[87] These assertions show that al-Ghazālī was supportive of war as a last resort. His concern for the fate of prisoners of war on both sides of battle (between Islamic versus infidel forces) positions him on the humanist side of war ethics dealing with *jus in bello*. Al-Ghazālī distances himself from some of his contemporary jurists, whose literal approaches to scripture and hadith were only detrimental to the unfortunate fate of prisoners.

Theological perspectives aside, a major question, however, remains: what was al-Ghazālī's view of the religious "others"? This specific notion determines the foundation of one's attitude towards war in physical and nonphysical realms. Here, al-Ghazālī has a dual approach. In a book written for Caliph al-Mustazharu Billāh (d. 1094), al-Ghazālī becomes quite militant and kerygmatic in condemning the Bātinī's (Ismā'īlī Shi'as).[88] Chapter 8 of *Al-Mustazharī* focuses entirely on the rule of sharī'a law, its charges of unbelief (*takfīr*), and the corresponding punitive measures – some of which were as severe as execution.[89] Later, he changes his radical views on other faiths and sects, and accepts that people of other religious, denominational, and theological orientations may well reach salvation. His book, *Faysal al-tafriqa bayn al-Islām wa'l-zandaqa* (*On the Boundaries of Theological Tolerance in Islam*) develops this notion further.[90] A much more flexible opinion of religious "others" as expressed in this book harmonized better with al-Ghazālī's esoteric and mystical belief that man's real enemy is his own carnal soul. Here, the final and mystical al-Ghazālī is the one speaking.

Al-Ghazālī's moderated position towards religious "others" is well reflected in his revised judgment of those "saved" (*al-nājīya*) and those condemned to eternal hellfire.[91] He broadened the categories of believers eligible for salvation and, by the same token, reduced the number of categories of disbelievers punished in hell. The only ones condemned were those who had full knowledge of Islam but failed to believe the three principles of Islamic faith – namely, the unity of God, the prophethood of Muhammad, and the existence of the Day of Judgment. Those who misperceived or erred in their faith could claim a measure of salvation, as long as they did not attribute lying to the prophet Muhammad and did not advocate unbelief (*kufr*).[92] Al-Ghazālī frequently warned against the hasty and unscrupulous condemnation of people. He questioned jurists' self-proclaimed judgmental authority: "How could the jurists, purely on the basis of his mastery of Islamic law (*fiqh*), assume this enormous task? In what branch of the law does he encounter the skill and sciences (necessary to distinguish between belief and unbelief)?" [93] Turning to theologians, he raises the same question: "Why should one of these parties (Mu'tazila or Ashā'ira) enjoy a monopoly over truth to the exclusion of the other?"[94] "Most of the Christians of Byzantium and the Turks of this age [al-Ghazālī's contemporaries] will be covered by God's mercy."[95] This last position has important implications for the cause of just war, for, in theory, it deprives army authorities from a religious justification to declare jihad against an enemy innocently ignorant of Islam. Al-Ghazālī's most militant position in the *Faysal al-tafriqa* turns out not to be against the heretic aliens, but against a slew of Muslim philosophers, theologians, and Sufis: "Those who rush to condemn people ... any ... school as unbelievers are reckless ignoramuses ... For challenging others with one's knowledge is a deeply ingrained human instinct over which the ignorant is able to exercise no control."[96]

One can conclude that in the early phase of his intellectual life, al-Ghazālī had a strong inclination towards a political realism that did not tie the hands of rulers with moral concerns in war. War, in other words, in the hands of the ruler did not need justification and was a matter of his discretion. Such moral laxity, he perhaps thought, was a necessary precondition for a political philosophy that puts a state's stability and security above all other political goals. As the mystical interpretation of Islam came to hold prominence over all other notions for the older al-Ghazālī, he became, according to Goodman, "far more interested in the spiritual and moral struggle for self-conquest than in the worldly struggle for dominion – even in the name of his faith."[97] The end result of this moral shift, as discussed above, was the appearance of many inconsistencies in al-Ghazālī's theory on ethics of war and peace. But the evolution of his perspectives brought him increasingly from a battle with the religious "other" to a battle with the carnal "self." Some scholars may still cite statements from the older al-Ghazālī's last works before his death, which can still be interpreted as dehumanizing religious "others." I am not contesting such observations, nor do I claim consistency in his views on war and peace. But a moral shift is certainly evident in the latter part of al-Ghazālī's life, which provides far more flexibility in defining an enemy than his earlier ideological position could permit.

Forgiveness in Politics

Nasīr al-Dīn Tūsī (d. 1274), one of the most prominent authorities in the history of Shi'i scholarship, expanded on Miskawayh's perspective on the philosophy and ethics of friendship. He developed his moral philosophy in *Nāsirean Ethics* (*Akhlāq-e nāserī*), which is an adaptation and translation into Persian of Miskawayh's *Tahdhīb al-Akhlāq*, with two extra chapters on economics and politics that Tūsī added to the former text. Tūsī was in full agreement with Miskawayh on the importance of friendship and love as cardinal virtues. He alludes to the superiority of love above justice; "The reason for this idea," Tūsī asserts, "is that Justice requires artificial union, whereas Love requires natural union; at the same time, the artificial in relation to the natural is like an outer skin, the artificial imitating the natural … Thus," Tūsī concludes, "it is obvious that the need for Justice (which is the most perfect of human virtues) in preserving the order of species, arises from the loss of love."[98] Given this perspective in a normative system where justice is inferior to the bond of love, it is not surprising that war in general – and even just war and warrior heroism – does not happen to be an interesting focus for Tūsī. He nevertheless does not miss the opportunity to advise rulers on just causes for war, just conduct in war, and just conduct after war.

Tūsī's main contribution to ethics is his work on politics – namely, in his discussion of "the management of states" (*tadbīr mudun*). When he describes the five classes making up the "virtuous city," he refers to the fourth as the "holy warriors."[99] It was these "holy warriors" who defended the city's ramparts against the aggression of nonvirtuous cities. Noticeably, no reference to offensive or expansionist war appears in his definition of holy war.

Tūsī comes closest to the ethics of war when he provides clear advice on the moral cause and conduct of war in a chapter on "The Conduct of Kings" (*Sīrat-e mulūk* in Persian), a treatise belonging to the genre of "mirrors for princes" (advice useful for princes in their leadership conduct). Addressing war, its morals, and qualities, Tūsī advises the following:

> The utmost effort should be made to win over enemies and to seek agreement with them, and matters should so be ordered (as far as possible) that the need for fighting and warfare does not arise. If such need docs befall, two cases only present themselves: Either one begins (hostilities) or one is the defender. In the former case, the first requirement is that one's purpose shall be only Pure good and the quest for Faith, and that one is on guard against any seeking after superiority or domination; next, one must fulfil the conditions of prudence and misgiving. Moreover, one should not embark upon warfare without prior confidence in victory; nor should one go to war with a following that is not of one mind in any circumstances whatsoever, for in passing between two enemies lies great peril ... So long as it is possible to disperse enemies and to root them out by contriving and the use of stratagem, it is anything but prudent to employ the instrument of warfare. Ardashīr Bābak says: "One should not chastise with a stick where a whip suffices, nor employ a sword where a club will serve." The last of all contrivings should be (a resort to) warfare: "The final remedy is cauterization." There is nothing reprehensible in creating confusion among one's enemies by resorting to all manner of stratagems, deceptions and false dispatches, but in no circumstances is it permissible to employ treachery ... In war, regards should be had to the profit made by merchants, and one nor should proceed to endanger men or equipment so long as there be no expectation of great gain ... Once victory is gained, scheming should not be abandoned, nor should there be any lessening of circumspection and prudence; but, in so far as may be, whoever can be captured alive should not be killed, for there are many advantages in taking prisoners (such as making captives, holding as hostages or ransom, or placing under an obligation), but in killing there is no profit. After victory, there should be absolutely no killing, and no indulgence of enmity and prejudice, for the position of enemies after victory is the same as that of slaves or subjects.[100]

As Fakhry has noted, for Tūsī war clearly was only to be waged in self-defence and only as a last resort.[101] Tūsī, however, discusses situations during which diplomacy failed and the ruler was thus compelled to initiate hostilities for the sake only of "Pure good and the quest of the Faith." The vague quality of terms like "Pure good" and "quest of the Faith" are open to voluntary interpretation with the potential to be abused by rulers seeking war. But living in the era of warlords with standards set by Mongol callousness, Tūsī has gone to important extents by reminding warlords and world conquerers of the realm of just cause for and conduct in wars.

Importantly, in the above passage Tūsī comes close to the three standard principles known in modern literature on the ethics of war as justice at war, after war (*post bellum*, denoting humanitarian treatment of the conquered enemy), and proportionality (denoting the significance of a realistic assessment of winning and assurance of more benefits in war than costs). His emphatic tone in forbidding treachery in war, in modern international-relations parlance, has no meaning but respect for bilateral treaties that must not be broken unilaterally by countries or private citizens.

Tūsī's recommendations on the treatment of prisoners of war are expressed in terms of cost and benefit, but between the lines one can discern humanitarian concerns.[102] He concludes this section of the text with reference to a legend about Alexander the Great and his teacher Aristotle. The legend, related to ethics of war, claims that when Aristotle learned Alexander was killing residents of an already defeated and surrounded city, Aristotle critically questioned the behaviour and reminded Alexander that forgiveness as a virtue was expected from kings, much more so than from the commoners or the lay public. Tūsī quotes the following from Aristotle's letter to Alexander: "While you had an excuse for killing your enemies before victory, what is your excuse, after victory, for killing your subjects?"[103]

This short analysis of Tūsī's views on war and peace demonstrates the need for a thorough study of his actual political philosophy during his life under Mongol rule. That he transformed Hulagu Khan, one of the most powerful military figures of history, into a patron of science, art, and rational theology demonstrates the power of the political philosophy of peacemaking and conflict resolution as envisioned and practised by Tūsī in the heart of the thirteenth century. We can imagine that the key to Tūsī's monumental success, who first met with the Mongol warlord as a captive scientist in the camp of the Ismaī'īlī citadel of Alamūt, was perhaps an effective language of diplomacy, which he conveyed to the warlord (Hulagu Khan) thus: "The farthest of men from virtue are those who depart from civilized life and sociability and are inclined to solitude and loneliness. Thus, the virtue of love and friendship is the greatest of virtues, and its preservation is the most important task."[104] It is through this lens of political philosophy that Tūsī approaches the climax of his war ethics by addressing forgiveness in politics: "The employment of pardon by kings," he exclaims, "is a more excellent thing than its use by others, for pardoning when one is able (to do the opposite) is more praiseworthy." Tūsī's final words on forgiveness in politics is an allusion to a poem from an Arabic source unrecognized by Wickens:

I will take it on myself to forgive every sinner,
    Even though crimes against me increase thereby,
People come under one of three heads:
    Noble, surpassed in nobility, or equal but adverse.

As for the one above me, I acknowledge his worth,
  Wherein I follow what is due, that being obligatory;
As for thc one beneath me, if he be disinclined to
  Respond to my suggestion (what then?), though some may criticize;
As for my like, if he slips or blunders
  I show grace, for grace bids what is due.[105]

Towards Conquering One's Carnal Self

Unlike al-Ghazālī, who at the end of his life was inclined (although not consistently) towards a pluralist, mystical position on war and peace, Jalāl al-Dīn Muhammad Rumi Balkhī (d. 1273), who is a globally respected scholar of mysticism, became an early proponent of peace early in life. For centuries, Rumi has formed an important part of generations of Iranians' collective identity. His most important work, *Mathnavī-e Ma'navī* (henceforth referred to as *Mathnavī*), revered in Persian cultures as "the Qur'ān in Persian," does not offer much on the ethics of war, but the few allusions made to the subject are remarkable and influential.

In his prelude to chapter 6 of *Mathnavī*, Rumi tackles the question of war from an anthological perspective:

جنگِ ما و صلح ما در نور عین   نیست از ما، هست بَین الاصبعین
جنگِ فعلی، جنگِ طبعی، جنگِ قول   در میان جزوها حربیست هول
این جهان زین جنگ قائم می بود   در عناصر درنگر تا حل شود
چار عنصر، چار استون قویست   که بر ایشان سقفِ دنیا مُستویست
هر ستونی اِشکنندهٔ آن دگر   استن آب اِشکنندهٔ آن شرر
پس بنای خلق بر اضداد بود   لاجرم جنگی شدند از ضرّ و سود
هست احوالت خلافِ یکدگر   هر یکی با هم مخالف در اثر
چونکه هر دم راه خود را میزنی   با دگر کس سازگاری چون کنی؟
مینگر در خود چنین جنگِ گران   پس چه مشغولی به جنگِ دیگران؟
تا مگر زین جنگ، حقّت واخرد   در جهان صلح یك رنگت بَرد
آن جهان جز باقی و آباد نیست   زآنکه ترکیبِ وی از اضداد نیست
این تفانی از ضد آید ضد را   چون نباشد ضد، نبوَد جز بقا
نفی ضد کرد از بهشت آن بی نظیر   که نباشد شمس و ضدش زمهریر
هست بی رنگی اصول رنگها   صلحها باشد اصول جنگها
آن جهان است اصل این پُر غم وثاق   وصل باشد اصل هر هجر و فراق
جنگها بین کان اصول صلح هاست   چون نبی که جنگ او بهر خداست [106]

([The source of] our war and our peace is in the Light of the
Essence [of God]. It is not from ourselves: it is "between the two

fingers of God."[107]
[There is] war of nature, war of actions, and war of words –
There is a terrible war among the parts [of the creation].
[And] this world is enduring because of this battle. Look at the
[conflicting] elements so that [this problem] can be solved.
The four elements [soil, water, air, and fire] are [like] four strong columns: by means of
them the roof of the world is [kept] even and straight.
Each column [is] the breaker of the other. The column of water
is the destroyer of sparks [of fire].
Therefore, the foundation of the creation was [based] upon
opposites. Necessarily, we are battling because of loss and gain. Your states are opposed to one another, [because] each one
is contrary against another in [its] effect.
Since you are highway-robbing yourself every moment, how can you
act harmoniously with another person?
Look at the waves of armies of your states – each one in anger
and enmity toward another one.
[So] observe a great battle such as this within yourself [as well].
Therefore, why are you occupied with battle against others?
Or perhaps [you are helpless and hoping] God may buy you
back from [remaining in] this war [and] bring you to the single-
coloured world of peace.
That World [spiritual] isn't [anything] other than eternal and flourishing,
since it isn't intermixed with opposites.
This mutual destruction reaches [every] opposite from [its
corresponding] opposite. [But] when there isn't [any] opposite,
there is [nothing] except eternity.
The One [Who is] without equal has forbidden contraries from
Paradise, saying, "There will be no sun nor its opposite, extreme
cold, [therein]."
Colourlessness is the origin of colours, peaces are the origin of wars,
Perceive that wars, which are the origins of all peace, are like [the war of] the Prophet whose war is for God's sake.)[108]

The perspectives expressed in this piece are deterministic and present humans as prey to nature's forces. The very essence of the universe is based on conflict; and this conflict, in Rumi's view, is the ultimate driving force behind all creatures. The ongoing conflict results from the conflict between the four elemental substances: water, fire, air, and soil.[109] This runs contrary to the view held by the philosopher Ibn Sīnā, who believed that the driving force of the universe, and all therein, was love.[110]

Rumi's attitude towards war provides a deterministic reading of some Qur'ānic verses, especially in instances where the poet asserts that war could eliminate the root of corruption on earth.[111] He contends that wars could act as a purifying process or as a detour through which human beings could transcend this world. However, Rumi is also conscious and emphatically supportive of the just cause for war. As shown below, he questions how warriors engage in temporal battles when a far more important esoteric battlefield exists within every individual's soul. Mankind's greatest enemy lives inside the soul, effectively underscoring the futility of fighting with other humans.

To pronounce the above convictions, Rumi refers to a story narrated by a zealous warrior named 'Abbādī, who may have been a member of an Islamic Khārijī sect (an early fundamentalist theological school in Islamic history). 'Abbādī participated in seventy campaigns (*ghazwa*s) in an unsuccessful attempt to reach martyrdom. In 'Abbādī's words, expressed by Rumi: "Once I did all that I could with no success, I turned to esoteric battle against my carnal soul. But as I was busy with the 'greater jihad' (*jihad al-akbar*), I heard once again that the army drums are calling volunteers for a military campaign; my carnal soul was moved and I desired to join. But then I rebuked my soul and reminded myself that of course it is an easy way out through one strike, while people watch me in praise. It was then when I noticed the depth of my soul's hypocrisy."[112] Rumi references similar anecdotes and seriously questions the motives of the warriors, eventually concluding that resorting to external war is, in fact, an escape from the responsibility of fighting with one's own carnal self:

ای بسا خامی که ظاهر خونش ریخت   لیک نفس زنده آن جانب گریخت
آلتش بشکست و رهزن زنده ماند   نفس زنده است ار چه مرکب خون فشاند [113]

(How so many immature there were,
Who appeared having lost their blood for good cause,
While, their carnal souls were left to escape untamed
Their essences lost physical means [their bodies],
However their innate carnal thieves lived on. [my translation])

Elsewhere, Rumi points out the significance of the legitimacy of war (*jus ad bellum*) by depicting a heroic war scene in which 'Alī b. Abī Tālib releases a defeated enemy because the enemy had angered him. 'Alī's reason for the chivalrous act was that his own personal anger spoiled the pure motive for which ‘Alī originally fought.[114]

The philosophical and ontological causes of war aside, when it comes to explaining why sharī‘a has made certain kinds of wars duty bound, Rumi alludes to the great danger of empowering and arming the ignorant. He uses his powerful, metaphoric language to respond to the question:

[115] پس غزا زین فرض شد بر مومنان   تا ستانند از کف مجنون سنان

(War [*ghazā*] became incumbent upon believers
So that they can force the crazy man [*majnoon*] to give up his spears.
[my translation])

Clearly, this verse justifies the use of force for disarming lunatics. Rumi believes that the only legitimate reason to wage war arises from a collective obligation to preserve peace by disarming any irrational entity that is using power for impulsive, emotional urges. In volume 4 of *Mathnavī*, Rumi discusses the adverse effects of power (i.e., ignorance) and provides a metaphoric argument based on universal and nondoctrinal wisdom, which favours a balance between reason and the use of force.

Rumi recalls a Prophetic legend wherein the Prophet speaks to Muslim warriors returning from a legitimate war. Through the words of the Prophet, Rumi defines war with the external enemy as the lesser jihad (*al-jihad al asghar*), as compared with the greater jihad (*al-jihad al-akbar*), which he defines as fighting with the inner, carnal self:

ای شهان کشتیم ما خصم برون   ماند خصمی زو بتر در اندرون
[116] کشتن این کار عقل و هوش نیست   شیرِ باطن سخره‌ی خرگوش نیست

(Oh kings, we have slain the outward enemy
And yet a worse enemy within remained.
To slay this [enemy] is not the work of reason and intelligence:
The inward lion is not subdued by the hare.)[117]

Rumi asserts that the greater struggle is a more important task than the lesser. To illustrate, he juxtaposes a mountain with a needle to explicate the enormity of the task: “It requires divine assistance to uproot the mountain of the ‘self’ with a small needle that is the only instrument available to humanity.”[118] In this way, the Prophet warns Muslim believers that they must be permanently conscious that the carnal "self" is by far a more dangerous enemy than the "other," or the external enemy.

[119] سهل شیری دان که صفها بشکند شیر آ نست آن که خود را بشکند

(It is easy for a lion to break rows [of others];
The real lion is the one who breaks the carnal self. [my translation])

Rumi categorically rejects using the battlefield as a short cut to paradise. In the entire *Mathnavī,* there is no commentary promoting or praising jihad, except in an esoteric sense. This military pacifism, to a large extent, is not far removed from the Christian pacifist schools in modern debates over the ethics of war.[120] Perhaps the most significant question Rumi poses is asking how an entity can conquer another for a supposedly good cause before conquering his own carnal self. When someone, who has been defeated in fighting his internal evil, dominates another entity for whatever excuse, the result is a double defeat and no victor. A person in command of his or her carnal soul, however, will, by definition, lose every incentive to dominate someone else. The above perspective questions the entire institution of external jihad, revealing it as self-deception. Such a perspective challenges the theological heart of modern suicide bombings, which have unfortunately become so fashionable in recent history. In Rumi's view, a "suicidal jihadist" is nothing more than a cowardly soul mistakenly thinking that the act is a nonstop flight to paradise – or, in other words, an escape from the responsibility of navigating the difficulties and injustices of ordinary life. If Rumi was critical of a warrior who enthusiastically looked for an occasion of war as a short cut to paradise, we can conclude with certainty that he would have condemned modern suicidal bombing, which takes so many innocent lives.

Conclusion

Al-Fārābī, Miskawayh, and Tūsī share two important perspectives that can help curb ideological wars and conflicts. The first, and most important, is a universal sense of justice that is not culturally defined but instead is intrinsic in all individuals, societies, and cultures. Objective ethics (or reason-based ethics) reject the assumptions of voluntarism in determining justice. Within this extrareligious definition of justice, the notion of "holy war" gives way to "just war," with elements that translate between various cultures and religions. This notion has two implications:

1 War and peace are legitimate subjects for international and interfaith dialogue, as well as for negotiations, conventions, and contracts.
2 The acceptance of political pluralism; this framework does not leave much space for belief-based wars.

The second view shared by all three scholars is that human beings are, by definition, social entities that would lose their essences without society. Additionally, Miskawayh and Tūsī expand on the Aristotelian philosophy of friendship from the horizontal human-human to human-God relationship and promote a social life that enjoys and employs values higher than simply what sheer distributive or punitive justice entails. Needless to say, a justice-plus society within a moral space defined by forgiveness, magnanimity, and generosity produces little incentive for war and conflict.

Al-Ghazālī and Rumi, on the other hand, maintain that the esoteric world is both a far more expansive realm of life and by definition more important than the exoteric life; that is, it is the battleground within one's soul that is far more critical than any external wars encountered in the mundane realm.

As al-Ghazālī demonstrates through his work, the backbone of Islamic ethics is formed by mastering the virtues of self-control, forgiveness, and flexibility (*hilm*, *'afw,* and *safh*). These virtues protect human beings from anger, vengefulness, blaming others, and rigidity of mind. As these virtues are universal, it is unimaginable that they disappear once they reach beyond Muslim borders. If universally applied, ethics of forgiveness can promote tolerance and peace beyond interpersonal relations and well into civic, international, and interfaith arenas. Al-Ghazālī, who lived before the era of nation-states, could not be expected to think like Hannah Arendt and proclaim that without respect for contract and forgiveness, international relations become impossible.[121] His theology and ethics, however, provide enough concepts for the moral sustenance of interpersonal relations to help good communal relations by extension.

Whether focusing on the primacy of friendship and social life or on the human struggle towards self-purification by fighting the carnal soul, both notions seem to keep people from a life of domination marked by the use of force against different others and mother nature. It is hard to imagine that human civilization could continue without these concepts. It should not be surprising, then, that many modern Iranian theologians and intellectuals, as we will see in chapter 4 of this volume, have incorporated these classical ideas into their syncretic and civilization-conscious ideas.

3 War and Chivalry in the Annals of Iranian History and Ethical Imagination

که فتوت دادن بی علت است

(For chivalry is in generosity without cause.)

– Rumi[1]

Ayatollah Khomeini's grandson, Seyyed Hassan, who symbolically appears in the Iranian media as a representative of his grandfather's legacy, visited the first international conference on traditional Iranian sport culture, called *āyīn-e pahlavānī* (rules of championship; Persian), on 27 August 2013.[2] He was welcomed by senior figures of this sport, which has chains of clubhouses called *zurkhaneh* (lit. house of strength) in various Iranian cities. These clubs are "a place," in the words of Lloyd Ridgeon, "where men came (and still come) to seek physical, moral, and spiritual perfection."[3] One of the banners attached to the walls of the conference hall where the young Khomeini and other honorary guests were present depicted some of the most important principles and moral codes of this sport. These codes were: loyalty, faith, truthfulness, humility, forgiveness, chastity, altruism, and patriotism.

For the organizers of the conference, the visit by Hassan Khomeini was significant not only for a political reason but also for a symbolic one: his attendance showed a religious celebrity paying tribute to an ancient, chivalrous institution that promotes moral championship in traditional sports. These *zurkhaneh*s are the descendants of youth and chivalry clubs and of many guild institutions engaged in providing security for urban areas, specifically in locations where no strong central government or police force existed to provide security.[4] At times, members of these institutions engaged in battles, effectively increasing their influence on the formulation of the ethics of war in Islamic moral history.

As I will demonstrate below in part 2 of this volume, three Muslim civil wars during the short caliphate of ʻAlī b. Abī Tālib and the episode of Karbalā, briefly mentioned in the introduction, profoundly influenced Shiʻi war ethics and literature. These ethics were, however, transmitted to later generations not through juridical scholarship but through folk culture, epic literature, street passion plays, festivals and associations, such as *javānmardān*, *ʻayyārān*, and *zurkhanehs*. The suppression of the Shiʻa minorities by fellow Muslims throughout a good part of Muslim history redefined the notions of "self" and "other" for Shiʻi communities and convinced them to rely more on the human-reasoned, natural, and universal notions of justice rather than on the concept defined by the political expediencies of Muslim rulers.

This chapter explores how the Iranian/Shiʻi ethics of war and peace have been partially influenced by institutions of chivalry that have, except for a very brief period of time in Islamic history, remained nongovernmental and have promoted the ethics of championship and chivalry in war, beyond the military triumphalism. Also presented are the cases of two influential Iranian Muslim figures, Yaʻqūb Layth Saffār (d. 879) and legendary character Samak-e ʻAyyār, both considered as icons of morality in war and peace.[5] Whether or not these figures were influenced by pre-Islamic Persian, Arab, and Islamic cultures of chivalry, their stories and chivalrous conduct in war are presently imagined by the Iranian public as exemplary.

Modern scholarship on Eastern cultures and institutions of chivalry (such as the pre-Islamic Iranian *asbārān*) and on paramilitary entities in the Islamic era (such as the *ʻayyārān* and *futūwwa* associations, *javānmardān* and similar organizations) has received scant, but nevertheless significant, attention in recent years.[6] Most scholars concur that these social entities were impressed upon by moral principles that combine both Islamic and pre-Islamic universal codes of ethics. Scholars do differ on issues related to the actual history of these entities, but these debates have thus far had little impact on how the contemporary Iranian public views these entities.

The warriors connected to these organizations were active early on in Islamic history. While their code of conduct is comparable to European notions of chivalry, their contemporary public held mixed views of them. From vagabonds and vandals to voluntary protectors of urban security and defenders of borders, these warriors enjoyed a varied range of reputations – both positive and negative. It is important to note that Muslim and Christian chivalric institutions interacted during the Crusades. The European mercenaries, for example, became familiar with the ethics of *futūwwa* (manners of liberal youth), which was the Arabic equivalent of the Persian *javānmardī*, and as a result were influenced by the practices of honour, respect for their enemy, and respect for women in these institutions. The Islamic codes of chivalry embodied in *futūwwa* organizations, however, went beyond regulating the conduct of war. They laid the foundations for the regulation of guilds, or what is known today as syndicalism. They have also played an important role in Sufi institutions, though many of these aspects lie outside the scope of this chapter.

Roots of the *Futūwwa* Institutions

After the early periods of Islamic conquests, a number of paramilitary institutions emerged, operating in both civic and official capacities. Among the contemporary scholars who have most recently contributed significantly to the study of these institutions are Mohsen Zakeri, Mehran Afshari, D.G. Tor, and Lloyd Ridgeon, all of whom have provided critical literature and readings of the sources related to these institutions of chivalry.[7]

Zakeri's work demonstrates how the history of these institutions dates back to the pre-Islamic Sassanian Empire.[8] Two earlier scholars, Taeschner and Cahen, have argued that *futūwwa,* in its assorted forms, such as *fatā* (a pre-Islamic term incorporating the ideals of Arab nobility) and *'ayyārān* (a pre-Islamic term incorporating the ideals of Persian nobility), were well known in the centuries prior to al-Nāsir li Dīn-Allāh (d. 1225).[9] He was thirty-fourth Abbasid caliph, the only caliph to head *futūwwa* organizations.[10] According to Zakeri, "Taeschner concluded that one can assume what was preserved from the culture of antiquity in Babylonia and Iran was transferred to Islam under the rubric of *futūwwa.*" Cahen notes that "there was not a single town in the Iranian and pre-Iranian world from Central Asia to Mesopotamia, which did not have its *'ayyārūn* (Arabic plural for *'ayyār*)."[11] Zakeri states: "The nucleus of these groups consisted of the *asbārān* who were employed by the Muslims as soldiers, bodyguards, and police in Basra, Kūfa, and other major cities. It was through them that the social ideals of a noble warrior class were introduced to the Muslims, and the foundation was laid for the institution of *futūwwa,* in which these ideals were synthesized with Arab and Islamic ethical virtues … by the *dihqānān* who, as 'intellectuals,' were involved in non-military engagements such as the Shu'ūbī disputations and the … movement of the Mū'tazilites."[12]

The pre-Islamic Iranian middle class of *dihqānān* helped form the paramilitary *asbārān,* and in turn, war ethics.[13] Soon after the Mazdakite social reform movement was suppressed by the Sassanian court, a large number of free-minded *asbārān* joined the Islamic forces as volunteer soldiers dedicated to fighting against the remaining Sassanian forces.[14] They settled in Basra as the *asāwira* (Arabic plural of *āswār*) and in Kūfa as the *ahāmira* (the Arabic plural of *ahmar*, which is a title for free warriors and is contemporary with *asāwira*) and later joined forces opposed to the caliphate. They were employed as guards and auxiliary forces by the caliph's opponent 'Abd Allah b. al-Zubayr in Mecca and fought with him in the battle of Rabadha in 684.[15] A second group of free converts, called *mawālī,* made up a significant cavalry of soldiers for the 'Abbasid revolution.[16]

The *futūwwa* institutions followed their own moral standards in battles. These standards were partly rooted in the pre-Islamic, Iranian culture of *asbārān* and *dihqānān*, also partly influenced by Islamic norms and by the Arabic *jāhilīya* concept of *murū'a* or *murūwwa*.[17]

Another Iranian scholar, Mehran Afshari, supports Zakeri's thesis by arguing that "it is not too far from truth to say that before the appearance of Islam, this tradition [of *javānmardī*], built on an Iranian-inspired foundation, had reached the Arabian Peninsula and all territories adjacent to Iran."[18]

In the spirit of an identity debate about the roots of *'ayyārān*, Tor expresses doubt that '*ayyārān* as a para-statal organization appearing in early ninth-century eastern Iran had any connection with the proto-Iranian social groups. Based on traceable evidence, she suggests that the '*ayyārān* were motivated by volunteer-based Sunni jihadi groups (*mutawwta'a*), who were fervently defending the borders of Muslim lands.[19] In one of the latest studies on the roots of *futūwwa*, Ridgeon revisits the sources for the history of *'ayyārī* institutions and sheds doubt on Tor's assertions; according to Ridgeon, "Tor's depiction of Ya'qūb as *mutatawwi'* whose primary concern was highly idealistic in fighting heretical groups and empowering proto-Sunni orthodoxy appears over-exaggerated at times."[20] Whether or not *futūwwa, 'ayyārī*, and *javānmardī* organizations shared the same principles and ethics does not alter three facts:

1 All of these organizations were following, to some degree and with variation, codes of ethics in war not directly based on Islamic juristic sources.
2 Iranian scholars of chivalric institutions unanimously emphasize Iranian roots for these entities.
3 Within the entire expanse of modern Muslim states, there are no functioning non governmental organizations that are as connected to the legacies of the above-mentioned organizations as the Iranian *zurkhaneh* sport clubs.

The above facts point to a strong tendency for the present Iranian generation to balance elements of its dual Iranian-Islamic ethical identities.

Unlike preceding institutions, *zurkhaneh*s did not have a military function at political borders; however, their social status still influenced domestic politics and conflict-resolution approaches. A modern case exemplifying their influence involves members of a central *zurkhaneh* in Tehran, headed by a chief wrestler named Sha'bān Ja'farī (d. 2009). This group played a significant role in the return of Mohammad Reza Shah Pahlavi to the monarchy in 1953, after Iran's popular prime minister Mohammad Mosaddeq had forced out the Shah during a country-wide movement on oil nationalization.[21]

Chivalry Role Models and Initiators

There is no dispute among scholars of Muslim chivalry organizations that 'Alī b. Abī Tālib, the fourth caliph after the Prophet Muhammad and the first Shi'i imam, was a chief role model for a wide spectrum of Muslim institutions of chivalry. For French scholar Henry Corbin, the centrality of the person of 'Alī in all of the *futūwwa* organizations leaves no doubt about "the fact that the very concept of *futūwwa* has complete connection with Shi'ism and the Shi'i view of the Imamate [the spiritual leadership]."[22] The figure of 'Alī as the legendary founder of these institutions is an important binding thread for them. Perhaps the centrality of 'Alī as figurehead may be explained by his antidiscriminatory attitudes towards non-Arab converts in early Islamic history, something that attracted a large number of Iranians to 'Alī's camp. Additionally, the appearance of Salmān al-Fārsī (the first Iranian companion of the Prophet), as a Muslim hero and as an Iranian cofounder in the genealogy of these groups and societies, lent them a joint Shi'i-Iranian identity.

The values that 'Alī and Salmān represented helped form the codes of chivalry for these entities. Such values are embodied in the terms *javānmard, 'ayyār, fatā, āzāda,* and the like and also reflect "the highest social and ethical values of noble warrior: altruism, prowess, loyalty, sustaining the poor, and defending the oppressed."[23]

The *futūwwa* phenomenon reached its climax in the early thirteenth century, when Caliph al-Nāsir reorganized them and became a spiritual leader promoting their socio-political impact across the eastern lands of Islam. Al-Nāsir tapped these reformed associations for his political base. The *futūwwa* subsequently assumed the form of professional and guild organizations.

The moral mission of Muslim free warriors varied between the early seventh and mid-thirteenth centuries. At times, they served as a volunteer police force protecting cities and communities from crime and disorder. At other times, they were merely volunteer soldiers used in expansionist or domestic intrastate wars. However, they always observed particular codes of conduct for their activities.

Ethics versus Law (sharī'a)

Legends concerning 'Alī b. Abī Tālib's initiation of *futūwwa* established the core values for these associations. According to one account narrated by multiple Persian-language sources, the master narrative of *futūwwa* orders revolves around how the prophet Muhammad once heard about a Muslim man and women having an illicit encounter in a nearby hideaway. With his informant insisting on the immediate application of sharī'a punishment, the Prophet dispatched 'Alī for enquiries. 'Alī walked around the premises of this illicit hideaway with closed eyes, eventually going back to inform the Prophet that he had seen no one. The Prophet, realizing what 'Alī had done, praised him. He gave 'Alī the epithet of *fatā* (lit. well-mannered young) and made him drink from a symbolic cup of salt water, thus establishing the rituals for subsequent *futūwwa* orders.[24]

'Alī's actions in this story have significant paradigmatic implications for *futūwwa* members. 'Alī's behaviour suggests that sharī'a's punitive codes are considered deterrents rather than measures that must be strictly implemented irrespective of their actual social impact. Such flexibility encourages important traits like forgiveness, magnanimity, tolerance of errors, and the overlooking of minor sins, qualities that form an important part of *futūwwa* and *javānmardī* ethics.

The above tale provides another significant moral element when detailing what happens after 'Alī's return to the Prophet without a report. The Prophet utters the following proclamation, reflecting on his moral traits: "There is no chivalrous except Ali and no sword except *dhu'lfaqār* ['Alī's double-edged sword]."[25] This phrase reflects, in fact, the heart of the Iranian image of 'Alī's ethics of war. *Dhu'lfaqār* (lit. double edged) is a curved binary sword appearing in most of the imagined portraits of 'Alī in Iran and is considered by the public to be a symbol of justice. The Prophetic phrase, as mentioned above, referring to the two elements of chivalry and sword has become proverbial in the Persian language and signifies the necessity of balance between forgiveness and justice. In terms of the philosophy of ethics, unlike Christian ethics wherein forgiveness is defined as a duty, in Islam the forgiveness-justice ethical equation reflects on the fact that forgiveness is a virtue and justice needs to be always accessible so that the virtue of forgiveness can attain its maximum value as a highly advised moral option.[26]

The Esoteric-Ethical versus the Literal Interpretation

One of the core principles of *futūwwa* is the primacy of forgiveness (*'afw*) over retaliation-in-kind (*qisās*), both of which are also promoted by sharī'a. The Qu'rān allows punitive retaliation for crime cases but also provides more valued options of financial compensation and, at the highest moral level, forgiveness.[27] There is, moreover, a Qur'ānic emphasis on the proper way of implementing these measures.

Henry Corbin's reading of a *futūwwa* charter, written by Shahāb al-Dīn 'Umar Suhrawardī (d. 1234),[28] brought him to the conclusion that Suhrawardī held some principles of *futūwwa* above sharī'a, at least in the literal understanding of the word.[29] This contradiction is resolved only in Suhrawardī's esoteric exegesis of Qur'ānic legal verses. Suhrawardī suggests that if the Prophet did not select another person other than 'Alī to enquire about the illicit affair, it was because the Prophet was cognizant of the virtues of *futūwwa* that 'Alī embodied. These virtues belonged to a moral order higher than simply a strict adherence to the letters of the law. "Forgiveness," maintains Suhrawardī, "does in fact conform to the *shari'a*, but with a higher esoteric level thereof."[30]

'Alī as a role model and the *futūwwa* as a moral institution cannot be imagined without their existential relationship in Shi'i and Iranian cultures. Ridgeon argues that "the Persian *futuwwa* literature after Suhrawardī builds on this deep veneration for Ali, and may be considered one of the factors that facilitated the gradual adoption of Shi'ism in Iran, even before the emergence of the Safavid state in the sixteenth century, when it established Shi'ism as the 'national denomination.'"[31] This assertion provides clarity about the possibility that, among other ethical elements, the Shi'i ethics of war and peace were also influenced by normative elements in the *futūwwa* world view.

While Suhrawardī's esoteric reading of sharī'a may help resolve some of the conceptual controversies between ethics and law, there are other normative elements that go beyond the scope of conventional Qur'ānic understandings, including the concept of loyalty. Authors on the subject almost unanimously agree that a main principle of *futūwwa* is "the friend of the friend is a friend and the friend of the enemy is an enemy."[32] This ethical code of affiliations, with its implications for the ethics of war and peace, is echoed in the Shi'i principle of *tavallā wa tabarrā* (affinity with friends of the Shi'i imams and strict disassociation from their enemies), as will be discussed in part 2 of this volume. Another *futūwwa* principle dictates that members of the order must never commit treacherous acts against each other. These two principles tie personal and institutional loyalty together, effectively constructing a political element that, at times, may be at odds with modern views of liberal democracy.

The Concept of Enemy

A well-known principle of almost all *futūwwa* charters is the renunciation of one's rights and claims in favour of others due to viewing oneself as inescapably lower than all other creatures. Within such a moral world view, it is clear that establishing an antagonistic definition of "other," and therefore the enemy, is an extremely difficult task.

According to Melikoff, groups referred to by historians as *ghuzāt* (Arabic plural of *ghāzī* "religiously motivated warrior"), *fityān* (Arabic plural of *fatā* "young man of liberality"), *'ayyārūn* (Arabic plural of *'ayyār* "free-spirited warrior"), etc. formed a reserve of troops available to those needing them.[33] In such a capacity, they acted merely as mercenaries subsisting on war. However, other sources refer to this reserve of troops as servants of God who "clean the earth from the defilement of polytheism."[34] This latter capacity is highly ideological and seems to be in stark contrast to the former view. The difference in these characterizations holds important implications for these associations' concept of enemy and in their treatment of the enemy. In their capacity as mercenaries, they were hired by warlords and sultans, such as Mahmud Ghaznavi.[35] It is logical to expect that, as far as the ethics of war were concerned, the behaviour of these troops would have been a function of the orders and supervision of the commanders they served. In their capacity as servants of God, they upheld the law or fought holy wars, which more naturally would have enabled them to act according to their own conceptions of Islamic ethos. In reality, these groups acted with a variety of motives and according to a multitude of moral standards.[36] Certain reports show their inclination towards sheer cruelty and lawlessness; yet other reports, as shown below, also depict them as adhering to the highest principles and codes of chivalry in their encounters with enemies.

Ya'qūb b. Layth Saffār, Samak-e-'Ayyār, and Chivalry in War

Ya'qūb b. Layth Saffār (d. 879), a coppersmith who founded the Saffārid dynasty in eastern Iran, was a significant *'ayyārī* moral role model and bearer of standards in the Persian imagery of chivalrous institutions.[37] According to Sīstān history (specifically in the *Tarīkh-e Sīstān*, written by an anonymous author in the late twelfth century), Ya'qūb owed his power to his *'ayyārī* attitude, which was perhaps tied to his origin as a coppersmith. The text relates, "The reason for his ascendancy was that he always shared his provisions, in a manly manner, with others, hence his natural leadership among peers in any profession he might practise" (my translation).[38]

Ya'qūb maintains a reputation among many medieval history scholars as being the first ruler to challenge the very concept of the caliphate as an institution.[39] According to the *Tarīkh-e Sīstān*, Ya'qūb openly criticized the Abbasid caliphate, asserting, "The very foundation of the Abbasid caliphate has been based on deceit and treachery [*ghadr* and *makr*]. Don't you see how they [the Abbasids] treated Abū Muslim [the Iranian general who brought Abbasids to power and then was treacherously killed by them], Abū Salama, the Barmakids [Abbasid's two prominent viziers who served Harūn al-Rashīd and then were killed by him], and Fadl b. Sahl, despite all their services to that regime, lest anybody trust them?"[40] These prominent personages had once served the regime but were later disgraced and executed.

The *Tarīkh-e Sīstān* reports that Ya'qūb observed a high standard of ethics in his battles. For example, he refrained from initiating any battle against infidels before exhausting all peaceful alternatives. He refrained from confiscating the property or children of any convert and returned confiscated properties to defeated foes who later converted. In addition, he not only ceased to impose the poll tax (*kharāj*) on subjects with incomes below five hundred *dirhams* but also gave them alms (*sadaqa*).[41] Ya'qūb was relatively mild in his treatment of captives, mercifully releasing many. He also had a reputation for protecting the weak and acting fairly and is quoted as having said, "Fat is not found in a sparrow's belly; look for it in a cow's stomach" (my translation).[42] Ya'qūb's image in the *Tarīkh-e Sīstān* fits the classical model of an *'ayyār*. He adheres to certain universal virtues and principles, such as courage, generosity, fairness, truthfulness, support for the weak, and maintaining a degree of independence from official and central authorities. He also refrained from religious bigotry and, in fact, entertained a number of different religious denominations in his court.

Many *'ayyār*s, such as Ya'qūb, began their careers as leaders of a band of brigands, eventually acquiring a popular "Robin Hood" image through selfless actions. Ya'qūb, for example, never left his victims entirely helpless or molested women. In fact, he lived simply. In one proverbial anecdote, he and his gang entered a house intending to rob it. In the darkness, he picked out a glittering object, assuming it to be a precious gem. To his dismay, however, when he touched it to his tongue, he found it was merely a salt crystal. He immediately dropped it and ordered his gang to leave the house, saying, "It is utterly immoral to rob whoever has fed you" (my translation).

Another legendary *'ayyār* Samak-e-'Ayyār, originally introduced in twelfth-century stories, maintains a similar set of principles. In one legendary account, Marzbān Shāh sends Samak gifts, hoping to win his support in a war against the Chinese. Samak, however, refrains from accepting the gift. He points out to the Shah's representative that he fights only for just causes and not for bread.[43]

Samak is committed to his principles of bringing justice to unjust situations.[44] He repeatedly pledges to his comrades that he is a friend of their friends and an enemy of their enemies, and will not commit any act of treachery to a friend.[45] Although very rarely, the *'ayyārī* legends sometimes identify women as heroines in battle, as, for example, Samak's wife, Sorkhvard, who is depicted in the stories to be among female warriors.[46] In battle, Samak fights in the name of God and only after receiving permission from the king and chief commander. Before fighting, he recounts his heroic exploits to his enemies and declares his reasons for entering battle. Afterwards, he carefully respects the rights of his prisoners.[47]

Although the *'ayyār*s were notorious as outlaws, a careful examination of related historical accounts shows that they fought against domestic despotism. According to al-Tabarī, the *'ayyār*s joined the riots of 863 in Baghdad and Sāmarrā against the Turks who had killed the caliph. "The populace of Baghdad," al-Tabarī reports, "gathered, shouted out in protest, and called for action."

Negative Traits

The *'ayyār* also had a number of negative qualities. Cahen maintains that "our only information about social aspects of the *futūwwa* movement in early Islamic times comes in works by authors connected with aristocratic circles, who take no interest in it except in cases of its involvement in disorders, when they describe it as a bandit organization; they never credit it with ideological motives."[48] As testimony to this negative image, Hanaway writes that it is the *fityān* who "generally appear as trouble-makers, ready in times of breakdown of authority to harass rich merchants and other worthies by pillaging or threatening to pillage the shops or premises of any who would not pay them fixed sums of protection-money."[49] Other historical *'ayyār* figures, such as Ya'qūb Layth Saffār, and ahistorical figures, such as Shāhūy in the Persian epic literature of Ferdowsi and other poets, are often cast in a similar light.[50] While *'ayyār*s could sometimes act as policemen, as in Baghdad from 1028–33,[51] at other times they terrorized the population, as they did in Baghdad from 1135–44 – times when weak central governments failed to provide domestic security. Cahen and Taeschner state that "the three centuries from tenth to twelfth CE are full of tales of disturbances fomented by terror in which they took part, their exploits only ceasing at exceptional times under strong rulers [the Būyid 'Adud ad-Dawla and the three early Seljūqs]."[52] These and other examples from medieval literature confirm such negative characterizations and traits, essentially identifying the *futūwwa* with rowdies, brigands, and the plebeian parts of society that often harassed local populations.[53]

Kraemer argues that the general openness accompanying the Būyids helped launch a renaissance of sorts and provided the *'ayyārūn* with an opportunity to seize and abuse power. According to Kraemer, "In the civil disturbances under the Būyids, the *'ayyārūn* are often mentioned as active participants."[54] It is therefore not without foundation to say that these associations helped bring about the Būyids' downfall, though, according to Cahen, one of the Būyids, Abū Kālijār, had ties with them.[55]

The relationship between violence and sharī'a or, to put it in a different frame, the abuse of sharī'a is a significant discussion. As Tor has discussed, the Hanbalī and al-Shāfi'i schools of law were at least partially responsible for encouraging jihad as a personal duty, leaving it susceptible to misinterpretation and adaptation to personal frameworks.[56] The Shi'i school of law, on the other hand, by focusing on the "right authority" in war and delegitimizing jihad in the absence of the occult imam, in effect helped curb the abuse of religion for violence. The danger of loose religious authority creating, for example, a militant understanding of Islam, such as views advocated by al-Qaeda, the Taliban, or Daesh (ISIS) in our time, is an additional factor responsible for making the notion of suicide bombings religiously accessible. It should be no surprise that the same theological perceptions manifested today by Wahhabi and Salafi militants encouraged unregulated and violent behaviour among the free warriors of times past.

The Moral Common Ground

The social justice concerns of most *'ayyār*s help explain their popular support. Social justice was important in the third century of Islam (tenth century CE), when it rose to prominence. Rekaya has tied the caliph al-Ma'mūn's *mihna* (theological inquisition based on the Mu'tazili theology) of 833 to the aim of reforming the tax system in the countryside. Peasants had supported his rebellion against his brother al-Amīn. For many of the same reasons motivated by social justice, circles close to al-Ma'mūn declared that 'Alī b. Abī Tālib, who had already established a reputation as a social justice champion, was the "Prophet's best companion."[57]

A concern for social justice became common in the early formation of the Shi'i and the Mu'tazili schools of thought. This concern justified the interventionism of these groups, similar to the *'ayyārī/futūwwa* associations. At times this intervention was tantamount to denying the legitimacy of the head of state or, as Hodgson points out, the privileges of their administrations, the noble *kātib* clerks.[58] The criticism of these groups was not aimed so much at their support of social justice but at the spontaneous and arbitrary manner in which they pursued their goals. This is why thinkers like al-Ghazālī preferred an unjust ruler who established order over the chaos and disorder of competing claims to social justice.

The Triangular Chivalry-Crusades-*Futūwwa* Connections

In the decades before the 'Abbasid caliph al-Nāsir's rule (1180–1225), *futūwwa* organizations began to lose their significance.[59] Al-Nāsir's political insight, however, prompted him to overhaul and reorganize *futūwwa*, and to turn it into an instrument of power and social solidarity. He achieved this through a program of reform that positioned himself as the spiritual leader of the *futūwwa* associations, a move, as Hartmann asserts, that was more effective than a strong army at his service.[60] Such success was due to the fact that the *futūwwa* associations subsequently became "a framework for solidarity of all Muslims of all confessions and social ranks up to the princes."[61] The development of *futūwwa* associations in the thirteenth century was parallel with the rise of the concept of just war in Europe. The standard Christian canon law of just war appeared in the mid-twelfth century – only fifty years after the inception of the Crusades (1095).[62] Important to note is that that essential parts of *jus in bello* laws (codes and regulations pertaining to the conduct of war) were developed not by the church but by chivalric institutions. In the early nineteenth century, Hammer-Purgestall seems to have been the first to consider *futūwwa* as "Islamic chivalry," which in his opinion preceded European knighthood.[63] Whether the two sets of institutions share a common root has been a matter of controversy. However, there is consensus on two points: first, that *futūwwa* and related organizations such as *'ayyārī* preceded the European chivalry; and second, that there are striking institutional similarities (especially when the post-Mongol form of *futūwwa* intermingled with Sufism and turned into guild institutions).

Some scholars, however, have cast serious doubts on a common origin. Richard Frye, for example, argues that European chivalry was born of feudal societies, which were nonexistent in pre-Islamic Iran.[64] Yet many scholars do not hesitate to speak of feudalism in the Near East.[65] Christensen argues that the Sassanian horsemen held the status of "chevalier" as in European chivalry.[66]

What is significant is that many important Iranian authorities on this subject maintain that the pre-Islamic Sassanian prototype of *futūwwa* inspired and influenced European chivalry. Mahjoub, for example, has cited evidence of a German lord who sent an emissary to al-Nāsir in the early thirteenth century, requesting membership in al-Nāsir's *futūwwa* organization. Mahjoub asserts, "There is a very high probability that the European chevalerie order was copied from Islamic countries" (my translation).[67] Similarities in rituals and symbols suggest this very relationship. The wearing of trousers (*sarāwīl*), for example, symbolizing the virtue of chastity in both Eastern and Western organizations, stems from an ancient Iranian ritual, as Arabs do not normally wear trousers.[68]

Corbin cites d'Ors, who traces Zoroastrian ethics through a long evolution to the Christian chivalric codes of the thirteenth century. Corbin's main thesis is that philosophers like Shahāb al-Dīn Suhrawardī (d. 1191) transformed heroic Zoroastrian epics into mystical Islamic ones. The idea of the Shi'i occulted imam returning to earth to establish universal justice is very close to the notion of *Sushiant* in Zoroastrianism. Corbin agrees with d'Ors's suggestion that Shi'ism in fact facilitated Western culture's borrowing of the ancient Persian ethos. Narāqi, who translated and annotated Corbin's introduction to a book on guild/*futūwwa* constitutions (*futūwatnāma*), also agrees with these assertions.[69]

Islamic *futūwwa* and European chivalric associations share a number of common values and principles, such as an emphasis on truthfulness, fidelity, defence of the weak, generosity, and finally, the fight against injustice.[70] At the same time, however, there are some major differences. Four out of the ten main ordinances for chivalric orders relate to the concept of fidelity to the church and to a commitment to battle "disbelievers." Three provisions require scrupulous observance of the law of God, feudal duties, and a love for the country of one's origin. In contrast, *'ayyārī/futūwwa* associations have little loyalty for any state or religious establishment. Islamic associations, in fact, have strong tendencies towards transnational solidarity, because ethical norms that emphasize the autonomy of the individual and judgment based on reason have greater influence than sharī'a law.

The cosmopolitan tendencies towards transnationalism and religious pluralism are closer to the humanitarian spirit of Western just-war theories than are the faith-driven chivalric commandments. Was it possible, then, that the Crusades, which brought the European knights into contact with Muslim forces and their codes of war ethics, were the medium that facilitated the assimilation of some of the Islamic *futūwwa* war ethics into the principles of the European just-war theories? According to Hay, although the theoretical literature of humanitarian concerns in war appeared in the works of the clerical authors and legislators from at least the late tenth century on, the moral influence of this literature on the knights appeared no earlier than the thirteenth century.[71] Gratian's *Decretum*, which established Christian canon law and some of the principles of just war in the West by referring to the peace of God, appeared in the mid-twelfth century, at least half a century after the beginning of the first Crusade in 1095. More eloquent principles distinguishing Christian soldiers from civilians were reflected in the works of St Bernard of Clairvaux

(1090–1153),[72] raising the possibility of some Eastern influence. The Crusades began long before 1095, in theory and in practice, not only against Muslims or pagans but also against rebel Christians.[73] Although the Crusades appeared as "holy" wars in the European historiographies of later eras, the motives behind these wars were often a combination of various aspirations. Before the First Crusade, a number of like-minded campaigns were launched across Spain, the Baltics, and North Africa. Riley-Smith suggests a variety of motives for these enterprises, including a desire for land, spoil or profit, colonial experiments, simple-mindedness, and, of course, religious duty.[74] France asserts, "For the papacy a degree of control of the European expansionism was essential to preserve its own position and to prevent an unthinkable outbreak of religious pluralism." He adds, "It was the papacy that was anxious to sanctify war, most notably in Spain and more dubiously in England in 1066, as an instrument of control."[75] France believes that the anti-Muslim incentives of both the Spanish wars of *reconquista* and the Crusades were an invention of later historiographies.[76] Cahen maintains that, although the main justification of the later Crusaders was to assist Christians in the Holy Land, the result was "completely opposite to their avowed object."[77] Cahen notes, "From a cultural point of view, objective comparison leads to the categorical conclusion that where the West has acquired knowledge of Muslim civilization, it has done so mainly through Spain and Sicily and not through Western settlements in the East or Crusaders from the West; moreover, Islam as such nearly always remained misunderstood, and the few accurate ideas about it that the West finally acquired are due to the efforts of missionaries, in other words, work undertaken in an entirely different spirit from the spirit of the Crusades."[78] An important side effect of the Frankish attacks against Egypt and the Holy Land, according to Cahen, was that it intensified anti-Shi'i campaigns, resulting in the domination of an orthodox Sunnism across the entire area.[79]

At the same time, the Crusades did not provoke a countercrusade by Muslims, not even by the Turks of Asia Minor, whose invasion of Byzantine lands was used to justify the Crusades.[80] In fact, the religious intolerance shown by the Crusaders against Muslims, Jews, and even Eastern Christians undermined the tradition of tolerance and cooperation previously existing between Christians and Muslims in the Muslim world. The rivalry between the Byzantine and the Islamic caliphate was not always hostile; rather, many scholars and pilgrims frequently travelled between them. After the Crusades, the unfortunate Christian minority under the Egyptian Mamluk regime fell victim to the legacy of the savagery of the Christian crusaders.[81] In addition, the Christian Byzantine Empire also fell victim to the oppressive policies of Western Christians, leading to the occupation of Byzantium in the Fourth Crusade.

An Iranian reader of the above history would be specifically interested in knowing not only the conceptual and organizational relationships between *javānmardī/futūwwa/'ayyārī* and Western chivalry but also, and more significantly, the manifestation of all of the above in actual wars. This knowledge may only be provided through the study of the battles conducted by the Shi'i first imam 'Alī b. Abī Tālib, which will be discussed extensively in the second part of this volume. Beyond narratives about 'Alī's moral conduct in war, however, are fragments of chivalric images that do not meet the Shi'i moral standard but attract attention only because they have a reputation in the broader Muslim world. The Muslim warrior Salāh al-Dīn Ayyūbī, a legendary warrior in European literature, is one such figure.

Salāh al-Dīn's War Ethics: A Mixed Moral Legacy

Among legendary figures in the medieval Muslim world, there is hardly anyone whose ethical and humanitarian attitude in war has received as much admiration by both Western and Sunni Muslim authors as Salāh al-Dīn Ayyūbī (d. 1193). One of Salāh al-Dīn's closest jurist associates, Bahā' al-Dīn b. Shaddād (d. 1234), whose book is published in Iran in Persian translation, describes Salāh al-Dīn as "a paragon of chivalry, generous, extremely modest that had a welcoming face for any guests that arrived even if he were an infidel."[82]

The above image gives an Iranian Twelver-Shi'a reader mixed feelings. Salāh al-Dīn, as a great liberator of Jerusalem and defeater of crusaders, looks even better if he dealt chivalrously with his enemies. But the Shi'a reader cannot ignore the fact that it was also Salāh al-Dīn who suppressed the Shi'i population of Egypt and Syria at the end of the Fatimid era. A brief internet search in Persian language leads to numerous articles that are quite critical of Salāh al-Dīn not only because he terminated the Shi'i rule of the Fatimids in Egypt but also because, according to these sources, he betrayed his Shi'i superiors who brought him to political and military power. The National Center for Responding to Religious Questions (*markaz-e melli-e pasokhgoo'i be so'alat-e dini*) website presents an article that discusses how Salāh al-Dīn betrayed the last Fatimid caliph al-'Ādid, usurped his power, replaced all Shi'i jurists with Sunni Shāfi'ī jurists, massacred all Shi'i residents of Aleppo in Syria, segregated all Shi'i males from females to stall their future generations, forced the Egyptian public to celebrate 'Āshūrā (the annual Shi'i mourning festival commemorating the martyrdom of al-Husayn) as a national happy holiday, and officially excluded the Shi'i school from other recognized Muslim schools of law.[83] Other websites refer additionally to his act of executing the great Iranian philosopher Shaykh Shahāb al-Dīn Suhrawardī (d. 1191)[84] and burning a large number of books related to Shi'i scholarship in the Fatimid libraries.[85]

Needless to say that Iranian readers of Salāh al-Dīn history can hardly reconcile the above assertions with reports by Ibn Shaddād when he talks about Salāh al-Dīn's compassionate treatment of his prisoners: "When he took Acre," Ibn Shaddād states, "he released all the prisoners, about four thousand of them; he gave each expenses to allow them to reach their hometown."[86] In other narratives, Ibn Shaddād shows how Salāh al-Dīn meticulously observed Arab chivalric traditions.[87] Some sources refer to Salāh al-Dīn as being very pious, and on many occasions weeping during prayer and taking great joy in listening to the hadith.[88] Salāh al-Dīn is also presented in non-Shi'i sources as trustworthy, truthful, faithful to his pledges, even to the enemy, and often times keen to settle disputes by negotiation. These sources also mention that his attitude towards Jews and Christians was far better than how his enemies treated Muslims under their rule.[89] For Iranian readers of Salāh al-Dīn's biography, these qualities, if they were true in Salāh al-Dīn, belong to the moral paradigm of *javānmardī'*, *ayyārī*, and *futūwwa*. These readers are also cognizant that, Salāh al-Dīn's animosity with Shi'as aside, the economic situations of Egypt and Syria deteriorated under his rule due to his sixteen years of continuous military campaigns (1177–93).[90] Locked in a mixed feeling about Salāh al-Dīn, an Iranian solution to resolve the paradoxical narrative is to surmise that Salāh al-Dīn, originally an Iranian Kurd, was partially influenced by *'ayyāri* and *futūwwa* ethics long before departing with his uncle to Egypt.[91]

Salāh al-Dīn was born in Tikrit, a Kurdish city in modern Iraq. According to Ibn Shaddād, Salāh al-Dīn's father, Ayyūb b. Shādī (or Shādhī), was born in Dvin (or Dwin), an Armenian city under the Shaddādid rule, a dynasty that flourished from the tenth to the twelfth century in northern Iran.[92] Abu'l-Aswār Shāwur of Shaddādīds ruled over Dvin between 1022 and 1067.[93] The very name of this ruler identifies his ties to the pre-Islamic *āswārān* (*asbārān*) warriors and predecessors of *'ayyārān* and *javānmardān*. Salāh al-Dīn's ancestors came from the area where the culture of *asbārī* and *'ayyārī* had historic roots. However exaggerated this view may sound to an impartial reader, for an Iranian admirer of chivalry institutions, Salāh al-Dīn's family heritage explains his partially chivalrous conduct during wars against crusaders.

Concepts of Chivalry in Persian Ethics and Sufi Literature

As mentioned earlier in this chapter, *zurkhaneh* is an organization that still upholds a part of the Iranian-Islamic chivalry culture in the practice of sports in modern Iranian life. But the theoretical, the normative, and the narrative foundations of the *javānmardī, futūwwa,* and *'ayyārī* phenomena in Iranian culture are well preserved in Persian epic literature, "mirror for princes," in Sufi literature, and also in modern folklore. The literary, and even the institutional, connection between Sufism and *javānmardī* is expansive and beyond the scope of this work. What is relevant here is the ethical common ground shared among all three disciplines that have, at least in theory, called for the containment of war and violence in both the interpersonal and intercommunal realms of life.

Although *futūwwa* did not exist as a chivalry organization in the time of the Prophet, certain Qur'ānic terms were interpreted later on to invoke its spirit. These include *fatā* in Q. 12:30, 18:60, 21:60, and in the plural forms *fitya* and *fityān* in 12:36 and 62, 18:10 and 13. This last verse (18:13) ascribes a laudatory connotation to *futūwwa*, referring to the People of the Cave (*ashāb al-kahf*), who are described as "youths who believed in their Lord, and we increased them in guidance."[94] They emerge as significant symbols in the *futūwwa* world view.

In addition to the Qur'ān, Shi'i hadith is very rich in a proverbial literature that has created important ethical foundations for altruism and chivalry. One such of these hadith proverbs is the statement from 'Alī b. Abī Tālib: "People are either your brother in faith or your equal in creation." The point is to see how chivalry is defined and qualified in nontheological sources.

Two important sources of Persian literature that do not fall into Sufi categories but shed scattered light on the ethics of chivalry associations are the *Shahnameh* of Ferdowsi (d. 1020) and the *Qabusnameh* (a "mirror for princes" written by 'Unsur al-Ma'ālī Kaykāvūs b. Eskandar in 1082).[95] Both texts are important sources for Iranian ethics, and both denote the *'ayyār*s in a positive light. Hanaway notes that from the time of the earliest appearances of *'ayyārī* in Persian texts, the word itself is linked with *javānmardī*.[96] In the *Qabusnameh*, *javānmardī* is associated with wealth, generosity, magnanimity, and courage.[97] An entire chapter of the *Qabusnameh* is dedicated to *javānmardī*, detailing the various categories and classes under this rubric. The three cardinal principles of *javānmardī*, according to this source, are fulfilling one's promises, refraining from untruthfulness, and having fortitude in all affairs; in addition, the author emphasizes the importance of treating prisoners of war well and avoiding revenge.[98]

At a philosophical level, the *Qabusnameh* defines unique ethics of justice that are to be expected from a chivalrous person and that are also highly valuable in conflict prevention and resolution. It suggests that when it comes to fairness, people fall into one of four categories: those who are neither fair to others, nor expect others to be fair to them; those who treat others with no fairness, but expect to be treated with fairness; those who are fair to others and expect fairness in return; and those who enact fairness to others, but do not expect it back for themselves. This very last category of people is considered chivalrous in the *Qabusnameh* and in other sources of Persian literature.[99] In short, these sources set the ethical bar for chivalry at the highest level of magnanimity. Needless to say, war that is waged in the name of justice can hardly be justified at the justice-plus realm of ethics, where forgiveness and generosity define the general mode of social behaviour.

When it comes to Sufi sources, *javānmardī* and other connected notions find far deeper definitions, qualifications, and elaborations than they do within any other genres of Persian literature. Sufi literature entertains an expansive amount of forgiveness-laden hadith pieces (Prophetic quotations) that have turned into frequently used proverbial poetry or prose in colloquial Persian. An example is the Prophetic hadith of "forgiveness at power, self-control at anger, and humility at wealth." Many Sufi manuals promote these three advanced, moral traits within the context of Islamic chivalry. Clearly, the first two codes have direct applications in the realm of ethics of war and conflict resolution.

Similar reflections on relationships between power (both physical and political), forgiveness, and charity are attributed to prominent and chivalrous Iranian icons like Pūrīyāy-e Walī, who lived in the early fourteenth century. Ridgeon cites Pūrīya, who is mentioned in Husayn Gārzagāhi's *Majālis al-'Ushshāq*,[100] a Sufi source typifying chivalrous traits:

گر بر دگری خرده نگیری مردی   گر بر سر نفس خود امیری مرد ی
[101] مردی نبود فتاده را پای زدن   گر دست فتاده ای بگیری مردی[۱۰۱]

(If you can dominate your own self, you are a man.
If you do not find fault with others, you are a man.
It is not manly to kick the fallen.
If you take the hand of the fallen, then you are a man. [my translation])

Jalāl al-Dīn Rumi defines several important aspects of chivalry in the same justice-plus space of magnanimity:

که فتوت دادن بی علت است   پاکبازی خارج از هرملت است
زانکه ملت فضل جوید یا خلاص   پاکبازانند قربانان خاص
نی خدا را امتحانی میکنند   نی در سود و زیانی میزنند

(For devotion [*futūwwa*] consists in generosity without cause:
gambling [one's self] clean away [pure self-sacrifice] is outside of
[transcends] every religion.

> Forasmuch as religion seeks [divine] grace or salvation, those who gamble [everything] clean away are [God's] chosen favorite.
> Neither do they put God to any test, nor do they knock at the door of any profit or loss.)[102]

According to Rumi, *futūwwa*, or chivalry, stands at the highest level of devotion and ethics, because it transcends the rational self-interest logic upon which every ordinary person acts. God's favourite people act on the moral level of selflessness that extends beyond ideological realms, leading to the denial of doctrinal selfishness. Within this perspective, chivalry as a realm that stands beyond the justice paradigm attains a nonideological, universal, and advanced moral status. In such a normative space, conflict of interests has no cause, and war and violence lose their relevance.

The above example of Muslim chivalry in its idealistic form might seem disconnected from the real history of some chivalry institutions, such as the *'ayyār*s, who in the course of medieval life manifested many instances of moral misbehaviour. As Tor notes, reports of the *'ayyār*s' cases that include unjustified violence, transgression, plunder, rape, and murder were plenty in the tenth century, in Baghdad for example.[103] But since the early eleventh century, as chivalry and Sufi ethics merged in Persian literature, chivalry has evolved to be portrayed as a noble discipline, which, just like Sufism, promotes a universal justice-plus and sharī'a-plus system of values that can rescue society wherever and whenever doctrinal schools and law fail. It acts like an extrareligious guarantee against ethical chaos, specifically when the interaction between modernity and conservative values create moral vulnerability and institutional gaps in conflict resolution.

Shi'i politics have become domestically and internationally assertive and active since the Islamic Revolution in Iran and have also become radicalized as a result of the eight-years-long Iran-Iraq War, which brought a millennium of Shi'i political pacifism to an end.[104] Time is still needed to see whether such monumental events will put an end to the institutional independence of Shi'i *ulama* from the government – a key distinction between Shi'i and Sunni institutional history. Whether this happens or not, the study of the discipline of chivalry, with its deep roots in both Iranian and Islamic identities, can serve as a normative check and balance against militant tendencies, both within and outside of the Muslim world. Such a study of Iranian chivalry, and a renewed dialogue between it and the notions of Western chivalry, may certainly reveal radicalism, as would any thorough exploration of a normative common ground between the East and West.

At the end of the Crusades, when Western chivalric institutions were exhausted and looking for a theme, better than war, to become their practical focus, they found inspiration in their Muslim counterparts and began to reorient their focus from war to a romantic courtesy to women.[105] This was one of the reasons that Muslim literature produced in Spain became the source of European romantic literature. Thus the Persian language, with its courtly literary history and its vast influence on the Asian cultures between Iran and China, spoken beyond Iran in a number of Central Asian countries, is exceptionally resourceful in terms of Sufi and chivalry peace literature. This language, which also embodies a vast amount of medieval rationalism, currently places Iran in a strong intellectual and political position to foster international dialogue that may reveal the bankruptcy of war in our time.

Conclusion

Considered through a historical binary Iranian-Shiʿi prism, the ethical norms of Muslim conduct in regular wars declined under the Umayyad caliphate and afterwards. However, parts of the ethics of chivalry that resulted from the legacy of the first Shiʿi imam (ʿAlī b. Abī Tālib) were preserved across a good part of Muslim history by entities like the *futūwwa* and *javānmardī* organizations. With some roots in pre-Islamic Iranian and Arab cultures, the Muslim practice of chivalry reappeared strongly between the mid-ninth to early thirteenth centuries, when Yaʿqūb Layth, Salāh al-Dīn Ayyūbī, and the Abbasid caliph al-Nāsir reinforced both the legends and the institutions of Muslim chivalry. Moreover, narratives about the legendary Samak *ʿayyār* mixed fact with fiction, provoking a strong and long-lasting public imagination about chivalrous Muslim warriors in Persian culture.

The presence of ʿAlī b. Abī Tālib and the first Persian convert to Islam (namely Salmān Fārsī) as the chief initiators and masters in the above-mentioned organizations strongly evidences an overwhelming sympathy among many of these institutions towards mixed Iranian-Shiʿi identities. The fact that the Abbasid caliph al-Nāsir, who reorganized the *futūwwa* organization, has been accused by historians of having Shiʿi sympathies indicates that the integral Shiʿi-chivalry connection was abundantly clear in the perception of medieval Muslim historians.[106] The indispensable and triangular relations between Iranian, Shiʿi, and chivalrous ethical identities manifest themselves in various genres of Persian literature, art, and history.

The *ʿayyārī*, *futūwwa*, and *javānmardī* codes of ethics within modern Iranian culture find organizational homes in the traditional guild and sports clubs of *zurkhaneh*s, which are still functioning in Iran and, to some extent, within all Persianate societies. This normative and institutional construct, however, does not serve a specific religious organization or school of politics, due mainly to its universalist approach and its historic links to ancient Iran. It maintains a deep influence over vast sectors of Iranian society and Iranian moral identity. In effect, the ethics of *javānmardī*, together with elements of the Sufi world view, are arguably the most powerful guarantors against the emergence of a long-lasting religious fundamentalism and violent extremism in Iran, as compared to some of Iran's neighbouring countries.

Despite being sandwiched between a few states where war, violence, and suicide bombings have become a normal part of everyday life, having experienced one of the longest modern wars, and moreover, having experienced tensions with the West over its nuclear program, Iran seems to be a relatively less violent and a more stable country compared to most of its neighbours. Perhaps an explanation may be found in a cultural mould that benefits from the binary system of Islamic and *javānmardī* moral traditions. Symbolically this dual system is represented by mixed attributes of two historic characters: Salmān Farsī, the first Persian Muslim convert who served the Prophet Muhammad as a close companion and chief military advisor and strategist; and ʻAlī b. Abī Tālib, the first male Muslim convert who also became the first Shiʻi imam. Both were key figures in early Muslim wars and military victories. At the same time, both of these figures appear on almost all genealogies of Muslim chivalry and *futūwwa* organizations as the prime initiators of these orders. It is possible that this interlink hints at a binary ethical source for the ethics of war and peace in Iranian and Shiʻi culture.

The philosophical and theological relations between power, justice, religion, altruism, and the ethics of magnanimity, forgiveness, war, and peace together do not present an easy-to-solve matrix of political philosophy. This chapter argues that in certain instances of their political and intellectual histories, Islamo-Persian institutions acting on ethics of *javānmardī* and *futūwwa* have come close to providing a moral solution. A syncretic normative system, by definition, should reduce causes of violence. This seems therefore, a necessity in giving civilizational posture to any culture.

The unprecedented inhuman, subhuman, and in instances subanimal violence and large-scale war crimes that Daesh (ISIS), the Taliban (in both Afghanistan and Pakistan), and radical militants in Israel have mastered in recent Middle East history are undeniable proof that religious traditions alone cannot guarantee ethics in wars.[107] We need other supplementary normative sources that can act as checks and balances against militant, irrational, and immoral interpretation of religions. The universal and transreligious ethics of *javānmardī*/*futūwwa* has frequently acted as a moral balancer in Iranian history. It is not hard to imagine that without such balancing codes of ethics, Iran, having experienced a revolution, a very long war with Iraq, and devastating economic sanctions against her economy, could emerge with as much tendency to violence as the above actors.

If a parallel study of the ethics of chivalry in the East and in the West cannot provide alternatives for interfaith dialogues aimed at peacemaking and conflict management, it certainly has a strong potential to offer these ventures new dimensions and conceptual depths. For historic, strategic, and theological reasons, and through her binary source of ethics that includes codes of *javānmardī*, modern Iran can certainly play a major role in realizing the goal of mutual comprehension and peace.

4 Modern Iranian Intellectuals on the Ethics of Enmity and Nonviolence

جنگ هفتاد دو ملت همه را عذر بنه
چون ندیدند حقیقت ره افسانه زدند

(Leave aside the squabbling sects and their divisions: all seventy-two of them,
Bereft of the Truth, they set out to hunt a Chimera.)

– Shamseddīn Mohammad Hafez[1]

Enmity or "enmification" has received considerable attention in modern ethical enquiry. Anthony Coates argues that the concept of the enemy plays a role in the moral posture of wars. He believes that without a *limited* concept of the enemy, the ethical conduct and moral restraint of war become totally irrelevant. "The enemy," he contends, "is never the Other" and cannot be placed "beyond the moral pale."[2] This chapter will briefly explore how a number of contemporary influential Iranian theologians and intellectuals have narrowed the definition of "enemy" and, in effect, limited its relevance and ramifications. The chapter will shed light on how the most significant ethical norms that inform the Iranian national and collective psyche on war and peace are under critical scrutiny and have become transitional. It will discuss moral approaches outside strict religious discourses that are helping such epistemological transitions in relation to concepts of hostility and positive peace.

The history of Muslim views on war is often based solely on the rich legal literature of Islam and neglects the wider relevant material and conceptual approaches present in other categories of Islamic literature and discourses. The present chapter aims to bridge this gap and help the reader to see how a robust normative syncretism in intellectual Iran is in the making.

The Question of the Enemy and Modern Iranian Theology

Carl Schmitt states, "Just-war leads to total enmity and total war"; Anthony Coates maintains that to limit wars is to accept that "the enemy is never an enemy in totality; the enemy is never the Other."[3] Combined, these eloquent formulations may lend themselves to complete accuracy. Memories of the Iran-Iraq War are still alive in the minds of the current Iranian generation. They remember well that a major reason the war stretched out over such a long period of time was due to, in the Iranian mind, the absolute evilness of Iraq under President Saddam Hussein. There was no hope for a negotiated settlement with Iraq as long as Saddam was in charge. The war affected not only the bodies of those involved but also the minds of many Iranian intellectuals, theologians, philosophers, and ethicists.

In Iran, the negative experience with war played a major role in the emergence of a new theological posture vis-à-vis the notion of absolute enemy that was symbolized by the United States of America. This chapter identifies a number of influential Iranian theologians, intellectuals, and artists whose perspectives have helped moderate the concept of the enemy and reveal the evil but hidden dimensions of war and violence.

Well known and read in Iran and in many other Muslim countries, Seyyed Hossein Nasr has been a prominent spokesman of a philosophical school known as the perennial philosophy (*hikmat-e khaledeh* in Persian). Nasr has an impressive repertoire of philosophical commentary about classical Muslim works, including the peripatetic philosophy of Ibn Sīnā (d. 1037) and the transcendental philosophy of Sadr al-Dīn Shīrāzī, also known as Mullā Sadrā (d.1640). Although he is generally known to be more of a traditional philosopher, his universalist approach has provided solid elements for intercultural and intellectual bridge building between the West and the East. The essence of his perennial philosophy is that the divine truth is not subject to or limited by cultural nuances, and can therefore be appreciated and accessed by all cultures. In Nasr's own words:

> Although, being a Muslim, I naturally have my roots in the Islamic tradition, which I know better than others, my exposition of the perennial philosophy is not personal and individualistic and has its roots in an anonymous wisdom to be found wherever tradition has flourished. I have known many Christian, Jewish, Hindu and Confucian scholars and thinkers of note who have found my exposition to be applicable to their own tradition as well, and I have carried out many dialogues on the basis of my understanding of the perennial philosophy with those belonging to

> other religious traditions. Among them the scholars who have accepted the traditional point of view have been able to identify themselves with my perspectives while they remain firmly rooted in their own tradition.[4]

The above statement, which allows access to the most Real in any tradition, by definition delegitimizes cultural and religious difference as a cause of war.

Nasr's universalist position and its inter- and intracultural peace-building potential is well addressed by Reza Shah-Kazemi, comparing Nasr's universalism with religious pluralism of the Christian theologian John Hick. Shah-Kazemi notes, "Whereas Hick sees the religions as being so many 'cognitive responses,' on the part of man, to the ineffable Real, Nasr sees the religions as so many Self-revelations of the ineffable Real to man."[5] By implication, Nasr's religious universalism does not force various religions to compromise their particularities for peaceful coexistence. Shah-Kazemi concludes that in Nasr's universalism "fidelity to the particularities – including the exclusivist particularities – of one's own faith determines one's ability to open up to the other with tolerance and respect."[6]

While Nasr has acted as an articulate critic of Western Islamophobia and modern materialism, his philosophical view remains in open conversation with some of his most significant Western counterparts, such as Frithjof Schuon and Giorgio De Santillana. Nasr's conservatism does not find itself in conflict with universal rationalism; this is due in part to his incorporation of mystic theology with the perennial and rational arguments, which have been used to facilitate Muslim-Western philosophical dialogue beyond political and cultural borders.[7] Such questions about humanity versus enmity are found in the histories of both Eastern and Western societies. These questions deserve to be highlighted, for the pursuit of answers to these challenging musings can form the basis of a rich, peaceful understanding between disparate cultures.

Nasr stands out as a staunch traditionalist among modern Islamic theologians, accepting the authenticity of many Muslim classical theologies, philosophies, and jurisprudential traditions. His traditionalism is better understood in contrast with the Wahhabi fundamentalist school, which rejects a greater part of Islamic intellectual and institutional history as heresies.[8] Naturally, it is far more difficult to define an enemy in Nasr's perspective than to do so within Wahhabism, which rejects more than a millennium of Muslim history.[9] Nasr is known for his critical view of various trends in modern Western thought, specifically when such thought relates to theories of clash between religious traditions across the globe. His criticism, however, does not totally demonize the modernist schools with which he has held theological and philosophical conversations for years. He refers to many "ironies" in the Muslim-West relationships, reflective of an actual and useful millennial engagement between the two civilizations. The first irony in these relations, Nasr contends, is that at the time that some major Muslim philosophical works, encompassing ancient Greek thought, were being translated from Arabic to Latin – thus creating the impetus for the Western Renaissance movement – a number of Christian theologians considered Islam as heretic. The second irony is that during the Enlightenment movement in Europe, Muslim rationalist philosophies and theologies, such as the works of the Mu'tazili school in Islamic tradition, were being used by leading European intellectuals to criticize the Christian church. The third irony resulted during the post-Enlightenment era, when Western thinkers, bored of rationalism, found Islamic romantic literature to be a useful and rich literary counterbalance to emulate.[10] The European hostilities towards Muslim cultures nevertheless did not diminish in either era.

A thorough examination of Nasr's "ironies" argument demonstrates that his most severe criticism is not as much against intellectual shortfalls of Western civilization as against its irrational, hypocritical, and immoral hostilities towards Islam. Nasr's argument is a qualified critique of the Western enmification of Islam as a religion, as a culture, and as a cooperative civilizational counterpart from which the West has tremendously benefited. When it comes, however, to his perennial philosophy and universal rationalism, he sides as much with his Western mentors, such as Frithjof Schuon, as with his Eastern ones, such as Mohammad Hossein Tabātabā'ī, the greatest Shi'i Qur'ānic exegete and philosopher of the twentieth century.

Importantly, Nasr's theology of war and peace is consistent with his universalist philosophy. He categorically rejects the concept of jihad in Islam as having an authentic militant connotation. Conversely, he considers jihad as an inner and esoteric struggle that is connected to the performance of all five pillars of Islam – namely, testifying the unity of God and the prophethood of Mohammad (*shahāda*), daily prayer (*salāt*), fasting in Ramadan (*sawm*), giving alms (*zakāt*), and performing pilgrimage (*hajj*).[11] To show the lower value of external jihad as distinct from inner spiritual struggle, Nasr reminds his reader of a Prophetic hadith, saying, "The ink of scholars is more precious than the blood of martyrs."[12]

Nasr rejects suicidal bombing even as a measure of defence. He stresses, "Although defense of oneself, one's homeland, and one's religion and the overcoming of oppression remain religious duties, the regulation of warfare, especially the protection of the innocent, that is, nonaggression against noncombatants, and dealing with the enemy in justice, also remain part and parcel of the religion and essential to it; they cannot be cast aside with the excuse that one is responding to a grievance or injustice."[13] Nasr agrees that without justice there is no peace, but to curb the emotional tendencies of his fellow Muslims in the implementation of punitive justice, he advises them against militant extremism: "Muslims," Nasr asserts, "must seek justice, but with humility and charity, not in self-righteousness, ever aware that absolute justice belongs to God alone and one of the cardinal meanings of the *shahāda* is 'there is no justice but the Divine Justice.'"[14] Nasr's rejection of the theology of revenge seems to be in perfect concordance with his perennial philosophy, which at its core resists fragmenting humanity along doctrinal fault lines.

Among contemporary Iranian religious intellectuals, there are a few other influential theologians who stand above the rest in laying significant philosophical and theological foundations for nonviolence and peace. Abdolkarim Soroush, Mohammad Mojtahed Shabestarī, Mohsen Kadivar, Mostafā Malekīān, Abolqāsem Fanā'ī, and Maqsood Farāsatkhāh, most with both seminarian and modern education, have collectively produced a literature subjecting Islamic jurisprudence to modern universal and critical ethics.

Using a hermeneutical approach, Shabestarī criticizes Islamic essentialism, maintaining that the Qur'ānic scripture has mostly attempted to make people recognize God as the supreme creator of both worlds; this, however, Shabestarī asserts, is attempted by the scripture with minimal intrusion into social morality. This prominent Iranian theologian, who has full credentials both in seminarian and modern study of hermeneutics, maintains that, ethically speaking, the Qur'ān never tried to present the final and best moral choices to humanity; instead, he argues, the Qur'ān merely presented normative advice that was time sensitive and relatively preferable within its historical and cultural context. That is why, he contends, the Qur'ānic injunctions were always put in the comparative moral frame of "the better," rather than the superlative choice or "the best."[15] Shabestarī's view of Islam presents a faith with the maximum respect for human moral choices, customs, and traditions. A God that minimally intervenes in human affairs does not provide much legitimate ground for religiously induced war and violence. "The Qur'ān," Shabestarī argues, "is an interpretation of truth, rather than the truth itself."[16] Such a view is naturally adaptable to all other religions, which are themselves also subject to interpretations beyond absolutist approaches. In Shabestarī's view, faith is a function of liberty, freedom, and open criticism – and by implication, no legitimate hostility may arise from mere difference of opinions.[17]

In one of the boldest positions that Shabestarī has taken against the conservative understanding of religion in modern Iran, he compares the methodological approach of the Iranian jurists to the violent theology of the so-called Islamic caliphate in Syria and Iraq headed by Abu Bakr al-Baghdādī. Al-Baghdādī and his followers in ISIS (the Islamic Government of Iraq and Syria, an offshoot of the fundamentalist al-Qaeda) presented their savagery in cold-blooded butchering of at least seventeen hundred Iraqi Shi'i soldiers and many civilians in Mosul when the city fell in June 2014.[18] In a short article "If Daesh [*dowlat-e eslami-e eraq va sham*, an abbreviated title in Persian for ISIS] Asks Shi'a Jurists," published by Shabestarī on his website on 16 July 2014, he addresses the theoretical roots of religious violence in the following words:

> The monumental danger of followers of Daesh, al-Qaeda, al-Nusrah, and Taliban in our present world stems from the theoretical foundation of their interpretive perspectives [of religion] rather than the lack of it. The unprecedented savage crimes of Daesh, no doubt, are condemned. Their existence not only threatens the territorial integrity of Middle Eastern states and peace in this region, but they are a menace for global peace at large ... The question, however, is that if Daesh's caliph al-Baghdadi, who proclaims himself to be a puritan Muslim and the executor of Islamic sharī'a, asks Shi'a jurists the following question, what should be their answer? "What foundational and methodological difference between my approach [al-Baghdadi's] in presentation of Islamic sharī'a and that of yours has caused so much [of your] verbal curses against me?" ... If al-Baghdadi further asks the official jurists, "You have the same approach in the field of Islamic sharī'a as I and Ibn Taymiyya do in maintaining that rules of sharī'a as stipulated in the texts of the Qur'ān, and hadith must not be subject to interpretation and must be executed on literal reading of these texts." What would be the answer of [Shi'a] jurists to these questions? Can it be: "Oh Mr. Baghdadi! The Islamic sharī'a is exactly the same as you state, but they cannot be implemented in the modern era." Or they may alternatively say, "Mr. Baghdadi! You implement sharī'a in a savage way and this is not right!"? ... Scrutiny in the science of hermeneutics during the last three centuries have demonstrated that, unlike what Ibn Taymiyya claims, avoiding interpretation of a text is an interpretation. The belief that the Qur'ānic and hadith texts encompass eternal and unchanging moral, social, political, and economic orders valid for all humans in all eras is a false theoretical premise for the interpretation of Islamic texts. This [belief] is the root cause of all dangers and all severe or milder violence in the Muslim world. (my translation)[19]

Shabestarī conveys two central points in the above article: First, if the official Shi'i clerics abhor the savage and criminal behaviour of ISIS in war, they should be mindful that this behaviour has a theological foundation, which makes it far more dangerous than if it were instigated by occasional urges for violence. Second, such violent theology is the natural result of a wrong interpretive methodology that transcends the Muslim sectarian Shi'i-Sunni divide. Therefore, Shabestarī portrays Daesh's savagery at war as a frame that shows the monumental scale of crimes caused by a specific theology, but also as a mirror that reflects the spectrum of potential for violence that similar radical theologies at home (Iran) may instigate.

Mohsen Kadivar, a renowned figure in modern Iranian-Shi'i scholarship and a cleric with a seminarian education, has been highly critical of traditional Shi'i jurisprudence.[20] He maintains that because of "the many religious prejudices that the Shi'i traditional jurisprudence has advocated against women, Sunni Muslims, non-Muslims, slaves, and laymen," this jurisprudence is in dire need of reconstruction.[21] Kadivar suggests that when it comes to human relations, based on the very first principle of the Shi'i theological school, namely, justice, he (Kadivar) is religiously obliged to prefer moral codes offered by the Declaration of Human Rights over codes of traditional Shi'i jurisprudence.[22] Kadivar's proposal for the moral reconstruction of Islam law is summarized as follows: "Each and every [non worship related] sharī'a precept had three particular characteristics in the age of revelation:

1 It was deemed to be rational by the conventions of the time.
2 It was deemed to be just by the conventions of the time.
3 In overall comparison with the precepts stipulated by other religions and rites, it was deemed to be a better solution.

In the light of these three characteristics, all these precepts were progressive solutions in the age of revelation, and laid the groundwork for a successful religious system. Collective human reason did not have better solutions at the time, and rational conduct endorsed these precepts and did not consider any of them to be unjust, violent, degrading or irrational."[23] He suggests that presently Muslim jurists must apply the same standards. Needless to say, this position substantially reduces the potential for various interfaith, denominational, and gender conflicts often caused by discriminatory legal or social statuses defined by theology.

Unlike Kadivar who, because of his bold critiques, had to leave Iran, Mostafā Malekīān, a prominent theologian living and teaching in Iran, has also increasingly advocated for the primacy of ethics over law and jurisprudence. In one of his articles, delivered in Tehran in the fall of 2013, Malekīān identifies six sources of social morality, including ethics, law, social etiquette and customs, religion, expediency, and aesthetics. After introducing each source, he emphasizes that various scholars confuse the aforementioned six normative sources without their hierarchical distinction. The significance of such a necessary distinction, he concludes, becomes clear whenever an individual is caught between conflicting injunctions, as advised by two or more of the six sources over the same criterion or subject. As such, they should always favour ethics over the other five sources.[24] For Malekīān, universal ethics have absolute superiority over other normative sources of social morality. If adopted globally, Malekīān maintains, these universal ethics can render all politically, culturally, and religiously instigated conflicts unjustified. Simply stated, universal ethics nullify all notions of cultural enmity produced by non-ethical sources of social morality.

In his theological contemplations against violence, Malekīān argues that art can curb violence through five distinct factors, three of which relate to aesthetics, one to imagination, and the last to creativeness. First, the ability to enjoy art, he argues, by nature curbs urges towards violence. Second, such an ability is tantamount to the ability to be less self-centred. With less focus on the carnal self, the probability to be in clash with others is less. Third, because the criteria for art evaluation are highly cultural, speculative, and based on human taste, the appreciation of art exposes the observer to a vast realm of pluralism, which curbs a polarized world view and by default violence. As a fourth factor – and impressed from the political philosophy of Simon Weil, Iris Murdoch, and Hannah Arendt, specifically Arendt's *Eichmann in Jerusalem: A Report on the Banality of Evil* – Malekīān argues that with the lack of imagination an otherwise normal and even moral character has the potential to become a criminal, for a criminal can never imagine himself in the position of his victim. An important function of art is to instigate imagination. Finally, Malekīān argues that artists, like all mothers, have experienced the pains and sufferings of giving birth to a human being or an artistic creation. He concludes that thus a creator is far less inclined to destructive violence by being cognizant of all hardships of creations. Between these lines, Malekīān reminds the highly artistic Iranian society that any tendency to violence in this society is tantamount to having lost its artistic senses and in effect its connection with its ancient civilization. He boldly reminds his audience that it is no wonder, save a few exceptions like Nelson Mandela and Václav Havel, that all prisoners of a political regime become torturers in the next one. Imprisonment kills the senses for art, and without art the vicious cycle of violence finds many causes for continuation.[25]

One of the latest emerging theologians Abolqāsem Fanā'ī has educational background in both Western theology and Shi'i seminarian studies. In his book *Aklāq-e dīn shenāsī* (The ethics of religious studies), he advocates for the primacy of universal ethics over all other normative sources of social life. Like Kadivar, Fanā'ī limits the normative validity of traditional jurisprudence to reason and human rights. He maintains that the discipline of ethics as "the sharī'a of reason" is pre-eminent in relations with both law, or "the sharī'a of customs," and jurisprudence, that is, "the sharī'a of revelation."[26] Fanā'ī proposes reconstructing the presently deficient jurisprudence, which he believes needs a modern philosophy of jurisprudence, rather than producing a modern positive jurisprudence.[27] Fanā'ī complements his jurisprudential reform proposal by suggesting that the translation of religious texts does not guarantee the relevance and the correct understanding of these texts; instead, he argues, such texts should be culturally translated.

Like Abdolkarim Soroush, Fanā'ī believes that for its full appreciation and implementation in modern time, the essence of faith in general, and Islam in particular, must be liberated from the culture and history of its birthplace. For example, Fanā'ī refers to Muslim wars during the formative period of Islam in Arabia and argues that if early Muslims had been granted permission to go to war, it would have been a legitimate retaliatory measure against polytheists depriving Muslims of their basic human rights – including the right to religion. In modern times, however, now that Muslims are relatively free to practise and advertise their faith in non-Muslim countries, religious wars have no foundation. Moreover, Fanā'ī points out, the modern world provides various methods of diplomatic conflict resolution, which, ethically speaking, render resorting to war unjustified and unethical.[28]

More Robust Than Ideology

Abdolkarim Soroush, perhaps the most influential Iranian theologian since the advent of the Islamic Revolution in Iran, advocates a nonessentialist approach to Islamic tradition. Soroush, like Nasr, is highly influenced by Muslim mystic thought. But unlike Nasr's conservatism, which considers collective Muslim traditions to be essential, Soroush believes in an inevitable reform to liberate the Islamic faith from its history and geography. For Nasr, a reformed Islam is no Islam. For Soroush, an unreformed Islam is doomed. One such example of a necessary reform is the need for Muslim cultures to embrace the modern notion of human rights. Soroush has boldly criticized many Muslim traditions, specifically those pertaining to theological jurisprudence. He has tried to open Muslim cultures and minds to Western political philosophies and ethics. Soroush's cultural self-criticism and his nonessentialist and universalist moral approach, by definition, reduce the possibility of enmifying the West in an ideological context.

Soroush's book *More Robust than Ideology* is perhaps one of the most important works for the postwar generation in Iran, effectively altering its view of Islam as a global, political ideology.[29] This book, which appeared first as an article published in the popular Iranian periodical *Kiyan* in the mid-1990s, sent intellectual ripples throughout the country. It criticizes Iran's use of Islam as a political ideology that hypocritically adopted and at the same time rejected communist ideology. He demonstrates that, during Iran's early revolutionary years, a number of influential Muslim leaders spoke about Islam within the framework of competing communist ideologies, thereby using Islam to mobilize masses for political agendas, when in essence the form and content of their politics did not differ from the politics found in the socialist bloc. This approach, Soroush contends, was successful in precipitating regime change but suffered the same absolutist pitfalls befalling various other communist regimes. Soroush argues that the two most problematic concepts of the communist systems, among many more adopted by Iran during the 1979 Revolution, were those of "absolute enemy," "perfect leader," or "a class of official interpreters" of religion.[30] He notes that Islam was able to survive only as a culture-friendly religion and not as the fairly modern and failed phenomenon of political ideology. "Ideologizing religion," Soroush argues, "means making it suitable for fighting and combat." For Soroush, the roots of the militarization of religion lie in some foundational characteristics of ideological systems. He summarizes some of these characteristics in the following excerpts:

> So the first important characteristic of ideology is that it acts as a weapon … With a revolutionary theory, which is the same as ideology, a person realizes what he should do and what he should tear apart, and that he should tear decisively (sewing and attaching are different matters, and as we say, ideology aims at tearing rather than sewing).
>
> … If some lines of thoughts seek to act as weapons, they will have to be accurate, clear and decisive (which is the second characteristic of ideology). This is why ideology never reflects philosophical questioning, scientific doubts and agnostic indulgence. An ideologist does not respect everybody simply because he contains an element of truth. On the contrary, he easily draws a line between supporters and opponents of his ideology and his ideology is quickly turned into party manifesto. Vague ideas which lend themselves to different kinds of interpretations and which blunt the ideological weapons are easily discarded … If we take firmness, clarity and sharpness to be descriptions of ideology, we shall immediately confess that weapons are made to suit type of enemies, and kind of combats (the 4th characteristic) ... We want to say that an ideology's survival depends on existence of an enemy.
>
> … Ideology, in this sense needs a leader or a special class of interpreters. An important aim of ideology is to tell us which direction to follow and which direction to not follow.
>
> … Our whole remarks revolve round a collection of ideas [imbedded in ideology are], characterized mainly by the followings. Firstly, it is worthy of fight (this

fight is political and idealistic, meaning that ideology is politics), so it suppresses and also creates enemy. Secondly, it seeks clarity and conclusiveness in human problems to such an extent (such as determinism, volition, the end and beginning of the world and mankind, etc.) that it ends in dogmatism. Thirdly, it includes and produces the need for a formal class of interpreters. Fourth, it seeks uniformity of idea, and does not tolerate plurality of opinions. Fifth, it approves of movement rather than search for truth. Sixth, because of these characteristics, it claims perfection and comprehensiveness, is indifferent to wisdom, rears followers, demands faith, is sometimes imposter and breeds hatred.

... Alas, rather than producing unifying love, ideologies have encouraged and generated unifying hatred, as is testified by historical samples of ideologies ... Those people who get united round the axis of hatred, love themselves because they hate enemies. In fact if these enemies, who are sometimes imaginary and fictitious, did not exist to incite hatred, that love would not be provided. Pure love and alliance is the one which is not preceded by hatred.

The most useful tools in the battle arena are dogmatism, conclusiveness and unquestionable obedience, and to resort to love and hatred instead of wisdom ... Ideologies give free rein to wisdom only to the extent that do not oppose the[m]. They do not tolerate anything more than that. That is why this question had arisen for all ideologies, as to what they should do with "wisdom." Fascism had really found its way. This ideology did not consider wisdom to be worth a penny, and worst of all was that it beheaded and sacrificed wisdom and science not for the sake of love, but for hatred.

... In ideological societies, leadership too, takes the form of military command, whereas in a religious society, leader means a model, that has combined all religious virtues in a way that shows such a combination possible, and that the person is a perfect example as viewed in that school, both in theory and in practice.

... Marx used to say that the only way to reform capitalism is to kill it ... No ideology can be reformed. The only way to reform an ideology is to execute it ... It must be exterminated and substituted by another ideology. In principle, the internal progress and evolution of a system is possible only when that system is flexible, and when reasoning and new development within it is feasible. If it is not possible, then one has to destroy the edifice in order to reform it and construct another building on its ruins.

... An ideology knows enemies more than it knows friends, and produces enemies more than friends.

... Religion is rather like air and sea which flows along streams and rivers but cannot be contained in them. Everyone can sit on the shores of this sea, and benefit from secrets, amazement, gems, salt and fish, etc.[31]

After establishing that the ideologization of religion will necessarily transform it into an antagonistic dogma and effective means of social edification, Soroush argues that by definition such a metamorphosis runs counter to the spirit of the most fundamental characteristics of religion. He stresses, "As Mowlavi [Rumi] says: 'The only function of religion is to cause amazement in you.' God Who is the origin, the essence and the origin of religion, is the most surprising creature, and His words, deeds and attributes are also amazing. How can we make these unfathomable depths so shallow so that they [fit] in several superficial principles?"[32] Soroush concludes, "Religion is a balance, a torch, a string, a ladder and a path. None of these is turned to a particular direction, and ideology that seeks to give a direction to religion, takes the balance, string, path and the ladder properties from it."[33] By criticizing an ideologized concept of religion, which gives religion a militant posture, Soroush effectively argued that certain conceptual fallacies of the political absolutism of communism copied by Iran had put this country at odds with many non-Muslim, as well as Muslim, cultures. This was an important contribution to underlining the conceptual and practical borders between theologies of war and peace.

Weakness as a Virtue

A separate argument that Soroush asserts in relation to the ethics of hostility is his definition of "the virtue of weakness." In a speech delivered in May 2013 at the University of Waterloo (Canada), he questioned why so many classical Sufi thinkers and mentors expressed their deep appreciation for lacking the power to harm others. To the modern mentality, Soroush argues, a real occasion for appreciation should arise when someone *does* have the ability to harm but chooses not to. To a conventional mind, the paradigm of conscious and voluntary power containment sounds far more interesting than a paradigm that appreciates weakness as a cause of no harm.

By referring to the following proverbial couplets from Shaykh Muslih al-Din Sa'di of Shiraz (d. 1292) and Khawjah Shamseddin Muhammad Hafez (d. 1390), Soroush sides with the latter paradigm:

[34] کجا خود شکر این نعمت گزارم   که زور مردم آزاری ندارم

(Where am I to thank the blessing
That I lack the strength of harming people?)[35]

[36] من از بازوی خود دارم بسی شکر   که زور مردم آزاری ندارم

(Very grateful am I to my arms
Because I lack the strength of an injurer of men.)[37]

In defence of this position, Soroush refers to the proverb "Power corrupts; absolute power corrupts absolutely," pointing out that the great gnostic teachers, such as Sa'di, were cognizant of this power paradigm and knew well how human history suffers from the lack of powerful figures who are able to resist the temptations of power abuse. Soroush turns to modern international relations and alludes to numerous cases where modern Western cultures produced weapons of mass destruction (WMDs) and became victims of the power paradigm trap. He suggests looking at the immoralities of Western powers in terms of the production and use of nuclear, biological, and chemical weapons. Muslim cultures, in turn, Soroush maintains, should not compete but celebrate their weakness in this arms race. He concludes, "Knowing that in the course of our history, we have also had many immoral records in waging unjustified wars, yet, we should feel proud that we have fallen behind in developing both the knowledge and the power of mass destruction."[38]

For Soroush, a conscious endeavour to remain underdeveloped in acquiring destructive weapons may be well appreciated only if we are ready to accept an alternative paradigm to the dominant and conventional power obsession. Soroush's view is morally far more defensible than today's popular paradigm of deterrence based on the mutual power of destruction that perpetuates enmity and institutionalized otherness.

A year and a half after Soroush delivered his lecture on the virtue of weakness, he was shocked, like many other Iranian intellectuals, by the news of the *Charlie Hebdo* tragedy in Paris, which was carried out on 7 January 2015 by two Muslim terrorists. The terrorists killed twelve staff members of the periodical, claiming retribution for what they considered a blasphemous presentation of the Prophet Muhammad through satirical cartoons.[39] In response to this act of terror justified by the perpetrators on religious grounds, Soroush published an article in which he argued that the postcolonial revivalist Muslims have unfortunately focused more on the revival of "Islam as an identity" rather than on "Islam as a source of knowledge or salvation." This, for Soroush, is the main cause of the current fashionable violence among fundamentalist Muslims, who do not balance their political zeal with knowledge of Islamic ethics.[40]

The remedy for this situation and the effective way to suppress monstrous phenomena such as Daesh, Soroush suggests, is the Persian word *danesh* (knowledge). He invites Muslim scholars to work hard, by distinguishing the moral essentials of Islamic faith from its historical and legal accidents, to put ethics before the rigidified body of sharī'a and liberate Islam's soul from its outdated forms. A return to the "preorthodoxy" phase of Islam, Soroush contends, will grant us the chance to have fresh contemplation about articles of faith, law, and theology, such as "disbelief, belief, permissible [*halāl*], forbidden [*harām*], the nature of revelation and prophecy, rights, duties, jurisprudence, and theology." "The antidote to most urges for violence," Soroush stresses, "is to transform the closed legalistic society to an open moral society." He adds, "We need to open our [duty-based] jurisprudence to ethics and rights."[41]

While the above article focuses primarily on the Muslim identity crises, it nevertheless briefly criticizes Western cultures for abusing their freedom of speech by producing culturally sensitive and blasphemous literature, the dissemination of which is neither a duty, nor a social utility, nor a virtue in various ethical systems. He adds that jihadists' violence is partly a reaction to the Muslim sense of security lost through violent Western incursions.

To complete his antiviolence argument, Soroush once again reminds his Muslim audience about the virtue of weakness, on which many great Muslim thinkers elaborated long before modern technology proved the extreme evils of destructive power.

The paradigm of weakness as virtue referenced by Soroush has a Qur'ānic source in relation to Genesis's story about Cain and Abel. According to the Qur'ān's tale, Abel's gift to God was accepted, while Cain's gift, given insincerely, was not. This made Cain jealous of his brother and prompted him to threaten his life. Abel's response to the life threat, as reflected in the Qur'ān, is telling: "If you should raise your hand against me to kill me – I shall not raise my hand against you to kill you. Indeed, I fear Allah, Lord of the worlds. Indeed I want you to obtain [thereby] my sin and your sin so you will be among the companions of the Fire. And that is the recompense of wrongdoers" (Q. 5:28, 29). Abel's strategy is not to retaliate but to rationalize a pacifist position in this conflict of mundane nature in exchange for a greater reward in the afterlife. Abel's position, however, predictably does not save his life, as Cain eventually murders him. But the virtue of weakness, as reflected in Abel's position, hints at an eschatological equation that results in more than the psychologically soothing possibility of a revenge for Abel in afterlife. This story lends itself to the notion that any premeditated, unjustified harm to another transfers a part or all of the victims' unrelated life sins to the eschatological record of the murderer.

A number of Prophetic-hadith narratives in various primary sources provide further eschatological rationale for pacifism.[42] By warning potential aggressors of the eternal implications of aggression, Abel's pacifist theology stands sharply against the theology of violence as practised in suicide bombing, which unfortunately has become fashionable among Muslim extremists.

Abel's approach, in effect, derationalizes the policy of mutual harm or chain revenge that is presently responsible for the global arms race under the doctrine of deterrence. Under a theoretical framework where the virtue of military weakness in this life leads to a strengthened spiritual position in the next, the human tendency towards punitive justice has a better chance of giving way to the ethics of benevolence and forgiveness.

Against Paradigmatic Violence

Among the contemporary Iranian sociologists of religion who have produced a substantial amount of scholarship on Iranian higher education methodologies, Maqsood Farāsatkhāh has emerged as an influential voice. In addition to a number of published books on the subject, he regularly publishes articles in his academically popular website.[43] In an article that appeared on his website on 25 April 2014 as a part of his longer article on Shi'i typology, Farāsatkhāh focuses on violence as a conceptual paradigm with deep influence on contemporary Muslim theologies. By examining specifically theological debates that have methodologically and conceptually influenced Iranian public, academic, and also seminarian minds since the establishment of the Islamic Republic of Iran in 1979, Farāsatkhāh comes to a striking conclusion: the dominant paradigm in most intellectual and theological debates in Iran during the past few decades has been the paradigm of war rather than peace.[44] As an example, the author refers to what he calls "the most subtle, the most gradual, and the most sociological subfield of the megaproject of critical Shi'i studies, namely, Shi'i reformism."[45] "But even in this field of Shi'i studies," Farāsatkhāh points out, "– most conspicuously represented by Ali Sharī'atī again the dominant paradigm is that of war: Religion Against Religion."[46] Echoing the critical voice of Soroush on Sharī'atī, Farāsatkhāh stresses that despite the fact that Sharī'atī was personally of a peaceful character, his intellectual paradigm was the paradigm of war.

In *We Iranians: A Historic and Social Contextextualizing of Iranian Ethos,* a well-researched and well-documented book published in 2015 with exhaustive factual charts and graphs, Farāsatkhāh demonstrates that Iranian rulers before and after Islam ruled on average 14.68 and 11.31 years respectively. These figures manifest chronic political instability throughout all Iranian history. "The political instability increased in the Islamic period. Approximately half of rulers among all Muslim dynasties ruled for less than ten years. This is close to the presidential life span of nonmonarchic and democratic governments that run on the principle of circulation of power and elections."[47] Farāsatkhāh concludes that the above facts could only point to the roots of psychological insecurity in the historical Iranian mindset, which often provided motivation for militarism and the prominence of militants in political hierarchy. "The macroparadigm of war rather than peace," Farāsatkhāh argues, "has dominated our intellectual discourses. This means we have no interest in getting to agreement while holding onto our intellectual differences. There is no ground [in our culture] to hold peaceful dialogues about diverse ideas."[48] Farāsatkhāh then refers to numerous historical examples, such as the emergence of the idea of apostasy in early Islamic history or of dividing the whole world into two confronting realms of *dār al-īmān* (the abode of faith) and *dār al-kufr* (the abode of disbelief). Other examples of methodologically antagonistic posture are reformism, fundamentalism, and traditionalism working against one another and the conceptual reluctance of advocates of these schools towards any possible compromise or even dialogue. Farāsatkhāh refers to the old dichotomy of the "salvific sect" (*ferqe-ye nājiyeh*) against "gone-astray sects" (*feraq-e zalāl*) as another historic concept that proposes that only one religious denomination has the chance to lead to human salvation; this is yet another manifestation of war paradigm. He mentions that it was indeed against this sectarian exclusive, salvific power that the fourteenth-century poet Hafez took stance when he condemned all sectarian confrontational and exclusivist claims in the following proverbial line:

جنگ هفتاد دو ملت همه را عذر بنه   چون ندیدند حقیقت ره افسانه زدند

(Leave aside the squabbling sects and their divisions: all seventy-two of them
Bereft of the Truth, they set out to hunt a Chimera.)[49]

In conclusion and in relation to the dominant confrontational approach in Muslim theological debates, Farāstkhāh puts the onus on a teleological or duty-based ethical system. In his opinion, unlike utilitarian ethics, teleological ethics (*akhlāq-e ghāyat andīsh*) pays little or no attention to the objective results of actions, thus this normative system's strong potential to instigate violence.[50]

In his succinct but foundational article, Farāsatkhāh invites postrevolutionary Iranians to look at the socioethical inconsistencies and moral flaws of the dominant political ideology as the real causes of many problems with which modern Iranian society is still struggling more than three decades after the 1979 Revolution. He shows how a narrowly defined concept of justice based on zero-sum game lays at the heart of a belligerent theology that has contributed to the development a polarized society caught in the vicious circle of violence and retribution. Even a cursory examination of Farāsatkhāh's books and many other articles, as appear in his official website, demonstrates that one of his major scholarly goals is to help and encourage the development a self-critical approach within Shi'i seminarian and academic studies. His main effort seems to focus on inviting serious attention to the view that historic Shi'ism has developed a theology that represents a suppressed-minority mentality fighting for equal rights. This theology, however, has lost relevance to the present time and space. There is an urgent need to transform Shi'i theology into a self-critical and, at the same time, self-confident theology that can lead to and sustain constructive dialogues with religious others in international and interfaith arenas.

Like Shabestarī, Soroush, and Fanā'ī, Farāsatkhāh pays attention to a theoretical and epistemological change that modern Iranian religious intellectuals have pioneered in their approach to the relationship between ethics and religion. In a speech delivered at Tehran University on 1 December 2014, Farāsatkhāh pointed out that the Iranian traditionalist approach to "religious ethics" has given way to "ethical religion" during the last few decades of Iranian history. The result, he maintains, has been an effective overhaul of the Shi'i traditional paradigms in relation with sociopolitical issues.[51] The new approach towards the moralization of religion, Farāsatkhāh maintains, had two specific orientations of what he calls 'action-based' and existential. The existential approach, he points out, as exemplified in the works of Ali Sharī'atī (d. 1977), had both a positive and negative result. On the positive side, Sharī'atī was able to use his version of "ethical religion" to politically mobilize the Iranian youth and university students. The flip side of this mobilization, as Farāsatkhāh – just like Soroush – maintains, was the ideologization of religion, which later on became a root cause of rigid mindedness and violence.[52] It is in reaction to this social violence, Farāsatkhāh concludes, that another turning point in Iranian social ethics is presently in the making: a moral shift from the previous focus on social ethics with philanthropic tendencies to a present focus on individual ethics that prioritize individual and personal hedonism. Farāsatkhāh concludes that through such multiple sociomoral shifts, the present Iranian society is unfortunately jumping into postmodernity without having fully experienced modernity. Between the lines, Farāsatkhāh conveys that the advent of political and ideological Islam in Iran since the 1979 Revolution has produced unnecessary social polarization and violence. In reaction, the current Iranian generation, in its experience of what he calls "intellectual dilution," is becoming highly introvert and socially passive.[53] This last conclusion is one with which a secular Iranian intellectual like Ramin Jahanbegloo may disagree.[54]

The Political Economy of Generational Enmity

Homa Katouzian, currently an Iranian professor at Oxford University, is internationally known as a scholar with novel insights about Iranian history. In an article titled "The Short-Term Society: A Study in the Problems of Long-Term Political and Economic Development in Iran," Katouzian demonstrates how a culturally chronic enmity between various Iranian generations has impaired Iranian political and economic development. As for the mechanism of this systematic generational clash, the very first paragraph of his article is telling:

> Iran was a *short-term society* in contrast to Europe's *long-term society*. It was a society in which change – even important and fundamental change – tended to be a short-term phenomenon. This was precisely due to the absence of an established and inviolable legal framework, which would guarantee long-term continuity. Over any short period of time, there could be notable military, administrative and property-owning classes, but their composition would not remain the same beyond one or two generations ... In Iran, property and social positions were short-term, precisely because they were regarded as personal privileges rather than inherited and inviolable social rights.[55]

Katouzian argues that such a politico-economic phenomenon manifests itself in many fields of Iranian culture, even in her urban development and building construction habits. He accurately points out that the concept of landmark building hardly exists in Iran, because when a generation disappears, the following one demolishes all buildings made by predecessors, so as to claim full authority over the past.

By borrowing the real-estate terminology of "pickaxe building" (*sākhtemān-e kolangī*), Katouzian touches upon a part of historic Iranian culture that systematically disrupts and destroys her own generational achievements. This phenomenon can only result from an insecure psychology that looks at history and nature as a zero-sum game, wherein any new gain must be established on someone else's loss. To complement Katouzian's important insight, I would argue that, for exactly the same reasons as he enumerates, Iran is also a "short-cut society" in the sense that she lacks a due-process culture. People in this culture, knowing that the next generation will soon take over, are in so much of a hurry to secure their share of the mundane that they have no time for due process. The end result of these short-term and short-cut societal habits is a systematic, unrelenting, and generational conflict that, unless checked by a cultural metamorphosis, will keep Iran as her own perpetual enemy. The good news is that diagnosis of a sickness is a great part of its cure. Katouzian has done very well in the discovery of a psychocultural problem that has been too obvious and too common to be truly recognized.

Philosophical Nonviolence and Disarmament in Rhymes and Melodies

Known as the most influential and prolific modern Iranian poetess, Sīmīn Behbahānī (d. 2014) has become one of the greatest and most memorable voices against war and violence of postrevolutionary Iran. As Farzaneh Milani put it, "Her body of work is the voice of a nation in search of itself."[56] Behbahānī's open and bold criticism of war and violence, specifically those justified on religious grounds, has given her a unique intellectual status among poets in modern Iran. Behbahānī, in the words of Milani, "ponders the conflicts between the forces of extremism and moderation, repression and freedom, revenge and reconciliation, religious fundamentalism and political absolutism."[57] As the end of the eight-year-long Iran-Iraq War failed to bring Iran any sense of military victory, and the news of its end brought the public to a state of shock, Behbahānī questioned the logic of war altogether in the following words:

> Our tears sweet, our laughter venomous
> we are pleased when sad, and sad when pleased
> happy when heart-broken, heart-broken when happy
> we wash one hand in blood, the other we wash the blood off
> we cry as we laugh at the futility of both these acts
> eight years have passed; we have not discovered their meaning
> we have been like children, beyond any account or accounting,
> ... we wished for a war, it brought us misery
> now repentant we wish for peace
> we pulled wings and heads from bodies
> now seeking the cure we are busy grafting
> will it come to life, will it fly
> the head we attach, the wing we stitch?[58]

The significance of Behbahānī's candid anti-war stance cannot be fully appreciated unless one is familiar with the institutionalized martyrdom culture in Iran. As chapter 8 of this volume demonstrates, even in 2014, twenty-six years after the ceasefire in the Iran-Iraq War, lamentation literature about the abrupt ending of war – short of a military victory and facilitated through the UN mediation – is still abundant. In the line "we cry as we laugh at the futility of both these acts," Behbahānī tackles an important question that deals with one of the deepest layers of the postrevolutionary and postwar Iranian collective ethico-psychological confusion: the legitimate sources of happiness and sadness. For the Shi'a community this is a long-lasting mental struggle between the real and duty, between the natural state of mind and feeling that enjoy peace, and a duty-bound allegiance to sadness that has resulted from historic suppression of Shi'i minorities. The wide gap between "is" and "ought to be," irrespective of some philosopher's position that there are no productive and consequential relations between them, is nevertheless a cause for mental tension. Perhaps

Behbahānī is asking her countrymen this question: where is a theology of happiness in Shi'i Islam?

Behbahānī's unrelenting critique of war and its culture extends to the question of accountability for human life. War by nature is insensitive to the number of lives lost and war veterans' quality of life, particularly those who are disabled. When war becomes ideological, the situation worsens, as even a slight sensitivity to numbers is considered a sin. Within this sensational space, anyone who dares to question the futility of war is viewed as someone who intends to sabotage the product line of a factory that is producing battle champions and martyr role models. This attitude informs the heart of the line in which Behbahānī proclaims, "We have been like children, beyond any account or accounting." The postwar (*post bellum*) attention of the above piece is also striking in its eloquent demonstration of the plight of war veterans. What is the meaning of life for a bird without wings, for a body without a head, both in physical and in spiritual senses?

Behbahānī has written many poems that invite ideologues' attention to what is going on beneath the shimmering skin of "glorious martyrdom." She frequently depicts tragic details of the miserable lives of mothers who have to deal with their lost children for the rest of their lives. One such poem titled "The Necklace," composed a few months after the end of Iran-Iraq War, takes the reader to the heart of just one of hundreds of thousands heartaching mothers. As Milani describes it, "By crystalizing a mother's pain into art, 'The Necklace' makes readers witness the nightmarish consequences and long-term implications of war."[59] Milani's eloquent interpretation of the piece sheds important light on the unconventional dimension of the *post bellum*: "The dead soldier's boots and his mother's wretchedness are all there to see. The parameters of the battlefield have thus been stretched unbearably. Ironically enough, the poem so blurs distinctions that it articulates a new conception of war in which dead soldiers are not the only casualties and their mourning mothers become new kind of combatants. Behbahānī defines another kind of war here, one in which a corpse refuses to be buried and finds reincarnation in boots. Rejected by the earth, this grief-stricken mother can't even take refuge in death. She is condemned to live and carry her pain."[60] In addition to the above, what may add to the pain substantially is if the mother loses the confidence that her son's life was a necessary price for bringing his country to peace with Iraq through the 1988 negotiations. Behbahānī's attention to the pain all mothers have to bear in any war indeed offers a gender balance to the study of the ethics of war. "The Necklace" as translated by Milani and Safa reads:

Anxious, agitated, sad,
her face uncovered, her head unveiled,

not afraid of arrest or policeman,
oblivious to the order to “Cover! Conceal!”
Her eyes two grapes plucked from their cluster,
squeezed by the times to fill a hundred barrels of blood,
mad, really mad, a stranger to herself and others,
oblivious to the world, beyond being awakened even by the deluge,
a particle of dust adrift in the wind, without purpose or destination,
lost, speechless, bewildered, a corpse without grave,
carrying around her neck a necklace of curses and tears,
a pair of boots tied together belonging to a dead soldier,

I asked her: What does this mean?
She smiled: my son, poor child, sitting on my shoulder,
hasn’t taken off his boots yet.[61]

The graphic details of the miserable life of disabled war veterans as reflected in the following piece speak volumes in a few rhymed couplets. Through his peculiar movement with only one leg, the disabled veteran invites attention to the meaning, or lack of meaning, of his life:

شلوار تا خورده دارد مردی که یک پا ندارد
خشم است و آتش نگاهش، یعنی تماشا ندارد
رخساره می تابم از او، اما به چشمم نشسته
بس نو جوان است و شاید از بیست بالا ندارد
بادا که چون من مبادا چل سال رنجش پس از این
خود گرچه رنج است بودن، بادا مبادا ندارد
تق تق کنان چوبدستش روی زمین می نهد مهر
با انکه ثبت حضورش حاجت به امضا ندارد
بر چهره سخت و خشکش پیدا خطوط ملال است
یعنی که با کاهش تن، جانی شکیبا ندارد
گویم که با مهربانی، خواهم شکیبایی از او
پندش دهم مادرانه، گیرم که پروا ندارد
رو میکنم سوی او باز، تا گفتگویی کنم ساز
رفته است و خالی است جایش، مردی که یک پا ندارد

(A man with a missing leg
has one leg of his pants folded.
Anger burns in his eyes.
Is this a spectacle, they cry?
Though I turned my face away,

his image lingers in my eyes:
his extreme youth, less than twenty, perhaps.
I pray he will not be like me:
Have to suffer another forty years.
Yet, the suffering that comes with existence
Is impervious to such entreaties.
My feet were quick,
yet how difficult the path was for me.
How will he manage with just one leg?
Tap, tap, he stamps the pavement with his cane,
though he needs no signature
to register his presence.
My tender smiles turned to thorns and daggers in his eyes.
Used to rough treatment,
he has no appetite for tenderness.
Lines of bitterness mark his cold, parched face.
It's as if, with his body diminished,
his spirit too had lost its resilience.
To help him hang on, I thought, I would offer him
some kindness and motherly advice.
But I realized it was more than he could bear.

I turned to him to initiate a conversation.
The spot where he stood was empty.
He was gone, the man with a missing leg.)[62]

Behbahānī's critique of war is not absolute. Where she finds a just war of resistance, she does not miss a chance to praise heroic combatants, whether young or old or a child:

O, History! Record this epic of resistance
record the tale of this season of blood
record the stone thrown by a sparkling child
record the ax which was carried by a caring elder ...
record the shout of all those who carried out "Death or Honor"
those who embraced death with courage
O, History! Record it all; record it.[63]

Patriotic resistance war aside, Behbahānī's voice, expressing her unrelenting resolve to reconstruct the country over war ruins, has penetrated Iranian hearts far more than any other works. The following lines, simple and yet so eloquently expressed in Persian, were memorized almost immediately after their composition by the Iranian public and were frequently chanted as a postwar national anthem:

> My country, I will build you again,
> if need be, with bricks made from my life.
> I will build columns to support your roof with my bones,
> I will inhale again the perfume of flowers
> Favored by your youth.
> I will wash again the blood off your body
> with torrents of my tears.[64]

"The death-defying poems" of Behbahānī, as Milani has accurately termed them, provide a view of the ethics of war in which heroism and patriotism must struggle very hard to find a war justification. She adheres to the notion of defensive just war, but only an unavoidable one that defines the borders of national dignity. Even within these narrow borderlines of a legitimate war, she does not miss a chance to draw her readers' attention to multidimensional war tragedies. In the end, she firmly stands for war only as a defence and only as a last resort. Behbahānī's poems on war and peace therefore have great potential to be used effectively as a political philosophy of peace in approaching conflict resolution. They can be translated easily into other languages, cultures, and media expressions. Behbahānī's thoughts on the inhumanity of war have inspired many other Iranians who have tried to transmit her message to different languages and media.

Behbahānī's rhymed and rhythmic words are often echoed in the Iranian musical space. It is no exaggeration to say that one of the most popular national figures in modern Iran is Mohammad Rezā Shajarīān, a classical vocalist, who because of his influential and powerful voice has engraved so much of classical and modern Persian poetry on people's hearts and minds. Both Mohammad Rezā and his son, also a very popular singer in Iran, have together performed Behbahānī's political poetry. The Shajarīāns have expanded the realm of their music far from romantic entertainment into the very heart of political dialogue in Iran. In 2009, when the Iranian presidential election caused street clashes, the senior Shajarīān chose for his very popular performance an antiviolence poem from one of the most renowned contemporary Iranian poets Fereydoon Moshīrī (d. 2000). The performance soon became a theme for collective singing in various social gatherings. A translation of the poem that Shajarīān performed in many cities inside Iran and also abroad, under the title "Language of Fire," is as follows:

تفنگت را زمین بگذار
که من بیزارم از دیدار این خونبار ناهنجار
تفنگ دست تو یعنی زبان آتش و آهن
من اما پیش این اهریمنی ابزار بنیان کن
ندارم جز زبان دل،
دل لبریز مهر تو،
تو ای با دوستی دشمن!
زبان آتش و آهن زبان خشم و خونریزی است
زبان قهر چنگیزی است
بیا، بنشین، بگو، بشنو سخن شاید
فروغ آدمیت راه در قلب تو بگشاید
برادر گر که میخوانی مرا،
بنشین برادروار، تفنگت را زمین بگذار،
تفنگت را زمین بگذارتا از جسم تو این دیو انسان کش برون آید،
تو از آیین انسانی چه میدانی؟
اگر جان را خدا داده است چرا باید تو بستانی؟
چرا باید که با یک لحظه غفلت، این برادر را به خاک وخون بغلطانی؟
گرفتم در همه احوال حق گویی و حق جویی
و حق با تو است ...،
ولی حق را- برادر جان به زور این زبان نافهم آتشبار نبای جست!...
اگر این بار شد وجدان خواب آلوده ات بیدار
تفنگت را زمین بگذار...[65]

(Lay down your gun, as I hate this very abnormal shedding of blood.
The gun in your hand speaks the language of fire and iron,
But I, before this fiendish tool, have nothing but, the language of the heart,
The heart full to the brim with love for you, who are in love with the enemy.
The language of fire and iron is the game of fury and bloodshed.
It is the language of Genghis Khan. Come, sit down, talk, hear.
Perhaps the light of humanity will get through to your heart, too.
My brother, if you want me, sit down for a brotherly chat. Lay down your gun,
So that the human-killer leaves your body. How much do you know
about the ethics of humanity?
If God has bestowed the soul, why then you take it away?
Why, in the twilight of ignorance, do you want to roll and wrap up your brethren
in dirt and blood,

The God-given soul? Let's suppose you are right, my brother, in seeking and telling the right and correct things.
But we ought to not seek even righteous things through the fire-spewing gun.
If it once happens that the pangs of conscience bother you,
Then lay down your gun.)[66]

Within these few lines, rhymes, and melodies, Shajariān sings more than a sentiment: he sings a powerful theology of peace, philosophy of disarmament and conflict resolution, which denies any human being justification for taking any God-given life. The piece has a touch of bitter satire. Force and bullets can hardly promote any spirituality! War therefore, especially when it carries a religious banner, is oxymoron.

Moshīrī, the poet of the above piece, enjoys an impressive imagination to speak for peace:

تیر صدای
ربود از دهان کلامم را
ستاره پرپر شد!
نسیم از نفس افتاد،
رنگ ماه پرید،
دگر کجا ببرم حرف ناتمامم را؟

(The sound of a bullet,
robbed my lips of words.
The star trembled,
the breeze lost its breath,
The moon paled.
Where else should I take my unfinished word?)[67]

The poet's skill in expressing much in a few words reaches its culmination in the following verse, which has become proverbial and questions the moral grounds for possibile homicide, irrespective of the cause:

در چشم من, شمشیر در مشت
یعنی کسی را میتوان کشت.[68]

(In my eyes,
holding a sword in hand
can only hint at the possibility of homicide. [my translation])

The philosophical mockery of war and the futility of violence echo well in another art genre in Iran: the cinema. The remarkable works of modern female Iranian filmmakers, such as Rakhshān Banī Etemād, provide a good example.

War's Inhumanity through the Prism of the Iranian Cinema

The Iranian Revolution of 1979, followed immediately by the Iran-Iraq War, entangled the majority of politically active Iranians in a matrix of polarized politics across ideological borders. Meanwhile, Iranian cinema, religiously disapproved before the revolution, forced itself back into social life within a shorter time than expected and became an influential medium in making and expressing public opinion. Soon after its inception in 1980, the Iran-Iraq War became an important theme for postrevolutionary modern cinema. A number of films branded officially as "the sacred defence cinema" (*sinamay-e defa'-e moqaddas*) focused on the heroism of war combatants; but importantly most of the films produced by renowned film directors reflected on the inhumanity of war and the injustice that war had inflicted upon the Iranian people. Significantly, no film, as far as I know, depicted the radical interpretation of war as a blessing. Exceptions are a series of entertaining and half-satirical films called *The Dismissed Ones* (*ekhrājihā*), made by a fundamentalist-turned-film director Masood Dehnamakī, which show how pious war-front warriors exercise deep sincerity in their selflessness and acts of chivalry – a fine moral space that cannot be found among city dwellers. Although this space is certainly true, Dehnamakī nevertheless does not appraise war as a moral blessing. In his edited volume *New Iranian Cinema: Politics, Representation and Identity*, Richard Tapper provides an accurate account of postwar films in Iran: "In Ebrahīm Hātamikīā's later [film] *Scent of Yusef's Shirt* (1996), we see how 'the task of post-war Iranian cinema becomes the task of mourning itself.' In post-war films, the 'world of lost souls replaces earlier cinema by moving the battleground, from the Iraqi border and the body, to Tehran and the soul ... battle and trance are incorporated in the search for bodies, for POWs and for meaning after the war.'"[69]

Iranian female film directors made a remarkable difference in exposing the inhumanity of war and violence irrespective of their cause(s), be it legitimate or unjustified. In their 2005 film *Gilāneh* based on a scenario authored by Banī Etemād, filmmakers Rakhshān Banī Etemād and Mohsen Abdolvahhāb focus on the life story of a rural family whose young male members are either killed in war or have become disabled. Gilāneh, the single mother of the disabled soldier and a pregnant daughter who has lost her husband in war, carries both the psychological and also the physical burden of the miserable long-lasting situation and struggles to keep the family's hope against all odds. Significantly, the unfortunate woman's reliance on religion is completely directed towards healing her son and comforting her daughter rather than claiming credit for men's patriotism and sacrifice. The film leaves a deep impression on observers about the hidden yet monumental depth of war inhumanities; this feeling is best expressed by the film reviewer David Shasha:

> In "Gilaneh" we are shown a kaleidoscope of human suffering amid the rubble of man's inhumanity to man. This suffering is filled with pain yet is ennobling in some sense. The self-abnegation of a character like Gilaneh who does not question the ways of God is a profoundly moving case study of the ways in which human beings face their traumas. As in "The Best Years of Our Lives," "Gilaneh" looks at the ways in which war devastates human beings and marks them for life. There is no escaping the mad screams and the silent suffering that suffuses the lives of those who struggle to overcome their nightmares, who just as often are left bereft of all hope and joy.[70]

There are many more films in this genre worth mentioning, such as *Bashu, the Little Stranger*[71] and *From Karkheh to Rheine.*[72] With the rise of regional terrorism, specifically the rise of the terror state Daesh (ISIS) in Iran's neighbourhood, Iran seems to be giving a whole new attention to the film industry as an effective medium in pursuing antiterror, antifundamentalist public, political, and moral campaigns. The common moral thread connecting the central arguments of these films is composed of two or three notions: war is evil; it inflicts far more suffering on both sides of battles than what the official media and ideological propaganda can address; and silent women, children, and disabled war veterans pay monumental, incalculable, and unaccounted prices for ventures that only superficially produce a heroism that symbolizes patriotism and religious piety. They all pose the serious questions of whether and why this price is a necessity. One such example is the film *The Prophet*, directed by Iran's renowned film director Majīdī Majīdī, which was screened in late 2015.

In the article "Sparrow's Chirping and the Controversy about the Prophet," Elaheh Najafī predicted that Majīdī's film *The Prophet* would attract much attention and controversy once it was screened at international film festivals such as the Berninale Festival. As Saudi Arabian religious authorities and a number of other Sunni scholars from conservative circles protested against presenting the figure of the Prophet Muhammad in feature films, Majīdī responded with the following words: "This time, with the weapon of culture and art [the screening of the film on the character of the Prophet Muhammad], we want to battle violent activists [Muslims] who have stolen the sacred name of the Prophet

Mohammad. With the support of Dirham and Dinar [reference to Arab currencies in the Persian Gulf], all they [Saudis] do in Iraq, Syria, Lebanon, and Pakistan is plundering, burning, exploding, and beheading by the scale of hundreds ... Through this film, people will see a prophet who will disarm and disclose the true face of pseudobeliever terrorists."[73] According to Najafī's estimation, this most expensive film production in Iranian history may have cost Iran between $350 million to one billion dollars. Notwithstanding the precarious Iranian economy thanks to Western sanctions, spending even a fraction of the above estimate echoes a clear message: the Iranian officials who have been spending systematically on propaganda films to keep the memory of the Iran-Iraq War alive, and who have been critical of war-critical film products, are now shifting their direction against regional militant violence. The film was screened in Iran in September 2015, and according to official Iranian news, public attendance and ticket sales only a month after the screening had surpassed all records in the history of Iranian films. Majīdī has successfully demystified Prophet Mohammad's youth and made his character accessible for laymen. With a tender figure shown always from behind, a soft voice that does not cause awe, an attitude that is consistently graceful and affable, this Mohammad bears no resemblance to a prophet who could produce such world views as those held by Daesh, Taliban, or Boko Haram. It is no wonder that the film was immediately opposed by Sunni fundamentalist clerics in Saudi Arabia and even in India.[74]

Towards a Theology of Nonviolence

Among current Iranian intellectuals who have paid some scholarly attention to the ethics of war and peace, many have criticized violence from various philosophical, theological, jurisprudential, and historical perspectives. But hardly anyone has paid as much systematic attention to the rational, universal, and faith-based foundations of nonviolence as Rāmin Jahānbegloo did in his *Introduction to Nonviolence*. To me, the most significant aspect of Jahānbegloo's approach is that, in his effort to present a universally acceptable foundation for nonviolence, he remains sensitive and responsive to cultural and religious aspects of and factors in various societies. His inclusive approach, therefore, provides a promising opportunity to encourage interfaith and international dialogues on nonviolence across the globe.

Quite frequently and emphatically Jahānbegloo takes a stance against what he calls "the absolute secularization of nonviolence dialogues." At the same time, he does not miss a chance to assert, "Both secular and religious dialogues pertaining to democracy should be accommodated."[75] Significantly,

Jahānbegloo's goal for nonviolence dialogues goes beyond establishing democratic political systems; he aims for the creation of a moral space that can help our current humanity in its struggle to transcend what I call "cold peace" in interpersonal and intercommunal relations. "Through dialogue and the nonviolent process of recognition of others," he argues, "a 'moral togetherness' will be constructed."[76]

As an Iranian scholar who paid a high personal price for his political views,[77] and therefore based on direct experience, Jahānbegloo offers his nonviolent theory to his Muslim home in the following words: "Nonviolence ... must be built on dialogical mechanisms that re-examine the existing power relations in Muslim societies. In order for this to occur, a shift must be made away from 'belligerent citizenship' to 'dialogical citizenship.'" He further adds, "Exclusion of religion from the Muslim public sphere can be destructive to the social fabric of community, but neither does it mean that the Muslim public sphere should undergo a theologization."[78] This is, of course, a very good wish, but as history and specifically Shi'i history has taught us, the theologization of political injustices has hardly been resistible in various societies. Suppressed societies tend to perpetuate their memory of suppression by theologizing catastrophic events that await retaliation sometime in future history. Should we then be proactive by contributing to the development of a theology of nonviolence? Jahānbegloo does not claim to have produced such a theology, but his arguments certainly do provide many rational, religious, and empirical ingredients and frameworks for a Muslim theology of nonviolence.

Jahānbegloo provides a brief review of some important Qur'ānic verses that are frequently used by Muslim modernists in current interfaith discourses, but his more important contribution is his successful endeavour to provide factual narratives about politically active Muslim role models for nonviolence. Jahānbegloo's focus on the two Indian Muslim activists Khān Abdul Ghaffār Khān (d. 1988) and Maulānā Abul Kalām Āzād (d. 1958) presents a version of Islamic political activism that is in full agreement with the Gandhian philosophy of nonviolence. Both figures were in close association with Mahatma Gandhi's nonviolent movement for Indian independence and freedom, but significantly both defined their political philosophy by parameters of an Islamic world view. As Jahānbegloo has asserted, "Ghaffār Khān started forming his philosophy of nonviolence before he came in contact with Gandhi. His nonviolent action drew its inspiration from the Qur'ān and the Prophet Mohammad, in contrast to Gandhi, whose ideals were largely inspired by the *Bhagavad Gita*, the New Testament, and the writings of Thoreau, Ruskin, and Tolstoy. Abdul Ghaffār Khān used to say: 'I did not learn secularism from Bapu [Gandhi's nickname]. I found it in the Qur'an.'"[79] Likewise, Jahānbegloo mentions,

"Āzād defines 'secularism' not as a lack of religion and spirituality in the public sphere, but as equal respect for all religions. This approach fundamentally criticizes a mono-religious or a mono-secular public sphere. In his pluralist approach," Jahānbegloo concludes, "Āzād invites Muslims, Hindus, Buddhists, Sikhs, Parsis, and Christians to live together in an enlightened climate of understanding, tolerance, amity, mutual respect, and regard for each other."[80]

Extending his insight on political nonviolence to modern Iran, Jahānbegloo argues that the 1979 Iranian Revolution "was a great political change that heralded the return of massive and long-term violence to the annals of modern Iranian history."[81] But three decades after the revolution, Jahānbegloo argues that the peaceful uprising caused by the controversial Iranian presidential election in 2009 marked "the end of a long period of violence and the beginning of a period of new political thought in Iran."[82] As far as Iranian political culture is concerned, Jahānbegloo seems to be generally accurate. The outbreak of the unprecedented violence by Daesh (ISIS) in Iraq and Syria in the summer and fall 2014, however, proved that the Middle East still has a long way to go before it can fully embrace nonviolence as a viable approach to political expression. I therefore read Jahānbegloo's conviction with some reservation, where he concludes: "The genie of nonviolence has been let out of the bottle in the Middle East; neither the old or the new regimes are confident that it can be put back."[83]

Conclusion

This chapter provided an overview of some prominent, modern Iranian intellectuals' rethinking about enemy, theologies of enmity, and nonviolence. Together, these scholars, poets, and artists, each through his or her own specific and novel approach, have influenced Iranian-Shi'i society's concept of the enemy. Some of these intellectuals offer a critical assessment of traditional Shi'i jurisprudence and theology from both within and out of the methodologically seminarian space. They all believe in a notion of objective, rational, and universal ethics that transcend not only cultural nuances of history and geography but also any rigid legalism within religious traditions. By nudging jurisprudence and international relations towards these rules of ethics, these theologians, intellectuals, and artists contribute to the ethics, conflict resolution, and theologies of peacemaking.

Despite these contributions, the effective reconstruction of the ethics of enmity and nonviolence is still hampered by the lack of a necessary and complementary scholarship and art on the ethics of forgiveness. In a moral world view where justice is the primary moral focus, the ethics of forgiveness in war is the best thing modern political philosophy can produce. But forgiveness is a particular virtue that is discussed most substantially within religious frameworks and traditions. Therefore, society needs more than modern theologians and political philosophers to reconstruct the ethics of war and forgiveness. This process requires the full engagement of the jurists who have, rightly or wrongly, dominated religious institutions for a good part of Muslim history. Equally, it demands serious endeavours by secular intellectuals, poets, and artists who should redirect their challenges against religion to challenges against old paradigms that have impaired both the religious and the secular in their uncreative moral convictions.

This chapter demonstrated that many Iranian intellectuals are increasingly presenting arguments in favour of the moralization of religion, as opposed to defining morality by the official religious framework. Such intellectual moralization represents indeed a very powerful, auspicious, and significant turning point and a remarkable achievement for Iranian philosophical and theological history. But at the same time one may ask whether this leap of virtue, or more accurately speaking, leap of moral paradigm, could develop into a civic friendship that will bring all Iranians to their mystical home after decades of struggling with various ideological, real, and imaginary "enemies"? It will be necessary to examine how Iranian religious scholars and their critics respond to this question in part 2 of this volume.

PART II

The Jihad Jurisprudence: Its Developments and Critics in Iran

Part 2 of this book examines how war and peace, as concepts, institutions, and histories have been subject to re-examination, redefinition, reframing, and reform by modern Iranian-Shi'i jurists. This new generation of jurists is distinct from its predecessors in assuming direct political responsibility for administering the affairs of state in war and peace. Some of these jurists are benefiting from all the luxuries of power, wealth, and status, but almost all of them are deprived of the scholarly comforts of previous generations who could copy and paste old dictums and traditional opinions that had little or no implications for the practice of the state. The fortunate result of this historically remarkable situation, as relates to the subject of this volume, has been the emergence of a thriving and critical new scholarship on the laws and ethics of war and peace that can perhaps be called the first genuine body of Shi'i scholarship in the field. Part 2 of this volume serves as an introduction to this emerging scholarship.

5 War and Peace in Shi'i Primary Narratives and Sources

صلاح ذات البين افضل من عامة الصلاة و الصيام

(I heard from your grandfather, the Prophet, that conflict-resolution [*salāh dhāt al-bayn*] is more important than the recommended daily prayers [*salāt*] and fasting [*siyām*].)

– 'Alī b. Abī Tālib, in his last will to his children[1]

Nothing is more inviting of divine retribution, greater in (evil) consequence, and more effective in decline of prosperity and cutting short of life than the shedding of blood without justification.

– 'Alī b. Abī Tālib, in his letter to his governor of Egypt, Mālik al-Ashtar[2]

This chapter provides an overview of some traditional Shi'i historical narratives and hadith collections that have informed and influenced Iranian scholarship and public opinion on the ethics of war and the ethics in war. These sources have helped Shi'i-Iranian jurists develop a position on jihad and further understanding of jihad's theological status, conditions, limitations, forms, goals, and ethics concerning war.

Background

Before considering the specific sources of Shi'i ethics of war and peace, a short overview of the theory and the practice of jihad in Islamic history is necessary. As an aid, a summary translation of two encyclopedic articles, one on jihad and the other on ethics in war, are provided below as appendixes 1 and 2.

Modern scholars of pre-Islamic Arabia barely question the notion that the tribal campaigns and raids in the arid Arabian lands were, in fact, standard means of economic survival and conventional modes of economy for the Arabian tribal system. Most Muslim scholars of the early Prophetic wars justify these wars as "wars of liberation" necessary for enduring peace, or what is known in modern parlance as "a war to end all wars." Some contemporary scholars of Islam, based on early sources such as the biography of the Prophet by Ibn Ishāq (*Sīrat rasūl Allāh*), maintain that the Prophetic wars were not aiming to expand the Islamic state beyond the Arabian Peninsula.[3] Following the Prophet, however, a united Arabia, now possessing a fresh ideological energy, was geared towards territorial expansionism. The power gap created by many decades of wars of attrition between the Persian and the Byzantine Empires also helped this program and motivated the Prophet's successors to expand the Islamic state far beyond the borders of Arabia. By bringing significant wealth to the young Islamic state, these rapid conquests and stunning number of victories convinced many earlier generations of Muslims that their expansionist wars were definitely sanctioned and approved by the Almighty God.[4] Significantly, this perception was shared among the conquerors and the conquered alike.[5]

The win-win philosophy of ideological wars (material rewards if one lives, and honour and paradise if one dies) created some difficult moral questions. For instance, the sense of divine mission, while resulting in extreme courage and fearlessness on the battlefield, did not take into consideration the toll of lives lost on either side. How could a warrior, presuming himself to be serving in God's army, care much about the life or well-being of a perceived enemy of God? How could an ideology, with a strong eschatological orientation like Islam, encourage a consideration of preserving life on battlefields? In light of these questions, Muslim jurists were driven to establish strict laws of war. Many early war chronicles (known in Arabic as *futūh* literature) refer to the war standards and norms established by the Prophet Muhammad early on, when he was still involved in intra-Arab and tribal campaigns.[6]

The first caliph, Abū Bakr (d. 634), issued an important decree regulating the moral conduct of Muslim campaigns in Byzantine and across Persian lands.[7] Military success under the second caliph, 'Umar b. al-Khattāb (d. 644), helped influence the views of later jurists. By the time 'Umar was assassinated, the Islamic Empire had expanded to include Persian and Roman territories. These successes excited some subsequent Sunni and Shi'i jurists in the following centuries to such an extent that they believed that a military conquest should be obligatory for all Muslim caliphs each year.[8] The Khārijīs (an Islamic sect that rebelled against the fourth caliph, who are widely known as the forefathers of modern Muslim fundamentalists) went even further, declaring jihad to be one of the main pillars of Islam.[9]

The popularity of jihad and the abuse of this institution by Muslim territorial expansionists caused an epistemological confusion regarding the real meaning of Arabic terms such as jihad (struggle for self-control), *qitāl* (reciprocal armed engagement), *harb* (actual battle), *ghazwa* (tribal military campaigns), and *murābita* (frontier battles) – all of which denote various modes of struggle, war, defence, and battle. Muslim jurists were conscious enough to use the word *harb* (war) for battles and military campaigns that had nothing to do with religious duties. The term jihad, nevertheless, soon gained a mercurial nature that has persisted till today. Contemporary Muslim militants have shown little hesitation in declaring jihad against their Muslim opponents. This has been the case not only in Egypt, where the term has been used to promote regime change, but also among militant groups under Saddam, in post-Saddam Iraq, and now in the territories under Daesh (ISIS), which has systematically terrorized Muslims and non-Muslims alike.[10]

One of the most important points argued by the article in appendix 1 is that, in essence, jihad had originally been used as an institution for defence and only later transformed into an institution devised for ideological and territorial expansionism. Epistemologically, jihad was first defined within the esoteric realms of human life, rather than within the exoteric; it was, in fact, a new spiritual approach to moral self-discipline, rather than a means for doctrinal impositions. Significantly, the article identifies the two most influential elements in forcing the drastic metamorphosis of the term "jihad": the war-prone social structure of Arab tribes and the heavy dependence of the early Islamic empires on volunteer fighters. The disconnection of jihad from its moral context helped its legalization and instrumentalization in terms of furthering territory-expansionist goals.

As mentioned in appendix 1, the interplay between "jihad" (the struggle with one's own carnal soul), '*qitāl* or *ghazwa* (war that can be offensive or defensive), '*fath* (expansionist war), and '*difā*' (strictly defensive war) was catalysed by more than political turns of fortunes and ambitions of the early empire builders: it was also catalysed by Muslim jurists and Qur'ānic exegetes who were caught intellectually between the moral ideals of Islam, the political realities of their time and space, and the fashions of war in their era. This fact, however, should not result in an entirely negative image for Islamic jurists, as they did manage to contain many absolutist tendencies of their contemporary political systems. The fact that almost all Muslim jurists defined jihad on the basis of collective obligation (*fard kifāya*), rather than on the grounds of individual duty (*fard 'ayn*), greatly contributed to containing conflict. By attaching considerable legal weight to the question of right authority in war, the majority of Shi'i jurists also tried to curb pervasive urges for offensive wars.

Moreover, by expanding the institution of defence from the realm of the secular to the sacred, Muslim jurists created political instruments, such as *jihadīyya*s, that could, in effect, compare with the relatively modern concept of military deterrence. Both encyclopedia articles (appendixes 1 and 2) show that, despite the many ups and downs of the theory and practice of war in Muslim history, war has rarely appeared as an opportunity to offer a sacrifice to God. To the contrary, war has appeared mostly as a necessity, even when not defensive. In short, the Islamic juristic traditions never viewed war as a goal in and of itself, nor did it view war as a testing ground where one could prove his piety. The above point has a special significance in the face of the current trend of suicide bombing, which has no roots in Islamic law.

With this brief background in mind, we now turn our focus to exploring master narratives that lay at the foundation of the Shi'i ethics of war and peace, within the context of a number of the intra-Muslim civil wars that have been central in defining the Shi'i political identity.

The Four Wars Determining Shi'i Ethics of War

Upon assuming political leadership of the Muslim community between 656 and 661, the fourth caliph and first Shi'i imam, 'Ali b. Abī Tālib (d. 661), was confronted with wars wherein Muslims were fighting against Muslims for the first time. A vast amount of literature has been written about the reasons, consequences, and historic significance of these three first Islamic civil wars. These three wars encompass the Jamal, or Camel (656), during which 'Alī confronted the Prophet's last wife 'Āyisha and her chief allies Talha and Zubayr; the battle at Siffīn (657) against the Muslim governor of Syria, Mu'āwiya b. Abī Sufiyān; and the battle at Nahrawān (658) against radical insurgents identified later on as Khārijīs. These battles, especially that at Siffīn, are responsible for the most serious theological and political schisms in the history of Islam.[11] However, they were also important in setting the moral and legal framework for codes of conduct in intra-Muslim battles (known as *bughāt* wars).[12] The domestic insurgency that 'Alī encountered during his caliphate lacked a precedent; as a result, he had to set new legal codes to regulate intra-Muslim wars.

As caliph, 'Alī was fully engaged in the above wars, participating in the battles and supervising war tactics, strategies, and rules of engagement in his capacity as the Muslim community's chief commander and also chief scholar. This combination of political status and religious authority established 'Alī's actions as the standards for intra-Muslim wars. The standards applied generally to the entire Muslim community but more specifically to his Shi'i followers, who believed 'Alī to be their first imam and, among the first four caliphs, the only legitimate successor of the Prophet. In his capacity as the Prophet's successor, 'Alī therefore became the most important standard bearer of ethics and laws of war in Shi'i history and school of law; thus it will be instructive to examine a few of 'Alī's most significant statements on the ethics of war, which inform both Shi'i scholars and the public.[13]

An Ethics for the Enemy

As the first Shi'i imam, 'Alī was respected by the majority Sunnis as one of the four rightly guided caliphs and, as mentioned above,[14] also as the supreme role model and chief initiator for almost all institutions of chivalry, both in the Sunni and the Shi'i traditions (the *futūwwa*, the *'ayyārī*, and the *javānmardī* institutions). The following war-related invocation reflects 'Alī's understanding that perhaps the most difficult part of war is refraining from excesses, extremes, and most importantly, from infringing on the rights of the enemy. "Oh God, if you make us win, protect us from transgressing our enemy; if you let our enemy win, then honour us with martyrdom and protect our friends."[15] The following passage reflects some of 'Alī's moral advice and codes of conduct for intra-Muslim conflicts, as frequently cited in various civil war chronicles:

> Do not initiate the battle before the belligerents do, for this is yet another proof of your right motive. In case you win the battle, do not trace a deserter, do not kill the wounded,[16] do not mutilate, nor disclose private parts of the deceased. If you enter the enemy's camp, do not tear off shield curtains, do not enter any house except with my direct order; no plunder; no harm to women even if they curse and insult you, as they are not in control of their emotion. Beware that we refrained in the Prophet's time to bother polytheists women, and in *jāhilī* time if a man harmed a woman, he would have been the subject of blame and humiliation for a long time.[17]
>
> Neither shout loud in the battlefield, nor publicly curse our opponents; show patience, forbearance, and kindness to your own forces; do not leave your brother alone with the enemy; do not execute any of the prisoners of war;[18] hatred for them (enemy) should not lead you to fight before inviting them to guidance and exhausting your pleas before them.[19]

'Alī's view against the killing of the innocent noncombatants (*safk al-dimā'*), as also reflected in his letter to Mālik al-Ashtar ('Alī's governor in Egypt), stresses the gravity of murder without justification. The following passage is frequently quoted in many sources of the Shi'i literature, for it signifies the spirit of *jus ad bellum*, or just cause for war and the primacy of peace.[20] 'Alī writes:

> Mind that you do not throw away the offer of peace, which your enemy may himself make. Accept it, for that will please God. Peace is a source of comfort to the army; it reduces your worries and promotes order in the state.
>
> But Beware! Be on your guard when the peace is signed for; certain types of enemies propose terms of peace just to lull you into a sense of security only to attack you again when you are off your guard. So you should exercise the utmost vigilance on your part and place no undue faith in their protestations.
>
> But, if under the peace treaty you have accepted any obligations, discharge those obligations scrupulously. It is a trust and must be faithfully upheld, and whenever you have promised anything, keep it with all the strength that you command, for whatever differences of opinion might exist on other matters, there is nothing so noble as the fulfilment of a promise.
>
> This is recognized even among non-Muslims, for they know the dire consequences, which follow from the breaking of covenants. So never make excuses in discharging your responsibilities, and never break a promise, nor cheat your enemy. For breach of promise is an act against God, and none except the positively wicked acts against God.
>
> Indeed Divine promises are a blessing spread over all mankind. The promise of God is a refuge sought after, even by the most powerful on earth, for there is no risk of being cheated. So, do not make any promise from which you may afterwards offer excuses to retract, nor go back upon what you have confirmed to abide by, nor break it, however galling it may at first prove to be. For it is far better to wait in patience for wholesome results to follow, than to break it out of any apprehensions.
>
> Beware! Abstain from shedding blood without a valid cause. There is nothing more harmful than this, which brings about one's ruin. The blood that is wilfully shed shortens the life of a state. On the Day of Judgement it is this crime for which one will have to answer first. So, beware! Do not wish to build the strength of your state on blood for, it is this blood, which ultimately weakens the state and passes it into other hands. Before my God and me no excuse for wilful killing can be entertained.
>
> Murder is a crime, which is punishable by death. If on any account the corporal punishment dealt by the state for any lesser crime results in the death of the guilty, let not the prestige of the state stand in any way of the deceased relations claiming compensation.[21]

The above advice may be rightly considered as a Shiʿi doctrinal manifest that pronounces the primacy of peace. The phrase "The promise of God is a refuge sought after, even by the most powerful on earth" should sound familiar to scholars who are familiar with Hanah Arendt's proverbial proposition that forgiveness and promise are the only remedies that can reduce humans' fundamental anxieties and sufferings, caused by the irreversibility of the past and the unpredictability of the future.[22] Promise is indeed the foundation of peace, and precisely because its authority, as pronounced in the above advice, is not confined by religious parameters, it advocates global peace.

Persian Shi'i literature addressing the codes of chivalry in war frequently references the legendary anecdotes wherein 'Alī, during the early Prophetic military campaigns, meticulously stressed the just cause for war. The story of 'Alī's battle with 'Amr b. 'Abdawūd, a polytheist who participated in one of the wars against the early Muslim community, gained proverbial fame and attention in Persian literature because of Rumi's narration of it in his *Mathnavī*. According to the narration, and as reflected in *sīra* literature, 'Alī was about to finish off 'Amr in a person-to-person battle when 'Amr spat on 'Alī out of contempt. This resulted in 'Alī releasing him at once, since the spitting provoked anger in him, effectively corrupting the just cause of his combat. Because so many Iranians memorize a good part of this poem as culturally significant, the full text is provided below in Persian, followed by its translation in English:

از علی آموز اخلاص عمل   شیر حق را دان مطهر از دغل
در غزا بر پهلوانی دست یافت   زود شمشیری بر آورد و شتافت
او خدو انداخت در روی علی   افتخار هر نبی و هر ولی
آن خدو زد بر رخی که روی ماه   سجده آرد پیش او در سجده‌گاه
در زمان انداخت شمشیر آن علی   کرد او اندر غزااش کاهلی
گشت حیران آن مبارز زین عمل   وز نمودن عفو و رحمت بی‌محل
گفت بر من تیغ تیز افراشتی   از چه افکندی مرا بگذاشتی
آن چه دیدی بهتر از پیکار من   تا شدی تو سست در اشکار من
آن چه دیدی که چنین خشمت نشست تا چنان برقی نمود و باز جست
آن چه دیدی که مرا زان عکس دید   در دل و جان شعله‌ای آمد پدید
آن چه دیدی برتر از کون و مکان   که به از جان بود و بخشیدیم جان
در محل قهر این رحمت ز چیست   اژدها را دست دادن راه کیست
گفت من تیغ از پی حق می‌زنم   بندهٔ حقم نه مامور تنم
چون خدو انداختی در روی من   نفس جنبید و تبه شد خوی من
نیم بهر حق شد و نیمی هوا   شرکت اندر کار حق نبود روا
او به تیغ حلم چندین حلق را   وا خرید از تیغ و چندین خلق را
تیغ حلم از تیغ آهن تیزتر   بل ز صد لشکر ظفر انگیزتر[23]

(Learn how to act sincerely from Ali,
God's lion, free from all impurity:
During a battle, he subdued a foe
Then drew his sword to deal the final blow.
That man spat in Ali's pure face, the pride

Of every saint and prophet far and wide:
Ali put down his sabre straight away
And, thought he was on top, he stopped the fray.
The fighter was astonished by this act,
That he showed mercy though he'd been attacked:
"You pointed your sharp blade at me before,
But then you simply dropped it on the floor –
Greater than fighting me what did you see
That you eased up in your attack on me?
What did you see beyond both being and place
That you spared me though I spat in your face?
Mercy in wrath's place! I don't understand
Why you would choose to shake a dragon's hand!"
He said, "I use my sword the way God's planned,
Not for my body but by God's command;
When you spat in my face, my self was moved:
I lost my temper though that's disapproved,
Thus both God and my passions had their shares
But sharing's not allowed in God's affairs.
His clemency's sword had redeemed this way
So many souls in bodies made of clay;
Sharper than iron's sword is mercy's blade,
Much more successful than an army's raid.")[24]

Rumi's rather extensive commentary on the narrative clearly addresses the question of just cause for war in 'Alī's view, but goes even further to connect his ethics of war to those established by the Prophet. In the following lines, Rumi stresses that the cause of the Prophetic wars was durable peace:

جنگ پیغامبر مدار صلح شد   صلح این آخر زمان زان جنگ بد
صد هزاران سر برید آن دلستان   تا امان یابد سر اهل جهان
باغبان زان می بردشاخ مضر   تا بیابد نخل قامتها و بر
میکند از باغ دانا آن حشیش   تا نماید باغ و میوه خرمیش[25]

(The Prophet's wars brought peace which all had sought,
Our peace these days stems from the wars he fought;
Though he slew thousands who showed enmity
This was so men could gain security:
The gardener trims the branches that cause harm
To cultivate a straight and tall date-palm,

And any weeds he finds he will uproot
So that the garden thrives and bears much fruit.)[26]

‘Alī's three wars against groups of Muslim insurgents (*bughāt*) offered the occasions to establish codes of ethics for intra-Muslim wars. These codes were, for obvious reasons, stricter in observing the rights of the enemy and also did not provide the victors with economic benefits, since collecting treasure and booty from defeated Muslims was strictly forbidden by ‘Alī. To that point, the norm was for belligerent Muslims on opposite sides to treat each other better than when facing nonbelievers.

The battle of Karbalā, wherein ‘Alī's second son, Husayn b. ‘Alī (d. 680), was invited by Kūfan dissidents to challenge the corrupt rule of Yazīd (the second Umayyad caliph, d. 683), resulted in al-Husayn's martyrdom. This incident raised entirely new questions.[27] This fourth intra-Muslim war was an important episode in two respects. First, martyrdom became a measure of political protest. Second, because of the savage way in which al-Husayn's camp was dealt, and because Yazīd's thirty thousand troops against an army of less than a hundred breached all of the moral codes of war, it revealed the moral decadence of the Umayyad system, and the concept and the definition of the "enemy" changed in the Shi‘i mind. In other words, in declining to accept Yazīd's rule, even at the cost of his own life, al-Husayn effectively educated future generations of Muslims to hold a critical view of, and maintain a conscious stance on, their contemporary politics. Some Shi‘i scholars, such as Askarī, argue that before the Karbalā tragedy, the caliph's methods of ruling and political conduct were highly sensitive to public opinion; afterwards, however, politics and faith were separated.[28] Al-Husayn's political protest was essentially a corrective stance against this separation.[29]

The war between al-Husayn and Yazīd's forces was, by any standard, uneven and unethical, especially when considering the extent to which al-Husayn's troops (numbered less than one hundred) were far outnumbered by those of Yazīd's (about thirty thousand, according to most reports). But why did those thirty thousand troops fighting against the Prophet's grandson, knowing the difference in strength and numbers, not spare even the suckling infant of al-Husayn? Why did these thousands of troops insist on setting the women's tents in al-Husayn's camp ablaze? For al-Husayn, the ethics of war were not solely based on religion; he expected that a basic and universal sense of liberality and chivalry, intrinsic in all men, would tame beastly urges. This notion is reflected in some of his last words aimed at his murderers. Abū Mikhnaf, the author of one of the oldest historical accounts of the Karbalā tragedy, depicts the scene as follows: "Shimr, together with about ten foot soldiers from Kufah, moved towards the place where Husayn had placed his belongings and his family. Husayn tried to go near that place, but they prevented him from doing so. Husayn said to them, 'Woe to you. If you have no loyalty to religion and are not concerned about the Day of Judgment, then at least conduct yourselves with civility and fairness in matters of this world. Stop the wicked and ignorant men from hindering my access to my family and belongings.'"[30] This statement contains significant elements related to ethics in war and also sits well with Shi'i theology in that, like the Mu'tazilī school, the Shi'i school believes in the extrareligious and universal sense of justice. This sense of objective justice, as the very first principle of Shi'i theology, as we shall see in the following chapters, has motivated Shi'i jurists to embrace and contribute to modern codes of conduct in war.

For Shi'a suppressed as a denominational Muslim minority, various narratives of the Karbalā tragedy soon became rich sources that demystified and shed light on the plight of the sect and on all hardships it continuously faced in the annals of Islamic history. The inhumanity of the final battle, the unprecedented callousness of Yazīd's troops in breaking every code of ethics at war, in war, and after war – when they forced al-Husayn's sister Zainab and family to march to the caliph's court, accompanying the severed head of the Prophet's favourite grandson in humility – these images all in all brought Shi'a to their Walzerian understanding of Islamic history. Walzer states, "For war is the hardest place: if comprehensive and consistent moral judgments are possible there, they are possible everywhere"; he adds, "War strips away our civilized adornments and reveals our nakedness."[31] The Karbalā tragedy therefore became a judgmental paradigm by which the Shi'a could see the naked moral structure of politics without piety. Nominal Muslims could be the fiercest enemies of Muslims. It is therefore no exaggeration to say that the absolute lack of ethics of war in Karbalā was probably the most significant and paradigmatic factor in the making of the Shi'a world view, theology, and political philosophy. Symbolically, al-Husayn's martyrdom became the final and definitive proof for the Shi'a that a truly legitimate government must be directed by an infallible agent, a charismatic figure whose divinely supported capacity and piety can protect him from all moral pitfalls and whimsical urges of absolute political power.

The above can explain why one proverbial phrase, used frequently during Iran's 1979 Revolution, during the Iran-Iraq War, and even as the country struggled with economic sanctions, says, "All days are 'Āshūrā, and all lands are Karbalā."[32] This slogan, which appeared in Shi'i literature long after the advent of al-Husayn's martyrdom, provided an alternative to a classical Muslim view of history that, since the eighth century, had become standard for the majority Sunni Muslims. This latter view essentially divided the whole world into the abode of peace and the abode of war (*dār al-Islam* and *dār al-harb*). Alternatively, the Shi'i perspective saw a divisive fault line running through the world, separating not only Muslim believers and nonbelievers but also, and more significantly, the abode of real Muslim believers (*dār al-īmān*) from nominal ones (*dār al-Islam*). Over the centuries, as a robust amount of epic Shi'i literature and master narratives were in the making, figures like Mu'āwīya and Yazīd became antiheroes, more so than any non-Muslim or disbeliever. Like a mirror image of the proverbial Prophetic hadith that proclaims the carnal soul as far more robust an enemy than external enemies,[33] the inner enemy presented a fiercer threat to the Shi'i community than the outside disbelievers did. Consequently, the divisiveness and violent political polarization occurring in various Muslim societies since the Karbalā incident, which have pitted Muslims against Muslims across sectarian lines, find full symbolization in the modern-day suicide bombings taking place almost daily in Iraq and elsewhere in the greater Middle East.[34]

The savagery of the forces of Yazīd aside, the narrative of the Karbalā tragedy included episodes that symbolized the loneliness of Shi'i communities in the annals of Muslim history. The following scene reported by the early Muslim historian al-Tabarī about a sensational conversation in al-Husayn's camp the night before the battle is telling:

> Husein spent the whole night readying his weapons and chanting dirges. When his young son 'Ali, who was sick and lying in his tent, heard him chanting that way, he began to weep. Then all the women began to scream and sob. Husein said to them: "Do not weep, for it would rejoice the enemy." Then, raising his eyes toward heaven, he cried out: "Lord, you know they swore an oath to me and have broken it. Grant me vengeance over them!" Then he called together his supporters who had followed him and spoke to them in these terms: "Whatever happens to you, it is you yourselves who have prepared it. It is not I pushed you into war. We are few, and the enemy is strong. As for me, I have made the sacrifice of my life. Not only did I not lead you into war, but I free you from your oath. Let all those who would like to leave go!" They replied: "O son of the apostle of God, what excuse could we give your grandfather on the day of resurrection for having abandoned his son in such a place, into the hands of his enemies? No we have sworn our lives to you!" So Husein prepared himself for battle.[35]

For a Shi'a reader of the above episode, the tragic encounter is multilayered. The battle is unjust in terms of its cause, the lack of proportion in numbers, and the fact that it occurs between Muslims. But the reader also finds al-Husayn freeing his few friends from any obligation to keep their earlier commitments to support him. Here, al-Husayn's reluctance to persuade his companions to undertake a fateful destiny and his willingness to encounter the enemy alone demonstrate his ultimate and chivalric sensitivity to the codes and ethics of war; but his words and actions also symbolize Shi'i loneliness as a legitimate cause for its political quietism.

The Karbalā incident helped define Shi'i political philosophy for the generations that followed. The tragedy taught the Shi'as that there was no legitimate grounds for giving political or defensive support to the corrupt, oppressive, and unjust caliphs, such as Mu'āwīya and his son Yazīd, whenever the latter faced non-Muslim threats. About six centuries later, when the Mongol warlord Hulagu Khan moved to attack Baghdad and remove the Abbasid caliph, a Shi'i scholar named Ibn Tawūs (d. 1265) declared in a *fatwa* that a disbeliever who is a just ruler is preferable to an unjust and oppressive Muslim ruler.[36] Therefore, it is safe to say that the Karbalā tragedy substantially contributed to Shi'i political quietism. In the following section, this chapter will explore how Shi'i sources reflect upon this political pacifism, which has implications for Shi'i ethics of war. However, it is important to examine first the early development of the ethics of war in mainstream Muslim juridical thought as a point of reference in helping to explain the Shi'i differences and contributions in the field.

The Islamic Canon Laws of War and al-Shāfi'ī's Influence

Early on in Islamic history, extensive literature in each of the four authoritative fields of jurisprudence (*fiqh*), traditions (hadith), biographies (*sīra*), and exegesis (*tafsīr*) contributed to the first major collection of Islamic canon law on war. This collection appeared in Muhammad b. al-Hassan al-Shaybānī's *Sīyar* (c. 804).[37] Significantly, this treatise appeared about four centuries before the first collection of Christian canon law, found in Gratian's *Decretum* (c. 1140).[38] Because *Sīyar's* content goes beyond mere regulations on war, Philip Jessup compares it with the work of Hugo Grotius (d. 1645), known as the father of Western international law.[39]

Readers of al-Shaybānī's *Sīyar* might mistakenly conclude that the text indicates that normal relations between the Islamic and non-Islamic worlds were that of a state of war. This misreading may be due perhaps, as John Kelsay points out, to the fact that as an Abbasid judge (*qādī*), al-Shaybānī, presupposed the connections between Islam, the Abbasid's imperial state, and its territorial pursuits.[40] However, as Khadduri stresses, "the object of war was not the annihilation of the enemy," and jurists "made no explicit statement that the jihad was a war to be waged against unbelievers solely on account of their disbelief (*kufr*)."[41] Further details of the laws of war, as provided by Shaybānī, confirm that an elaborate body of law, related both to the cause of war (*jus ad bellum*) and to the conduct of war (*jus in bello*), was devised by early jurists as a way to regulate, limit, and reduce the human casualties of war.

Al-Shaybānī saw the world from a Manichean perspective as divided into two spheres: one made up of Muslims and the other compromised of non-Muslims. But as a student of Abu Hanīfa, and just like other early Hanafī and Mālikī jurists, Shaybāni appears to have advised the caliph to prosecute war only when the inhabitants of the abode of war (*dār al-harb*) came into conflict with Islam.[42] As both Sālehī-Najafābādī (a prominent Shi'i jurist, d. 2006) and Khadduri explain, "It was al-Shāfi'ī who first formulated the doctrine that the jihad had for its intent the waging of war on unbelievers for their disbelief and not merely when they entered into conflict with Islam ... jurists who came afterward, and up to the very decline of Islamic power, merely introduced refinements and elaborations of these basic principles."[43]

Al-Shāfi'ī promoted the more militant Syrian school of thought, thus making it the normative theory. Despite his radical political tendencies, he also suggested a new realm of thought in international relations called the "abode of covenant" (*dār al-'ahd*), which based Islamic international relations on contractual law. In this way, he softened the belligerent content of the "others," thereby reducing, to a certain extent, the inevitability of clashes between Muslims and non-Muslims. Nevertheless, by viewing jihad as an inalienable principle of Islam and granting it a systematic practice and implementation at least as important as the other major pillars of faith, al-Shāfi'ī and his followers made the institution of jihad more available to territorially expansionist rulers who needed to resort to periodic wars for political and economic reasons. The position in support of primary (offensive) war and the interpretation of jihad as an eternal, permanent, and collective duty to fight against disbelief was so radical that even staunch traditionalists, such as Ibn Taymīya (d. 1327) who opposed rational philosophy, denied this interpretation and labelled jihad as religion's greatest compulsion.[44] Ibn Taymīya stressed, "Muslims have allowed war because the enemy has authorized war."[45] This defies the dichotomy of *dār al-Islam* and *dār al-harb*, which are the foundations of the Islamic view of the globe. Conversely, the political geography introduced by many other Muslim jurists includes a multiple of abodes such as peace (*al-sulh*), contract (*al-'ahd*), amnesty (*al-amān*), dissimulation (*al-taqīya*), faith (*al-īmān*), and others.

Al-Shāfi'ī played a key role in theorizing a dichotomic political philosophy. Also influential in this view were the jurists from the beginning of the second century of Islamic rule, who only minimally studied the expansionist wars of the early caliphs and the Umayyads. Later on, the Qur'ānic exegetical controversies about war became numerous, though these conflicts were not produced outside of a historical context; rather, they were byproducts mirroring the conflicts found in other arenas of Muslim life and history.

Jihad in the Mirror of the Shi'i Hadith: The Roots of Political Quietism

The fate of the four tragic wars of Jamal, Siffīn, Nahravān, and Karbalā permanently changed the political outlook of the Shi'i leadership within the caliphate. The first three civil wars exhausted 'Alī b. Abī Tālib, who was ultimately martyred in an act of terrorism by plotters who were dissatisfied with the results of these wars. The fourth war, which was more tragic than all the others, permanently and incurably wounded the Shi'i memory. Reflections on and juristic conclusions from these histories, which appeared as the content of many Shi'i hadiths, originated mostly from – or were otherwise part of a chain of hadith reports linked to – the founder of the Twelver-Shi'i school of law, namely Ja'far al-Sādiq.[46] Presently, the most authoritative and frequently used collection of hadiths used in Shi'i seminarian circles by clerical students is *Wasā'il al-shi'a ilā tahsil masā'il al-sharī'a* written by Muhammad Hassan Hurr al-'Āmilī (d. 1692).[47] This collection addresses the topic of jihad (*kitāb al-jihad*) in two sections: the first addresses jihad against the enemy, and the second details jihad against one's own soul (*al-nafs*).[48]

As indicated in this hadith literature, al-Sādiq takes a position on armed jihad that is clearly distinct from the practical function of this institution under the Umayyad (661–750) and the Abbasid (750–1258) caliphates, which used jihad as an instrument of territorial expansionism. Al-Sādiq candidly opposes jihad as it was understood and utilized both by the public and political authorities. For example, as the following passage demonstrates, al-Sādiq questioned 'Abdul Malik b. 'Amr (one of his Shi'i followers) about the legitimacy of the very fashionable expansionism in the name of jihad: "O 'Abdu'l Malik," al-Sādiq said, "I do not see you to have left for war in the regions your fellow countrymen have left for." 'Abdu'l Malik responds, "Where do you mean?" He replies, "Jiddah, 'Ubbādān (western Iran), al-Masisa, and Qazwīn (northern Iran)." "I responded," 'Abdu'l Malik relates, "I have waited for your command and your leadership." Al-Sādiq answers, "Yes, indeed, I swear to God we would have been ahead of them [the warriors who already left for expansionist jihad] if I saw any good in that venture [expansionist wars]."[49]

Similarly, al-Sādiq's father, Muhammad b. 'Alī al-Bāqir (the fifth Shi'i imam), states, "I do not know in this era any jihad other than the greater and the lesser pilgrimage [*hajj* and *'umra*] and protecting one's neighbour [*al-jiwār*]."[50] Al-Sādiq quotes 'Alī b. Abī Tālib, who stated: "A Muslim will not go for jihad accompanying those who do not believe in the rules and [who] fail to implement God's command regarding the booty ... Such a person, once he dies in this place [battlefield], dies as a supporter of our enemy, a culprit in usurping our rights, in shedding our blood, and therefore his death is a *jāhilī* [pre-Islamic][51] death [i.e. of no eschatological value or reward]."[52]

The above passage establishes that the moral aspect of conduct in jihad (*jus in bello*) is inseparable from its just cause (*jus ad bellum*). In other words, by virtue of the above, illegitimate conduct in a war negatively affects the legitimacy of its cause. However, there is more to this statement. The hadith addresses the question of the right authority for war and, more importantly, the very goal of it. It suggests that expansionist wars do not bring religious credit to the fighter and in fact may inflict damage to the real cause of Islam. It rejects the conventional assumption that one of any two warring parties must be on the right side of the conflict, for both can be on different wrong sides. By implication, the mere fact that a war is taking place between a Muslim and non-Muslim force does not automatically obligate Muslims to participate in the war. Another hadith attributed to al-Sādiq states, "If a person strikes people with his sword and calls them to himself, and if there is someone among Muslims who is more knowledgeable [about the will of God] than he, then he is certainly misguided and false."[53] The two hadiths above clearly assert that participation in war must be a calculated, well-informed decision. They serve as a clear warning against making jihad a way of life, a risk-free, win-win occasion in which one may find a short cut to paradise or, alternately, gain a hefty fortune by seizing war spoils. In referring to a "*jāhilī* death in war," the statements are reminders that jihad, in being abused by empire builders, has become an official excuse to revive the pre-Islamic Arab lifestyle that looked at war as a normal course of economic life.

The fact that Shi‘i readers of early Islamic history could not find any trace of ‘Alī's participation in the caliphate's expansionist wars is of tremendous significance and raises a very curious question. It is true that during his relatively short-lived caliphate, ‘Alī b. Abī Tālib was entangled in the web of extensive civil wars. In effect, civil wars did not render his regime any capacity for territorial expansion. True as this may be, ‘Alī's meticulous sensitivity to matters of justice does not provide any basis for assuming that had he had the chance, he would have instigated an unprovoked war. Post-Prophet Muslim history tells us that ‘Alī, while giving council to other predecessor caliphs, never personally participated in any expansionist war. Moreover, ‘Alī's criticism of the abuse of jihad is reflected in other Shi‘i hadith narratives, specifically those related to his sermons on jihad.

‘Alī b. al-Husayn (the fourth Shi‘i imam) responds to a critic who wonders why he (Ibn al-Husayn) undertook pilgrimage instead of jihad, citing the Qur'ānic verse 9:111.[54] Ibn al-Husayn asks his critic to read a specific verse

(9:112) which established the necessary qualities for jihad warriors.[55] He then reminds the person that without those qualities jihad loses its legitimacy.[56] Ibn al-Husayn clearly conveys two points: most or all of the wars in his time were pursued in the name of jihad, though for nonreligious mundane purposes; additionally, he emphasizes the moral preconditions for actors in armed jihad. In other words, he sets two important criteria for legitimate jihad, the right intention and the right moral character of the jihad actor (*mujāhid*). It seems to me that the latter condition adds a significant Shi'i element to the six standard provisions of *jus ad bellum*: namely, just cause, right authority (who decides for war), proportionality (between the inflicted damage and war's ultimate goals), last resort (war is used only after all other means of conflict resolution have failed), the reasonable hope of success, and right intention.

Several hadiths reflect on questions about the appropriateness of waging offensive war in the absence of the twelfth imam (al-Qā'im or al-Mahdī, who went to occultation in 941). 'Alī b. al-Husayn responds, "I swear to God that none of us will come out before the coming [*khurūj*] of al-Qā'im, or else it will be like a newly born chicken just out of its shell that will be taken by kids as a plaything before it can develop its wings."[57] One hadith assumes an even stronger tone, quoting al-Sādiq saying, "One who bears the flags [of jihad] before the coming out of al-Qā'im is a false deity [*tāghūt*] who serves other than God the most Powerful, the Magnificent."[58] These statements clearly advocate more than political quietism: they delegitimize fashionable expansionist jihad and by implication make offensive jihadists responsible for their acts of commiting homicide and unnecessary bloodshed.

The majority of jihad-related hadiths in Shi'i sources emphasize two essential points: first, in the absence of a right authority, armed jihad loses justification; second, jihadist campaigns under the Umayyads and the Abbasids had worldly or unjust motives and were therefore illegitimate. Consequently, Shi'i authorities were at pains to disassociate the term jihad from that of general warfare.

The question may arise about whether the Shi'i eschatological theory of legitimate offensive war under al-Qā'im could cause the Shi'i just-war theory to suffer an inconsistency. One may also ask if the theoretical postponement of the Shi'i final offensive war under the messianic imam could have political implications in current history. For example, could Ayatollah Khomeini, who established his political legitimacy by ruling on behalf of the occult imam, have been motivated by this theory to assume the responsibility of continuing the war with Iraq, despite the fact that Iraq was pushed back to international borders in 1982 after two years of war?

As will be discussed below in chapter 7, Ayatollah Khomeini was primarily against bringing an Iranian offensive war to Iraqi territory. His insistence on continuing the war with Iraq was rather predicated on punitive justice, meaning that the aggressor regime of Saddam Hussein had to be personally punished. In order to evaluate better the possible political implications of the Shi'i theory of the final just war, it is necessary to examine the thriving modern literature on the subject, which will be addressed in the discussion of martyrdom in Shi'ism below in chapter 8. Here, however, it will suffice to note that the master hadith for the coming of al-Mahdī (al-Qā'im) refers to the following concept narrated from the Prophet Muhammad: "If there were to remain in the life of the world but one day, God would prolong that day until He sends in it a man from my community and my household. His name will be the same as my name. He will fill the earth with equity and justice as it was filled with oppression and tyranny."[59] This hadith clearly promises an indefinite yet sure final justice on earth. To facilitate this very goal, Shi'i just-war theory lends the legitimacy and the authority of the final war to al-Mahdī so that he could end all wars and all historic injustices on earth. In effect, however, the Shi'i final just war and war for justice is introduced as the responsibility of an imam, which is, in the words of Mahmoud Ayoub, "pushed out of world history altogether and into eschatological time."[60] According to a number of scholars, the deferment of justice is an effective way to help a suppressed minority society to survive and tolerate current hardship.[61]

In response to the fashionable and profitable expansionist wars by early Muslim caliphs, the Shi'i categorical denial of the legitimacy of these wars is echoed in a much larger body of hadith literature collected by the "Book of Jihad" in *Wasā'il*. Through a specific epistemological approach to the question of jihad, Shi'i hadith literature focuses on jihad against one's carnal soul or, in other words, a spiritual struggle to bring one's own vices under control. The redirection of the meaning of jihad from the exoteric to the esoteric realm is well manifested in the fact that the section of *Wasā'il* on spiritual jihad is twice as large as the section on armed jihad. In it, the Shi'i authorities take a tough position against a human's own carnal soul, which could potentially be a much more dangerous enemy than disbeliever forces who threaten Muslims from outside their territories.[62] This position could have impacted Muslim domestic politics in that, as a minority community during the Umayyad and the Abbasid eras, the Shi'a faced systematic suppression and persecution by fellow Muslims. Each of the first eleven imams were imprisoned, poisoned, or martyred by claimant Muslims – not by foreign disbelievers. The nominal ideological self, as an extension of the carnal self, was in reality a more significant enemy than the infidel "other."

Jus ad bellum and *Jus in bello* in Hadith

The chapter on exoteric jihad in *Wasā'il* is short, but nevertheless it elaborately regulates warfare style. Chapters 16–24 address and emphasize many moral grounds of *jus in bello*, as listed below:

- Sanctity of covenants, contracts, and treaties (*'ahd, 'aqd, mīthāq*)
- Respect for amnesty (*amān*) given to the enemy in combat
- Equal validity of amnesty given by all ranks of Muslim combatants
- Prohibition of the use of poison (*samm*)
- Prohibition of the initiation of actual battle in any war
- Prohibition of attacking the elderly, women, children, and the disabled of all faiths
- Ban on night attacks and, above all, the absolute ban on resorting to perfidy or treachery (*al-ghadr*). The hadith literature clearly distinguishes between treachery and perfidy (*al-ghadr*), which is absolutely forbidden, as it involves a unilateral breach of a contract or treaty, and ruse (*al-khud'a*), which is tantamount to a tactical deceit as a form of war itself (*al-harbu khud'a*).[63]

Chapter 27 of *Wasā'il* explores the proportionality of forces. Army size matters, and according to several hadiths, once enemy forces are more than twice that of Muslim fighters, fleeing the battle is permitted. This chapter indirectly opposes deliberate martyrdom (as it is a form of suicide attack) and instead brings rational calculations into wartime decision making, effectively drawing a clear line between suicidal missions and obligatory defence. Within such a rational space for war, as described by this authoritative source, war must not be abused as an institution for a deliberate, dramatic show of a willingness to sacrifice one's life for God as a proof of religious piety. These positions delegitimize romantic and emotional causes for war. Elsewhere the "Book of Jihad" emphasizes that while a Muslim must not initiate a battle, he could not escape a battle unless, as the above hadith notes, the proportion of troops is more than two against one.[64]

Wasā'il chapter 67 condemns intra-Muslim conflicts. A Prophetic hadith asserts that when two Muslims clash without justification, both the murdered and the murderer end up in hell.[65] This hadith opens important doors for serious negotiations between sharī'a law and international conventions on human rights. A Muslim should not oppress another; but oppression and aggression, even from a fellow Muslim must not be tolerated either. A submissive individual, tolerant of oppression, cannot claim any spiritual credit for his submission to unjust Muslim acts; he will be considered a culprit in the act of oppression.

The hadiths collected in chapters 24–7 suggest that Shiʻa authorities had a difficult time explaining to their followers why ʻAlī b. Abī Tālib treated his domestic enemies so leniently. In response to their doubts and questions, these authorities argue that it was exactly because of this leniency that subsequent Shiʻi enemies have tolerated the Shiʻi community so far. Some raise questions as to why ʻAlī was more lenient towards enemy fighters in the battles of Jamal and Nahrawān than in the battle of Siffīn. Authorities explain this by noting that in the former cases ʻAlī was cognizant that the remaining enemy forces did not have a centre wherein they could regroup, and therefore they were no longer considered a threat. In the Siffīn conflict, however, Mu'āwīya had a solid base of power and could regroup his defeated forces.[66] As such, ʻAlī b. Abī Tālib had to adjust his war conduct according to the circumstances of the occasion – if the enemy camp regrouped, additional bloodshed and war would be inevitable.

Hadiths 5 and 7 (chapter 25) demonstrate how ʻAlī resisted pressure from his troops to seize and distribute booty after the battle of the Camel. ʻAlī ordered all war spoils to be returned to their owners. When some soldiers protested, he replied, "Who will take Umm al-Mū'minīn (the Prophet's wife ʻĀisha, a chief leader of the defeated insurgent army) as his share?"[67]

Other hadiths suggest that the Shiʻi's messianic twelfth imam, al-Qā'im, will be less lenient after he reappears on earth to bring justice and equity. While ʻAlī feared that his enemies would retaliate against his community in the future, al-Qā'im would have no such concern.[68] A substantial amount of the Shiʻi hadith literature demonstrates the mounting frustration of the Shiʻi community over the first few centuries of Islamic history. Statements about al-Qā'im's inflexible manner in dealing with his enemies were probably reassuring to the oppressed Shiʻas, who thought that a quietist position had not brought them any ease within the larger Muslim community.

Chapter 49 confirms the legitimacy of the Zoroastrian faith (*al-majūs*) as an authentic divine religion.[69] According to a number of hadiths, Zoroastrians have the same status as the "people of the book" (*ahlu'l kitāb* or *dhimmī*) and had to be protected by Muslim governments. By the same token, they had to pay the poll tax (*jizya*) if they chose not to convert to Islam.

Chapters 23, 24, and 32 discuss *jus in bello*, or the treatment of prisoners of war, specifically as it relates to the obligations of the Islamic state to feed prisoners well, even if they are to be executed the next day.[70]

A number of important hadiths address the cause of war, or *jus ad bellum*. In one hadith, ʻAlī b. Mūsā al-Ridā (the eighth Shiʻi imam, d. 818) writes the following to the Abbasid caliph al-Ma'mūn (d. 833): "Jihad under a just imam is obligatory [*wājib*]; also whoever is killed while defending his life, his property, and his own safe travel is considered a martyr [*shahīd*]. It is forbidden [*harām*] to kill any disbeliever in the abode of dissimulation [*dār al-taqīya*], except in retaliating a murder or opposing an insurgent [*bāghī*], and these latter measures may be taken only in case one's own life is not at risk ... It is also forbidden to take any property of one's opponents or others; and concealing one's belief in the abode of dissimulation is obligatory" (my translation).[71] This hadith demonstrates not only the Shi'i rulings on the codes of conduct for the minority Shi'i Muslims but also the very restrictive nature of the use of force according to Shi'i legal and moral opinions. The only justifiable reason to fight a disbeliever is due not to credal disbelief but rather to his acting against such basic human rights as the right to life, property, free passage, free choice of residence, and security.

In addition to the realms of the abode of covenant (*dār al-'ahd*), the abode of peace (*dār al-Islam*), and the abode of war (*dār al-harb*), Shi'i hadiths include a new realm called the abode of dissimulation (*dār al-taqīya*). This realm reflects the circumstances of a minority Muslim community living in a non-Muslim state or, given its precarious situation, a Shi'i minority within an Islamic state. The Shi'i hadiths create a major paradigm shift in the global Muslim outlook. Accordingly, as previously mentioned, the line between the abode of peace and the abode of war is not the same as the borders between the Muslim and the non-Muslim territories (as was the conventional perspective in the Muslim world); rather, it is a line between where Muslims of all schools could freely practise their sharī'a, even if these lands were administered by non-Muslims, and where they could not do so, even under a Muslim administration. A significant and immediate implication of this perspective is that, in theory, the Shi'i school has no urge to convert the whole world to Islam. According to this new world view, the ultimate conversion of the world is deferred till the time when the twelfth imam (al-Qā'im) will reappear. The above assertion does not theoretically oppose expansionist wars in an absolute time frame but effectively renders obsolete all justifications for expansionist wars before the time of the Shi'i eschatological realm (the end of history when al-Qā'im ends his occultation).

Shaykh Mufīd, a Shi'i theologian and one of the most prominent founders of Shi'i theology (d. 1022), made a clear distinction between the political and the religious perspectives of the global map. He emphasized the difference between the abode of Islam (*dār al-Islam*) and the abode of faith (*dār al-īmān*). In Mufīd's view, Muslim political rule does not guarantee that the true faith of Islam is being practised.[72] Part of Mufīd's political philosophy, as reflected in his book *al-Jamal*,[73] refers to various opponents of 'Alī who were, in Mufīd's view, only nominally Muslim. Thus, according to Mufīd, political rule by nominal Muslims, by implication, could not create a legitimate Islamic sovereignty.[74] In other words, a legitimate Islamic state entails a believing, practising Shi'i Muslim head of state.

The Demilitarization of Jihad

In early Islamic jurisprudence, jihad (in its various interpretations and applications) was discussed not only as an approach vis-à-vis unbelievers but also as an instrument for commanding right and forbidding wrong (*al-amr bi'l-ma'rūf wa'l-nahy 'an al-munkar*) – both at the individual and collective levels.[75] These principles are, to various degrees, moral obligations incumbent upon all individuals and upon all modes of conduct, in both private and public domains (depending on the various views of different Islamic schools). The principles were generally designed as a system of checks and balances meant to limit unjust rulers and also allowed individuals to act as a moral force to protect private society from committing immorality.

Among the various theological and legal schools of Islam, the Shi'i (*imami*) school is profoundly quietist regarding the use of force in the implementation of the principle of commanding right and forbidding wrong. As Michael Cook states, "If we concentrate on the traditions that have something substantive to say, we can readily detect a quietist strain which befits the general character of early Imāmism."[76] This Shi'i quietism limits the performance of the principle in several ways: First, it limits the obligation of jihad only to the strong and knowledgeable members of the community. Second, they must also be knowledgeable enough about the religion to discern exactly where the principle applies for the obligation to become incumbent. By establishing several conditions regarding the implementation of the principle of commanding right and forbidding wrong, Shi'i imams and scholars managed to – at least in theory – curb the use of violence as a legitimate moral and legal instrument. This was accomplished by stipulating six general preconditions for jihad: (1) the need for certainty that a supposed offence is indeed wrong; (2) evidence that the offence will continue; (3) determination of the efficacy of the measures taken against a wrong; (4) avoiding danger to life; (5) avoiding danger to property; and (6) the action taken against wrong must not itself be evil.[77]

The above points conform to the body of the Shi'i hadiths presented in this chapter. Shi'i literature's approach to the questions regarding confronting non-Muslims, as well as to the principle of commanding right and forbidding wrong within Muslim society, generally and coherently reflect the Shi'i quietist position on the use of force within real history. An important by-product of this approach is the expansion of the very meaning of jihad from mere physical engagement to other domains that encompass peaceful actions and expressions. In short, defining multiple realms of actions, including spiritual practice, under the rubric of jihad helped to demilitarize jihad, at least within the realm of Shi'i ethics and jurisprudence of war.

Conclusion

By shedding light on the impact of four early civil wars in Islamic history, this chapter explores how these events ultimately influenced Shi'i thought on the ethics of war and, in effect, how the lack of these ethics in the battle of Karbalā formed its political philosophy. A brief examination of the most authoritative collection of Shi'i hadith literature demonstrates how the leadership of this Muslim minority, including all eleven imams of Twelver Shi'ism, focused its systematic war and peace teachings on intra-Muslim relations rather than on territorial expansion. Given the fact that the Shi'i represented a suppressed minority, the ethics of war reflected in the collection of Shi'i hadiths reveal a defensive undertone. Due to the lack of power and the absence of necessary sociopolitical components, the Shi'a dream for political justice – a virtue that all social minorities desire, at least in theory – was ultimately postponed and left to an eschatological messianic institution that was to emerge at the end time.

Gradually, as the marginalized Shi'i communities began to prioritize self-preservation, the prevailing black-or-white Muslim view of dividing the whole universe into unbelievers and believers yielded in Shi'ism to grey areas of a real pluralistic world. Early Shi'i communities learned that being a Muslim and part of the mainstream Sunni community did not amount to political and moral credibility or security. Direct experience taught them that an oppressive Muslim has less legitimacy in ruling over other Muslims than does a just person who exists outside the faith. This very perspective enabled Shaykh Mufīd, one of the founding fathers of Shi'i theology, to formulate a justice-based extrareligious political philosophy in the early eleventh century, with which a good part of the contemporary Muslim diaspora identify a thousand years later. They feel freer to exercise their faith outside their homelands than they do inside.

For various sociopolitical and historical reasons, the notion of extrareligious and universal justice was the founding principle for Shi'i theology. As a result, Shi'i primary sources for the ethics of war and peace offer the remarkable potential to align with contemporary humanitarian standards of war, as compared with sources from rival Sunni schools. The more important question, however, is whether this potential was realized by Twelver-Shi'i jurists and moral philosophers, which will be examined below.

6 Traditional Shi'i Ethics of War and Peace Untested: Jihad, Ideology, Revolution, and War

The primary function of all the prophets and their scriptures was conflict resolution.

– Mohammad Hossein Tabātabā'ī[1]

A common and vast literature on details pertinent to just cause for war (*jus ad bellum*) and just conduct of war (*jus in bello*) exists between all Muslim schools. This literature, which according to war historian David Nicolle ranks the Islamic ethics of war as one of the top two most elaborate and humanistic legal systems in the classical and medieval world,[2] contains detailed moral positions on the many humanitarian factors of war. What follows is an examination of contemporary Iranian-Shi'i traditionalist jurists' position on the ethics of war before the Islamic Revolution of 1979. Such a study will clarify, first, the relationship between Shi'i primary sources and positive laws on war and peace and, second, the significance and the extent of critical thinking on jihad evident in Shi'i scholarship after the Iranian Revolution.

As discussed above, Shi'i narratives and hadith literature on jihad carried two messages with significant implications for the ethics of war: First, in the absence of right authority, war was illegitimate, save defensive wars; and second, the border between the abode of Islam (*dār al-Islam*) and the abode of war (*dār al-harb*) was not territorial but rather a legal distinction and a direct function of the freedom of religious practice or expression. This literature also contains an esoteric message: the real enemy is either inside the human soul or within one's own community, and the major jihad, as the Prophet had said, is with the carnal self, the Satan from within. In other words, Muslims' worst enemies were Muslims. Such a demilitarized notion of jihad and de-enmification of the religious other could potentially play a significant role in more effectively delegitimizing war, as well as in emphasizing the need for the right authority in war. The narratives of ʻAlī's chivalrous ways of treating his enemies, together with the narratives of the savage and most inhumane ways in which ʻAlī's son, al-Husayn, and his companions were treated, benchmarked both the best and the worst ethical standards for *jus in bello* (ethics in war) in the Shiʻi sources, as discussed above in chapter 5. Parsing out the ethics of war was difficult, however, as the Shiʻi followers of the imam did not codify these narratives and standards into a body of laws until they no longer had access to a living imam. The last imam went into occultation in 941.

From an overall perspective, Shiʻi scholars and scholars of Shiʻism, to my knowledge, do not disagree that "quietism" is perhaps the most accurate term that can generally define the Shiʻi position on jihad during the first three centuries after the demise of the Prophet Mohammad (632–941). In the next phase of Shiʻi history, a greater part of Shiʻi jurisprudence, including official rulings on jihad, was initially developed by Shaykh Mohammad b. al-Hasan Tūsī. Tūsī borrowed many provisions from Sunni jurisprudence, including the jurist Ibn Idris al-Shāfiʻī's rulings on the laws of war, whose radical views on expansionist jihad served the ambitions of empire-building caliphs.[3] Al-Shāfiʻī ruled that, just like a pillar of faith, at least one military incursion into non-Muslim territories is incumbent annually upon the head of the Muslim state, arguing that the inherently valuable practice of jihad should not be left unattended and obsolete.[4] Beginning with Tūsī, all major premodern Twelver-Shiʻi jurists followed al-Shāfiʻī's dictum,[5] among them prominent scholars and authorities such as Abu'lqasim Najmeddin Jaʻfar b. Hasan Muhaqqiq Hillī, Hasan b. Yusuf b. Mutahhar al-Hillī, ʻAlī b. Hossein Karakī, and Mohammad Hasan Najafī.[6]

One could conclude, then, that the influence of a popular dichotomous and deterministic world view as invented by Abu Hanifa and his student al-Shāfiʻī (*dār al-harb* and *dār al-Islam*), which predicted that ultimately the non-Muslim world would adopt Islam by force or free will, played a role in leaving al-Shāfiʻī's ruling on the obligatory expansionist jihad unchallenged. A disconnect resulted among Shiʻi master narratives on war, hadith sources, the practically quietist Shiʻi position on jihad on the one hand, and the practically untested body of Shiʻi jihad jurisprudence on the other hand, which did not escape al-Shāfiʻī's radical influences for more than eight centuries. These conceptual inconsistencies and extra-Shiʻi influences aside, the Shiʻi jurisprudential view on war and peace had three major characteristics during the eight centuries between the two prominent Shiʻi scholars, Tūsī (d. 1022) and Najafī (d. 1849). First, Shiʻi jurisprudence interpreted the early Islamic jihads as legitimate and necessary measures needed to provide civil liberties, specifically freedom of religious practice and expression. In theory, this meant that offensive wars initiated to establish the religious truth (*jihad al-haqq*) were legitimate but only under the right authority – as long as the "right authority" was a qualified imam. Second, the presence and the permission of the right authority, that is, of an infallible imam, were integral and essential factors in legitimizing war. Third, the legitimate cause of jihad was based not on territorial borders or the nominal titles of political systems (i.e. Islamic land or state) but rather on whether the Shi'as could practise their sharī'a in full freedom or not.[7]

The above background will aid in understanding and evaluating the critical works of the contemporary Iranian scholars in the field. It is against this backdrop that one can measure the major scholarly contributions of Morteza Motahharī (d. 1979) and his mentor Mohammad Hossein Tabātabā'ī (d. 1985), who are considered in Shi'i-Iranian seminarian circles as the top two most influential contemporary Shi'i scholars.

Tensions between Political Duty and Moral Liberties

Tabātabā'ī has conducted one of the most elaborate and critical Shi'i treatments of classical Qur'ānic exegesis in his voluminous magnum opus *Al-Mīzān*. His treatment of the question of jihad, its conditions, and its qualities is not limited to one specific section of his exegesis but is scattered throughout various chapters, within his abundant perspectives and analyses of various jihad- and war-related verses of the Qur'ān.

In addressing just cause for war, although Tabātabā'ī acknowledges the legitimacy of ideologically offensive wars, he points out that the phrase "in the way of God," repeated frequently in the Qur'ān demonstrates that, as far as scripture is concerned, the cause of war is more important than its results.[8] This notion does not coincide with the relatively more result-sensitive, modern consequentialist just-war theories. Tabātabā'ī, nevertheless, emphasizes that the goal of war cannot be total dominance or victory over non-Muslims, but rather war should be limited and sanctioned only for defending legitimate human rights, based on what he terms "common sense and natural law embedded in the nature of human being [*fitra*]."[9] Following this spirit of universal rights, Tabātabā'ī is conscious of the law of proportionality within war and therefore supports the just-war maxim, namely, that the gains of war must be more than its losses.[10]

Tabātabā'ī rejects the instrumentalist view of war that, in the spirit of social Darwinism, claims to keep the world's corruption at bay. The Darwinist natural conflict, Tabātabā'ī stresses, cannot save humankind from corruption, for it destroys social diversity; rather, he asserts, the types of war supported by the scripture protect the very fabric of society.[11] "An effective defence of a human's basic and intrinsic rights," he asserts, "entails the expansion of jihad as a duty [*hukm*]."[12] According to this principle, which informs Tabātabā'ī's central social theory, fulfilling such a duty is intrinsic to human nature because of the desire to maintain order within one's community. In short, sustaining basic rights and order as dictated by human natural instincts constitute central causes for "natural jihad." From Tabātabā'ī's perspective, once members of a society resist this duty (jihad), it leads to chaos and, ultimately, to war.[13]

Thus far, Tabātabā'ī has attempted to interpret jihad as a means of protecting order, human rights, and social diversity. In other words, Tabātabā'ī interprets jihad as an institution that protects an intrinsically pure and moral society from going astray. However, in considering a society that has already gone astray and is in need of moral reform, he considers the second function of jihad as an instrument of legitimate corrective coercion. In a morally consequentialist spirit, he asserts that war is sometimes necessary for imposing beneficial social norms upon certain people (i.e. conversion). In his exegesis on the Qur'ānic verses encouraging war against polytheists, Tabātabā'ī claims that since Islam is the essence of humanity, forcing a misguided generation to accept Islam is tantamount to forcing them to be human.[14] Coercing one generation to accept the laws of nature, he believes, is acceptable because the (natural) law has to be observed, either willingly or through force. The next generation of a morally coerced society, he concludes, will have no need to be under compulsion, presumably because they are convinced about the merits of a moral society. Through this line of reasoning, Tabātabā'ī ultimately concludes that an offensive war, aiming to establish divine law and order, is not in essence offensive; rather, it is defensive mainly because it is a moral necessity.[15] Regarding the scriptural permissibility of corrective wars practised by pre-Islamic prophets, as reflected in the Qur'ānic verses 3:146, 5:24, and 27:37, Tabātabā'ī again denies that these wars were offensive on the same basis as he explained above.[16]

It is not surprising that Tabātabā'ī's consequentialist reasoning in his ethics of war echoes the views of John Stuart Mill in supporting war against immoral states whose economies are based on slavery:

> A war to protect other human beings against tyrannical injustice; a war to give victory to their own ideas of right and good, and which is their own war, carried on for an honest purpose by their free choice is often the means of their regeneration. A man who has nothing, which he is willing to fight for, nothing, which he cares more about than he does about his personal safety, is a miserable creature who has no chance of being free, unless made and kept so by the exertions of better men than himself. As long as justice and injustice have not terminated *their* ever renewing fight for ascendancy in the affairs of mankind, human being must be willing, when need is, to do battle for one against the other.[17]

Some readers of Mill's ethics of war have concluded that with slavery-based economies in mind, for Mill, preventing a tyrannical majority from suppressing the basic rights of a minority provides a moral pretext for state intervention through war.[18] In Tabātabā'ī's broader ideological perspective, however, the difficult endeavour to justify unprovoked "primary wars" on moral grounds, echoing the conviction of many classical Muslim exegetes, did not save him from facing three dilemmas: first, the Qur'ānic assertion that faith is not of a compulsory nature;[19] second, the reality of mixed motives for territorial expansionism in the post-Prophetic history of Islam; and third, similar utopian logic used to justify many modern international wars. He did not live long enough to see how Western powers waged wars as a means of exporting democracy to tyrannically ruled states, such as Iraq and Afghanistan, but he could see a similar line of war justification across Islamic history. In short Tabātabā'ī's support for moral offence raises the same question that is well known in Western literature on the ethics of war, that is, whether or not force should be used to protect and preserve values.[20]

The shift between Tabātabā'ī's liberation theology as discussed above and his categorical condemnation of early expansionist wars in Islamic history does not happen smoothly. He unequivocally rejects the expansionist policies of the Prophet Mohammad's immediate successors. These wars, he claims, exhausted early Muslim society by forcing their focus towards war and material gains instead of towards spiritual development.[21] He denies that such expansionist policies, in terms of motives and consequences, were substantially different from those pursued by Alexander the Great or Genghis Khan. "If Islam had sanctioned expansionism," he contends, "it was for the implementation of righteousness, social justice, and the spiritual education of people, rather than to establish Persian-like or Roman-like empires, slavery, collection of booty, and unlimitedly adding to court treasures."[22]

Tabātabā'ī also mentions that 'Umar b. al-Khattāb (d. 644), the second Muslim caliph, removed the phrase "Seek the best of all deeds" (*Hayya 'alā khair al-'amal*) from the daily call to prayer, replacing it with the phrase "Prayer is better than sleeping" (*As-salātu khairun min an-nawm*). This latter invented phrase, which did not put daily prayer before jihad, helped serve 'Umar's expansionist policies at the cost of reducing Muslim spirituality.[23] In short, Tabātabā'ī rejects the notion that the post-Prophetic territorial expansions of the Muslim world, which occurred as a result of the first three caliphs' policies, were necessary or even useful parts of Islamic history.

Addressing the very important question of the relationship between spiritual power and politics, Tabātabā'ī maintains that the basis of the Prophet's decision making on matters of war and peace had nothing to do with revelation but was a function of the collective views of the Muslim community.[24] All of the Qur'ānic verses rebuking the pacifism attributed to some of the Prophet's companions criticize their reluctance in joining war campaigns that were already decided upon through expert consultation. In other words, there were no Prophetic military campaigns initiated in a purely offensive and unprovoked manner, either by the Prophet's decree or by a scriptural injunction. Tabātabā'ī stresses that, according to the Qur'ānic verses 2:212 and 3:64, "the primary function of all the prophets and their scriptures was conflict resolution."[25] Here, the scholar counters his first account of Prophetic wars, to a degree, by asserting God's noninterventionist policy within the realm of Muslim political and military affairs.

Tabātabā'ī finds it astonishing that, from the Prophet Muhammad's twelve thousand companions who outlived him, only five hundred hadiths that dealt with the very important matters of jurisprudence remain. This amounts to only one hadith per twenty-four companions. Tabātabā'ī believes that this lack of hadiths resulted from the Umayyads' ban, for obvious political benefits, on the accumulation of the much-needed jurisprudential hadiths, while at the same time they rewarded the collection of all literature that promoted the personal images of the first three caliphs over the fourth, 'Alī b. Abī Tālib (the Umayyads' enemy).[26] Therefore early on in Islamic history, the personal dispositions of specific political figures overshadowed and subdued matters of principle. As a result, the war policies of the first three caliphs were justified and left without criticism.

While Tabātabā'ī is quite candid and bold in criticizing the general war policies of the early caliphs, he remains partially apologetic regarding traditional Islamic exegeses on questions related to causes of wars (*jus ad bellum*). He also does not add much to what his medieval predecessors had discussed on the qualities of ethics in war (*jus in bello*). These shortcomings have received important criticism by another contemporary Shi'i scholar Sālehī-Najafābādī. But before leaving Tabātabā'ī's arguments on war legitimation, it is important to identify the most significant tensions with which his view on war struggles and which may have caused inconsistencies in his argument: questions of the freedom of moral choice; a social-justice-based Shi'i version of Gutierrezian liberation theology, which also informs Shi'i eschatology; the reality of territorial expansionisms in Islamic history; the traditional Muslim exegetical methodology that predominantly overlooks historical contexts of revelation; and expediencies and paradigms of modern life such as the nation-state concept that has rendered the *dār al-Islam* and *dār al-harb* division of the world irrelevant and obsolete.

The solution to the complex matrix of factual and epistemological elements presented above may be found by answering two fundamental questions:

1 Should sharī'a be a function of ethics or ethics a function of sharī'a?
2 Can we replace the traditional linear methodology of Qur'ānic exegesis with a contextualist methodology, such as the one the Syrian scholar Muhammad Shahrūr (b. 1938) offers according to his "limits" or "range theory"?

Shahrūr argues that traditional Qur'ānic exegeses create serious tension with aspects of modern life because they have adopted a linear approach to scripture, in the sense that all later verses abrogate preceding verses whenever a tension arises between the two. As a result, all more limiting and strictly legal Qur'ānic verses are given priority over moral, lenient, and flexible injunctions. Based on his criticism of the the traditional methodology, Shahrūr suggests that, alternatively, a range approach will save exegetes from numerous abrogations and will offer a range of alternative choices to parallel sharī'a rulings, all of which may be considered "Islamic" and applied flexibly according to the expediencies and circumstances of time and space.[27]

Tabātabā'ī's own methodology, known as interpreting the Qur'ān by Qur'ān, has helped him to be occasionally critical of traditional Qur'ānic exegesis but not systematically, as expected by his later critics. On the positive side, his bold criticism of early Muslim expansionist policies has certainly paved the way for the emergence of new critical Shi'i scholarship on the ethics of war.

Ideology and Jihad

Morteza Motahharī (d. 1979), one of the most erudite Shi'i jurists of the late twentieth century, formulated the philosophy of jihad within modern discourse in a whole new language. As a student and commentator of Tabātabā'ī, Motahharī was greatly influenced by his mentor, although at times he does criticize his mentor's philosophical views. Instead of dwelling on classical and medieval juristic sources, he discusses scripture by utilizing a discursive and novel method to establish the meaning of jihad in his own exegesis.

After citing the Qur'ānic verses "And if God had not repelled some men by others, the earth would have been corrupted" (2:251) and "For had it not been for God's repelling some men by means of others, cloisters and churches and oratories and mosques, wherein the name of God is mentioned often, would surely have been pulled down" (22:40) in his seminal article on jihad, Motahharī adopts a consequentialist and instrumentalist view of war. "War that is transgression," he asserts, "is utterly evil, while war that means standing erect in the face of transgression is utterly good and is one of the necessities of human life." Therefore, he concludes, "the existence of armed forces, the duty of which is to prevent aggression, is an absolute necessity."[28]

Like most modern Sunni scholars, Motahharī altogether avoids matters relating to the conduct of war *(jus in bello)* and primarily develops new insights into the causes of war (*jus ad bellum*). He enumerates a number of legitimate war categories required by jihad, such as wars waged to aid oppressed people, with or without the oppressed party having requested the intervention. He contends, "It is permissible or rather obligatory for us to render aid to the oppressed regardless of whether they appeal to us for help." Many early Muslim wars, according to Motahharī, were fought on these grounds.[29] Another legitimate cause of war, in his opinion, is the necessity to remove obstacles (including political systems) that hinder people's free access and their response to the invitation to Islam. In other words, it is completely legitimate to fight in favour of people isolated from the call for truth, as well as against regimes suppressing freedom of speech.[30] Defensive wars, which include defending one's life, wealth, property, land, independence, and moral principles, are also all legitimate.[31] But within this list, he stresses priorities: "There exists something superior to the rights of individual or nation, something more sacred, the defense of which in accordance with the human conscience has stronger priority than the defense of individual rights. And that something is rights of humanity."[32] He continues, "No one should have any doubts that the most sacred form of jihad is that which is fought in defense of humanity and for the promotion of human rights."[33] In addition to the above, he maintains that another legitimate cause for jihad is to help universal morality: "There is a possibility that one fights not for the sake of aggression, nor in defence of oneself or one's human values, but for the universal expansion of human values."[34] Here again, this reasoning is not far from some of the West's justifications for waging war to promote democracy.[35]

Motahharī's view of the freedom of belief is novel within Islamic theology; he is, however, candidly against the freedom of any belief not rooted in what he calls "the original uncorrupted thought."[36] However, the question as to what the qualities of this "original thought" actually are is left unanswered, opening up the potential for a closed and self-serving logical circle that clashes with the proverbial Qur'ānic verse against coercive indoctrination, "There is no compulsion in faith" (2:256). In keeping with this line of thought, the legitimate categories of war proposed by Motahharī come close to being identified with the hegemonic ideological wars, such as communism versus democracy, that were quite popular in the developing world during the 1960s and 1970s. In addressing the freedom of belief, Motahharī seems to take a more radical tone than his mentor Tabātabā'ī. As an influential and pioneering thinker of his generation, Motahharī was reactive to the rival Marxist revolutionary propaganda and its absolutist utopianism. Given the respect imparted to Motahharī as the chief Iranian theologian closest to Ayatollah Khomeini during the 1979 Revolution, it is not surprising that his views above were codified in the constitution of the Islamic Republic of Iran.[37]

In theory and by implication, Motahharī denies any merit to a democratic system created by an ignorant society that, in his opinion, could be justly conquered as a way of informing them about truth, humanity, and human rights. Here, Motahharī fails to pay attention to the fact that notions such as "truth," "humanity," and "human rights," if not partially speculative in the age of hermeneutics, are presently expansive and fluid. Even in some of the most conservative Muslim societies, one may face questions like "Whose truth?" and "Whose definition of humanity and human rights?" Moreover, his view lacks an elaboration on the mechanisms of making decisions on war. He also fails to examine Muslim jurists' traditional views on war critically, thus validating those views from a fundamentalist perspective. However, his emphasis on the essentiality of "humanity" and "human rights" in any given society brings him closer to objective and universal Mu'tazilī ethics, as well as to modern international law, though it is in contradistinction to traditional, duty-based jurisprudence.

Examined from a different angle, Tabātabā'ī and Motahharī's exegetical works on jihad in the Qur'ān demonstrate strong theological inclinations to a natural-law perspective that is well-defined and categorized by such Christian and Muslim ethicists as Edward Vacek and Anver Emon. Vacek divides the whole theoretical spectrum of Christian ethics into three categories: divine command, natural law, and mutual love. While the central drive of the divine-command theory is based on human obedience, the natural-law theory looks at "right" as, in the words of Vacek, "that which fulfills human nature and/or that which conforms to rightly exercised human reason … Since the structures of this world embody God's wisdom and goodness, it makes good sense for us to live in accord with these structures."[38] From an Islamic law perspective, Emon recognizes two trends among Muslim jurists who, in varying degrees, accept natural law as a framework for their ethical approach to religion. He calls the first group "Hard Natural-Law jurists," who believe that jurists can utilize reason as a source of law; these jurists give an ontological authority to reason. "Soft Natural Law jurists," however, accept reason only as an epistemological instrument in their jurisprudence, because they believe that an absolute authority on reason limits God's omnipotence.[39] Tabātabā'ī and Motahharī, both from a Shi'i theological background, lean closer to hard natural-law jurisprudence. They clearly struggle in their treatment of jihad to find reasonable justifications for wars pursued by various prophets. The fact that both authors are staunch critics of the expansionist wars waged during the post-Prophetic caliphal era demonstrates that, in their view, the universal authority of reason is far more powerful in developing an ethical world than is war.

Perhaps the most serious question, which begs an answer from Tabātabā'ī and Motahharī in the era of multiple nation-states, is related to the mechanism of making decisions on international interventionism. Christian von Wolff (d. 1754), a scholar of international relations who was influential in the development of the modern approach to the laws of war, stated that "no nation can assume for itself the functions of a judge."[40] How, then, do Tabātabā'ī and Motahharī envision moral interventionism when already more than two Shi'i majority nation-states exist in our time? To my knowledge, neither scholar provides a clear answer to this question; thus their political philosophy suffers a theoretical lacuna.

In addition to the works of Tabātabā'ī and Motahharī, several other significant treatises and exegeses on jihad were written before the 1979 Islamic Revolution, for example, Mohammad Mojtahed Shabestarī's "Jihad in Islam" (1969). In this work, Shabestarī, presently known as one of the leading progressive theologians in postrevolutionary Iran, introduces Islam as a universal ideology with its own specific economic, legal, ethical, social, and political systems that seek to dominate the entire world. "Islam," he contends, "looks for a revolution, not in a specific society, but in the global arena, and wants to expand its worldview to the rest of the world, to all international fields, and to all societies." He concludes, "In this connection, jihad in Islam is not but armed defense to support the expansion of the mentioned revolution."[41] Shabestarī also considered the armed insurgency against the incumbent monarchy, gradually taking shape in Iran during the mid-1960s, as a legitimate jihad.[42] Shabestarī's ideological view of Islam coincides with that of two influential contemporary authors on jihad and martyrdom, namely 'Alī Sharī'atī (d. 1977), known as the architect of the 1979 Iranian Revolution, and Sālehi-Najafābādī (d. 2006), an author and seminarian critic of traditional jurisprudence. Not much later, in the course of the revolution, however, Shabestarī changed positions and became one of the boldest critics of ideological politics.[43]

Conclusion

Struggling with the realities of an Islamic history coloured by many wars driven by territorial ambitions, with the eruptive force of the communist-leftist ideologies of the mid-twentieth century, which justified the extensive use of force and violence for political goals, and with their religious obligation to contain violence within a moral framework, Tabātabā'ī and Motahharī developed a compromising political philosophy. During the decade before the revolution, when a monumental political change in Iran was in the making, Tabātabā'ī and Motahharī – as beacons of Twelver-Shi'i scholarship in the twentieth century – tried to present a reinterpretation of the traditional theories of jihad and Shi'i ethics of war and peace that could instigate moral interventionism and limit the use of force all at the same time. On the one hand, these two influential scholars faced challenges from Iranian leftists, who branded all religions as "opium" causing political numbness. On the other hand, they had to respond to the Western critics of Islam, who accused this religion of promoting conversion by force. Unlike many of their classical predecessors who, under the umbrella of political quietism, did not feel obliged to fill the gap between traditional jurisprudence of war and the political realities and expediencies of their own time, Tabātabā'ī and Motahharī were caught intellectually in the heart of such contentions. But this was not yet the end of their intellectual dilemmas. The gap between the Shi'i master narratives and the traditional positive jurisprudence of war and peace, a good part of which was adopted from Sunni laws, was another monumental challenge for both scholars. All of the above contentious factors, in effect, produced such a complex moral, political, and jurisprudential matrix that could hardly be resolved by one or two scholars, even these two extraordinary and erudite scholars.

The result of such an impossible situation was a half-apologetic, half-critical political exegesis and philosophy that were supposed to bridge the multilayered historical, moral, and epistemological inconsistencies. By permitting offensive war on moral and ideological grounds, Tabātabā'ī and Motahharī rendered new interpretations for jihad that, in effect, rode the line between freedom of religious choice and the collective duty to fix the world morally. Jihad then seemed to be a universal obligation to protect and promote human rights.

The above formulation, however fit to serve revolutionary and war goals, nevertheless suffered from many inconsistencies that required an entirely new critical reading of Shi'i ethics of war and peace; yet, it offered an important impetus for the Shi'i seminarian circles and beyond to read history and moral traditions critically. Together, Tabātabā'ī and Motahharī provided a fertile intellectual ground for the next generation of Shi'i scholars who placed morality above the ephemeral expediencies of any specific political system.[44]

It is noteworthy that almost all of the scholarly arguments and literature on jihad and martyrdom produced in Iran in the decade before the 1979 Revolution, and utilized for the revolution, dealt with the causes of war (*jus ad bellum*), with the exception of some abstract and scant references to the qualities of conduct within war (*jus in bello*). This gap in scholarship has fortunately been filled by the unfortunate calamities of the Iran-Iraq War. The following chapter further details the emergence of new Shi'i theologies on war and peace, which signifies a turning point in Shi'i-Iranian scholarship. The study of this modern scholarship will be necessary not only to facilitate understanding of the transitions in Iranian and Shi'i political and theological philosophy, but also to highlight perspectives and literature that can increase and assist Muslim participation in the global dialogue on conflict resolution and peacemaking.

7 Postwar Revision and the Reconstruction of Modern Iranian-Shi'i Ethics of War and Peace

It is not morality that rests on religion but religion on morality.

– Kai Nielsen[1]

The Islamic laws of war, which were canonized a few centuries earlier than were Christian laws, gradually fell behind the pace of development of its counterpart laws in Western legal literature and tradition. Muslim scholars of applied ethics lost touch with everyday politics. More significantly, because jurisprudents claimed exclusive rights over political theory, the scant number of Muslim political philosophers after the time of al-Fārābī contributed very little to scholarship on the ethics of war and peace. This lack of scholarship led to the freezing of rational, philosophical, and theological Islamic traditions that, at their peak, had laid the foundation for the European Renaissance. The loss of the tradition of *ijtihād* (juristic independent reasoning) exacerbated the situation. The divorce between law and ethics deprived Islamic jurisprudence of critical reasoning.

This chapter discusses how a new spirit of *ijtihād* has been revived in Iranian-Shi'i culture over a couple of productive decades. This section delves into modern critical literature related to the ethics of war as produced by Iranian-Shi'ite jurisprudents, beginning with the end of the Iran-Iraq War in 1988. The chapter explores how a new trend of critical thinking by postrevolutionary, postwar Iranian clerics with experience in both war and in international politics provided new perspectives on traditional legal views in both domains of justice of war (*jus ad bellum*) and justice in war (*jus in bello*). The goal of this chapter is to examine Iranian-Shi'i scholars' postrevolutionary shift in their views on various aspects of war, the new jurisprudence resulting from the aforementioned, and the way in which these updated perspectives inform Islamic laws and ethics of war.

The Iran-Iraq War and Its Moral Controversies

With hundreds of thousands dead on both sides, a larger number of injured or disabled, and more than $1.2 trillion economic damage (a modest estimation), the Iran-Iraq War forced a turning point in the development of modern Shi'i literature on the ethics of war.

The shock of the Iran-Iraq War, a battle that impacted tens of thousands of noncombatant civilians early on, positioned Shi'a clerics in one of their most precarious situations in the history of Shi'ism. The hard realities and high costs of war – material and spiritual – challenged both the clerics as commanders of war and, by implication, their traditional jurisprudence in its relevance and application to battlegrounds. As for *jus ad bellum,* nobody questioned the legitimacy of Iran's justifications for the cause of war, for it was purely of a defensive nature – at least during a good part of the war's lifespan when Iraqi forces were still in Iranian territory.

When the United Nations Security Council (UNSC), after a week of silence on the Iraqi invasion, called on both Iran and Iraq to sign a ceasefire via the UNSC Resolution 479, Iranian authorities immediately rejected it because the invading Iraqi forces were still inside Iranian territories. A ceasefire could only help to solidify the occupier's position. This rejecting stance was agreed upon by many top-ranking Iranian political and military leaders, who in the early days of the revolution thought of the United Nations as nothing more than an instrument for facilitating world domination by the superpowers. Unfortunately, the negative precedence set by Resolution 479 caused Iran to respond to UN Security Council resolutions negatively for a long of time after. Assured of the UN's political bias in favour of the aggressor, Iranian authorities did not seriously examine consecutive UN resolutions on war between 1980 and 1987. Iran's voluntary absence from all Security Council deliberations on the Iran-Iraq War left Iraqi diplomacy in the council unchallenged. The end result was the council's adoption of a stream of politically biased resolutions that gave Iran just more justification to reject them. Such a politically vicious circle almost guaranteed that *jus ad bellum*, or the question of the legitimacy of continuing the war, would not receive Iran's proper attention.

The main controversies among Iranian authorities, however, arose in relation to *jus in bello,* or the extent of the war's impact and the morality of the war's conduct – a subject more important for the UN Secretariat than for its Security Council. Questions such as whether the Iranian air force should retaliate against Iraq's bombardment of cities, given that Iraq was not only a Muslim country but also the country with the biggest Shi'i population after Iran, were not easy to answer. But nonretaliatory policies could further encourage Iraqi forces to press on with attacks, while nondiscriminatory attacks against Iraqi cities could result in the deaths of many more people and provoke popular support for Saddam Hussein. Moreover, such attacks could infringe upon traditional Islamic laws of war. It was a complicated situation, even a moral paradox. Iranian war chroniclers have reported that Iranian air-force commanders pressed the country's top leadership for permission to undertake retaliatory attacks on Baghdad, only to be frustrated when their requests were denied.[7] Of course, international institutions, such as the International Committee for the Red Cross (ICRC), also exerted pressure on both sides to refrain from breaching international humanitarian laws of war, such as the 1949 Geneva Conventions and Additional Protocols of 1977 prohibiting the targeting of civilians and civilian targets. Iran's highly ideological and revolutionary regime, which believed that the war was instigated primarily by the superpowers rather than by Saddam Hussein, did not care much about what it considered the UN's selective and arbitrary show of humanitarian concerns in a war fought by proxy with the West.

In 1982, two years after the war began, Iran's successful push to force Iraqi troops out of Khorramshahr in western Iran transitioned the war into a new phase. The victory boosted the morale of Iran's fighters, war commanders, and public alike. The Organization of the Islamic Conference (OIC) dispatched a delegation to Tehran to mediate peace between Iran and Iraq. Rumors circulated that some regional Arab states (specifically Saudi Arabia), fearing that the war would continue to spread to neighbouring countries, enticed Tehran to accept peace with an offer for impressive financial compensation.[3]

Ayatollah Khomeini, the official commander of armed forces according to the Iranian constitution, was initially interested in seeking a peace resolution but altered his position once the leading commanders of the Revolutionary Guard (IRGC), overwhelmed by the excitement of the recent victory, insisted that a total military defeat of Iraq was possible and that stopping at the borders was a poor military strategy.[4] From that point on, the quality of the war and the very continuation of the war (*jus ad bellum*) became matters of concern and the subject of controversy between Iran's leadership and its international and domestic critics.[5]

In the last six years of the eight-year-long war, Saddam, fearing a massive defeat, pursued a policy of "peace or total war." This meant that, short of a peace agreement, Iraq would know no bounds or limits in war, which effectively excused Iraq's use of chemical weapons. Iran, on the other hand, was interested in gaining a territorial upper hand and thus pursued a policy of limited, conventional war, which, contrary to the Iraqi position, meant war would continue justifiably but only within the bounds of international laws of war. The immediate result of these policies was demonstrated in Iran's keen interest in entertaining the ICRC and the UN Secretariat's imposition of humanitarian limits on Iraq's war policies, while Iran itself tried to comply. Iraq, on the other hand, pretended to be in full compliance with the Security Council's resolutions in the pursuit of a genuine ceasefire. In other words, Iranian diplomacy, which was totally alienated from discussions surrounding *jus ad bellum*, focused on *jus in bello*. Iraq, however, did the complete opposite. Iraq's use of chemical weapons in Halabja in 1988, the UN Security Council's reluctance to pressure Iraq against using chemical weapons (which were used against Iran between1983 and 1988),[6] and the absence of an Iranian ceasefire, brought Iran to a serious jurisprudential impasse. This situation stirred deliberations among the clerics in charge as to whether Iran could and should retaliate in kind. During controversies about Iran's nuclear program, many Western analysts speculated that Iran's interest in this field was the outcome of the above-mentioned bitter impasse in which Iran was once locked.

The main reasons for continuing the war after its turning point in 1982 were twofold. First, the strategy of irregular war, as Iran's Revolutionary Guards believed, entailed an offensive posture.[7] Second, the unexpected victory in retaking Khorramshahr boosted the ideological zeal and self-confidence of Iran's army to such a level that "the punishment of the aggressor" – in terms of a religious duty – was deemed both necessary and plausible. The idea of "punishment," which emerged during the second phase of the war, was interpreted to mean punishing not only Saddam and his regime but also all of his foreign culprits as well. "War, war till the eradication of sedition in the world" (*Jang jang tā raf'-e fetneh*) became the most popular war slogan in Iran between 1982 and 1988. Militant protagonists created this slogan and used it as the main justification for the prolonged war. This meant that Iran had a corrective, universal mission in the world and that war was an essential instrument for implementing this divine mission. It was in the spirit of this universal mission that the second official slogan, "The way to al-Quds [Jerusalem] passes through Karbalā," also came to be. This latter slogan functioned as two specific reminders to the warriors: first, that the ultimate goal for the war was to reach the greater enemy, Israel; and second, that the liberation of the Iraqi territory was necessary for the liberation of Palestine. In other words, the slogan reminded the warriors that they were fighting for the cause of the whole Muslim world, and the prolongation of the war was therefore fully justified on theological, teleological, and perhaps eschatological grounds.

The Iran-Iraq War finally and abruptly came to a highly emotional and controversial end after eight years. Because the international isolation of Iran during the war deprived the country of sophisticated weapons, the resulting lack of an indigenous defence industry prompted Iranian war strategy to rely on manpower and on mobilizing young volunteers en masse. Such mobilization made use of Shi'i martyr culture, as well as the institution of jihad, which had incidentally seen an emergence just before the revolution.

Iran's sudden and surprising acceptance of UN Security Council Resolution 598 in July 1998 was a major shock to many Iranian ideologues, as well as to the public at large. Moreover, it revealed the implausibility of most war slogans. Short of "the eradication of sedition" or "corruption in the world," as these ideologues expected, the war ended with Saddam still in power and with Iran's military position no better than it was six years before when Iran pushed Iraqi forces out of western Iran. In short, six full years of war had resulted in an outstanding amount of human and economic loss, making it difficult to justify its costs morally, both in terms of finances and life. This bitter realization was reflected in the final, proverbial statement issued by Ayatollah Khomeini that equated accepting peace with Saddam to "drinking the chalice of poison."[8] Nevertheless, for over two decades after the war's end, no Iranian authority save Ayatollah Montazerī (who was under house arrest) and Mahdī Bāzargān (Iran's first prime minister following the 1979 Revolution) dared to question the futility the war's six-year-long second phase.

At an unofficial level, however, a serious trend of critical thinking regarding both the ethics at war and the ethics in war gradually took shape among Iranian scholars, inside seminarian circles and outside. Some scholars, such as Mohaqqeq Dāmād and Eskandarī, did not directly connect their arguments about the ethics of war to the Iran-Iraq War case, while others, such as Sālehī-Najafābādī, unequivocally expressed in their reassessments of the ethics of war in Islam the negative impressions left by the tragedies caused by the Iran-Iraq War.[9] More recent authors, such as Sāber Adāk, who witnessed the full extent of the political and psychological side effects of the war on Iran's domestic and foreign policies, went beyond mere criticism of jurisprudential perspectives to challenge the war-laden and classical Islamic historiography of the Prophet Muhammad's life, which is dominated by war narratives. The remainder of this chapter will discuss some of the above treatises that represent new approaches by Iranian-Shi'i jurists to the ethics and laws of war and peace. These jurisprudents have initiated a new trend of scholarship that, in effect, is redefining jihad or, better to say, liberating jihad from its historic misappropriations in the course of history. If one can imagine a positive outcome of the long war, this scholarship is indeed one such result.

On the Defensive Nature of Armed Jihad: War as a Measure of Talion (*Qisās*)

Some of the post–Iran-Iraq War juristic treatises written on jihad in the Persian language emphatically stress jihad's defensive nature; they provide a moral and universal foundation for armed jihad. In other words, they introduce armed jihad as a universally justifiable institution that conforms to the present norms of international law. Onc prominent jurisprudent, Mohammad Hossein Eskandarī, suggests that the sole legitimate cause of war (*jus ad bellum*) in Islam is the principle of "retaliation-in-kind" or *qisās* (talion/retaliation). *Qisās* is traditionally considered a punitive, penal law code (*hoqūq-e jazā* in Persian) applied to murder cases or incidences of bodily harm to private citizens. Eskandarī, however, extrapolates this concept to include the laws of war. He suggests that in their nature, there is little to no difference between murder as individual-scale violence or the large-scale violence that is war. According to Eskandarī, a legitimate war is to be waged only for retaliation-in-kind, making it defensive-punitive by definition.

Eskandarī reminds his reader that the penal law of *qisās* is among one of the most controversial questions in classical jurisprudence. He concludes that, according to Qur'ānic verses, *qisās* is only a right (*haqq*) and not an obligatory duty (*taklīf wājib*), for the Qur'ān unequivocally calls upon those entitled to this right to forgive and settle conflicts through other recommended approaches, such as through financial compensation (*dīya*) or forgiveness (*'afw*). Eskandarī concludes that war as a notion of retaliation-in-kind is only an option and not a duty for Muslim communities, which preferably should seek peaceful means to settle conflicts.

Through an exhaustive examination of various juridical views of both Shi'i and Sunni scholars on *qisās,* Eskandarī enumerates the many limitations to implementing this law. He refers to, for example, the views of various jurisprudents on the following key Qur'ānic verses related to retaliation:

> And in it We prescribed for them: a life for a life, an eye for an eye, a nose for a nose, and an ear for an ear, and a tooth for a tooth, and retaliation for wounds. Yet whosoever remits it out of charity, that shall be an atonement for him. Those who do not judge by what Allah has sent down – it is they who are the wrongdoers. (5:45)

> O you who have faith! Retaliation is prescribed for you regarding the slain: freeman for the freeman, slave for slave, and female for female. But if one is granted any extenuation by his brother, let the follow up [for the blood money] be honorable, and let the payment to him be with kindness. That is a remission from your Lord and a mercy; and should anyone transgress after that, there shall be a painful punishment for him. (2:178)

> There is life for you in retribution, O you who possess intellect! Maybe you will be Godwary! (2:179)

> The requital of evil is an evil like it. So whoever excuses and conciliates, his reward lies with Allah. Indeed He does not like the wrongdoers. (42:40)
>
> And if you retaliate, retaliate with the like of what you have been made to suffer, but if are patient, that is surely better for the patient. (16:126)
>
> A sacred month for a sacred month, and all sanctities require retribution. So should anyone aggress against you, assail him in the manner he assails you. And be wary of Allah, and know that Allah is with the Godwary. (2:194)
>
> Fight in the way of Allah those who fight you, but do not transgress. Indeed Allah does not like transgressors. (2:190)[10]

According to Eskandarī, while the law of retaliation-in-kind was clear on certain physical injuries, such as the loss of an eye, ear, or limbs, jurists of various schools of law have not been able to agree on other types of injuries or methods of retaliation. He refers to an exemplary classical case wherein a man killed another by beating him to death with his cane, an act amounting to torture. The case was presented to various jurists to determine the measures of retaliation-in-kind. Following the two hadiths cited by Eskandarī, Ja'far al-Sādiq ruled that the murderer must be delivered to the family of the murdered, though they could not execute him by torture; the execution, rather, was to be be simple and by a sword.[11]

All Shi'i jurists, according to Eskandarī, have reached the same conclusion about the limited scope of the law of retaliation-in-kind. Some jurists, like al-Shāfi'ī, support retaliation-in-kind without limits. Eskandarī criticizes a contemporary Sunni exegete, Mohammad Rashīd Ridā, who based on al-Shāfi'ī's ruling concludes: "I add to the ruling [of al-Shāfi'ī] that in war too retaliation-in-kind must be strictly observed exactly as in the case of murder. Therefore, whenever the enemy fights the Muslim forces by canon, fire weapons, or chemical warfare, they [Muslims] must retaliate by the same means; or else jihad will lose its function, which is on the one hand the prohibition of oppression, sedition, hostility, and aggression, and on the other hand the establishment of freedom, security, justice, and doing good."[12] Eskandarī rejects this conclusion and instead stresses that the Qur'ānic concept of retaliation-in-kind – when applied to war – is concerned with the results of a criminal action rather than with the method by which an injury was inflicted upon a victim. In other words, the application of the law of *qisās* should equate to war against war and not chemical weapons against chemical weapons (given the indiscriminate impact of WMDs). He asks, What if a person or a group rape women or men, be it in war or peace? Obviously, retaliation-in-kind in this case, Eskandarī contends, does not make sense; in fact, it would be ridiculous if one were to say to an individual who murdered his brother, "Now that you have killed my brother, I will kill yours."[13]

Eskandarī concludes that no act of retaliation-in-kind should inflict damage on an innocent third party. He categorically rejects the use of weapons of mass destruction by Muslims because indiscriminate killing has no legal or moral basis in sharī'a. By referring to Q. 16:126, he reminds his readers that this verse (cited above) was revealed when the Prophet visited the mutilated body of his beloved uncle Hamza during the battle of Uhud. Stricken by deep sorrow and anger, the Prophet vowed to kill in retaliation seventy Meccan polytheists of the Quraish tribe; however, the verse consequently reminded the Prophet that he could not go beyond a proportional measure of retaliation, and that exercising self-control instead would be morally more fitting. Eskandarī concludes, on the basis of the Prophetic incident and its related verse, that the phrase "retaliation-in-kind" is not "similarity in form of the reaction," as some jurists have concluded; instead, the proportionality of damage to the enemy is an integral part of Islamic laws of war.[14]

Given the above argument, Eskandarī arrives at conclusions important for the ethics and laws of war in terms of both the cause and quality of war. He maintains that because sharī'a is sensitive about the limits of retaliation-in-kind, measures at the personal or collective levels (that is, in terms of civilian or international relations) must be decided by the state. He cites a hadith by al-Bāqir (the fifth Shi'i imam), which asserts that all measures of retaliation not approved by the imam (religious authority) must be penalized.[15] In Eskandarī's view, another factor limiting both the scope and quality of retaliation-in-kind involves the conventional norms (*'urf*) of various societies and historical periods. For example, once slavery became a universally obsolete practice in modern times, it could not be applied to prisoners of war held by Muslim forces.[16] Similarly, he rejects the classical dichotomy of the abode of peace (*dār al-Islam*) and the abode of war (*dār al-harb*) in traditional Muslim political philosophy, maintaining that even if one does classify the world's political map into these domains, there is no reason to believe that the only relationship defined between these two domains is limited to a state of war.[17] In his view, the basis for international hostility according to Islam is an act of war and aggression rather than disbelief in God.[18]

It is important to note that by methodologically and morally removing the categorical distinction between private and public law in the application of retaliation-in-kind, Eskandarī paves the way for applying forgiveness in civic and international relations. The Qur'ānic injunction regarding the three alternative options that a private individual could choose in penalizing a murder can be also applied to war. At the legal level, the option is retaliation-in-kind. The second option of accepting material compensation enters a moral realm advised by the Qur'ān. At the highest moral level, the scripture exhorts forgiveness. Needless to say that if the third piece of advice is applied in collective relations, it will open a whole new chapter in universal peace and conflict resolution.

How Ethics in War Can Serve Ethics at War

Another jurist Mostafā Mohaqqeq Dāmād treats armed jihad from a different angle, with similar conclusions to Eskandarī's.[19] In his elaborate treatise *Protection of Individuals in Times of Armed Conflict under International and Islamic Laws*, he covers many areas of both *jus ad bellum* and *jus in bello*.[20] This work offers a comparative analysis defining the entire body of Islamic traditions on *jus in bello* within the context of modern humanitarian international law. As for the legitimate causes of war in Islam, Mohaqqeq Dāmād emphatically asserts, "All Mālikī and Hanafī, most Shāfi'ī and Hanbalī and many Imāmī [Shi'i] *faqīh*s [jurisprudentsts] have expressed the view that the purpose of jihad and war is to keep the enemy's bellicosity at bay." He then concludes, "Thus, war must be waged with the enemy for his aggression against Muslims and Islam, not that he must be killed because he is an infidel."[21] He asserts that killing someone for an alternative belief system is forbidden because "killing non-belligerent citizens is prohibited in the *sharī'a* law." Pointing out the Prophetic order to save many categories of civilians in war from death, including women, the elderly, and children, Mohaqqeq Dāmād further emphasizes, "Had merely being a non-believer been justification for death, any non-Muslim individual would have had to be killed."[22]

The author indicates that an opposite view held by some followers of the Shāfi'ī, Shi'i, and Zāhirī (a school of law known for its literal interpretation of texts) schools suggests the cause of fighting in Islam to be disbelief, adding, "In certain works, Shāfi'ī has preferred this opinion."[23] He further notes, "Proponents of this view also authorize the killing of the elderly, children, the blind and the invalid."[24] Mohaqqeq Dāmād, however, asserts that this latter view is in the minority and based solely on a weak hadith from a hadith transmitter, Samrat b. Jundūb, who lacks credibility among jurists and has incorrectly interpreted the Qur'ānic verse 9:5.[25]

On the meaning of jihad, Mohaqqeq Dāmād concludes, "Taking into careful consideration the definition of jihad in the Islamic law and war in the international law, it becomes clear that, in both cases, jihad and war take place for public interests of a state, against a foreign enemy."[26] The only difference, it seems then, is that war is waged for material goals whereas jihad, by definition, is waged in pursuit of spiritual ends.

In his examination of the laws of war, Mohaqqeq Dāmād observes that most Muslim jurists have categorized the main questions pertaining to *jus in bello* to include the following:

- Who should be fought
- Who should be killed
- Who should be protected
- How a war should be fought
- Which acts are authorized and unauthorized in war
- Rules of dealing with prisoners of war (*istirqāq*)
- Rules concerning war spoils
- Rules and conditions concerning the protection of peoples of other faiths (*dhimmī*)
- Rules of poll tax (*jizya*)
- Rules concerning the enemy's buildings and properties after victory
- Rules concerning peace agreements and amnesty.[27]

Contrary to the minority view in the Shi'i school that permits killing women and children who take part in war, Mohaqqeq Dāmād argues that most Twelver-Shi'i jurists would absolutely prohibit this, "even if they take part or render assistance to enemy in wars."[28]

The author refers to an important methodology in Islamic law, specifically to "fixed" and "changing" laws. He maintains that some obligatory rites, like prayers and fasting, belong to the first category, while laws granting concessions and permissions to Muslims, such as ownership and property, are subsumed under the second category. Mohaqqeq Dāmād asserts, "Most rules and regulations regarding the Holy War in Islam belong to the second [changeable] category, as they do not constitute fixed or invariable rules, but depend upon the discretion of the Islamic state."[29]

Mohaqqeq Dāmād's comparative analyses of traditional humanitarian laws of war in Islam and those of modern international law resulted in three general conclusions: First, Islamic law is highly compatible with much of modern international law. Second, wherever it lags, the changeable nature of the Islamic laws of war and the contractual possibilities built into Islamic law enable Muslim states to bridge the gap easily and legally. Third, in many fields, Islamic legal provisions pertaining to war and its conduct are more progressive than present modern international law. One case in point is the following:

> The regulations of Geneva Conventions pertaining to armed conflict of a non-international nature are less bold [than the Islamic norms] and their guarantees are

> much weaker than those contained in the provisions pertaining to international armed conflict. The philosophy underlying the division of the Convention provisions on humanitarian law into two protocols is, itself, based on the desire to withhold the greater guarantees from combatants in non-international armed conflict. The Islamic system, on the other hand, takes a diametrically opposite stance. It takes a more sympathetic view of armed conflict with rebels and Khārijites, offering them rules and guarantees that it withholds from polytheists and apostates engaged in international armed conflict.[30]

The problem with the above assertion is that terms such as "apostates"[31] and "polytheists" do not carry any negative weight in modern international law. In the context of modern, secular international law, rights are equal irrespective of one's belief system. From this perspective, one can conclude that both modern international humanitarian laws of war and the comparable traditional Islamic laws suffer from some kind of discrimination. It is from a neutral perspective that one can address the shortcomings of present international law in protecting domestic dissent.

Mohaqqeq Dāmād, however, provides a comparative picture of Islamic and modern international humanitarian laws of war, demonstrating that the differences between the two are nonessential and can be bridged with little effort on the part of modern Muslim jurists. He illuminates how Muslim states can embrace present international laws of war based not only on secular premises but also on norms that genuinely conform to Islamic traditions. Mohaqqeq Dāmād's main contribution to the field brings him close to humanitarian approaches by Hugo Grotius (d. 1645) and Jean Jacque Rousseau (d. 1778), both of whom, according to James Johnson, made *jus in bello* a domain conceptually and morally independent from *jus ad bellum* and believed in the full protection of noncombatant civilians vis-à-vis state administrations that involve wars.[32]

By shifting the legal basis of jihad from a mix of offensive and defensive causes in traditional law to a purely defensive one, Eskandarī and Mohaqqeq Dāmād provide their own theories of armed jihad based on personal *ijtihād* (independent juristic reasoning). Their theories, however, are based less on a critical reading of the past than on the necessities and expediencies of modern international relations. This significant gap was effectively bridged by other post–Iran-Iraq War scholarship.[33]

The Critical Reading of Traditional Sources

In contrast to the above methods, and in connection with his highly controversial treatises on the theory of martyrdom, Sālehī-Najafābādī, a seminarian scholar well known in theological circles for his bold views, has produced a new treatise on the topic of armed jihad in Islam. Like Eskandarī and Mohaqqeq Dāmād, Sālehī-Najafābādī introduces armed jihad as a strictly defensive measure. Unlike the other scholars, however, he criticizes the entirety of traditional jurisprudential literature on jihad, denying an authentic link between the literature and the meaning of jihad in the Qur'ān and in Prophetic practices.

Sālehī-Najafābādī asserts that, beginning with Shaykh Tūsī (d. 1067), all Shi'i jurists have acceded to al-Shāfi'ī's erroneous rulings on jihad, while al-Shāfi'ī himself relied on a notorious hadith forger in this field.[34] All such jurists, in Sālehī-Najafābādī's opinion, rewrote Islamic history based on their juridical views rather than on historical and textual facts.[35] These jurists, according to Sālehī, distort both the *sīra* (Prophetic biographies) and the scripture. The legitimacy of offensive war in Islam and "awkward" rulings are exemplary misinterpretations, such as the one developed by al-Shāfi'ī espousing the necessity of at least one offensive war a year for the Islamic state.[36] He expresses astonishment about al-Shāfi'ī's incorrect conclusion that all Qur'ānic verses limiting Muslim wars to defensive undertakings were abrogated by one verse, Q. 2:193.[37] An extensive range of both Sunni and Shi'i jurists accepted the ruling without scrutiny, such as the following: Hanafī b. Humām (d. 1456), Shaykh Tūsī (d. 1067), Ibn Idrīs Hillī (d. 1202), Allamah al-Hillī (d. 1325), Shahīd-e Thānī (d. 1558), Mohammad Hasan Najafī (d. 1849), and Ayatollah Kho'ī (d. 1992).[38] Such a view, Sālehī-Najafābādī asserts, defies the principle of the primacy of peace in Islam, as stipulated in many Qur'ānic verses.[39] Moral political philosophy aside, Sālehī-Najafābādī also criticizes the *fatwa* on offensive jihad from a methodological angle. He questions Najafī's assertion that the ruling has been based on consensus attained by all Shi'i jurists, "although," Sālehī-Najafābādī asks, "he [Najafī] knew that the *ijma'* [consensus] on this matter was absent because Saykh Tūsī had originally taken this *fatwa* from Imam Shafi'i, whose legal opinion and proofs are totally unacceptable."[40]

After criticizing the *fatwa* of offensive jihad as an annual political obligation, Sālehī-Najafābādī then invites the attention of his jurist colleagues to Shi'i sacred history and the way it defies the *fatwa*:

> The jurists have stated that Muslims are obliged, based on textual evidence and consensus, to launch an offensive war once a year even if the unbelievers are not hostile and at peace with the Muslims. If this were really the case, then one would expect Imam 'Ali, during his short caliphate, to obey it. And yet he did not. Is not this proof that God did not demand such an activity, because if He had, surely the Imam would have acted upon it?

> If the jurists have no response to this question, then the equitable thing to do is to distance themselves from this *fatwa*, and to ensure that Islam's reputation from this point onward is no longer tarnished by its custodians' claim that they are obliged to attack and kill peaceful unbelievers. This *fatwa* has been – and remains – a source of irreparable damage to Islam's honor and stature, as well as an injustice that the jurists have inadvertently imposed upon this divine religion!"[41]

Regarding *jus in bello*, Sālehī-Najafābādī provides a new reading of the Qur'ānic verses related to war without resorting, like most classical exegetes, to multiple scriptural abrogations. He maintains that all major jurists of both the Sunni and Shi'i schools, in an effort to be comprehensive, neglected to scrutinize individual legal topics; instead, they copied from one another extensively, gradually creating rigid laws irrelevant to scripture, to Islamic tradition, or to contemporary life. The Qur'ānic tone in addressing the issue of prisoners of war, as reflected in Q. 8:70, is compassionate, hopeful, and conciliatory.[42] The Qur'ānic verse Q. 47:4 establishes guidelines for their treatment: Captives are treated as people deserving of pity, guidance, and benevolence.[43] Either they should be unilaterally freed without precondition, or relatives or other benevolent institutions, such as a state, tribe, or other social organization, should be allowed to purchase their freedom.[44]

Sālehī-Najafābādī presents a striking case of misreading and misinterpretation that challenges traditional exegetical views of Q. 8:67, which reads: "No apostle should take captives until he has battled and subdued the country; you desire the vanities of this world, but God wills [for you the reward] of the world to come; and God is all-mighty and all-wise." Sālehī-Najafābādī explores many classical and modern exegetical commentaries on this verse, ranging from the works of al-Tabarī (d. 922) to those of Tabātabā'ī. These exegetes conclude two important points: first, that the Prophet must have executed all prisoners of the Badr War (the first Muslim-Meccan polytheist war in 624), as they were captured before the war's termination; and second, that this judgment established a portion of the permanent laws dictating the treatment of prisoners of war. The verse in point, however, simply maintains that Muslims waging war must not focus on material gains (for example, taking prisoners in the hopes of getting ransom) before the war's end.[45] In Sālehī-Najafābādī's opinion, the grave consequence of such misinterpretations is that scholars of theology and exegesis, like Tabātabā'ī, have invented a history that contradicts the actual events in the battle of Badr, during which captives were actually released either by ransom or by applying grace. Based on their misinterpretations of the verse, Sālehī-Najafābādī suggests that these exegetes astonishingly concluded that all other prophets had executed their prisoners of war![46]

Based on consensual juristic opinions (*ijmā'*) of identical Sunni and Shi'i rulings on the laws of war, Sālehī-Najafābādī constructs a hypothetical war simulation demonstrating the serious and deeply inhumane implications of such rulings. The full account of the simulation is described as follows:

> Suppose in a hypothetical war case, there is a report that the Islamic forces have captured twenty thousand prisoners of war from the enemy, of whom ten thousand have been captured during the battle and the rest surrendered after war's conclusion. The two distinct groups of prisoners of war each have been kept in a corner of the battleground next to a large poster that describes their status and facing the other group. The Islamic commander (ruler) is also stationed in his special chair ready to seal the fate of the prisoners of war and close the war's chapter. His speaker reads a statement on his behalf. A representative of the international media is present there too, reporting on the details of the concluding stage of the war. According to the statement just read on behalf of the commander, the prisoners of war that surrendered at the end of war will be subject to Islamic graceful treatment based upon Q. 8:70.
>
> The speaker continues reading the verse: "If God finds some good in your heart, He will reward you with something better than was taken away from you, and forgive your sins, for God is forgiving and kind," the speaker reads. He continues: "Now that your fate has brought you here, do not be heartbroken because by virtue of Islam's protection you will receive full respect and you are free like all other human beings, for God has created every individual free; the kind arms of Islam is wide open to embrace and serve you, and you can choose wherever you want to live in the abode of Islam without being forced to convert, as we read in the holy book: 'There is no compulsion in matters of faith'" (2:256). "Or you are free" the speaker reiterates, "to go back to your homeland as you wish," the speaker reiterates. "In order for you," he continues, "just to remember the affable position of Islam on prisoners of war, we will present each of you with a frame quoting the Qur'ānic verse I just read for you; at this juncture I call upon you to grab your gifts and proceed to the reception arranged to honour your departure."
>
> At this juncture an international media reporter asks the speaker whether the ceremony is over. He retorts: "This was the Islamic ruling on the first group of prisoners of war who were just released based on Q. 47:4, which gives us two choices of either releasing them on ransom or let them free by grace, and we chose the second option to enhance the international reputation for Islam."
>
> As this scene has raised a great hope in the heart of the second group of prisoners of war and expecting the same ruling on themselves, suddenly a number of executioners enter the scene each carrying a sharp sword ready to follow orders. The speaker reads a new statement: "This second group of the prisoners of war

who were captured before the termination of the battle will be executed in the form that an opposite hand and leg of each will be severed and they will be left to die," he announces. At this point the prisoners will be brought before the executioners in ten groups each of a thousand, and their arms and legs will be severed as ordered, and their still-alive bodies thrown in a large ditch that was prepared in advance. The moaning and crying of thousands of the unfortunate tortured and mutilated prisoners of war who will suffer for long before their death will fill the air as millions of television spectators around the world are watching this dreadful tragedy, while the Islamic commander and his staff are observing the scene in cold blood and emotional indifference, satisfied that they have just implemented their religious obligation [*taklīf shar'īya*], and will be duly rewarded by the Almighty.

After a break during which all the mutilated captives lost their lives, the floor was open for questions from the media. A reporter asked, "Why did you free the first group of prisoners with such respect and so graciously and execute the second group by torture. Did the latter pose serious threat against you?" The commander of the Muslim forces answers: "No, they did not pose any threat; we just executed them to fulfil an obligatory law based on a hadīth from Talhat b. Zaid." Another reporter asked, "Does this ruling limit you to execute them by such torture or does it give you other options as well?" The commander: "No, we could simply behead them instead." A reporter asked again: "But for the first group, you chose to free them without ransom in order to promote the international image of Islam, haven't you?" The commander: "The jurists, based on the text of '*sharh-e lum'a* [a collection of sharī'a rulings] in vol. 1, page 260, have ruled, about the specific methods of their execution, that we do not need to care for public exigencies [i.e. public image, expediency, etc.], thus we just did what we liked without caring for extra pains the prisoners of war had to suffer from." A reporter: "What kind of law or social necessity would entail that you execute a group of captives with such a callous method, while releasing another group so gracefully and with utmost respect?" Another reporter adds: "And what amazes us further is that you delivered frames of a Qur'ānic verse to the first group, according to which you must have been graceful to all the prisoners of war, without exception!" The reporter continues: "According to Arabic philologists, the word *al-asrā* used in Q. 8:70 becomes universal and covers all types of prisoners of war because of the letters *al* [definitive article in Arabic] coming before the word. What then could possibly justify your prejudice against the second unfortunate group?" The commander: "It is true that the ruling of Q. 8:70 applies to both types of the prisoners; however the hadith of Talhat b. Zaid excludes out the second group from the general amnesty granted by the Qur'ānic verse to all." The same reporter argues: "Does this single hadith have such an authority to delimit the Qur'ānic verse!?" The commander: "Well, the hadīth of Talhat b. Zaid is known

> to be among the weak hadith and therefore lacks authenticity; however, since a number of well-known jurists have formed and issued a consensus [*ijmā'*] ruling on it, the consensus remedies the weakness of the hadith, thus its treatment like an authentic hadith and thus its authority to delimit the Qur'ānic verse." Another reporter: "Is it justice, that a few thousand prisoners of war, against the very text of the Qur'ān, be executed through torture in such a tragic method, and thereby the callous act would tarnish the international image of Islam, and all this, just on the basis of a weak hadith?!" The commander responds: "So far this has been the ruling of all the well-known jurists, the renowned Allāma Hillī [d. 1325] has even stressed, 'This is the ruling of all our jurists'; having said this, I have to conclude this session by adding that our jurisprudence is very progressive and welcomes new rulings on this matter, provided that we have new legal reasoning [*ijtihād*] which rejects both the weak hadith and justifiability of remedying it by the jurists' consensus, in which case [in the face of the new ruling] we will treat all of the prisoners equally, gracefully, and with respect. Our sincere hope is that such *ijtihād* would take place soon and benefit our Islamic society *inshā'allāh* [God willing]." – End of the jurist's war-gaming scenario.[47]

Sālehī-Najafābādī's bold and very articulate criticism of these jurists' views extends beyond the above rulings to include the most important features not only of cross-border war but also of the domestic insurgents who instigated armed resistance against the incumbent regime (*bughāt*). He criticizes the views of both Sunni and Shi'i schools, finding them to be opposite extremes. The Shi'i school, he notes, applies the law of insurgency only when the ruler is an infallible imam, dictating that domestic armed struggles against other kinds of rulers are not subject to the severe punishment that the former case evokes. On the opposite side, Sālehī-Najafābādī mentions that all Sunni schools and Zaidī Shi'a jurists reject and condemn insurgency against the ruler of the Islamic state, even if that government is totally corrupt. Sālehī-Najafābādī concludes that both views are unrealistic and that the law against insurgency may only apply when the head of state runs a just government. He welcomes Ibn Khaldun's opinion that because al-Husayn's revolt against Yazīd was indeed against a corrupt regime, al-Husayn was right, should not have been subject to the law of insurgency, and is actually a revered martyr.[48]

The tension between scripture and jurisprudence – the letters and spirit of law and ethics – and its ends and means, as reflected in the scenario constructed by Sālehī-Najafābādī, is an affront to any moral thinker. The above scenario proves that the inconsistencies inherent in the approaches of traditional Islamic law lead to an impasse in modern implementation. For Sālehī-Najafābādī, law itself could not be an end in and of itself; rather, jurisprudence must be cognizant of the moral consequences of its rulings. In short, Sālehī-Najafābādī concludes that, early on in the history of jurisprudence, jurists' views on war were influenced by militant political systems rather than by reason. This effectively set the tone for their successors. The jurists of later generations accepted these views without scrutiny. Later, when faced with serious inconsistencies between their views and the primary sources (such as the Qur'ān), they invented their own history in order to make their ruling appear rational. Warfare, Sālehī-Najafābādī asserts, lost its concern with justice and humanitarian values under the Umayyads, the Abbasids, and the Sultānates.

What is the remedy when it comes to the tension between hadith literature and the moral soul of the scripture? Sālehī-Najafābādī's answer is to resort to a general rule: "All hadiths that do not agree with the Qur'ān are to be set aside."[49]

Sālehī-Najafābādī's exceptionally bold and critical views on jihad brought Shi'i scholarship on the subject to a monumental turning point. Following its publication in 2007, his book became a bestseller in Iran.

The Ethics of War Caught between Theology, Power Politics, and Law

One Iranian jurist Davoud Feirahī, who is also a professor of political science at Tehran University and impressed by Sālehī-Najafābādī, has written extensively about the impact of political power on medieval jurisprudence. Feirahī, acquainted with Western theories on the relationship between knowledge and power (as explored in the works of Michelle Foucault), notes that the Ash'arī-Shāfi'ī schools that were followed in the vast Muslim territories during medieval Islam focused on the following: the political theology of predestination, the predominance of revelation over reason, and the authoritarianism of the Arab tribal systems when mixed with Persian structures of monarchy. The environment produced by these factors resulted in a largely unchallengeable climate for the powerful medieval sultans.[50]

Feirahī mentions that al-Māwardī (d. 1058), one of the very few and most important medieval Muslim authors on politics, coaxed Muslims to show absolute obedience to their rulers, no matter how the rulers had acquired their power. He did so by referring to a Prophetic hadith narrated by Abū Huraira, which details how the Prophet informed Muslims about the future appearance of both righteous and corrupt rulers, both of which were to be obeyed as a religious duty.[51] To al-Ghazālī, al-Māwardī, and many others, ruling by usurpation and through the use of force (*taghallub*) was a common medieval practice and legitimate – as long as the rule provided security and stability for the community, effectively showing a preference for strong rule over just rule.[52] In Feirahī's opinion, Shi'i political jurisprudence failed to change medieval political authoritarianism. He points out that early on, during the formation of Shi'i political theory, conformist jurists devised a pragmatic and instrumentalist view of law that permitted cooperation with an unjust ruler (*al-sultan al-jā'ir*), justified by the notion that such services would benefit people in their general legitimate ends.[53]

By attempting to replace a malign despot with a benign one, medieval Muslim thinkers kept their pen in the service of the authoritarian sword. By doing so, they reversed the spirit of early Islam that had put the pen above the sword.[54] Feirahī does not write directly about the philosophy of war held by medieval Muslim conquerors but instead provides an in-depth analysis about the transformation of the knowledge-power equation to the power-knowledge hierarchy in Islamic history. He poses a particularly significant Foucaultian question: why did the men of sword subdue knowledge in the political structure of Muslim states, despite the fact that knowledge was the true source of political authority in early Islam? This question seriously challenges the expansionists' popular philosophy of conquer-convert, a philosophy which, as noted above, Tabātabā'ī candidly condemns.[55]

Feirahī has written two key articles on war. In the first, he discusses the relationship between three war-related areas in Shi'i jurisprudence: breaching conventions and treaties or perfidy (*ghadr*), terror (*fatk*), and suicide attacks (a modern notion not yet discussed exhaustively among Muslim jurists, but known in modern Arabic as *istishhād*).[56] He points out that the overwhelming majority of Sunni jurists permit "offensive jihad" (*jihad al-haqq* in Arabic; *jihad-e ebtedā'ī* in Persian usage), which is defined as an offensive war initiated to expand the world of Islam, as reflected in al-Shāfi'ī's main treatise *Al-Umm*.[57] Very few Sunni jurists, including Shaykh Mohammad Abduh (d. 1905), support limiting jihad to only defensive wars. In contrast to Sunni jurists, almost all Shi'i jurists reject starting an offensive war in the absence of an infallible imam (one of the twelve imams) and his command. Feirahī notes that very few Shi'i jurists, such as Sālehī-Najafābādī, reject the legitimacy of any offensive war with or without the presence of an imam; instead most believe that all legitimate wars or armed jihads must be defensive by definition in the absence of imams. The majority view is reflected in major treatises on jihad (*kitāb al-jihad*), including Feiz Kāshānī's *Al-Sahāfī*, Sayyid Ali Tabātabā'ī's *Rīyād al-Salikīn*, and Shaykh Muhammad Hasan Najafī's *Jawāhir al-Kalām*. Najafī specifically refers to a hadith by 'Alī b. Musa al-Ridā (the eighth Shi'i imam), which unequivocally prohibits any offensive war against infidels in the absence of the occulted twelfth imam. Feirahī points out that according to the predominant view of the Shi'i majority, even defensive war is limited *only* to situations in which the freedom of Muslims to engage in religious practices and rituals is threatened or when a dominating infidel power threatens their general freedom, residences, and properties.[58]

The question of offensive or defensive war becomes increasingly sensitive in cases where a Muslim nation is caught between a domestic, nominally Muslim, suppressive regime and a threatening disbeliever/non-Muslim power intending to occupy Muslim land. A direct quotation from Najafī, as analyzed by Feirahī, clarifies the Shi'i position:

> The Author of *Jawaher al-Kalam* [Najafī] considers two conditions for defensive jihad: (a) that Muslims are invaded by the infidels, given that the invasion threatens the foundations of Islam, and (b) that it is intended to dominate over the lands of Muslims and results in Muslim slavery, homelessness, and loss of properties. In this situation, it is obligatory for all Muslims, including men and women, the healthy and the ill, the blind and the invalid, etc., to perform jihad in any ways and there is no need for the permission of an imam and for other conditions of the offensive jihad to be met. This perspective is exactly reflected in the *risalat al-'amalīya* [a book of collection of *fatwās*] of the contemporary Shi'i authorities [*marja'-e taqlīd* in Persian].
>
> In his jurisprudential analysis of defensive jihad, the author of *Jawahir* assumes a hypothetical situation in which defensive jihad is forbidden and even considered prohibited [*harām*]. Reference to this jurisprudentially hypothetical situation is significant in this chapter because it has similarities to the present situation of the Shi'as in Iraq and clearly explains the jurisprudential bases of the political behavior of the Iraqi Shi'as and the *ulama* [religious scholars] in their reactions to the Baath regime and the American invaders.
>
> Sheikh Mohammad Hasan Najafī states: "Should jihad not be one of the principles, it is one of the necessities of Shi'ism. Yes, sometimes it is forbidden, and sometimes it is said to be religiously prohibited; if the infidels threatened to politically dominate parts or all of the lands of the Muslims nowadays, but they allowed Muslims to perform their Islamic rituals and did not interfere in their [Muslims'] religious affairs, in this case, jihad would be forbidden or religiously prohibited because doing harm to one's self without religious permission is not allowed. However, this hypothesis, apparently, comes under the prohibition of murder at the time of occultation because it is helping an illegitimate government against a similar one. But, if the infidels intend to eradicate Islam and its rituals as well as abolishing the name of Muhammad and his religion, then, there is no doubt in the obligatory nature of jihad, even if such jihad would necessitate assisting a tyrannical ruler; however, the true intention [of the Muslims in jihad] should be fighting against the eradication of Islam and its rituals by the infidels but not supporting the tyrannical ruler."[59]

Feirahī's case applies to the United States' occupation of Iraq, in the sense that as long as the Iraqi people enjoy full freedom to practise their faith and live freely under occupation, the Shi'i sharī'a does not justify armed struggle against the American occupiers of Iraq.

Regarding the second area, Feirahī maintains that there is no legitimate ground for terrorism in any Shi'i sources. He refers to an authentic Prophetic hadith that unequivocally and unconditionally condemns acts of terrorism: "Faith delimits terrorism; therefore the faithful should never commit terrorism."[60] To this Feirahī replies, "In fact one of the most knowledgeable contemporary Shi'a clerics, Ayatollah Hoseinali Montazerī renowned for many bold and politically risky positions, has reminded Muslims of the significant Shi'i historical precedent against the use of terrorism." In reference to the Karbalā tragedy, Montazerī points out that al-Husayn's emissary in Kūfa, Muslim b. 'Aqīl, had a unique opportunity to use terrorism against Ibn Ziyād, the commander of forces against al-Husayn. If realized, however, such an act could have changed the fate of Karbalā and al-Husayn in 679. The opportunity was deliberately missed by Ibn 'Aqīl on account of a hadith he had heard from the Prophet prohibiting acts of terror in Islam.[61]

In Feirahī's opinion, suicide attack, called *istishhād* in modern literature, is without precedent in sharī'a. In essence, he argues, modern Shi'i jurists find little justification for this act, as it involves not only the act of suicide, which is forbidden in sharī'a, but also committing blind, indiscriminate terror.[62]

As for treachery (*ghadr*), Feirahī references a hadith by al-Sādiq that reads, "Muslims may neither resort to perfidy, nor order an act of treachery, nor support in war those who commit treachery."[63] In Feirahī's opinion, this position implies that the ban against a "unilateral breach of contract" (an accurate translation of *ghadr*) is absolute in Islamic sharī'a and cannot change in war or peace. Muslims, therefore, may not resort to any act in contravention to the bilateral or international treaties accepted and signed by their respective governments.[64] In a separate article, Feirahī mentions the following rules in order of importance: the primacy of peace; the necessity of serious effort to restore peace; and the prohibition of offensive war in the absence of an infallible imam. These rules also ban the initiation of battle in the war field; cursing the enemy during battle; the use of weapons of indiscriminate killing; attacks on monks and monasteries; attacks against women, children, and the elderly; beating women in battle; the destruction of buildings; killing of animals and trees; terrorism (*fatk* in Arabic); the unilateral breach of bilateral or multilateral contracts; in addition, these rules emphasize the protection of prisoners of war and amnesty for ambassadors and emissaries.[65] Feirahī's short article was prepared to provide succinct answers for the mounting curiosity of both the Iranian public and students regarding Islam's position on war. It reflects on the fact that Iran's postwar generation increasingly questioned the merits of war as a means of advancing ideological agendas. The endless bloodshed in Iraq, often the result of suicide bombings, has also added to the public's outrage and questioning. It is important to note that Feirahī's cross-disciplinary approach to the ethics of war and peace, combined with his active and continuous dialogue with both seminarian and university students, has prompted him to raise bold questions on the relation between religion and violence. During a round table discussion on "Salafism" sponsored by the *Great Islamic Encyclopedia*, Feirahī suggested a need for serious enquiry into what he called "the criminalization of religion," that is, a need to study how religion can be abused and turned into an instrument of crime by psychopaths and criminals.[66]

A Humanistic Revision of the Laws of War

Ayatollah Hoseinali Montazerī ranks among the major grand ayatollahs in Iran who have gained respect for boldly criticizing official positions and practices. In the most important modern treatise on the theory of the guardianship of jurisconsult (*wilāyat-e faqīh*), published in Iran before the 1979 Islamic Revolution, Montazerī dedicates a full chapter to jihad and defence.[67] In that particular chapter, he notes in an apologetic tone that, although Shi'i jurists have divided the topic of jihad into two subtopics of offensive (*ebtedā'ī*) and defensive (*defā'ī*), jihad in all cases should be considered a defensive measure. Similar to Motahharī's proposals, the chapter stresses that jihad exists primarily as an institution to protect human rights, humanist values, and state security. Within this general definition, Montazerī also includes preventive wars against potential aggressors within the category of legitimate jihad.[68]

In the spirit of the above-mentioned definition of jihad, Montazerī, who was one of the leaders of Iran's 1979 Revolution, became a voice of political threat against leaders of Iran's neighbouring countries, especially in the early days of the revolution. He supported continuing the war with Iraq after 1982, which he later explained away by claiming that the position was forced on him because he was duty-bound to support Ayatollah Khomeini's policies. Long after the end of the Iran-Iraq War, and in a rather unprecedented tone of self-criticism, he stated, "I remember that in one of my speeches on the anniversary of Revolution, I confessed that we have committed many mistakes for which we need to make repentance." During the war, Montazerī asserted, "We chanted many improper slogans, and I, myself, was among those who, in the name of revolution, caused tension in our relations with other countries." This political and legal turning point is well reflected in Montazerī's juridical emphasis on the sanctity of respecting international treaties, including diplomatic immunity.[69] After he was dismissed from his official position in 1989, Montazerī emphasized that he was originally against continuing the Iran-Iraq War after 1982 and insisted that he was sorry that Iran rejected and left unheeded so many other countries' peace mediations. He then stipulated the "primacy of peace" as a principle in his legal writings.[70]

In the latter part of his political life, Montazerī became a staunch promoter of peaceful, friendly relations with non-Muslim countries.[71] In speaking about war, he also paid attention to right conduct in war (*jus in bello*), making specific references to the rights of prisoners of war, as well as to their right to be freed soon after war's termination.[72] The above examples demonstrate how Montazerī's involvement in revolution and war caused a major theoretical transformation in his views on war and jihad. He has formally apologized for his previous radical interventionist positions. More importantly, he has stressed that decisions on national matters of war and peace are of a consultative nature and subject to the views and votes of the public, rather than solely to the discretion of the supreme leader.[73] Such a view clears the institution of jihad from any notions of being a preordained, divine order accessible only to authorities of religious emulation (*marāje'-e taqlīd* in Persian).

It is public knowledge in Iran that Montazerī's critical position on Iran's war policies contributed to his dismissal from Iran's theocracy. The sharp division between him and Ayatollah Khomeini over war was highlighted by Iran's former prosecutor general Ayatollah Mūsavī Tabrīzī. In a published interview, Tabrīzī states that only thirteen days before Ayatollah Khomeini accepted a ceasefire between Iran and Iraq, Ayatollah Montazerī had encouraged the Iranian leader to do so but was only met with a firm rejection. Ayatollah Khomeini told Montazerī that "any doubts about the war [its legitimacy] is tantamount to treachery against the Apostle of God."[74] Tabrīzī adds that a few days after this exchange, two letters – one from the commander of the Revolutionary Guards, Mohsen Rezā'ī, and one from then Prime Minister Mir Hossein Mousavī – informed Ayatollah Khomeini about facts and figures of war and the state's precarious economy. Both reports conveyed, in essence, that the country's bankrupt economy and costly war could not continue if based on rational and conventional calculations. Both reports were saying implicitly that, between accepting a ceasefire with Iraq and continuing a war that was tantamount to collective martyrdom on a national scale, there was no other option. It was at this juncture that Ayatollah Khomeini accepted a ceasefire with Iraq and stated that the offered alternative was nothing more than lip service.[75] Later on, it was revealed that Rafsanjani, then the Iranian commander of war, did not see any possibility of a military victory and encouraged the writing of the aforementioned letters as a means of getting Ayatollah Khomeini's consent in accepting a ceasefire.

In light of the above events, the remaining question is what it was within the system that prevented or hampered informing Ayatollah Khomeini about the war's realities, including a mounting international consensus against Iran's war strategy. Why did he not pay attention to the possibly valid grounds of Ayatollah Montazerī's request for peace? Montazerī's response to these questions was that Ayatollah Khomeini's charismatic leadership and the incorrect, absolutist interpretation of the "guardianship of jurisconsult" (*wilāyat-e faqīh*) as the foundation of the Iranian political structure prevented a rational flow of critical thought regarding Iran's state affairs. As a result, and as the case of Ayatollah Montazerī's political dismissal proved, no one among the rank and file of the country dared to question the state's war policies without risking their own political status.[76]

At a theoretical level, Ayatollah Montazerī's arguments against prolonging the Iran-Iraq War were no different than questioning an authoritarian, nonconsultative system of decision making on the legitimacy of the continuation of war (*jus ad bellum*). Such a practice, in Montazerī's view, was not only incompatible with the tradition of the Prophet Muhammad, who always consulted with his companions on matters of war, but it also defied the sense of conventional reason, recognized as an important foundation of Shi'i law. "The consultative nature of decision making on war in Islam," as Montazerī has put it, by implication causes a theoretical tension with the Shi'i juristic majority view that permits offensive war only under the rule of an infallible imam. Perhaps this very tension prompted Montazerī to reject the legitimacy of any unprovoked offensive war in Islam. However, this significant contribution to the field of just-war theory was not Montazerī's most important juristic contribution; rather, his introduction of apology and forgiveness into politics represented a more novel, significant, and unprecedented advance in the history of Iranian and Shi'a clerical politics.

A Criticism of Reading Islam's Early History through War Narratives

This chapter explored above how Mohaqqeq Dāmād tried, in his first book, to present a universalist, rationalist, and semiapologist account of the ethics of war in Islam.[77] A few years later, however, he published some very bold articles in Persian; in which he appeared as an unequivocally firm critic of some Shi'i jurisprudential positions on the legitimacy of war (*jus ad bellum*). In these articles, Mohaqqeq Dāmād presents strong evidence supporting the illegitimacy of the notion of a "sacred war" within the framework of Islam; such evidence includes a reminder to his Persian readers that all wars waged against the first and third Shi'i imams were waged illegitimately and wrongly justified as "sacred" by their Muslim enemies.[78] He further argues against the so-called "sacred war," or pseudojihad, as it was the illegitimate institution used by the Umayyads to justify their expansionist wars; thus, Mohaqqeq Dāmād concludes, the abuse of jihad has inflicted the worst damage to Islam.[79]

Mohaqqeq Dāmād also takes aim at some of the most prominent Shi'i scholars for their support of offensive campaigns, including Shaykh Tūsī, Shahīd Thānī, and the senior contemporary authority Ayatollah Abulqāsim Kho'ī.[80] He argues for the primacy of peace in Islam, which he believes to be firmly established by the Qur'ānic systematic advice imparted to the Prophet, effectively denying him any authority to use force in the name of religious conversion. He emphatically rejects the binary political perspective held by some classical Muslim jurists who viewed the world as divided into the two realms of *dār al-Islam* (the abode of Islam) and *dār al-harb* (the abode of war).[81] This view, Mohaqqeq Dāmād believes, overlooks the Qur'ān's nonauthoritarian posture on conversion, as well as the Prophet's tradition of religious tolerance. Significantly, Mohaqqeq Dāmād here avoids any apologetic stance in reviewing the works of his Shi'i predecessors, a clear sign of the authentic use of reason as one of the four standard sources of Shi'i jurisprudence.

Mohaqqeq Dāmād's bold criticism of classical Shi'i literature on the ethics of war resonates with the work of Saber Adāk. Adāk goes a step further than Mohaqqeq Dāmād in his criticism of the traditional view of war in Muslim cultures by also examining all primary sources related to early Muslim wars. He even goes so far as to criticize the militarization of the Prophet Mohammad's biography, written by the famous biographer Ibn Hishām. Adāk points out that, through a dominant classical approach, the "biographies of the Prophet [*sīra*s], specifically narratives about his life after emigration to Medina, have been presented through the prism of war, thus naming phases of his life as *al-Maghāzī* [the Prophetic wars]"; this misperception, Adāk notes, is testified in the works of biographers, such as al-Wāqidī.[82] Such an approach, in Adāk's view, leaves readers with the impression that the Prophet's most important accomplishments were these wars.

Adāk underscores the fact that the aggregate time the Prophet spent in wars all together amounts to less than a year of his decade-long residence in Medina. Why then, Adāk asks, should the whole life of the Prophet be viewed in the framework of military campaigns?[83] He further asserts that a systematic trend of hadith forgery exaggerating the war campaigns, under the Umayyad dynasty and according to Arab cultural tastes, contributed to the emergence of a whole genre of war-based biographies. These biographies, in turn, legitimized the illegitimate, as was the case with the Umayyads' expansionist ambitions. Adāk stresses that these war-based biographies eventually produced biased historical accounts even of the Prophet's famous peace treaty, al-Hudaybiyya, which was adapted to be called the “al-Hudaybiyya military campaign” (*ghazwa al-hudaybīya*).[84] Adāk adds that governance and power politics were not essential to the Prophet; rather, these activities were residual effects resulting from his mission.[85] The Prophet faced such severe sanctions, boycotts, conspiracies, and the threat of being expelled that he had to resort to force only to protect the intellectual liberty of early Muslim society.[86] Adāk highlights that not a single credible biographer has detailed reports of the Prophet rejecting peace initiatives or breaching contracts signed – not even in relation to his staunchest enemies.[87]

The tragic encounter between Medina’s Muslims and one of its Jewish communities, known as Banī Qurayza, prompted Adāk to question the alleged carnage dooming the community’s fate. According to early Muslim biographers like Ibn Hishām, leaders of this tribe allied themselves with Arab polytheist tribes before attacking Medina. This alliance was in direct contravention to the peace treaty that they had made earlier with the Prophet. The Banī Qurayza’s penalty was subject to an arbitration that was delegated to one of the tribe’s own former members who had converted to Islam (Mu‘ādh b. Jabal), resulting in a verdict that asked for the execution of all Jewish males. Various sources have estimated that anywhere between four hundred and one thousand males were executed. Adāk challenges these reports and highlights their inconsistencies, maintaining that the Umayyad and Abbasid dynasties most likely exaggerated, if not concocted, these stories to justify their violent policies, which were imperative for the two dynasties to preserve their despotic regimes. Adāk suggests there could be an alternate scenario wherein later Jewish sources created the narrative to colour Islam as violent and bloodthirsty, while setting up a courageous image for the Banī Qurayza.[88] Adāk asks, How is it possible, as many narrators of the story have claimed, for anyone to believe that some seven hundred people were detained at the house of one the Prophet’s companions? How and why, as the composers of the story claim, would Islam’s Prophet accept an arbitration and verdict based on Jewish tradition? Why, he further muses, would the Prophet have asked only one or two people, as the biographers have reported, to carry out all executions? And why would mass executions be carried out in the middle of a market and in the presence of crowds? Adāk concludes, based on the fact that the Prophet never in his life engaged in acts of vengeful violence, even against the Meccan polytheists who fought him for so many years, that the story was totally fabricated or, at best, heavily exaggerated.[89] Adāk strongly criticizes Muslim biographers of the Prophet for profiling him within the framework of war, for overembellishing the war narratives, and for neglecting the inconsistencies in their reports. He concludes that all Prophetic military campaigns were either defensive or preemptive and waged with the single aim of preserving the right of early Muslim society to practise freely and to undertake invitation for religious conversion. He adds that during his lifetime the Prophet showed only tolerance and respect to monotheists and hypocrites alike. Clashes with Medina's Jewish tribes, Adāk stresses, had nothing to do with faith but were in fact a result of breached contracts and military conspiracies perpetrated by the latter group; thus, Adāk notes, the interfaith clashes, while situational, historical, and accidental, were certainly not theological.[90] Compared with scholars like Motahharī and Tabātabā'ī, both of whom came close to justifying primary and offensive ideological wars as a way to secure human rights, Adāk denies the legitimacy of any offensive war. He is a refreshing voice among modern Iranian scholars, who often criticize the entire genre of early Prophetic biographies for its theoretically biased approach, as well as for its disproportional fascination with military campaigns. This war-prone historiography, in Adāk's view, is responsible for overshadowing other qualities of early Muslim society.

Hasan Yousufī Ashkevarī, a clerical voice for reform on many jurisprudential grounds, takes an even bolder step in his view on jihad by criticizing jihad's inclusion among the extended list of pillars in the traditional juridical classification of the pillars of Islam.[91] He suggests that this notion has lost its function in modern life and must be removed from the list of pillars in new jurisprudence scholarships. Ashkevarī argues that because the legitimacy of defence is self-evident in modern society, there is no need to consider it a pillar of Islam. Otherwise, he warns, jihad's function advances beyond defence and becomes an instrument in expansionist wars. Ashkevarī maintains that jihad was included in the list of pillars during the second and third Muslim centuries because, like so many other tribal customs adopted from tribal Arab societies within the framework of sharī'a, armed jihad also entered jurisprudential thoughts with a legitimate, if not circumstantial, function for its time. But just as slavery became an obsolete institution in our time, expansionist wars have also lost legitimacy.[92]

An increasing number of like-minded Shi'i scholars and authors on the ethics of war and peace are emerging with many elaborate and erudite approaches and perspectives. Among them Abdolmajīd Soodmandī, Fāzel Meybodi, Seyyed Mohammad Saqafī, and Mohammad Esfandīārī stand out, all with jurisprudential credibility. In his short treatise titled *War and Peace in Islam: A Critical Review of Shi'i Jurist Perspectives in the Mirror of the Qur'ān and Tradition,* Soodmandī argues that for various historical and political reasons a great number of Shi'i jurists have conceptually accepted offensive wars under the authority of an infallible imam, thus rendering the concept of permanent peace with non-Muslims theoretically impossible. He examines a number of methodologically juristic approaches to solve this problem conceptually, but the final and more stable solution, he argues, would be to accept the concept of offensive war as irreconcilable with the Qur'ān and Prophetic traditions.[93] In the end, Soodmandī's final and more reliable solution is to reach a compromise between the bulk of Shi'i traditional jurisprudence on war and peace and a new ethical exegesis of the Qur'ān and Prophetic traditions in order to accommodate the paradigms and parameters of modern international relations based on nation states. He finds a shift in the moral approach to war far easier than a jurisprudential excercise in this field.

Meybodī argues that the only acceptable war in Islam is one that enforces the rule of law rather than a specific belief system. He argues that all of the Qur'ānic sword verses belong to such a context, and disbelief is never a cause in any of the Prophetic wars. The dichotomy of *dār al-Islam* and *dār al-kufr*, Meybodī argues, is a completely obsolete and irrelevant concept in the age of nation states. Meybodī categorically rejects the concept of the sacredness of martyrdom: "Human beings," he stresses, "have come for life and peace"; as proof, he argues emphatically, "We do not have a single case for the participation of an infallible imam in an offensive war."[94]

In the same spirit, Saqafī discusses all of the letters that Prophet Mohammad wrote to various contemporary rulers of his time, inviting them to Islam. "None of these short letters," Saqafī argues, "demonstrates a threat to war."[95]

Mainstream Iranian clerical scholars such as Eskandarī, Mohaqqeq Dāmād, Feirahī, Adāk, Ashkevarī, Soodmandī, Meybodī, and other like-minded scholars may have asked to go too far in initiating a major jurisprudential overhaul of Shi'i Islamic traditions and rules. However, their attempts certainly represent genuine exercises in bold and independent juristic reasoning (*ijtihād*), promising the emergence of modern-day Shi'i jurisprudence.

Conclusion

By the time the Revolution erupted and achieved success in February 1979, Shi'i theology and Qur'anic exegesis of jihad had begun to undergo a robust process of rethinking and reconceptualization. However, jihad had yet to face another epistemological and functional challenge and turning point only a year later. With revolutionary emotionalism and idealism still culminating in Iran, Iraq invaded. The outbreak of one of the longest wars in modern history, combined with the political isolation of Iran resulting from its neighbours' deep fear of the regional spread of revolution, pushed Iran into an impossible situation. Moreover, a full-fledged theocracy was now in charge; the clerics needed to make hard decisions about the details of war, foreign policy, and the state's economy by themselves. All of these factors collectively tested jihad in both theoretical and practical senses unprecedented in Shi'i political history.

Direct clerical involvement in the revolution, followed by eight long years of war with Iraq, effectively changed and reshaped the way Shi'i jurists thought about the ethics of war, and the ethics in war and postwar. Various scholars who were politically active during the 1979 Revolution, in the Iran-Iraq War, and in postwar peacemaking developments (such as Montazerī, Sālehī-Najafābādī, Mohaqqeq Dāmād, Eskandarī, Feitahī, Kadivar, Adāk, and Ashkevarī) played significant roles in facilitating the monumental transition in the Shi'i ethical view and reconceptualization of war and peace. These scholars have produced new concepts and arguments encompassing several important aspects of the subject matter. First, although their field of study is, in theory, limited to law and jurisprudence, they managed to take a predominantly ethical stance in their jurisprudential and moral analyses. They remained conscious of how various sociopolitical and historical situations, as well as how the structures of various political systems, may have adversely influenced the views of Muslim jurists throughout history. These scholars also closely observed the devastating results of the Iran-Iraq War and were well aware of the bitter realities of war, which extended beyond superficial state propaganda and emotional, fantastical, and epical evaluations of war and martyrdom. These shared experiences moved them to use genuine *ijtihād* to transform the traditional laws of war into a more universally justifiable and objective-based system of ethics. They did this without severing the relationship between tradition and the necessities of modern life; this factor remained especially important because if modern jurists wanted their evolving views of religious laws to influence the status quo, the lay public had to be swayed, especially in an era when traditions held strong, popular appeal. Many of the authors discussed in this chapter presented their views within the scholarly framework of tradition, rather than outside of it.

Another factor assisting the spread of this new critical thinking is related in part to a shared rationalist Mu'tazilī theology adopted by Shi'ism during its early formation. Discerning moral rights from wrongs as a rational exercise provides modern Shi'i thinkers with a great theological tool, not only in avoiding domestic fundamentalism but also in criticizing the global fundamentalism presently impeding Muslim reform and advancement.

Sālehī-Najafābādī has employed *ijtihād* in its deepest sense and thus felt free to criticize the well-established, traditional premises of war jurisprudence without reservation. Through a morally consequentialist perspective, Montazerī applied hard lessons learned from the 1979 Revolution and the Iran-Iraq War to revise many of his previous legal positions, as well criticize the very political system he had helped create. Montazerī should also be credited for his pioneering role in introducing apology and forgiveness into Shi'i politics and jurisprudence. A new generation of jurists, including Feirahī, Adāk, and Soodmandī, has read political history and the history of law while remaining conscious of how the medieval authoritarianism of political systems has influenced their contemporary jurisprudents and the need for overhauling this jurisprudence.

Mohaqqeq Dāmād and Eskandarī, despite their different approaches to the ethics of war, focus on one common point: they both suggest that even if a war waged is defensively, the rights of individuals and noncombatants should not be overlooked. This idea contradicts a significantly negative attribute of war in the annals of history, wherein a spirit of collective heroism, romanticism, and idealism, or, in short, triumphalist aspirations insensitive to the rights of the individual, has prevailed. War cultures, whether traditional or modern, are indifferent to the number killed or injured, an attitude that clearly contradicts the famous Qur'ānic view that one equals all and the notion that "if one kills one person without justification, it is as if he has killed all mankind" (5:32).

Unlike their predecessors, all of the authors mentioned in this chapter discuss both *jus ad bellum* and *jus in bello* systematically and with methodological consistency. This is a great achievement with enormous potential to open constructive discourse between Muslim scholars of war and peace and their international and Western counterparts.

In his bold criticism of traditional historiography, Adāk is perhaps addressing his contemporary Iranian compatriots, whose involvement in an eight-year war pushed many towards a more militant world view. He reminds his readers that none should fall into the trap of engaging in violence out of loyalty to a sacred history or due to a tribal misperception that warring is the most heroic way of life. If over two decades after the end of the Iran-Iraq War a few Iranian militants continue to lament the triumph of peace and diplomacy over military might, then scholars like Mohaqqeq Dāmād, Adāk, Ashkevarī, Meybodī, and Saqafī have a key audience in serious need of learning that what ultimately prevails in shaping a society is the power of culture – not the culture of power.

8 Terrorism and Shi'i Theologies of Martyrdom, Nonviolence, and Forgiveness

It is far easier to fight for principles than to live up to them.

– Alfred Adler

An excess of morality may be more dangerous and more harmful than any moral deficit.

– Anthony Coates[1]

Violence justified under religious context is probably as old as religion itself. The pagan idea that gods' sentiments can be manipulated by offering human or animal sacrifice is ancient. All theologies of violence and sacrifice have one philosophical premise: the ultimate test proving one's loyalty to the Divine is voluntary physical harm to one's own body or to those of others. This anthropomorphistic theology, which was supposed to end after God stopped Abraham from sacrificing his son for God's sake, unfortunately kept reappearing through extremist tendencies across various religious and pagan traditions.

An exemplary case for such religious violence appeared in the theology of active and systematic martyrdom among ancient Christian Donatists. "Being a martyr," Debra Kelly explains, "was just one of the things that they aspired to. Known for their tendency to gravitate toward extreme violence, members of the sect carried massive clubs that they called Israelites. Those that were completely ready to become martyrs would attack people on the streets with the goal of forcing these random people to fight back and to kill them, fulfilling a lifelong goal of martyrdom. It was the ultimate way into heaven, after all, and it was considered especially good if the person doing the killing was a member of the church or any variety of town official."[2] The self-inflicted carnage did not stop there for this sect and culminated in voluntary drowning or jumping from mountain cliffs. Perhaps it never crossed their minds that the unnecessary destruction of what God calls in the Qur'ān his masterpiece (human being)[3] could be the most impious and blasphemous act among all crimes.

Because one does not possess his/her body in the Islamic world view, suicide and terror have the same status in Islamic jurisprudence across all denominations. The German journalist Jurgen Todenhofer has rightly said, "Terrorism has as much to do with Islam as rape has to do with love."[4] But the frequency of Muslim suicidal terror in current world politics has made it easy for many Western observers to think of Islam as a legitimizer of violence. Some Western scholars, such as Bernard Lewis and Michael Walzer, explain the cause of Muslim terrorism, according to Talal Asad, as "the failure of Muslim countries to modernize, a failure that explains the scapegoating of the United States and Israel by Muslim immigrants in Western countries."[5]

For mainstream Muslims, this phenomenon appears heretical, with little background in Islamic tradition. The suicidal carnage, however, practised beyond any specific political border and moral order, reaching a very high level of brutality as exemplified in monumental cases of mass terror by Daesh in Mosul,[6] Peshawar,[7] Nigeria,[8] Paris,[9] Lybia,[10] and Ankara,[11] is an undeniably soul-shaking, modern reality. What adds to the complexity and irony of the matter is the fact that Muslim acts of suicidal terror are increasingly taking more Muslim lives than non-Muslim. In other words, most current Muslim suicidal acts are callous, cruel, thoughtless, and large-scale self-destruction in more than one dimension. For precisely this very reason, it is hardly convincing to frame this carnage as a Muslim reaction to non-Islam or to modernity, as Lewis and Walzer believe.

Although the ideological and institutional father of Muslim suicidal terror is al-Quaeda, with roots in Saudi Wahhabism, acts of mass terror by Muslims reached their peak in modern Middle East history with Daesh (ISIS) in Iraq and Syria. In a rather short time, Daesh – itself a more radical offshoot of al-Quaeda – left such a high score of mass terror that its father (al-Quaeda) or sister (Taliban) organizations were made to look moderate in comparison. The only way for a mainstream Muslim theologian to imagine reconciliation between the strictly forbidden act of suicidal mass terror, which is categorically condemned in traditional Islamic sharī'a, and its current, fashionable practice by the so-called jihadist-salafis is to consider the contemporary loose and arbitrary definitions of jihad and martyrdom.

Terror and suicide are strictly and unconditionally forbidden according to Shi'i scholars.[12] Legally speaking, any act of suicide is tantamount to homicide, and suicide mass terror, therefore, is a compound crime locked in an unsolvable matrix of legal and moral problems. As noted above in the review of

Ayatollah Montazerī's legal perspectives on human rights, the primary Shi'i antiterror narrative has firmly established that terror is forbidden, even when a possible single act of such a nature against Ibn Ziyād could have prevented the tragedy of Karbalā altogether;[13] but an unequivocal Prophetic hadith rejecting terror (*fatk*) prohibited al-Husayn's emissary, Ibn Aqīl, in Kūfa from using the opportunity for a preemptive ambush against Ibn Ziyād, who later on martyred al-Husayn. To a scholar of Shi'i law, this narrative speaks volumes about the categorical prohibition of suicidal terror (*istishhād*). But judgment about the legitimacy or illegitimacy of terror becomes complicated, as the conceptual borders between terror, martyrdom, and punitive violence tend to be vague and murky.

Presently, more often than not, acts of suicidal terror are presented as active martyrdom and/or legitimate punishment of the political enemy. The problem in Iran, however, arose from a different angle in her recent postrevolution history: the need for extensive manpower during the very long Iran-Iraq War forced Iranian clerical authorities to broaden the definition and the utilization of martyrdom. Importantly, as shall be discussed below, the comparatively short period of governmental sponsorship for and expansive definition of martyrdom did not last long, as postwar Shi'i theologians in Iran did not waste much time in rejecting any notion of martyrdom as an authentic means for political agendas.

In this chapter, I will discuss how the Iranian Revolution and war with Iraq brought a few traditional theories of Shi'i martyrdom under scrutiny by critical scholarship. I will argue that this scholarship, combined with the effects of the anti-Shi'a terrorism by Daesh and the Taliban, have helped to reframe the modern Shi'i view of martyrdom alongside a quietist-rationalistic position. Such a position, as noted by David Cook, views martyrdom within the moral framework of guilt and grief rather than as an institution that, in addition to serving political agendas, can facilitate free and shortcut flights to paradise.[14]

War and the Political Theology of Martyrdom

Comparatively little time elapsed between the February 1979 Revolution in Iran and the beginning of the eight-year-long Iran-Iraq War (both countries having a majority Shi'i population) in September 1980. The revolutionary zeal had not yet subsided when the war broke out. As a result, societal excitement, fed by a newly revived spirit of jihad and martyrdom, was readily redirected towards the institution of war. War kept the fire of the revolution alive; revolutionary enthusiasm and ideological sentiments fuelled triumphalist aspirations for the war. Western powers and the UN Security Council kept supporting Iraq.

The three sides of the equation fed each other, causing the prolongation of the war and causing failures in a number of external and domestic peace initiatives. Excited by the miraculous victory in toppling what was widely perceived as one of the most stable regimes in the region (the Pahlavis), the newly born Islamic Republic could not settle for anything less than exporting its revolution at least to the neighbouring region. This highly idealistic and romantic perspective could easily assimilate and employ concepts of a liberating jihad, and excite aspirations for a universal moral mission as a plan for ideological expansion. The missionary view of jihad had been welcomed previously by Motahharī, Sharī'atī, and other like-minded scholars and political activists who were pressed by the challenges of the rival Iranian Marxists for a competing ideological and universal program. The challenges of war, the international isolation of Iran after the hostage crisis, the early chaotic domestic politics resulting from the revolution, and the displacement of the ruling class all provided an even stronger incentive to rally the support of the Iranian youth. As it did indeed prove, a theology of necessary sacrifice and martyrdom was instrumental in mobilizing tens of thousands of young (including minor) volunteer fighters towards the war fronts. It is therefore important to discuss the different versions of this martyr theology and their relevance to revolution and war in Iran's modern history.

In order to begin an examination of the wide spectrum of Shi'i martyrology, one needs to examine various versions of a Shi'i master narrative: the Karbalā and al-Husayn's tragedy. An ongoing controversy continues among Shi'i scholars about al-Husayn's ultimate motive in rising up against Yazīd. The most enduring traditional concept, held by the majority of (Twelver) Shi'a, maintains that al-Husayn's move was based on the Islamic principle of "commanding the right and prohibiting the wrong," and served no political ambitions.

The second view, which has gained popularity since the thirteenth century, believes that al-Husayn knew that he would be martyred long before his actual confrontation with Yazīd and therefore went to Kūfa seeking his preordained martyrdom, which was supposed to provide an universal example for Islam. Morteză Askarī, a contemporary Shi'i scholar who has produced influential scholarship on the history and the theology of Karbalā, argues that the oath of allegiance in Islam (*bay'a*) is not always used necessarily for political power. The allegiance, called the first *'aqaba'* between the Prophet and some of his companions, for instance, encouraged conversions to Islam rather than serving political purposes.[15] Therefore, Askarī denies that the oath of allegiance given to al-Husayn by the Kūfans (who invited him for leadership) had established grounds for a power-seeking, political move on his part. The story revolves around al-Husayn, who was invited by political dissidents in Kūfa – the capital city of al-Husayn's father, 'Alī b. Abī Tālib, and a garrison city in Iraq – to lead the struggle against Yazīd.[16] However, once al-Husayn began his journey, many of the Kūfan inviters backed down, leaving the imam and his few companions as victims of a historic carnage in Karbalā. Askarī, however, believes that al-Husayn's intention was not to seek political rule; he knew in advance that this was a predestined and role-modeling occasion for martyrdom, which he embraced wholeheartedly and as a divine duty. This line of thought, of course, sounds familiar to Christology experts, who find close similarities between al-Husayn's conscious and deliberate martyrdom and that of Jesus Christ.

The third view is found in Sālehī-Najafābādī's highly controversial book *Shahīd-e jāvīd* (The immortal martyr). According to his perspective, al-Husayn actually did seek to overthrow Yazīd and seize political rule over the universal Muslim community, especially given the initial support of and invitation from the Kūfan residents.[17] Sālehī-Najafābādī rejects the conventional Shi'i view that al-Husayn's challenge against the Umayyads lacked a political motive and was solely a moral campaign against Yazīd's corrupt rule; in essence, the traditional position maintains that al-Husayn's motive, founded on a moral duty, served by using martyrdom as an effective and essential institution of political protest. Sālehī-Najafābādī argues against the depoliticization of the Karbalā tragedy and denies that al-Husayn had advance knowledge about the exact timing of his martyrdom, though he did know of its eventuality.

This very last point stirred a clerical uproar against Sālehī-Najafābādī's thesis in the heart of Iran's central seminarian city of Qom, when his book was published a few years before the Iranian Revolution. The standard view is that all twelve Shi'i imams were in possession of a divine knowledge (*'elm-e ladunnī*) about the timing and minutiae of the entirety of mundane and spiritual life. In fact, Sālehī-Najafābādī's thesis necessitated a modification in the traditional theory of knowledge held by imams, from a detailed to a more general level of knowledge; without this modification, the main point, namely al-Husayn's decision to seek the leadership of the Muslim community (*umma*), would have lost its foundation, solely because he should have known that he would not be successful.

In Sālehī-Najafābādī's opinion, in contrast to the view commonly held by the Shi'i public, al-Husayn's uprising was not a response to a predetermined divine call for his martyrdom; rather, Sālehī-Najafābādī maintains that once al-Husayn's military strategy against Yazīd failed, he was seeking an honourable truce, and only in the last stage of his encounter did martyrdom become an *imposed* alternative.[18] Contrary to Shi'i popular opinion, Sālehī-Najafābādī believes that the Muslim world did not benefit from al-Husayn's martyrdom; the martyrdom of the third imam, he argues, resulted in a century of corrupt Umayyad rule.[19] In other words, for Sālehī-Najafābādī, a living al-Husayn served the expediencies of the Muslim community (*umma*) far better than a martyred one. Through such a line of reasoning, Sālehī-Najafābādī initiates a very bold criticism of traditional Shi‘i sacred history, which holds implications also for Shi‘i eschatology according to which the occult twelfth imam will appear at the end of time to bring justice to al-Husayn's case.

By implication, Sālehī-Najafābādī rejects all forms of suicidal ventures and does not believe they can be justified under the rubric of "martyrdom." A just war, in his view, must be based on a rational calculation and a reasonable possibility of victory.[20] This view as stipulated in traditional Islamic laws of war resonates with a principle in modern just-war theory.[21] He also denies that the political leadership of the Shi‘i imams was divinely preordained; instead, he suggests that any legitimate political leadership (with the exception of the Prophet) must be based on popular will and by vote. Here, Sālehī-Najafābādī refers to an issue that, for more than three decades after the establishment of the Islamic Republic of Iran, has remained a subject of much theoretical and scholarly controversy, mainly since the official name of the Iranian regime itself, namely the Islamic Republic of Iran, contains the two notions of Islamism and republicanism. The compatibility of these constructs depends on various definitions of democracy and Islamism. The heart of this theoretical controversy in Shi‘i political philosophy hinges on the questions of the source of political authority and legitimacy and whether political leadership is ordained and appointed by God or by the people's vote.[22]

Sālehī-Najafābādī's ideas were considered to be the antithesis of ‘Alī Sharī‘atī's opinion on martyrdom. Both during and after the Islamic Revolution of 1979, Sharī‘atī's view was followed most widely by the Iranian revolutionaries and such underground militant activists in Iran as the Mojahedin Khalq Organization. In an existentialist spirit, Sharī‘atī defined martyrdom as an institution essential to the success of the revolution, stressing that martyrdom is not a passive notion embraced by the martyr when he has no other alternative choice but rather a conscious choice or an effective measure of political and moral protest. In his words, the "martyr enters the battlefield, exactly when the warrior [*mujāhid*] is defeated."[23] Sharī‘atī formulated the same notion in the following highly influential, sensational, and proverbial phrase, which was interpreted by Iran's modern critical scholars as a recipe for a violent and militant mentality: "If you are able, make your enemy die, and if you are not, die yourself." For Sālehī-Najafābādī, however, martyrdom is not to be deliberately sought, and the importance of al-Husayn's actions was not in his martyrdom but in his resolve to challenge a corrupt political regime.

Sharī‘atī agrees with Sālehī-Najafābādī in so far as he stresses the obligation of al-Husayn to seek a regime change; however, he disagrees with Sālehī-Najafābādī on the nature and significance of martyrdom. In Sharī‘ati's view, martyrdom is an active and existential institution substantially different from the passive Sufi or Christian concepts of martyrdom. Sālehī-Najafābādī's political activist perspective of al-Husayn's episode was welcomed by Ayatollah Khomeini's close associates, as well as by advocates of Ayatollahs Montazerī and Meshkīnī. The Iranian revolutionary clerical leadership agreed to support the scholarship of Sālehī-Najafābādī's book (as reflected in the book's introduction).

Challenges of Martyrdom for Political Establishment

After Sālehī-Najafābādī and Sharī'atī had presented their different interpretations of the Shi'i primary martyrdom narrative, Abdolkarim Soroush, one of the top Iranian religious intellectuals of the postrevolutionary era, tackled the question of martyrdom from a new angle. Like Ayatollah Hoseinali Montazerī, Soroush appeared soon after the 1979 Revolution as an ideologue of the new theocracy; however, like Ayatollah Montazerī and Shabestarī, Soroush quickly became one of its staunchest critics.

In a lecture on the subject of martyrdom delivered in Rockville, Maryland in late 2010, Soroush, now a voice for the Iranian dissident diaspora, stated that the Islamic Republic of Iran ironically finds itself at odds with and threatened by the revolutionary theory of al-Husayn's martyrdom. In Soroush's view, Imam Husayn's main goal in leaving his hometown Medina for Mecca, and later for Kūfa, was not to challenge the rule of Yazīd but to avoid casting a vote of allegiance for Yazīd's rule. In the end, he found himself surrounded by enemy forces and had no option but to accept martyrdom. Soroush said in his presentation: "There is no viable hard evidence to prove that Husayn wanted to make a revolution ... This, is a fabricated concept made for revolutionary needs, but has no real connection with Husayn's real incentive ... The 'Āshūrā event [the anniversary of al-Husayn's martyrdom in the Arabic lunar calendar] was expanded beyond its real proportion because Shi'as needed it to make a mythical and identity-making narrative that could also help them to deprive their enemies of reputable identity."[24] In Soroush's opinion, the revolutionary clerics entertained a new approach to al-Husayn's martyrdom that had no precedence before the 1979 Revolution. Soroush stresses that no past prominent Shi'i scholar had used the narrative to mobilize political protest and that such an approach was totally novel, with no trace of it found in Shi'i traditional scholarship. In the past, he contends, the narrative was used to motivate the achievement of spiritual goals; however, the revolutionary era completely changed the function of the martyrdom narrative. Soroush concluded his speech, saying that "with the consolidation of the revolutionary regime, the political establishment would try hard to bring back the traditional reading of the Karbalā tragedy, if only because it [the Islamic Republic of Iran] does not want the risk of keeping martyrdom as an effective instrument of political protest against itself." In short, Soroush maintains that the function of martyrdom, once again, has to change in order to mitigate any risk to the Iranian political establishment. An active and political jihad had been very useful so far, but it could not be a sustainable form of protest in terms of the regime's viability and stability.[25]

More recently, Seyyed Abdolhamid Zīyā'ī, the author of *The Sociology of Ashura Distortions* (*Jame-e shenas-e tahrifat-e ashura*), has offered one of the latest critical approaches to the concept of martyrdom in Iran. He tackles the Karbalā tragedy from a new angle, arguing against the prevalent and popular Shi'i theory of al-Husayn's predetermined martyrdom. According to this traditional perspective, Zīyā'ī points out, the third Shi'i imam had advanced information that he would be martyred in Karbalā. Zīyā'ī contends that, within the framework of Shi'i eschatological and intercession theory, this foreknowledge should have motivated him to welcome the tragedy as the necessary price to pay in order to gain the power of intercession, which could save Shi'i followers in the next life. Such an incentive, Zīyā'ī adds, amounts to the same suicidal action as strictly forbidden by sharī'a law. More importantly, it becomes a case of a logical and moral vicious circle and "self deconstruction," because al-Husayn becomes a victim of wrongdoings in order to save wrongdoers.[26] Such deterministic views of martyrdom, Zīyā'ī believes, were served and promoted by politicians like Mu'āwīya (Yazīd's father) who needed to legitimize their aggressive and corrupt policies. "No wonder," Zīyā'ī comments, "historians such as Ibn 'Asākir in his *History of Damascus* (*Tārīkh-e Damashq*) reports on twenty hadith mentioning how the Prophet and also 'Alī b. Abī Tālib predicted al-Husayn's martyrdom;" he adds, "Do not such predictions make Yazīd innocent?"[27] Zīyā'ī conclusively rejects the intrinsic value of martyrdom and stresses that it provides a value only if it is the last resort to serve a higher necessary moral goal that cannot be attained by any other means.[28] Zīyā'ī's criticism of the problem of martyrdom within its traditional framework of divine predestination could perhaps be summarized by the following conclusion: martyrdom is the last honourable solution, not the first.

Revisiting the Karbalā Tragedy in the Mirror: Daesh's Violent Theology

The celebration of 'Āshūrā, the much-revered annual Shi'i passion festival of Muharram and the commemoration of the martyrdom of Husayn b. 'Alī and his few companions, in 2014 opened a new chapter in Shi'i critique of the theology of violence. During the last three decades after the Iranian Revolution of 1979, the mourning festival had been used systematically by Iranian officials as an occasion to boost a sense of national resistance and protest against Western anti-Iranian economic sanctions and political pressures. Like the martyred imam, Iran had been projected as a victim country that was suffering many political episodes just because she desired to keep her independence from world powers both culturally and politically. What changed this narrative in the fall of 2014 was the emergence of Daesh terror in Syria and Iraq, which did not spare any effort in conducting a systematic policy of Shi'a cleansing in territories under its rule. Since Daesh came to power in the spring of 2014, thousands of Shi'i civilians and military personnel have died through mass executions unprecedented in modern Muslim history in terms of the magnitude and the callous styles of cold-blooded homicide.

The official Iranian propaganda attributing the very creation of Daesh terrorists to Western policies, even if effective in explaining the cause of war, could not settle the account of Daesh's ferocious behaviour. The Iranian public abhorrence of the horrendous mass executions under Daesh brought new questions to the Iranian media not only about the political but also about the theological genesis of violence in the Middle East. The rise of such politically charged theological questions would not simply settle for official references to the historic tendencies of Wahhabism towards violence; the Iranian public, as the following examples demonstrate, is now asking serious questions about the relationship between violence and religion at a broader transsectarian level.

For many Shi'i Iranian scholars, the calendar coincidence of the commemoration of the 'Āshūrā tragedy in the fall of 2014 with the appearance of a peak in violent war crimes by Daesh, the Taliban, and Boko Haram offered the perfect moment to review the tragedy of Karbalā through a new lens beyond the filters of grief and justice. November and December 2014 coincided with the Arabic lunar months of Muharram and Safar that comprise the season for the annual commemorations of the Karbalā tragedy. As usual, on the tenth of Muharram ('Āshūrā), one of the most significant marks in the Shi'i calendar, the ritual of collective mourning for the martyrs of Karbalā was performed in Iran and Iraq with the highest national and interstate participation and attention. The performance of this ritual in 2014, however, differed significantly from the regular annual processions: in the wake of Daesh's anti-Shi'i violence and massacres, the Iranian and the Iraq mourners transformed both occasions of 'Āshūrā and also 'Arba'een (the fortieth day of the tragedy) into a national-sectarian showdown against Daesh.

The political protest and demonstration reached its zenith on 'Arba'een, when governmental sources in both Iran and Iraq claimed that some seventeen million pilgrims marched by foot from various cities towards al-Husayn's shrine in Karbalā. There is no question that the official estimations on both sides of the historic march on 11 December 2014 were highly exaggerated, but even the lowest estimates spoke volumes about the historic event, which signified a surge in the transnational sense of Shi'i identity and solidarity. What prompted such a large and robust expression of identity was well attested by one of the pilgrims interviewed by a reporter: "This is the biggest," Aqil al-Turaihi said, "It's exceptional because the pilgrims consider this as an act of defiance in the face of the terrorist gangs of Daesh."[29] What al-Turaihi is addressing in simple words is that the multimillion-people Shi'i march was a protest against an unjust war and massive violence that breaches all moral codes of war in the East and West. More than anything else, it was a mass expression of abhorrence against violence. It was the most unprecedented style of collective commemoration of the Karbalā carnage that had ever taken place between 680 and 2014.The popular million-people march was not the only Shi'i reaction to the Daesh phenomenon. On an intellectual level, the occasion also prompted a chain reaction among Iranian theologians to discuss various aspects of the Karbalā tragedy and martyrology. Just like the popular rituals, the tone and essence of the intellectual contributions in 2014 also made an unusual difference compared with those of previous years: the focal point of intellectual attentions, adversely impressed by Daesh's systematic violence, was to argue that the martyrdom of al-Husayn and his followers in Karbalā was a tragedy imposed on them rather than embraced by them in a show of heroism or sacrificial pietism.

This new, fresh Iranian scholarship on martyrology not surprisingly opted to present the most nonviolent political and moral interpretation of jihad and martyrdom produced after the Iranian Revolution. Compared to the official theology of active martyrdom useful during the 1979 Revolution and the 1980–8 Iran-Iraq War, these freshly produced perspectives did not aim to promote martyrdom but indeed to condemn all violent jihadism, including acts sponsored by Daesh. Among many other Iranian scholars inside and outside of Iran, Mostafā Malekīān, Abdolkarim Soroush, Mohammad Mojtahed-Shabestarī, Mohsen Kadivar, Abdolali Bāzargān, Mohammad Soroush-Mahallati, and Mohammad Esfandīārī presented new perspectives about the Karbalā episode and religious violence, mainly with two central conclusions: first, that al-Husayn spent every effort to avoid the tragic encounter and violence, but to no avail;[30] second, that the cult of jihad and jihadism as propagated and enacted by Daesh has corrupt, unethical, and pseudotheological bases that must be contained by any means including countertheologies.

Soroush-Mahallati, an intellectual cleric residing in Iran, argues, for example, that the root cause of violent tendencies among Sunni fundamentalists such as

Daesh is Ash'arī theology, which rejects any notion of universal and objective sources for ethics.[31] This theology, he argues, prompts a religious person to deprive himself of reason as an independent and intrinsic source of ethics; consequently, such a person submits himself to a rigid understanding of traditional texts. By questioning why the Karbalā tragedy also involved war crimes, Soroush-Mahallati indicates 'Ash'arī theology as the responsible factor.[32] Even this argument may be problematic, in the sense that contemporary jihadi-salafi fundamentalists, such as Daesh followers, do not even go so far as to agree with the rational use of the Qur'ān and the Prophetic tradition as normative sources of Islam. They believe, rather, in acting upon the very letters of some early Muslim militant traditions, without caring for any hadith authentication. What is important in Soroush-Mahallati's opinion, however, is first, that modern Iranian clerics are paying far more attention to the significant impact of theological and philosophical perceptions on the practice of religion, and second, that the most sacred and pious acts, such as jihad or martyrdom, once enacted within a radical religious world view, can be transformed into a serious public evil.[33]

In search for pathological aspects of Muslim cultures and internal root causes of war and enmification, Esfandīārī delves into deeper analyses of the social psychology of Muslim communities and tackles a number of negative paradigms that, in his view, have brought Muslim communities to war with itself in modern times. Among such factors is giving more moral weight to equality than to brotherhood, as if brotherhood is worthless without equality.[34] This problematic perspective, Esfandīārī believes, is produced primarily by leftist ideas that have intoxicated Muslim ethos in modern life. It is in this spirit that Esfandīārī provides a critical reading of the views of 'Alī Sharī'atī, known as the architect of the Islamic Revolution of 1979 in Iran. He asserts, "In the works of some authors, one can see how they have predicated the credibility of brotherhood on class equality in the sense that brotherhood is futile without class equality. This is because, as they claim, brotherhood among the unequal will perpetuate inequality, just like a chain around hands and feet of the weak and the oppressed."[35] Esfandīārī argues that in reality "not only brotherhood is not conditioned by equality, but conversely, it is the equality that is a function of brotherhood … Whenever people consider themselves as brothers," he asserts, "it is only then that they will make efforts and take it as their duty to observe each other's rights … It is notable," he adds, "that the Qur'ānic principle of brotherhood was one of the three mottos for the French Revolution: freedom, equality, brotherhood … Non-Muslims, endeavored for brotherhood," Esfandīārī concludes, "while ironically, Muslims, did not come to moral awareness and thus lived non-brotherly."[36]

In Esfandīārī's moral pathology, the root causes for the emergence of non brotherly relations and violence among Muslims are predicated primarily on several character factors including the following:

We are only friendly with the one who agrees with us.
We consider tolerance and gentle manners as symptoms of a weak character and contentiousness as a sign of religious piety and revolutionary character.
We consider ourselves as a standard for judging about truthfulness.
We overlook all virtues of our adversaries.
We are impulsive in animosity and very slow in reconciliation.
We are talented in making enemies out of our friends, but rarely the other way around.
We exceed boundaries of justice in hostility.
We have little tolerance for criticism.
We focus more on differences than on commonalities.
We tend to perceive our adversaries as a total evil.
We perceive roughness as a measure of righteousness.
We transform all differences in taste and opinion into religious opposition.[37]

Esfandīārī's martyrology appeared in *'Ashura Studies: A Research on the Goal of Imam Husayn*, which he published in 2013, the same year that he also published *We Are All Brothers*. In his martyrology, Esfandīārī recognizes seven typical perspectives about al-Husayn's causes and goals on the way to his martyrdom. He categorizes these martyrdom perspectives as "defensive," "offensive," "mystical," "obligatory," "sacrificial," "political," and "reformist."[38] The first perspective defines al-Husayn's goal as merely defensive when he tried to protect his life after being asked by Yazīd to give his vote of political allegiance. The second view portrays al-Husayn's goal as seeking to establish his own caliphate by overthrowing Yazīd. The mystical perspective considers al-Husayn's goal as personal, in which he seeks personal nearness to God through martyrdom. The obligatory perspective looks at al-Husayn's motive as a measure of religious obligation in the context of Islamic law. In the sacrificial view, al-Husayn's martyrdom attains the same status as Christ's martyrdom, through which he obtains an intercessory status. The political martyrdom perspective considers al-Husayn's motive as a measure of political protest seeking to delegitimize the Umayyad's caliphate. Finally, the last perspective that receives Esfandīārī's personal support is martyrdom as an attempt at political reform. Esfandīārī warns against tendencies towards extremist readings of the Karbalā tragedy, looking at it either as an ultimate epic venture or alternatively as a revolutionary program. He portrays al-Husayn as a moderate reformist leader who made only rational decisions on his way to Karbalā, but whose decisions resulted in his accidental and tragic martyrdom.[39] By demystifying and politically rationalizing the Karbalā tragedy, Esfandīārī purifies martyrdom of the elements of legal necessity and defines it as an imposed tragic accident that should never be sought deliberately as long as other honourable and morally sound alternatives are available. This positon stands diagonally opposite to the offensive martyrdom and jihadism as propagated by Daesh theology.

Moderation and Nonviolence as Piety

All of the above Shi'i reactions to the theology of violence and the Daesh phenomenon, which are conceptually fresh, lead to one significant conclusion: by going to extremes in war crimes, violence, and inhumanity, Daesh has presented all of its neighbouring cultures – and specifically all Shi'as – with a full picture, or even an imaginative mirror, that shows the present and the potential evils of radical Islam or of any other militant ideology. Such an awakening conclusion has encouraged many religious circles in and outside of Iran to appreciate moderation and nonviolence not as a measure of religious laxity but as the manifestation of real, earnest, and deep religiosity. As a result, during the last two months of 2014 Iran hosted two major international conferences with the announced goal of promoting theologies of moderation and nonviolence within seminarian, academic, and policymaking circles.

The first international conference (International Congress on Extremism and Takfiri Threats), held in Qom in late November 2014, was sponsored by two grand ayatollahs Makārem Shīrāzī and Ja'far Sobhānī. According to official estimates, the conference received about seven hundred participants, including four hundred Sunni scholars from eighty countries. The first two operative articles of the conference's final resolution, read by a Sunni scholar at the conclusion of the session, are as follows:

1 Islam is a religion of peace, brotherhood, goodness and kindness, as The Holy Prophet of Islam (PBUH) declared the aim of his prophetic mission to be the completion of moralities, the secret to the spread of Islam and tendency to the Holy Prophet Muhammad (PBUH), as Holy Quran says, is compassion and kindness: "So by mercy from Allah, [O Muhammad], you were lenient with them. And if you had been rude [in speech] and harsh in heart, they would have disbanded from about you (3:159 Al-i-Imran)." Therefore all the Muslims especially Ulama [scholars of theology and jurisprudence] and elite should resort to the Prophet Mohammad (PBUH) and his household, and the religious scholars

should face not only the Muslims but also the followers of other religions peacefully and kindly and confront every violence from any religion.

2 In confrontation with the opposite thoughts, the holy religion of Islam has recommended us to [hold] the triple principles of wisdom, good advice and argument. So any offence towards the sanctities of other religions is forbidden and all Muslims should be aware of it and treat the followers of other religions with tolerance up until they have not committed anything wrong against Islam and Muslims.[40]

The second conference, held in Tehran in early December 2014, was titled "First International Conference on World against Violence and Extremism" and sponsored by the Institute for Political and International Studies (affiliated with the Iranian Foreign Ministry). The conference provided a forum for international participants from many countries to reflect on an Iranian initiative to curb global violence and extremism. The first two operative articles of the conference's final resolution are as following:

1 Welcome the proposal made by H.E. Hassan Rouhani that the United Nations proclaim the 18th December of each year as the day of "A World against Violence and Extremism," and request the Secretary General of the United Nations to recommend, in its report to the General Assembly at its seventieth session, a recommendation to that effect.

2 Stress on the importance of the public condemnation of all forms of extremism, violent extremism and terrorism by all states, religious leaders, politicians, and scholars.[41]

Apparently, the last two months of 2014 registered a turning point in the official Iranian perception of and approach to jihad, violence, and the question of martyrdom. The frequently pronounced antiextremist and antiwar posture of President Rouhani, which has proved to be helpful also in defining the spirit of the Iranian negotiations with 5+1 countries over Iran's nuclear program, has not missed any chance to be reemphasized at the highest international political level. His UN speech in the fall of 2015 was focused predominantly on the problem of violence and methods for its global irradication.[42] Another such case is a representative statement that the Irananian ambassador delivered to the UN Security Council on 27 March 2015. Significantly, this statement strongly condemns Daesh's excessive brutality, including "setting fires to houses and schools, enslaving the free, oppressing the vulnerable, killing the innocent with astonishing cruelty, beheading, burning and enslaving women and children, destroying Mosques, holy shrines, churches, temples as well as artifacts, and archeological treasures representing the rich cultural heritage of humanity."[43]

One may argue that the Iranian enthusiasm in the early revolutionary days to revive and fully embrace armed and ideological jihad and martyrdom, concepts that were found functionally and institutionally beneficial and vital for the sustenance of the prolonged Iran-Iraq War, came full circle in about thirty-five years. The very ambitious and intense Iranian endeavour to pioneer the development of a literature of nonviolence seems more serious than a temporary political tactic. The high cost of the Iranian ideological and radical foreign policy during the tenure of President Ahmadinejad has proven to be too detrimental for the country's economy to have a chance of revival. As a result, it is more probable than not that Rouhani's push for "A World without Violence" is a genuine "jihad for peace."

It is too early to predict how this course of events will affect the Shi'i martyrology in deeper theological and eschatological senses. David Cook is partially right in saying that unlike in Sunni Islam where "death is greeted by joy rather than sorrow ... in Shi'ism the dominant attitude towards martyrdom is grief."[44] The reason for this grief is rooted in early Islamic history: not only 'Alī b. Abī Tālib and his son al-Husayn, as the first and the third Shi'i imams, but almost all of the remaining imams of Twelver Shi'ism were martyred. As Cook has noted, according to the author of the most famous Arabic martyrology Abu'l Faraj al- Isfahānī (d. 967), up until 925 "close to 200 descendant of Muhammad through both the Hasanid and the Husaynid lines ... came to gruesome ends."[45] Cook adds, "After each failed proto-Shi'ite or Shi'ite uprising during the first 200 years of Islam, a large number of those people who felt that they should have supported a given descendant of the Prophet Muhammad felt intense guilt over having failed that person."[46] Grief and guilt may have been the true binary roots of Shi'i martyrology for a good part of her history, but they cannot fully explain the essence of modern Shi'i martyrology any longer. As some video-clips of the passion play that went viral on the internet during the 'Āshūrā of 2015 have symbolically demonstrated, antiviolence chants have become dominant in many public mourning processions across the entire country.

It is the combination of the senses of grief, guilt, and antiviolence that connects modern Shi'i martyrology with her messianic eschatology. As a result, a Shi'a, living between the unjust past and a certain but different political justice and vindication in the unforeseeable future, should not, in theory, feel an urge to be violent because even an inadvertent injustice will undermine the very first article of his faith (i.e. justice).[47] A violent Shi'i person, in other words, is a living oxymoron and theologically shooting at his own feet once he becomes a victimizer. For a Shi'a living in the second decade of the twenty-first century, the immorality of war and violence has become far more complicated than a question that can be answered by traditional theology.

When more than a hundred Saudi fighter-jet pilots who bombed Yemen for a whole month (April 2015) and killed many civilians, including four hundred children, were each promised to receive the prize of a luxury Bentley car (built only for millionaires) by the Saudi prince al-Waleed b. Tatal, the historically unprecedented corrupt relationship between petroleum, Wahhabi theology, and large-scale manslaughter of Muslims by Muslims called for more than a simple scholastic theology of peace and humanitarian jurisprudence.[48] A Jordanian reader of the news about Bentley rewards for bombing civilians responded to the news with these words: "So that's what it's all about ... 100 or 200 lives for a Bentley, that's how cheap human life is."[49] For a Shi'a, whether a victim is a Twelver Iranian or a Houthi Yemeni, and whether a young Kurdish Yezidi girl enslaved by Daesh or a Yemeni child killed with his mother by the cluster bombs killing indiscriminately, the situation requires an overhaul of perceptions of Muslim history, theology, and political philosophy.

The urgent need for this overhaul of course did not arise from isolated cases of violence but from systematic monstrous acts perpetrated by the hybrid Muslims who were aided also by petrodollars in their experiment with a Hollywood-inspired project that one may truthfully call *Daesh Jurassic Park*. The horrendous reality of this full-scale exhibition of inhumanity has cornered many people, including theologians, across the world to take a moral stance; but hardly any figure of authority came with such an elaborate and detailed position on the ethics of war as did Ayatollah Sīstānī, originally an Iranian and the most prominent Shi'i authority in Iraq, with millions of followers in Iran.

Daesh's systematic beheadings together with the Saudi Bentley booties hardly left any spirit of "jihad in the way of God" or what was traditionally known as just war in Islam and canonized in the eighth century by Muslim jurist al-Shaybānī. In terms of comparative history, the situation is not dissimilar to when the Christian theologians of the eleventh and twelfth centuries, according to Johnson, were prompted to promote "peace of God" and "truce of God" after they witnessed horrendous bloodshed across Europe in the tenth century. Johnson asserts, "From the breakup of the Roman Empire to the tenth century the just war ideas of the classical world and of late classical Christian theory were ignored in the development of Western culture. At the same time, the Germanic traditions on war had not yet solidified into the attitudes and customs of chivalry ... Lack of political unity reinforced the tendency toward general lawlessness on the part of those who bore arms."[50] This medieval situation sounds exactly like what is happening now in the occupied, borderless areas in Iraq, Syria, Libya, Afghanistan, Pakistan, and finally in Yemen.

Shi'i Authoritative Responses to Crimes against Humanity, Acts of Chain Revenge, and Terror in War

On 3 February 2015, Daesh forces demonstrated an act of cruelty and callousness in war that was considered a shock even to the most radical terrorist organization, such as al-Quaeda and its operatives. A video released by Daesh showed Moaz al-Kasasbeh, a Jordanian fighter pilot, who was captured on 24 December 2014 and burned alive as revenge for his participation in the Western allies' bombing of Daesh's forces. The professionally filmed scene of the utmost cruelty was conducted with a cold-blooded savagery unprecedented in the modern history of war crimes.[51] Later on it was revealed that Moaz's tragic fate was not a single case, but that, according to another report, Daesh had burned to death forty-five Iraqis in the western Iraqi town of al-Baghdadi.[52]

Crime and violence as the most striking characteristic of Daesh never fell short of innovative styles of terror, torture, callousness, and murder. On 15 February 2015, an affiliate branch of Daesh in Libya beheaded – in front of the camera – twenty-one Egyptian-Christian labourers who worked in that country and had been captured.[53] On 19 April 2015, the same war crime was reported when thirty Ethiopian-Christian labourers in Libya were shot to death and beheaded by Daesh affiliates.[54] As if various and numerous styles of beheadings did not excite Daesh criminals enough, a new style of execution became another murder fashion: smashing the head of victims by cement blocks. Scenes of such evil innovations so frequently photographed and scattered on the web have created a numbness for many eyes that now view these scenes as the normal course of life under Daesh.[55]

As scores of Daesh crimes against humanity extended from the most cruel acts against prisoners of wars, civilians, women, children, and all living creatures to museums and human cultural heritage, the world also witnessed a range of condemnations, though not enough, from various political and religious authorities. When Moaz al-Kasasbeh was burned alive, the rector of al-Azhar, the most authoritative source of the Sunni *fatwa*, issued the following juridical opinion: "In a statement released by the Grand Imam of Al-Azhar, Ahmed al-Tayeb condemned the killing of al-Kassassbeh, declaring that 'Islam prohibits the taking of an innocent life' and does not allow the mutilation or burning of anyone, even enemies at times of war. Continuing, the Grand Imam said that the Islamic State terrorists, who are fighting God and the Prophet Muhammad and are unjust and corrupted, deserved to be punished by death, crucifixion and dismemberment of their hands and feet."[56]

It is against the above background that the terms, implications, and significance of the most authoritative Shi'i response to war crimes in the history of the early twenty-first century may be fully comprehended: on 12 February 2015, the office of Grand Ayatollah Sayyid 'Ali al-Sīstānī in Najaf issued an authoritative advice on the ethics of war that establishes the newest and one of the most detailed and elaborate manuals for Shi'i conduct in war (*jus in bello*) in modern history (see the full text of the manual in appendix 4 of this volume). In this manual, comprised of twenty numbered articles, Ayatollah Sīstānī – who has a great number of followers in all Shi'a societies, including Iran – first proclaims that Islamic codes of war do agree with universal human wisdom. This assertion, by default, is supposed to draw the attention of warriors to all internationally accepted humanitarian laws and protocols limiting the scope and qualities of war. By disregarding this universal humanitarian wisdom, Sīstānī warns, no otherworldly credit can be gained from violence in war. The second article of the manual tackles the sanctity of life of women, children, and the natural environment; the next article addresses the just cause of war. The fourth article focuses on the sanctity of the "human soul." Sīstānī then warns against ambush and surprise attacks on the presumed enemy and immediately pays ample attention to the rule that the immunity of noncombatants in war may not be compromised.

In article 6 of the manual, the ayatollah pays specific attention to the illegitimacy of wars waged under the excuse of fighting religious heretics. He takes the occasion to address the great damage that the extremist Kharijites inflicted upon all of Muslim history because of their unjust wars against many Muslim factions accused of heresy by this group. The ayatollah then proceeds to article 7 in which he stresses Muslims' obligation to protect their non-Muslim neighbours just as they would their own immediate families.

In article 8, Ayatollah Sīstānī addresses the sanctity of property rights in Islam and warns warriors against plundering in hostile territories. Stressing the necessity of full respect for enemy corpses brings the ayatollah's ethics of war, as expressed in article 9, close to what Ferdowsi addressed: human beings, even bodies of enemies, deserve respect and decent treatment.[57] In this same article, the ayatollah warns against the verbal abuse of women.

In articles 10, 18, and 20, Ayatollah Sīstānī pays attention to the psychological roots of war by addressing the need for anger control, the prohibition of impulsive acts, and the avoidance of sentimentalism and emotionalism by warriors. As a standard in conduct of war, he advises that Muslim warriors must behave morally better than the enemy. This advice stands in the face of the blind chain revenge that has become fashionable in modern Middle Eastern wars – an unfortunate revival of the primitive pre-Islamic habits of Arab tribes.

As a clear assertion that war is not a solution but a significant part of the problem, article 12 of the manual pronounces that injustice cannot remedy corruption. In this connection, the subsequent article concludes that "military triumphalism at any cost" is antithetical to presumed justice sought through war. Article 14 pays attention to the traditionally established laws of amnesty in war. Ayatollah then addresses the need for compassion for fellow humans irrespective of their beliefs.

The spiritual tone of the manual is more manifest in its concluding part. Articles 15, 16, 17, and 19 invite warriors to pay specific attention in war to the use of human reason, good manners, spirituality, ritual prayers, and to standing as moral guards for each other.

Significantly, Ayatollah Sīstānī bases all of his moral advice on primary sources, including direct Qur'ānic and the Shi'i hadith injunctions, thus contributing to an authentic and authoritative modern Shi'i ethics of war. The manual scores a full contrast with the ethics of war as practised by Daesh and Saudi Arabia, both of which have promoted systematic Muslim fratricide on theological grounds. The above contrasts between the Shi'a and the Wahhabi ethics of war highlight theologies both of war and at war. The two schools, each in its own stance, manifest the naked bodies of moral systems.

The Theology of Forgiveness and Friendship

Theologically and theoretically speaking, martyrdom as the last resort to protect one's liberality and decency in life, unlike the jihadi-salafi view of it, has strong conceptual links with nonviolence almost by definition. But this politico-ethical equation has a moral and conceptually integral component that is missing from international and intranational modern politics: forgiveness.

Three decades after the Iranian Revolution and more than two decades after the end of the Iran-Iraq War, the question of forgiveness in politics and in international relations – itself a fairly new subject in scholarship – is gradually attracting serious attention from Iranian theologians. One significant case arose when Grand Ayatollah Sāne'ī from Qom offered a very new and promising solution for the US-Iran conundrum. On 16 December 2013, Carol Giacomo of the *New York Times* detailed her interview with Grand Ayatollah Sāne'ī:

> When it comes to Iranian clerics, Grand Ayatollah Youssef Saanei has long defied convention. Over the years, he has issued edicts that uphold women's rights. He also preached what in this society is a reformist political line and advocates

> rapprochement between Iran and the United States. Criticizing Ahmadinejad, Ayatollah Saanei said: "He introduced Islam as the religion of oppression and suppression inside the country" and also as a force for "animosity and violence and fighting outside the country."
>
> As a cleric who backed Rouhani early on, he endorsed the nuclear deal among Iran, the United States and other major powers and, invoking the late Nelson Mandela, he said that, "today the people in power in Iran and the people in power in the United States should forgive each other, should forget the past and start friendship."[58]

The ayatollah also suggested that if Israelis "get rid of their dangerous objectives and beliefs," there is a possibility that one day Iran could make some kind of accommodation with Israel.

For scholars familiar with Iran's highly ideological politics and previous sentimental foreign policy literature, it is abundantly clear that Sāneʻī's short but significant statement – which includes such terms as "Iranian forgiving of America" and "American forgiving of Iran" and "accommodation with Israel" – conveys a monumental change, not only from a policy perspective but also in terms of political philosophy and theology. Sāneʻī's unequivocal support for an officially disfavoured reformist faction in Iran caused him to lose official clerical credibility only among the Iranian political establishment. But as a trusted scholar in seminarian circles and an affiliate of Ayatollah Khomeini and the prosecutor general under him, Sāneʻī's scholarship can hardly be challenged, even by his foes. Most importantly, under Ayatollah Khomeini, Iran's seminarian circles considered Sāneʻī a leftist cleric with a radical position in his juridical practice; this was during a period of time when there were plenty of instances of government-sanctioned property confiscations and executions of those deemed to be "antirevolutionaries." Sāneʻī's transformation from a radical revolutionary jurist to a brave defender of universal human rights and an advocate for global peace truly represents the very metamorphosis that he symbolizes in Shiʻi political philosophy.

Sāneʻī's introduction of forgiveness into politics is not an isolated position. Ayatollah Montazerī was among one of the very first modern Shiʻi authorities who applied apology and forgiveness to politics. Cross-disciplinary scholars, such as Feirahī, have also touched on the theoretical foundation of forgiveness in politics.[59] In an article that he published on 3 February 2015 in the Persian virtual media, Feirahī argues that in the Qur'ānic context forgiveness is superior to retaliatory justice; as such, it should be preferred to the implementation of punitive justice specifically in international and civilizational relations. He stresses that it is time to reconsider justice-based political discourses in favour of forgiveness discourses, because punitive justice promotes violence in the course of retaliation. As a historic and Prophetic example, Feirahī points out that when the Prophet Muhammad defeated Meccan polytheists and entered the city, he gave three locations as amnesty to residents, as secure safe havens: the first, Masjid al-Haram where Ka'aba is located; the second, people's own homes; and the third, surprisingly, the residence of his chief enemy Abu Sufiyan. Feirahī argues that by granting such a sweeping amnesty, but more so, by declaring the very residence of his enemy a safe haven, the Prophet marginalized the foundation of violence. He concludes that civilizations cannot act upon vengeful sentiments; rather, they need to act upon the ethical mode of forgiveness that is superior to the mode of retaliatory justice. For this to happen, Feirahī suggests that large political entities, such as countries, must apply forgiveness first to their own constituencies and citizens.[60] In his short but significant article, Feirahī boldly ventures to argue for the liberation of high moral values such as forgiveness from the limitations of sentimentality and private life and encourages their applicability to politics not as an option but as an expedient political imperative.

Montazerī, Sāne'ī, and Feirahī represent examples of an increasing number of clerical scholars whose views prove that the traditional political philosophy of Shi'ism is morphing from its original position, defined by a theology of protest, to a more confident, nonreactive, inclusive, and cosmopolitan one.

Conclusion

As Iran moved closer to the 1979 Revolution, the concepts of jihad and martyrdom gained extensive use among Iranian revolutionaries needing to mobilize people against the monarchy. More importantly, the toppling of the monarchy necessitated an alternate political system, which was offered by Ayatollah Khomeini's theory of *wilāyat al-faqīh* (guardianship of the Islamic jurists – a theocracy). But the promotion of this idea, which contradicted the historic political quietism of Shi'ism, again required a political philosophy that could frame and justify Khomeini's theory within a Shi'i narrative. This new approach was effectively produced a few years before the revolution by Sālehī-Najafābādī, who claimed that al-Husayn's challenge against the Umayyads' rule was nothing less than a deliberate endeavour to establish a new political order. Sālehī's theory, however, was criticized for its deviation from traditional theories of jihad and martyrdom, implying that martyrdom in and of itself could never be a sacred goal and could only be valuable if imposed on a political contender.

While some clerics close to Ayatollah Khomeini praised Sālehī-Najafābādī's view on scholarly grounds, a greater majority of Sālehī-Najafābādī's Shi'i colleagues in Iran and Iraq opposed him, claiming that this interpretation diminished the sacredness of al-Husayn's martyrdom. Ali Sharī'atī, a sociologist by education and one of the main architects of the 1979 Revolution, tried to bridge the two sides in the martyrdom controversy. By taking the middle ground, he proposed that martyrdom, being an effective measure of political protest, was valuable in itself. This position helped many underground Muslim fighters understand the risks they undertook in confronting the Shah's regime.

The prerevolutionary and early revolutionary era in Iran forced Shi'i jurists to modernize the institution and the concept of jihad. Such newly defined notions of jihad, removed from their esoteric interpretations in early Shi'i jihad narrative and scholarship, proved to be very effective in catalysing the revolution and the ensuing theocracy. A full war was in the making, however, and militant jihad, coupled with a revived sense of sacred martyrdom, was an essential and indispensible fuel for the Iran-Iraq War machine.

The Iran-Iraq War, which ended without a decisive military victory, left the newly energized and reconceptualized institutions of jihad and martyrdom in the air. The two concepts had yet one more turning point to surmount after a tumultuous journey that refreshed memories of an important part of the old Shi'i protest culture. The violent rise of the Taliban in Afghanistan and Pakistan and Daesh in Iraq and Syria, and the shock of their extensive cruelty, callousness, and inhumanity in their intra-Muslim wars seem to have offered that needed turning point. As a result, Iran seems to have chosen the stance of a staunch supporter of nonviolence, both conceptually and institutionally.

More than three decades after the Iranian ideological revolution, the rational Shi'i institution of *ijtihād* is reviving with the goal to put moral expediencies above power politics and to embrace political philosophies of nonviolence and forgiveness. More importantly, this new *ijtihād* is putting the sanctity of life above martyrdom and justifies martyrdom only as the last honourable resort rather than the first in any armed encounter. Significantly, this new posture and the emerging theology of peace are not developments isolated to seminarian or intellectual circles. As the monumental, historic, multinational million-man Shi'i march to Karbalā during 'Arba'een of 2014 has manifested, the goal of this traditional march was no longer a symbolic allegiance to a theology of revenge but rather a show of Shi'i solidarity against violence and extremism. All of the above developments may appear to be in their preliminary stages, but as further details will demonstrate, they certainly indicate coherent, systematic, and multifaceted developments.

The next chapter will explore in further detail how the concept of jihad that helped in the Iran-Iraq War and was reformed by it is in the process of further reform through the Iranian nuclear crisis. In effect, the nuclear negotiations between Iran and the Western powers have led to defining a new field for jihad, which may be called "negotiation jihad."

9 Diplomacy in between Nuclear Technology and Antibomb Theology

Whoever kills a soul unless for a soul or for corruption [done] in the land – it is as if he had slain mankind entirely. And whoever saves one – it is as if he had saved mankind entirely.

– Qur'ān 5:32

The tragic military entanglement between Iran and Iraq – the two countries with the world's largest Shi'a populations – provides a unique case study for students of international and humanitarian laws in terms of war. The eight-year war was a multilayered and comprehensive battle. For Saddam Hussein, the moral concerns of war were among some of the least important issues. However, for Ayatollah Khomeini, who came to power shortly before the start of war and led a popular, highly ideological revolution, the moral aspects of the war posed serious concerns, especially given Khomeini's formal spiritual status in Iran and among Shi'a seminarians. He was the first head of state (both in terms of Shi'i and Muslim states) in the history of Islam to be both a high-ranking jurisprudent and an authoritative religious source, emulative for millions in the heartland of the Islamic world. As the ongoing civil war in Iraq proves, war has hardly stopped in Iraq since its invasion of Iran, even after the end of the Iran-Iraq War and the fall of Saddam.

From a macroperspective, this ongoing state of war has proven a major shock for the geopolitics and economies of the entire region. Given its vast impact on all aspects of Shi'a life in both Iran and Iraq, the Iran-Iraq War had serious theoretical, logistical, and security implications for Iranian and Iraqi domestic and foreign policymaking; it has also greatly impacted Shi'i theology and ethics of war and peace, which have rarely, if ever, been challenged within their traditional framework. While war has had a devastating impact on Iran,

Iraq, and many other regional countries, it has also served as a reality test in measuring the functionality of traditional views of jihad and theologies of war and peace.

The war formally ended after eight years of carnage and destruction. Between 1983 and 1988, Iranian forces fell victim to the use of chemical and biological weapons, which major world powers either aided or overlooked – a flagrant violation of the humanitarian laws of war as defined by various international conventions.[1] Could this bitter experience have encouraged Iran to try to access nuclear technology as a security/defensive instrument? Or did Iran genuinely become interested in acquiring nuclear knowledge for energy and medical needs, as well as for scientific development? In either case, the question is particularly worth consideration in a society as religious as Iran, where Islamic law weighs in on the use of weapons of mass destruction.

This chapter forms an introduction to the theology of nuclear arms from an Iranian-Shi'i perspective. As the course of Iran's complex negotiations with the six Western powers over nuclear technology has revealed, these negotiations and their various dimensions involve too many factors and dilemmas to be addressed by one article or even several books. I have, therefore, limited my focus here to only some theological aspects and implications of these negotiations. My main goal here is to demonstrate that during these negotiations both Iranian officials and Iran's seminarian scholars are presenting a new nuclear theology that will permanently influence the Shi'i ethics of war and peace.

The Struggle between International and Religious Laws: Prospects for Compromise

Ann Elizabeth Mayer believes that international law is religion neutral and therefore at odds with Islamic traditions and sees several problematic aspects, including "economic aggression, armed reprisal, state-sponsored terrorism, belligerent occupation, collective self-defense, collective punishment, multilateral peacekeeping force, disarmament schemes, war-crime tribunal and weapons of mass destruction."[2] She concludes that the only area of congruence between the two realms, namely between Islam and human rights, is honouring contracts.[3] Mayer may be right in some of her points, but the contentions she notes are not necessarily of a religious essence; they could, for example, be connected to certain cultural traditions without being attached to the moral foundations of specific religions. Conversely, one can argue that because religions claim sacred authority, they are tremendously helpful in controlling arms and managing disarmament. Most modern approaches to the ethics of war and strategic peace emphasize the necessary inclusion of religious discourse and traditions. The question of nuclear theology therefore deserves full attention in this chapter.

At the height of the nuclear crisis between the West and Iran, and perhaps as a result of public pressure and the hardships accompanying the West's imposed economic sanctions, the Iranian supreme leader Ayatollah Khamenei once again expressed his official position on nuclear theology, rejecting the production and the use of nuclear weapons on religious grounds. His jurisprudential decree (*fatwa*) that nuclear warfare was a "crime against humanity" instigated serious interest in interfaith dialogue on the theology of disarmament.

Ayatollah Khamenei's antinuclear decree was not new. On 10 August 2005, a document circulated by the Iranian representative at an IAEA (International Atomic Energy Agency) emergency meeting included the text of Khamenei's *fatwa*. The text clearly states, "The production, stockpiling, and use of nuclear weapons are forbidden under Islam, and the Islamic Republic of Iran shall never acquire these weapons."[4] Iran went on to host an international conference on nuclear disarmament on 17 April 2010, where the *fatwa* was reiterated: "We consider the use of such weapons [nuclear] as *harām* [a jurisprudential term that means "strictly forbidden"] and believe that it is everyone's duty to make efforts to secure humanity against this great disaster"; Khamenei emphatically mentioned in his statement "using or even threatening to use such weapons is a serious violation of the most basic humanitarian rules and a clear manifestation of war crime."[5] More than two years later, on 30 August 2012, Ayatollah Khamenei reiterated this position when addressing some 120 heads of state and officials at the Sixteenth Non-Aligned Movement Summit in Tehran: "The Islamic Republic – logically, religiously, and theoretically – considers the possession of nuclear weapons a grave sin and believes the proliferation of such weapons is senseless, destructive, and dangerous"; he added that Iran "proposed the idea of a Middle East free of nuclear weapons, and we are committed to it."[6]

In the above official statements, Ayatollah Khamenei speaks in political and jurisprudential terms, highlighting the direct implications for Iran's foreign policy, as well as for the followers of this school of thought beyond Iran's borders. They also have clear pedagogical bearings for the Shi'i ethics of war. One serious concern was how neighbouring Shi'i states could protect themselves against a nuclear Taliban or Israeli nuclear arsenal. The Shi'i community further wondered how Iran could ensure its safety, considering its less-than-good relations with the West, as well as how to mitigate the potential impact of the internal turmoil in Pakistan and the possibility of the Pakistani Taliban destabilizing their country. These concerns raised the possibility that perhaps the official Iranian position on the ban of nuclear weapons was a tactical measure rather than a strategic one. But if the *fatwa*, regardless of its strong terms, proved to be tactical, then the ayatollah would effectively be risking his religious authority and credibility, which he could not afford, given the many challenges that the relatively new theocracy is facing. Just as with Western legal traditions, where legal rulings create powerful precedence for future judgments, Shi'i *fatwa*s also hold longstanding jurisprudential implications for future rulings. Therefore, it is hardly imaginable that Ayatollah Khamenei could issue such a *fatwa* simply as a deceiving ploy against Western critics of Iran. Moreover, Ayatollah Montazerī, the second most powerful religious authority after Ayatollah Khomeini and handpicked by him, had taken a stance against both the production and the use of weapons of mass destruction, including nuclear weapons.[7] It seems then that Ayatollah Khamenei should not want, on religious grounds, to oppose the decree of a senior religious authority, despite the fact that Montazerī lost his political credibility in 1989 but not his jurisprudential authority even within the official Iranian establishment.

Khamenei's view on nuclear weapons has been well reflected in nonpartisan Iranian politics. During the conference on the Review of the Non-Proliferation Treaty (NPT), held at the UN headquarters in New York on 3 May 2010, heads of state of only two member states participated – Iran was one of them. The incentive of former Iranian president Ahmadinejad was apparent when he showed up in person rather than sending his foreign minister; this was, in part, to alleviate some of the West's political pressure on Iran regarding its nuclear project. However, the strong language Ahmadinejad used in his address, despite it being presented by one of the most radical Iranian politicians, is telling. Ahmadinejad emphatically asserted in his address that Iran had no plan to develop nuclear weapons because "the nuclear bomb is a fire against humanity rather than a weapon for defense."[8] He additionally challenged the double standard of Western countries on the matter and pointed to the irony of the United States – the only country to have ever deployed nuclear bombs and one of the top developers of a nuclear bomb stockpile – acting as the chief moral guard against it.

In response to Ahmadinejad's speech, former US Secretary of State Hillary Clinton sowed doubts about the real nuclear intentions of the present Iranian government. Despite the differences between Ahmadinejad and his successor President Rouhani, the official position of Iran against nuclear weapons and weapons of mass destruction could have not been expressed more strongly by Rouhani in his address to the Non-Aligned Disarmament Conference at the United Nations on 26 September 2013: "Any use of nuclear weapons is a violation of the UN Charter and a crime against humanity. Doctrines justifying such use are unacceptable ... As long as nuclear weapons exist, the risk of their use, threat of use, and proliferation persist. The only absolute guarantee is their total elimination." He concluded by repeating a statement expressed by the chairman of an earlier session: "No nation should possess nuclear weapons, since there are no right hands for these wrong weapons."[9]

Ayatollah Khamenei's *fatwa* encouraged other grand ayatollahs to issue similar decrees. In a meeting with Iran's head of the Atomic Energy Organization, 'Alī Akbar Sālehī, on 19 December 2013, Grand Ayatollah Makārem-Shirazi officially stated, "Just like the Iranian supreme leader, I, as a source of religious emulation, make an edict that the making of nuclear weapons is *haram* [strictly forbidden] in Islam."[10] After Ayatollah Makārem-Shirazi, at least three other grand ayatollahs came out with similar edicts. Grand Ayatollah Javādī Āmolī stated, "Scholars believe that possession and development of atomic weapons and WMDs are not permitted and have issued religious rulings in this regard ... Mass killing and genocide are forbidden by divine religions."[11] Grand Ayatollah Ja'far Sobhānī's edict came with a stronger tone: "Given the principles of Islam in regards to human beings and the respect it holds for mankind, utilizing atomic weapons is absolutely prohibited – even for deterrence purposes."[12] Grand Ayatollah Nourī Hamadānī also stated, "We do not allow the use of nuclear weapons."[13]

Perhaps the most categorically rejecting position was the *fatwa* issued by Grand Ayatollah Sāne'ī. In an interview with an Iranian seminarian periodical published in Qom (*Safir-e hayat*), Ayatollah Sāne'ī states, "The production, stockpiling, and use of nuclear weapons are banned and forbidden [*harām*] in Islam because in addition to human mass destruction, it destroys all living species, plants, and the environment. Also the nuclear radiation will contaminate vast territories for a very long time with many negative repercussions." He adds emphatically, "Therefore, I firmly believe that even if our enemies use nuclear bombs against us, we have no right to retaliation in kind ... It was based on the same logic, that during the Iran-Iraq War when we were subject to attacks against civilian and residential targets and chemical weapons, we did not resort to the law of retaliation." Ayatollah Sāne'ī then explains why his *fatwa* is not circumstantial and cannot be altered in the future.[14]

*Fatwa*s aside, Iran's President Rouhani has already made significant contributions to the theological discourse on peace. On 6 December 2013, in his address to the Fourteenth Conference on Research and Development (R&D), he pointed out, "The production of WMDs is against the *fatwa* of the supreme leader and therefore it is *haram*." He added that based on "reason and national interest" Iran did not and would not pursue efforts to acquire WMDs. Rouhani stressed, "Research is a sacred task, and as such research in the field of WMDs has no place in the Iranian defence doctrine."[15] Two points warrant additional exploration: First, on a theoretical basis, these statements contribute significantly to disarmament theology and have the full potential to engage Shi'i seminaries and seminarians in an interfaith and international dialogue on the modern ethics of WMDs. As this chapter further details, the nondiscriminatory, destructive effect of WMDs causes a major jurisprudential impediment in the way of both the production and the use of these weapons. Second, with the exception of Ayatollah Sāne'ī, it is not clear how Ayatollahs Khamenei, Makārem-Shirazi, Sobhānī, Nourī Hamadānī, and Javādi Āmolī individually developed their jurisprudential reasoning when issuing their *fatwa*s on banning nuclear weapons. Elaborate juristic discourses related to the aforementioned *fatwa*s can not only shed light on the nature of these edicts but can also help war and peace ethicists to expand these arguments to other fields.

From an exegetical point of view, the Qur'ān, as the most important source of Islamic law, provides many verses that can benefit jurisprudential inference. It unequivocally states that killing one innocent person equates to murdering the whole of humanity. Qur'ānic verse 5:32 reads, "Because of that, We decreed upon the Children of Israel that whoever kills a soul unless for a soul or for corruption [done] in the land – it is as if he had slain mankind entirely. And whoever saves one – it is as if he had saved mankind entirely. And our messengers had certainly come to them with clear proofs. Then indeed many of them, [even] after that, throughout the land, were transgressors." The message is telling: if killing one innocent person is tantamount to murdering all of mankind, and in light of the fact that weapons of mass destruction kill indiscriminately and on a very high scale, the use of any such weapons equates to murdering all of humanity several times over. Importantly since his election as president, Rouhani has frequently referred to this Qur'ānic verse as the foundation of his antinuclear-weapon doctrine.

In addition to the Qur'ān, Shi'i jurisprudential sources also provide ample reasoning against WMDs. Ayatollah Abolqāsem 'Alīdoost, a prominent scholar who spoke at a conference in Tehran on Nuclear Jurisprudence in March 2014, has referred to these sources elaborately. He states, "The most significant general principles that can be applied to the case of weapons of mass destruction are principles governing differentiation of targets, protection of the environment and ensuring safety and security of non-combatants during war and conflict."[16] After referring to a number of hadith passages reported from the Prophet Muhammad to this effect, Alīdoost refers to a statement from a founding father of Shi'i jurisprudence, Shaykh Tūsī, which may be a major source of the ayatollah's edicts against WMDs. Tūsī is quoted from one of his works, *Nahayat fi mujarrad al-fiqh wa'l-fatwa*, saying, "It is permissible to fight with infidels using all sorts of deadly tools except for poison. The dispensation of poison in their land is not permissible."[17] Alīdoost demonstrates how most Shi'i authorities after Tūsī have adopted his opinion that the use of weapons with indiscriminate effects should be banned. He concludes, "It should be borne in mind that the absolute prohibition [of weapons with indiscriminate harm, as reflected in the works of jurists following Tūsī] emphasize the impermissibility of such weapons, even if their use could lead to the victory of Muslims in war."[18]

The above-mentioned antinuclear-weapon commitment by Iran is pronounced in Tehran's Friday prayer, which is counted as the most significant gauge for Iran's public policy. On 1 May 2015, Ayatollah Imāmī Kāshānī, one of the few Friday-prayer leaders in Tehran, addressed Iran's commitment to nuclear nonproliferation in his sermon and justified its validity on the authority of an exclusive Shi'i primary source of jurisprudence and ethics of war. He stated:

> If the Islamic Republic of Iran has shown steadfastness regarding the peaceful use of nuclear activities and pronounces that she does not own nuclear weapons, it is because of her thoughtfulness and the logic of the 'Alavite [Shi'i] political philosophy ... All human-rights jurists of the world should be informed that the basis of our policies is the decrees of his eminence 'Alī b. Abī Tālib to his appointed governor of Egypt Malik al-Ashtar, whereby 'Alī advises his governor, "Never break your contract with a friend or an enemy, even if you find out, after commitment, that it is ultimately against your interest." Furthermore, 'Alī (peace be upon him) states to al-Ashtar that once you enter into a treaty with an enemy, you must know that contracts are a means for God to secure peace and tranquillity for all mankind, and therefore you must stay faithful to your promise and avoid cheating.[19]

From a political perspective, these new official positions demonstrate a significant doctrinal turning point in how Iran's clerical leaders view national and regional security. As Sohail Hashmi notes, it was not long ago when former President Mohammad Khatami (who was considered internationally a reformist president) congratulated Pakistan for its first successful nuclear test in May 1998.[20] In Rouhani's strategic policy, however, it seems that the doctrine of mutual deterrence and balance of power has yielded to the alternative perspective of regional and global disarmament. He knows well that deterrence may only work when both sides of the balance of power are expected to act rationally. Rouhani seems to be fully aware that the cult of suicide bombings, advocated primarily by Saudi Wahhabis who have a major influence on the Taliban and on Sunni fundamentalists in Iraq and Syria, may not stop at the nuclear threshold.

There is no question that the present Iranian political scene is not completely free of militant-minded politicians such as those found in the circle of former President Ahmadinejad. But the stunning defeat of this faction in the June 2013 Iranian presidential election, the pursuant shift in Iranian foreign policy, which has culminated in successful nuclear talks between Iran and six major Western powers, and the defeat of radical parliamentarians in Iran's parliament election in March 2016 all hint at a transformation in the political and defence doctrines of the country. This policy change coincides perfectly with the new theology and ethics of war emerging from within modern Iranian-Shi'i scholarship. Furthermore, due at least to the deep dissatisfaction with the official abrogation of civil rights under the presidency of Ahmadinejad, the Iranian public has shown little to no support for militarizing Iranian politics and economy. This attitude contrasts, for example, with trends in neighbouring Pakistan. As noted by Sohail Hashmi, "In the aftermath of the Pakistani [nuclear] test, Jama'at-i Islami [a fundamentalist political party] supporters dragged through the streets of Islamabad models of missiles with the words 'Islamic bomb' stenciled down their side."[21] Despite the fact that Iran is one of the few countries to have suffered from weapons of mass destruction, its streets have hardly witnessed military violence except for the regular army marches that signify their national security function. The present Iranian public, having experienced one of the longest and deadliest wars of the developing world, has no interest in another. The bitter memories and deep wounds of the last war, still fresh and still haunting in public life, prompted the Rouhani government to firmy deflect all domestic challenges against the successful conclusion of the 5+1 agreement.

Iran Emerging out of War Legacies and Theologies

During Iran's June 2013 presidential election, many signs highlighted the fact that twenty-six years after the end of the Iran-Iraq War Iran's politics, economy, society, and culture remain deeply affected by the horrors of war. Scholars Garrett Nada and Helia Ighani reflect on this premise:

> A quarter century later, the Iran-Iraq War looms over Iran's presidential election as if it happened yesterday. All six candidates participated in the grizzliest modern Middle East conflict as fighters, commanders or officials. Over the past month, the campaign has evolved into a feisty competition over who sacrificed and served the most in the eight-year war. A leading candidate lost a leg. Another candidate commanded the Revolutionary Guards. A third liberated an oil-rich frontline city. A fourth brokered the dramatic ceasefire. During the final debate on June 7, candidates

> invoked their wartime experience during the "Holy Defense," as it is officially dubbed in Iran, as a top credential for taking office. It clearly shaped the worldviews of all six, despite their disparate political affiliations as reformists, hardliners or independents. But experience during the 1980-1988 war is also emerging as an unspoken credential in facing the future, specifically a confrontation with the outside world over Iran's controversial nuclear program. The debate resonated with language of resistance that echoed from the war, which claimed up to 1 million casualties. Iran's presidential contest illustrates how the war generation is now competing to take over the leadership from the first generation of revolutionaries.[22]

The above piece is telling. The Iran-Iraq War continues to have multidimensional impacts on the Iranian mindset. But the result of Iran's 2013 presidential election, in effect, defied Nada and Ighani's conclusions. The war generation lost the election to an administration with well-planned strategies in terms of changing Iran's war-oriented political literature, theology, and diplomacy. President Rouhani and his administration have changed the way Iran interacts with the international community in less than a year after coming to office. Their perspectives on international relations effectively steered Iran away from the obsolete political paradigm of *dār al-Islam/dār al-kufr* (the abode of Islam/the abode of disbelief) dichotomy. Iranian foreign policy has moved from a Manichean zero-sum game world view to a pluralistic one based on win-win relations with all countries irrespective of ideological orientations of counterparts.

The ongoing tragedies in Syria, Iraq, Afghanistan, Pakistan, and Yemen have definitely shown Iranians that the national security, as well as the territorial integrity, of their country could be threatened and compromised as much by elements within the parameters of Islamism as by those outside. If Iran's previous administrations failed practically to appreciate the West's assistance in ousting the Taliban and Saddam Hussein from Afghanistan and Iraq, Rouhani's administration, having no illusions about the myths of pan-Islamism, seems to look for political alliances beyond ideological premises. Rouhani, in fact, has used every opportunity since his election as president to educate the public about ideological misperceptions and their negative implications in global politics and economy.[23]

The breakthrough Geneva agreement between Iran and the West is no less a result of philosophical and theological transformations than of the hardships faced by the Iranian economy in the face of economic sanctions. Clearly, Iran's articulate foreign minister Javad Zarif has never missed a media opportunity to share new theoretical frameworks for Iran's foreign policy.[24] But perhaps the Iranian endeavour to negotiate a peaceful solution for its controversial nuclear project has deeper roots in Iran's modern history. As military analyst Shahram

Chubin highlights, "Iran's approach to military power and strategy should be seen in the context of its recent history and its goals. The country has little experience of war in modern times ... Iranian history over the past century and a half had been free of war, until the 1980–88 conflict with Iraq, which Iranians call the 'imposed war' ... Iran has been the victim of invasions and occupations, but is itself rather passive. The CIA's clandestine history called this Iran's 'modern tradition of defeat.'"[25]

What makes Iran additionally less interested in flexing its political, rather than cultural, muscles is the fact that Iran is among one of the very few countries in the region never formally colonized by Western powers; this plays and has played an important role in Iran's national behaviour. As a concrete factor, the fact that Iran's arms expenditure is lower than that of its smaller Persian Gulf neighbours is telling. However, even more compelling is the fact that even in light of its other historical factors, as Chubin notes, "Iran has no martial tradition, and does not share neighboring Turkey's high esteem for the profession of arms."[26]

Three Historic Trends in the Shi'i Theology of Jihad

A macroperspective on the three trends of Shi'i *fatwa*s (authoritative juridical ruling) on jihad will serve as a necessary complement to the brief introduction to the emerging Iranian-Shi'i nuclear theology presented above. First, it is necessary to stress that Shi'i politics in Iraq had different turns and lessons as compared with Iran. The war that Saddam Hussein began with Iran in 1980 has not stopped in Iraq for more than three decades now. The country's sociopolitical fabric is heavily disturbed, to the extent that Iraq as a state is near collapse and terminal partition. The Iraqi Shi'as, thus far, have experienced a brief period of running the country; but they have also faced political fragmentation, external threats, and a host of domestic insurgencies. Iraq quite unfortunately has served as a perfect laboratory for all kinds of wars and conflicts – civil, regional, and international. It has been both the user and victim of all conventional and nonconventional weapons, except nuclear, in its modern history. On top of it all, Iraq has been affected by the ups and downs of Iran's domestic and international politics.

Perhaps all of these major and traumatic events experienced by the Iraqi Shi'as have cautioned its seminarian circles to become very prudent when it comes to taking authoritative positions on the theology of war and peace. When the shocking news of the fall of Mosul at the hands of the anti-Shi'a forces of Daesh (ISIS) reached Baghdad and Najaf in June 2014, Grand Ayatollah Sīstānī had little choice but to declare jihad against the Daesh forces. The declaration of jihad *kifaya* (which technically means a call to take up arms upon the necessity of defence and is not obligatory for the entire Shi'a community) that Ayatollah Sīstānī issued on 13 June 2014, however, was carefully formulated. The dictum formed an expected response from the highest religious authority in Iraq to the savage massacre of more than seventeen hundred Shi'i residents of Mosul and Tikrit – an act that was recognized by the UN human rights commissioner as a crime against humanity.[27] A day later on 14 June, out of concern that the jihad *fatwa* may cause uncontrolled retaliatory measures against the Sunni minority in Iraq and also out of concern that the *fatwa* may infringe upon the authority of the Iraqi government, the following addendum to the *fatwa* was issued by the ayatollah's office:

> **In the Name of God, the ever-merciful, the ever-compassionate**
> The Highest Religious Authority [in Najaf] calls upon all the citizens [of Iraq] – especially those living in mixed areas [i.e. areas that include Shi'a and Sunni residents] – to exert the highest possible level of self-restraint during this tumultuous period. And [we urge] all [ethno-sectarian] groups [i.e. Shi'a, Sunni, etc.] to behave in the most compassionate and kindest of manners. And [we urge those groups] to steer clear from sectarian- and untamed-nationalistic discourse that is to the detriment of Iraq's national unity. Moreover, he [the Highest Religious Authority wants to take this opportunity to] emphasize the need [for all citizens] to refrain from militant acts that are outside [the state's] legal frameworks; furthermore, [the Highest Religious Authority] calls upon the official state actors to take the necessary measures to prevent such actions [i.e. militant acts occurring outside official state avenues].[28]

Whatever the practical effects of the *fatwa* and its explanatory addendum, it was immediately received by the Iranian theological circles as a perfect example of a new emerging trend in Shi'i authorities' recognition of the territorial authority of government when it comes to jihad. It is public knowledge that during the leadership of Ayatollah Khomeini in Iran, he was always supportive of the Iranian government's war policies. But the difference is that Ayatollah Khomeini was himself the government, and Ayatollah Sīstānī, in contrast, has retained his independence from the Iraqi administration.

In an online article that appeared on a number of official and nongovernmental Iranian websites on 6 July 2014, the seminarian scholar Seyyed Hādī Tabātabā'ī concluded that the history of Shi'a jihad *fatwa*s is experiencing a third trend or phase. The first, according to the author, was a position that did not recognize any territorial boundaries and legitimate nonjuridical authority. During this phase, which extended for about eight centuries after the eleventh century, the predominant characteristics of most Shi'i jihad *fatwa*s were their universal nature and the recognition of the legitimacy of offensive and expansionist wars in the name of faith. The second phase began with Shi'a authorities who were contemporary to Ayatollah Khomeini, including figures such as himself and the other grand ayatollahs Seyyed Mohammad Shīrāzī, Mohammad Rezā Golpāyegānī, and Seyyed Sādeq Rouhānī. These authorities rejected the legitimacy of offensive wars and limited jihad only to defence and necessity. But they nevertheless spoke as a government.[29] The third trend of jihad *fatwa*s emerging in the post-Khomeini era has a local, nonuniversal nature, and is confined within borders of state laws, with full acceptance of the authority of legitimate governments – thereby recognizing the paradigm of nation-state, the separation of church and state, and respecting representative government.[30] By the time Iran and 5+1 Western countries finally came to full agreement on nuclear talks and began its implementation in the fall of 2015, a number of top Shi'i grand ayatollahs demonstrated their full acquaintance with many technical terms and foreign policy paradigms. Their calculated posture vis-à-vis the ups and downs of the two-year-long negotiations under Rouhani demonstrated three factors: First, they educated themselves with a new modern discourse that will affect their *fatwas* and theological stance on domestic and world politics. Second, they mostly acted within the parameters of national interest. Third, their jurisprudential posture showed a strong tendency to be predicated more on moral rather than on legal arguments. All of these factors together hint that the future generation of Shi'a seminarian authorities will interact heavily and negotiate positively with the secular parameters of international laws and will come to terms with the idea of the division of expertise in juristic and technical domains. Therefore, instead of having more grand ayatollahs in the future who feel confident to issue *fatwas* on all issues and in all fields of social life from A to Z, instead we will have grand ayatollahs with specific expertise. The net result will create smaller gaps between international and religious laws and ethics. Such a development is tantamount to a positive metamorphosis of Shi'i sharī'a laws as applied to the vast realm of international relations, including war and peace.

Conclusion

The direct engagement in the Iran-Iraq War provided Twelver-Shi'i jurists many practical lessons that encouraged them to adjust their traditional perceptions and state policymaking to correspond to the harsh realities of modern life. Compared to the Sunni majority, the politics and the jurisprudence of the Shi'i minority have developed either on the quietist side of the political spectrum (as they did for most of its history) or more often on the active-protest side, when the political space of the Sunni majority was open to the voice of sectarian others. Both of these historic postures of quietism and protest have undergone major transformations after the Iranian Revolution and the Iran-Iraq War. The exceptionally prolonged war with Saddam Hussein taught both revolutionary Iran and the Shi'i majority in Iraq that modern international relations require far more sophisticated policymaking than what traditional jurisprudential paradigms and a Shi'i absolutist sense of justice could accommodate.

The nuclear crisis added to these experiential and pedagogical developments. Hardcore realities and the large-scale damages inflicted upon Iran's economy and society by the Iran-Iraq War and by Western sanctions outweighed the huge sacrifices that the people were asked to make for keeping unrealistic, ideological state postures. More than three decades of nonstop public sacrifice ultimately exhausted and alienated a large number of people, prompting them to ask for economic and political transparency and accountability from Iran's political leadership. The shocking news of the unimaginable wealth procured by associates of Ahmadinejad's government hammered the final nails into the coffins of the *economy of sacrifice*, *unaccountability of state management*, and the *foreign policy of ideological Cold War*.[31]

The election of President Rouhani, and the major shift of political factions in favor of reform in the parliamentary election of March 2016 were not surprises in light of the above. Iran's ideological and sectarian policies needed to change and, as demonstrated in this chapter, did indeed paradigmatically transform. However, what ultimately helped the monumental policy changes may be traced to both a pragmatic approach to Iran's political and economic realities, as well as to the production and adoption of a new political theology that essentially provided rationally and morally justified frameworks for policy adjustments.

Iran's emerging nuclear theology, which is built on an increasing number of *fatwa*s and novel ethical approaches against the use, making, and stockpiling of nuclear weapons, is creating an important Islamic literature on disarmament and a conceptual precedence in modern Muslim politics. With its well-expressed concerns about nuclear weapons' ill effects on the global environment, this literature has the possibility of establishing an influential discourse with mainstream Sunni thought and with other religious traditions. The horrific actual and conceptual extremism of Daesh, the Taliban, and other jihadi-salafis will sooner or later convince other parties prone to regional sectarian politics to understand their common strategic stake. The increasing tendency of Iran to embrace the rational and humanistic theology of disarmament may indeed form a natural bridge that will allow moderate Shi'i and Sunni theologians to meet and help each other to combat transsectarian militant fundamentalism.

After centuries of political quietism and an outdated jurisprudence of war and peace that had lost its necessary ethical relevance to modern life, Iranian-Shi‘i jurists, ethicists, and theologians have each through their own specific discipline come close to a common humanitarian understanding about the perils of the global arms race. We are still far from having world religions contribute satisfactorily to strategic and durable peace-building discourses and institutions. The Muslim world, which is fortunately behind the West in arms production and use, is unfortunately behind its expected share in disarmament literature. Iran, however, seems to be emerging as a pioneer state with the intellectual and theological resolve to bridge this gap; this study has been an endeavour to demonstrate such bridge building.

Conclusion

Beyond a Minority Mentality: The Emerging Shi'i-Iranian Cosmopolitanism

Revenge, the end of politics, and justice, the beginning.

– Donald W. Shriver Jr[1]

Throughout this book, I have attempted to present a picture of how a multitude of sociopolitical and theological challenges in modern Iran, the experiences of a revolution, a very long war, and the intricacies of a theocracy have pressed Iranian intellectuals and Shi'i seminarian jurists to rethink war and peace both conceptually and morally. I have also tried to demonstrate how this process of moral rethinking benefited from a host of cultural, historical, philosophical, jurisprudential, literary, and institutional elements. The intellectual and theological reactions to the confluence of the above factors and processes have fostered the emergence of a growing and robust critical literature on war and peace, which is increasingly influencing the Iranian public, civil society, and also governmental policymaking in this country.

During the most formative years of Shi'i theology, Skaykh Mufīd took a major step in establishing justice as the first principle of the Shi'i school of thought and imama (the charismatic leadership of twelve descendants of the Prophet) as the second.[2] He explored the thoughts of Mu'tazila – an early theological school of Islam that advocated objective ethics – and interpreted Qur'ānic revelation as a confirmation of intrinsic normative instincts present in the soul of every individual. Among Mu'tazila's major dogmas was justice as both a religious and an extrareligious virtue.[3] The rival Ash'arī school of thought believed justice to be limited and defined by God's wills and deeds.[4] Shaykh Mufīd, however, along with a predominant majority of Shi'i scholars after him, shared the Mu'tazilī's universal concept of justice, which had direct implications for Shi'i ethics of war and peace.

Given that Shi'i societies have been political and social minorities during a good part of their history,[5] a universal and sometimes absolutist notion of justice seemed to be the best political guarantor of Shi'i rights, especially among those living within the majority Sunni Muslim populations. Importantly, when justice became the primary article of Shi'i dogma, it helped to define Shi'a relations with both sectarian others and non-Muslims. The historic focus of Shi'ism on justice can explain why the Prophetic statement "The political rule survives with unbelief, but not with injustice" has become proverbial in the political literature of this religious denomination.

In 1979, a prominent Shi'i scholar and jurist Ayatollah Khomeini ascended to the position of supreme leader of Iran during a massive revolution and became the highest authority in the present Iranian theocracy. He headed a unique political system that was supposed to end the many centuries of political suppression of the Shi'a throughout the course of Muslim history. Such a dream, however, did not last long; Iraq's invasion of Iran psychologically switched the Shi'i mentality back to the same old station of finding injustice as a norm in global affairs. Very soon, war became an episodic drama that revived the painful collective memories of Shi'ism's past – one that was difficult to resolve by negotiating with the same world powers that, in Iran's conspiracy-laden political view, were the main instigators of the war. In effect, to the Iranian psyche the world was still unjust, if not more so, and the country's revolutionary society could not find a chance to institutionalize and enjoy the fresh self-confidence gained in the course of the victorious 1979 Revolution. Iranians were driven back once again to a precarious defensive footing, both practically and conceptually. In effect, they embraced the same old idealistic, absolutist sense of justice; it was this political psychology that caused many peace mediations during the Iran-Iraq War to fail. The net result was the prolongation of the the Iran-Iraq War for six more years after 1982, when Iran managed to push Iraqi forces out of two major occupied cities, Abadan and Khorramshahr.

The perceived need for punitive justice against the Iraqi invaders, which symbolized a history of suppression encompassing the time between Husayn b. 'Alī's martyrdom in 680 and Iran's 1979 Revolution, was more than just a moral option; it was perceived as a historic, religious duty incumbent upon a nation. After all, the chant "I wish I were with you to experience the great victory of martyrdom" has been a proverbial Shi'i statement of allegience to al-Husayn for centuries. This phrase, deeply embedded into the consciousness of every Shi'i individual, was the most sincere conversation they had ever had with the soul of their martyred imams. This spiritual call, chanted for over a millennium, symbolized the irrelevance of the passage of time in the face of an unforgettable and unforgivable tragedy that became one of the most important Shi'a identifiers in its history. This connection with historic tragedy explains why some devout revolutionaries had little to no sensitivity towards the monumental human and material costs of the the Iran-Iraq War. Justice was always paramount in Shi'i theology, and now justice at war became a significant fixation as well – a commitment owed to mankind and history.

Ultimately and fortunately, in the midst of a national emotional entanglement with a utopian sense of justice, the Shi'i seminarian tradition of *ijtihād*, or scholarly independent reasoning, saved rational Shi'ism from traditional sentimentalism. Moreover, some of Iran's revolutionary leaders gradually became cognizant of the fact that they were not only responsible for the fate of Twelver Shi'ism but also in charge of an ancient country and civilization symbolized by Cyrus the Great, recognized as having authored the first known, universal declaration of human rights in history.

Ayatollahs Montazerī, Sālehī-Najafābādī, and Rafsanjani each in their own way engaged in open and discrete criticism of the war and the futility of its continuation. These criticisms, together with practical and financial stalemates, large-scale human tragedies, the exhaustion of Iran's armed forces, and the dissent voiced by many intellectual critics of war from Bazargān to Behbahānī, halted the perpetual war machine fueled by martyrdom enthusiasts.

The unexpected negotiated end of the Iran-Iraq War in July 1988, however, triggered a serious reevaluation of the philosophy, jurisprudence, ethics, and politics of war and peace. On the one hand, a considerable amount of government-subsidized war-related literature, including novels and soldiers' memoirs, were published periodically to convey an appreciative and nostalgic sense of the collective sacrifice experienced during eight years of war. The goal was to keep alive a culture of selflessness and Shi'i piety. This strategy could also guarantee the public's loyalty to protect Iran's nascent and fragile theocracy. On the other hand, and perhaps more importantly, some influential academic and seminarian literature produced during and after the war explored moral aspects of modern wars and the relationship between war and justice in the areas of religious tradition, universal ethics, and modern political philosophy. This bold and critical literature has encouraged theoretical reform of age-old concepts related to the ethics of war and peace in Shi'i Islam and Iran.

This book endeavoured to reflect on these reform literatures produced both within and outside of Iran's scholastic and seminarian circles. The robust intellectual, theological, and jurisprudential scholarship developing in Iran during the two decades following the Iran-Iraq War points to a new direction for the theological perception and definition of the enemy and the ethics of war and peace. The concept of the enemy, for example, is less and less ideologized. In effect, Iranian-Shi'i international relations began to shift from the idealistic, pan-Islamic solidarity imagined in the early revolutionary years to relations based on objective and universal moral perspectives, economic and strategic factors, state's bilateral interests, and modern paradigms in international relations. The remarkable shifts in Iran's foreign policy and political literature during Rouhani's presidency (as compared to that of his predecessor) should be credited at least in part to the above trends rather than to the economic sanctions against Iran alone.

An increase in a critical reading of traditional Islamic scholarship and Shi'i history, as well as a new-found tendency towards universal rationalism, human rights, and nonviolence in modern Shi'i jurisprudence, is well reflected in the works of Mohaqqeq Dāmād, Shabestarī, Sālehī-Najafābādī, Kadivar, Feirahī, and other like-minded seminarian scholars.

At a higher hierarchical and institutional level, the top Shi'i religious leaders and sources of emulation are showing an increasing sensitivity and response to moral issues related to international, interfaith, and intersectarian war and peace. Among these leaders, Grand Ayatollahs Sīstānī in Iraq, Montazerī, Sāne'ī, and Shirazī have seriously begun to reformulate the Shi'i ethics of war and peace based on a balance between human rights for the individual and for the community. They have also contributed to a thriving postwar (*post bellum*) literature that introduces forgiveness as an imperative moral construct in war and peace.

Grand Ayatollahs Makārem Shirazi, Sobhānī, and Āmolī have initiated, in various degrees, groundbreaking *fatwa*s on the ban of weapons of mass destruction (WMDs). At the official state level, Ayatollah Khamenei has pioneered significant jurisprudential positions against the production and the use of weapons of mass destruction.

Major moral philosophers, intellectuals, and ethicists, such as Bāzargān, Soroush, Malekīān, Fanā'ī, Farāsatkhāh, Esfandīārī, and others, are subjecting jurisprudence to universal ethics from outside the seminarian circles and world view. They have effectively argued that religion, religious rulings, and institutions must be accountable to rational morality, not the other way around. Scholars of Islamic and political philosophy, Persian chivalry, and Iranian history, such as Nasr, Jāhānbegloo, Zākerī, Afshari, and Kātouzīān, are effectively coalescing rational and moral Shi'ism and nonviolence with Iranian cosmopolitanism. Poets, singers, musicians, artists, and film directors, such as Behbahānī, Shajariān, Banī Etemād, and Majīdī, have launched monumental and globally effective campaigns against war and violence that have helped to develop a confident and civilization-conscious mindset in postwar Iran. All of these positive activities are not merely intellectual desires; rather, they demonstrate how the new Iranian generation actually thinks. This is why statements like "I am not a colonel, I am a jurist"[6] and "Extremism is a sign of a lack of self-confidence,"[7] by President Rouhani and his foreign minister Javad Zarif respectively, not only furthered their success during Iran's 2013 presidential election and parliamentary vote of confidence but also brought them national and international popularity, specifically after the monumental nuclear agreement between Iran and 5+1 industrial countries.

The significant setbacks during the Arab Spring (as, for example, in Egypt, where a popular revolution ended in the presidency of the military general el-Sisi) and the failed coup d'état in Turkey in July 2016 provide proper frameworks in which to assess political developments in Iran. Iran's peaceful government transition from the populist Ahmadinejad to the reformist president Rouhani, which resulted from a popular election that occurred at the same time that a military government in Egypt was engaged in killing unarmed protesters in Cairo, conveys a clear message. The postfundamentalist Iran has little to no interest in returning to outdated ideological dogmas. She is emerging as a conscious reader of history, reluctant to repeat its uncalculated habits, misperceptions, and impulsive reactions.

The above assertions may sound too rosy. Radical voices in Iran are still numerous even after the landslide defeat of radicals in the March 2016 parliamentary election. No question – some of Iran's militant interests and literature still sell in this country. As similar cases in the United States and in many other countries have proved, military industry, economy, and mentality that feed on crisis are a diehard. But the Iranian public and leadership can hardly overlook the tragic situations in Iraq, Egypt, Libya, and Syria that resulted directly from decades of military dictatorships in these countries. Iran's foreign minister Zarif reflected on this awareness aptly in his talk to Iranian military personnel in late October 2015, when he addressed the two faces of radicalism and compared the unfortunate fate of Iraq's Saddam Hussein with that of Libya's Muammar al-Ghadafi, one failed because of uncalculated overaction and the other for uncalculated inaction at a time when international relations are in a multifactored transitional mode.[8]

The tragic fates of Saddam Hussein and al-Ghadafi, and the violent and beastly faces of Daesh and the Taliban as reflected in the mirror of the universal ethics of war have brought Iran to appreciate the deep wisdom of a famous Persian proverb: "The wise Loqman was asked from whom did he learn his fine morality? He answered, 'From those who did not have it.'"

Perhaps the net result of the exceptionally long and very costly Iran-Iraq War may be summarized in the following conclusion: Shi'ism, historically a protest theology and cognizant of a millennium of suppression as a Muslim minority, found its opportunity during the Iranian Revolution and the Iran-Iraq War to pay its historic and ideological debt to its tragic history, which began with the episode of Karbalā in 680 and has been fraught with injustice ever since. The Shi'i theology of protest coloured by an absolutist sense of justice contributed many centuries later to the prolongation of the Iran-Iraq War. But ironically, it was the high scale of human and material loss in that war and observing the immorality of Daesh and the Taliban in their battles that encouraged the subsequent development of a thriving and critical Shi'i-Iranian scholarship on the ethics of war and peace. As demonstrated in this volume, such modern tragedies liberated Shi'i scholarship from the millennial grip of obsolete war jurisprudence. In the end, the inconclusive prolongation of war with Iraq and the violent and inhuman record of the Taliban and Daesh during their short history together symbolized the defeat of the political philosophy of revenge and of a moral perspective that thrives on sacrificial duties unconnected to the tangible and tragic realities of modern life.

As the memory of two devastating world wars in the twentieth century remains relevantly fresh, it is hard to dispute that a major cause of the Second World War was excessive punitive justice inflicted upon the losers of the First World War. Having had their own direct experiences with a devastating chain of regional wars, Iran, Iraq, and modern Shi'ism seem to have learned a lesson well expressed in the Qu'rān for over fourteen centuries: that is, the living world cannot survive with justice alone. Qur'ānic verse 45:35 unequivocally asserts, "And if Allah were to impose blame [punitive justice] on the people for what they have earned, He would not leave upon the earth any creature."

For any contemporary scholar, diplomat, or negotiator studying or engaging with the Iranian-Shi'i ethics of war and peace, it is important to understand how, in the mind of each and every Iranian, a theology of strict justice exists in permanent tension with a mystic philosophy of peace and benevolence. On the one hand, historical memories of political suppression and, on the other, peace-centric perspectives of Persian mystic mentors, such as Rumi, Hafez, and Sa'di, have influenced the Iranian public psyche. It is therefore no wonder that the poetic Iranian culture, almost by definition, has a strong tendency to "embrace the possibility of contradiction," a phrase borrowed from the great scholar of Andalusian literature Maria Rosa Menocal.[9]

Hamid Dabashi has concluded that the above tension causes a cultural clash between Shi'i protest theology and its cosmopolitanism. Dabashi maintains that during the Safavid era, the Shi'i cosmopolitanism won over the protest theology, because Shi'ism could express itself elaborately in the public space and by the vehicles of reason, art, and literature.[10]

Even a cursory study of the history of the Islamic Republic of Iran since 1979 demonstrates that the same trend has been on the rise for more than two decades in this country. Iran is seeing unprecedented and internationally recognized productions in film, music, calligraphy, painting, and other visual and performative arts. Additionally, as this work has attempted to demonstrate, in the emotionally charged fields of war and peace a sense of universal reason is on the rise in modern Shi'i-Iranian scholarship and policymaking. Do we, therefore, have all the necessary practical and conceptual elements required for the rise of Shi'i cosmopolitanism?

For Dabashi, the only unresolved question impeding Iranians from embracing a full, syncretic cosmopolitanism is a politico-theological paradox. This is the insoluble paradox between "Shi'i triumphalism," which requires an enduring sense of victimization to be considered legitimate, and an institutionalized theocracy, which cannot survive the stresses of international relations while maintaining the sense of permanent protest essential to Shi'ism.[11] In other words, Dabashi maintains that official Iranian Shi'ism is presently caught between political victory and moral defeat.[12] In Dabashi's own words, "The only way for Shi'ism to resolve its enduring paradox is to absolve it into the world at large and transform it from being at odds with itself to being at odds with a world at odds with itself."[13] Abdolkarim Soroush mentions this very point, though within a different framework. He states that Iran's official endeavour to maintain an ongoing revolutionary spirit in the country leads to a destabilization of the theocracy itself, because revolution by definition tends to change the status quo.[14]

This work has demonstrated that a reading of the present political, theological, and intellectual posture of Iran suggests that modern Iran is fully cognizant of the above paradoxes and is, in effect, moving towards practical solutions for them. Although the structure of the Iranian theocracy seems to be the same as it was before, it is gradually experiencing the emergence of pragmatic politicians in turbans, rather than theologians clothed in secular suits; this is what the French scholar Laurence Louer accurately terms "the secularization of Shi'a political Islam."[15]

If negotiations between Iran and the six world powers on the nuclear issue have taken far too many frustrating years, it can be blamed partly on the lack of a sophisticated language that can define the elements comprising Islamic-Persian culture, traditions, and a sense of security; a language that is not disconnected from Shi'i-Iranian history and theology is needed. These elements need to be translated not only into European languages but also into modern theologies that can facilitate cultural understanding. Moreover, a Western negotiator unaware of the history and background of a Shi'i-Iranian position towards war, peace, chivalry, mysticism, and friendship can hardly be expected to offer the confidence-building elements of which modern Iran needs to be assured.

Modern Shi'i jurisprudence on the ethics of war and peace is becoming increasingly open to universal wisdom, modern philosophy, etiquettes of chivalry, the politics of forgiveness, and the theology of disarmament. Seminarian pedagogies are moving beyond old juristic paradigms and are becoming open to the cultural sources of the great Iranian civilization. Because of this new openness, a serious interest is on the rise in Iran in finding Persian-speaking versions of Nelson Mandelas and Mahatma Gandhis, rather than Fidel Castros and Che Guevaras.

Many contemporary scholars agree that Muslim political philosophy has traditionally been subdued by the monopoly of jurists and jurisprudence. A survey of the presently thriving critical theology and scholarship of self-criticism in Iran demonstrates that the above trend has reached a historic turning point that requires close study with proper expertise; hopefully, this book has taken a step in this direction. I have demonstrated two significant trends: First, modern Shi'i jurisprudence is responsibly opening itself to criticism from ethicists and political philosophers. Second, this jurisprudence has also become self-critical and is re-evaluating a good deal of its outdated positive laws, which have been adopted uncritically from various sources.

Perhaps the most important point of this book is its argument that the Shi'ism of Iran's postrevolutionary era is moving away from its previously reactive, utopian, and ideological tendencies and is approaching a cosmopolitan posture that represents the truest sense of the broader Iranian identity. The current generation in Iran is looking for a type of politics and a religio-intellectual posture that incites a sense of belonging beyond political and denominational borders. In the early years of the twenty-first century, Vali Nasr's insightful book *The Shia Revival* caught the attention of many American policymakers. A strong regional Shi'i revivalism now seeks more than to display its desire for a just share in the Middle East's fortunes of politics and economy: it is trying to contain and transform a fundamentalist Islam that is detrimental not only to Iran's security and her neighbouring countries but also to Islam's global image. By discussing how modern Iranian intellectuals are shifting gears from ideological conformism to serious critical thinking in the areas of war and peace, I have tried to argue that a syncretic and civilization-conscious soul is emerging in Iran.

The story of this book is not yet finished. The study of the past and the present should hint at the future. As Iran shifts its international posture from one driven by revolution and reaction to one founded on cultural interdependence and cosmopolitanism, Iran is taking a fairer attitude in expecting her international counterparts to interact in the same spirit.

Many Iranians and Persian-speaking communities, including non-Muslims, revere Cyrus the Great as their common-identity maker. Cyrus is revered not just for his vast empire but more so for respecting freedom of religion and acting as one of the first human-rights advocates, as the famous Cyrus Cylinder bears witness.[16] The ancient king is also well remembered for having liberated the Jews from captivity in Babylon and for sponsoring and paying for the construction of the Second Jewish Temple in Jerusalem, a monument sacred to Jews to this day. In the wake of so many intrastate wars that are presently fragmenting the Middle East in both territorial and cultural senses, the historical reel played in reverse makes Cyrus look like the Middle East's great unifier. The Islamic Republic's early pan-Islamic aspirations and policies have hardly scored any success on any ground since the Iranian Revolution in 1979. Consciousness of these historical successes and failures makes the generation of postrevolutionary, post–Iran-Iraq War, and postsanctions Iranians interested in pursuing a different direction. The robust critical and humanistic thinking about the ethics of war and peace that is emerging in Iran truly represents the Iranian cultural reorientation.

On religious grounds, the lessons learned from past wars prove that certain hostile measures over the course of history have the tendency to form an integral part of enduring theologies. If the Karbalā tragedy in 680 could influence the prolongation of a war thirteen centuries later in the 1980s, then modern policymakers across the world must beware that even a short-term war can construct a hostile theology that can endure for centuries and victimize many future generations.

Finally, an unfinished business in conflict-resolution scholarship and practice must be addressed. It is fortunate that during the last couple of decades the world has been witness to a thriving trend of scholarship regarding the ethics of peace. In spite of this progress, at least two additional fields have been waiting for in-depth studies: the ethics of forgiveness and the ethics of friendship in politics. Indeed, all Abrahamic faiths, including Islam, have the strong potential to contribute to the notion of forgiveness in politics. Moreover, the legacies of such key figures as Mahatma Gandhi and Nelson Mandela have already provided important cases for serious study and scholarship in this field. Critics of "secular paradigm" in conflict resolution, such as Daniel Philpott and Gerald Powers, encourage the inclusion of religion in peacemaking approaches and efforts, making it hard to imagine that the ethics of forgiveness could make any substantial progress without religious contributions.[17]

Additional serious studies on civic forgiveness must be conducted in order to use this virtue more effectively in public discourse and international relations; this is also true of the ethics of friendship, which defines a realm beyond justice-based ethics. Friendship, especially in Islam, is a justice-plus cardinal virtue – a virtue that defies the predominant zero-sum paradigm in interpersonal and international relations. Muslim philosopher Abū 'Alī Miskawayh (d. 1030) argued that humanity is predicated on gregariousness, or the art of intimacy, and the role of a political leader is to maintain the public institution of social intimacy.[18] As such, friendship represents a moral world view that transcends a legalist framework for life and focuses on surpassing distributive or punitive justice in intercommunal and international relations. It can elevate our state of relations beyond the negative virtue of tolerance, as Gustave Niebuhr suggests in *Beyond Tolerance*. Friendship as a world view looks at others not as competitors in a race for scarce resources but as blessings and companions of fortune. Shi'i-Iranian culture, which helped Islamic humanism to flourish during the Buyid dynasty (934–1062) and has deep roots in gnostic world views, rational jurisprudence, and artistic-poetic abilities, has much to offer in promoting a necessary paradigmatic, moral shift in international relations.

If modernity alone has not yet matured us beyond the need for war, we need to be conscious that, as the historian Toynbee has mentioned, militarism has been the most important common cause of the downfall of twenty civilizations so far.[19] We also need to be aware that our behaviours in war, as Walzer has articulated, continue to test and may defeat any moral system by which we claim to abide.[20] Hardly anything seems to be more ironic than acting viciously in the name of any belief system and on behalf of a God who is supposed to be the Creator of those very "enemies."

Unfortunately, not many societies are conscious of the fact that fixing past injustices through punitive wars only comes at the high cost of future friendships. In the view of the great Iranian-gnostic poet Hafez of Shiraz, friendship and love must not be left to fate.[21] Under the current paradigms of international relations, even just wars and peace treaties do just this: they draw false lines of ideology or political identities over maps and claim that *I* am somehow different from *you*. Diversity is a blessing, and, as Martin Buber will agree, it is no cause for conflict.[22] When the blood finally dries, we are told to stop fighting – but never to start loving. Friendship, like any other skill, does not grow if not well conceptualized and institutionalized, especially during uncomfortable and difficult situations. While the process is slow and often trying, the potential gains for any such endeavour make the struggle a noble one. Some seven hundred years ago, it appears that Hafez got it right:

صد ملک دل به نیم نظر میتوان خرید   خوبان در این معامله تقصیر میکنند
قومی به جد و جهد نهادند وصل دوست   قومی دگر حواله به تقدیر میکنند

(One can purchase a hundred realms of heart with half a glance,
In this act, inefficiency, lovely ones present.
With efforts and struggle a crowd established union with the friend,
Reliance on fate, another crowd make.)[23]

The ethics of war and peace, like any other normative study, are not only impressed upon by religious traditions but are also influenced by such factors as literature, customs, epical and mythical narratives, institutions of chivalry, psychology, and even dreams and other relevant cultural sources and paradigms. In this spirit, the interplay between Shi'ism and Iranian culture claims a significant role in the formation of Iranian ethics of war and peace. My deepest hope is that reading through the literature and works of key authors and scholars in this field could help manifest the inhumanity of war to a point where the term "ethics of war" would sound more an oxymoron.

Whether we think of "war as the continuation of politics," as Clausewitz expressed it in his proverbial phrase, or consider politics as war through other means, as professional jihadist and weapon industries do, we are still prisoners locked into the same militant paradigm that worships violence as the means, goals, or both. Our collective liberation from this prison first and foremost requires our intellectual graduation from the kindergarten of morality, alternatively called punitive justice or living in the negative past. On a personal level, our religions or our concepts of religion must also improve. If we agreed with Kai Nielsen's wisdom, "It is not morality that rests on religion but religion on morality,"[24] a better future for all mankind could only be imagined and attained through a higher wisdom: *it is not friendship that rests on morality but morality on friendship.*

Iranian Shi'ism is conceptually rich for espousing this paradigm, but only if it is ready to depart from the theologies and eschatology of revenge. If the chief founder of Shi'i theology, namely Shaykh Mufīd, were alive today, I doubt he would have resisted a paradigmatic change in his moral focus from the realm of justice to the higher moral space of benevolence and bounty (*tafaddul*). It will perhaps be only through this change that Shi'ism can find and define its true meaning and its moral raison d'être in the twenty-first century.

APPENDIXES I & II

Appendixes 1 and 2 provide my translations of two entries in the *Great Islamic Encyclopedia* (published in Iran), one on jihad and the other on the Persian *jang* (war). These complementary articles discuss notions of both jihad and nonreligious war (*jang*). They also tackle developments in both realms of justice of war (*jus ad bellum*) and justice in war (*jus in bello*) in the history of Muslim juristic thought. The articles to date (2015) and to the extent of my knowledge are the latest well-sourced and most succinct encyclopedic articles on the subject matter produced by Iranian/Twelver-Shiʿi authors in the Persian language. Both articles represent Iranian critical thoughts on the ethics of war and will be important sources for relevant scholarships. Given their significance, I have decided to provide a rough translation of both articles not only because they are occasionally referenced in this volume, but also for the possible wider use by the reader.

The first article provides an overview of jihad and the development of various interpretations and implications of this notion in Muslim political and intellectual history. It demonstrates how the concept of jihad has been at times dynamically used, at times arbitrarily abused, and frequently has received modified interpretations by various Muslim political and religious figures, entities, and institutions. The article also provides an overview of important primary and secondary Shiʿi and Sunni sources related to the ethics of war and peace in Islam. The first article, although rich in tackling some aspects of ethics of war (*jus ad bellum*), is nevertheless more of a critical overview of the history of the concept than a scholarly attention to jurisprudential arguments about the justice of war in its technical meaning. Notwithstanding the difference between jihad as a concept that conveys religious wars and *jang* (or its Arabic equivalents *harb/qitāl*) as war in a secular or nonreligious sense, the second article in appendix 2 provides an overview of Twelver-Shiʿa laws in war (*jus in bello*).

The first article serves as a fresh prism through which one can see how contemporary Shi'i-Iranian scholars formulate a macrohistory of jihad in Muslim life and the development of this concept in the annals of Muslim and Shi'i scholarship. Since the goal of this book is not to provide a full account of jihad in broader Muslim scholarship, all of the original footnotes and references are not presented in the translation for two reasons: First, some footnote details are not directly related to the focus of this book and were not necessary here. Second, the text itself provides many references to significant sources. To better understand the dates and years as they appear in the text, I have added the corresponding Common Era dates to match the Arabic lunar (AH) calendar.

Appendix I

"Jihad": A Historical Overview of the Concept of Its Politics[1]

Jihad in the Qur'ān and Hadith

As one of the devotional and practical pillars of faith, the word jihad represents a wide range of struggles in the service of God. Developed from the three-lettered Arabic root word of *jhd*, the word *mujahida* conveys that jihad refers to a reciprocal, rather than a unilateral, struggle.

The frequency of the use of jihad and its various derivative words occurs forty-one times in the Qur'ān. A close analysis of the word jihad in the Qur'ān shows that it is predominantly defined within the epistemological realm of the Arabic term *fī sabīl Allah* [in the way of God]. Literally, *sabīl* in Arabic usage is related to following the right path while passing through a desert. As Izutsu points out, this notion is used as a metaphor in human-divine relations. The interconnection between jihad and *sabīl* in the Qur'ān explains the responsive nature of jihad. To understand this responsiveness, one needs to look also at another Qur'ānic phrase, namely *saddu 'an sabīl Allah* [blocking the way of God].[2] In the above context, jihad means "struggling to remove barriers blocking the way of faith." To understand this struggle in its historic context, one must hone in on the difficult situation faced by early Muslims in Mecca, where their practice of the new faith faced many hurdles, threats, violence, hardships, and wars perpetrated by the Quraish tribe [the leading tribe in Mecca]. As such, the practice of faith needed, and indeed endured, serious struggles and tests of steadfastness.

This wide range of difficult encounters and tensions risked alienating a new believer to the verge of deserting Islam, committing apostasy – or inclining towards hypocrisy and skepticism – as some Qur'ānic verses have warned. It is in this spirit that the Qur'ān defines [a broad sense of] jihad as a necessary defence (Q. 2:217, 218; 8:31; 11:12; 9:45; 63:8; 2:217, and 5:54). Faced with these threats, the Qur'ān stresses that the only winners are *mujahids* [active participle of the verb *jihad*].[3]

Later on, the interconnection between the three notions of faith, God's path, and jihad caused hadith literature to embrace an expansive meaning of jihad and to include a very broad range of notions such as: seeking legitimate provision; struggling with ego; performing the major and minor pilgrimage [*hajj* and *'umra*]; avoiding transgression against another human being; seeking knowledge; exercising piety in acquiring wealth; serving parents; resisting jealousy and rivalry with others in the pursuit of wealth; managing house affairs by women; keeping secrets of the house of the Prophet; and finally, fighting with polytheists.

The above list demonstrates how scholars' understanding of jihad in the very early Islamic periods overwhelmingly conveyed notions of mental discipline and keeping a person's own carnal soul under control. The next phase of epistemological expansion in the meaning of jihad includes almost any righteous act, including jihad, with mind, tongue, heart, limbs, and charity.

As we come close to the period of Islamic civil and expansionist wars, jihad was increasingly used for armed struggle, whether defensive or offensive. During the middle of the first Islamic century and its accompanying civil wars [specifically the Siffin war between 'Alī and Mu'āwiya at the time of the caliphate of 'Alī b. Abī Tālib], jihad was frequently used to draw fighters into the cause.

After this period, during the process of empire building and political consolidation, the usage of jihad became identical to *qitāl* [conventional war]. As the Crusade wars progressed, the tendency of exegetes of the Qur'ān towards militant interpretation of the scriptures became dominant – even when the text and contexts of verses were irrelevant to armed struggle. As a result, Qur'ānic exegesis faced serious difficulties. For example, while the militant interpretation of verses Q. 9:73 and 66:9 ordered war against Muslim hypocrites, in reality the Prophet never fought with them and, retrospectively, would be seen as failing to execute God's order.

With the development of various fields of Islamic disciplines such as exegesis [*tafsīr*] and jurisprudence [*fiqh*], jihad was widely used in association with a number of terms, such as *qitāl*, *harb*, *ghazw*, and *shahada* [martyrdom], all related to notions of war. As a result, and unrelated to the Qur'ānic and hadith contexts, the farthest notion of jihad from its original meaning permitted expansionist and primary [unprovoked or offensive] wars.

The metamorphosis of the meaning of jihad over many years, evolved to include a broad range of notions, from the Prophet's regular praise of jihad as a spiritual exercise to the militant interpretation of the word as practised today by radical groups. This is how the arbitrarily developed, radical meaning of jihad has become increasingly fashionable in a vast part of the Muslim world. The militant meaning of jihad was certainly useful for an expansionist political culture. In essence, the pre-Islamic Arab culture that viewed armed forays and plunders as a normal way of life, coupled with its need to attract a formidable influx of volunteer soldiers, corrupted the meaning of jihad and alienated it from its original esoteric context.

Another significant reason for such a metamorphosis was that the term *qitāl* [conventional war] was so conditioned in its legal use and by many limitations in the Qur'ānic context that it could not serve expansionist agendas. Conversely, jihad was used and advocated far more frequently and widely in the Qur'ān without attached conditions or preconditions. As a result, newly converted Muslims could not easily use *qitāl* for political or expansionist goals, thus widening the interpretation of jihad.

A final reason for the abuse of jihad is that in a few instances it sits next to the word *qitāl* in the Qur'ānic text, creating an excuse for some Qur'ānic interpreters to use these distinctly different terms interchangeably. In the end, frequent abuses of the word jihad resulted in considering the concept to mean primary or offensive wars in Islamic jurisprudence.

Jihad in Islamic Jurisprudence[4]

Generally speaking, in Islamic jurisprudence, jihad has been used only to denote war in the way of God. Other forms of jihad, such as one's spiritual endeavour to exercise self-control, are irrelevant to jurisprudence. It is important to note, however, that many jurists do discuss jihad in a broad sense as a pillar of faith in the context of benevolence and financing the expansion of Islam. The juridical emphasis on jihad has gradually become so strong that neglecting or escaping it came to be considered a cardinal sin.

Not all legitimate Muslim wars are necessarily considered jihad according to jurists. For example, if a Muslim living in a non-Muslim country has to defend himself against a non-Muslim invading force, his defence, while legitimate, cannot be credited as legal jihad.

The placement of discussions about jihad within the structure of most classical works of jurisprudence bears witness to the significance of the subject for jurists. In most juristic textbooks, jihad is discussed at the level of other significant pillars of faith, such as pilgrimage, alms giving, or daily prayers. Some Sunni jurists, however, have discussed jihad in the context of penal codes. There are also cases where jihad is discussed in biographical books or what is called *sīyar*.

Generally speaking, jurists present jihad in two parts: rules about the actor upon whom jihad has been incumbent and rules about the persons who are targets of jihad [the enemies]. Some texts also provide a third section addressing the rules dictating how to treat people of the book [followers of other Abrahamic religions] and regulations for sharing war booty.

Jihad as Duty

Muslim jurists remind their readers that the Prophet and his companions were not permitted to engage in any war for the entire period of their residence in Mecca, even during their early Medina years. Before the battle of Badr, Muslims were permitted to resort to war only when they were about to be attacked by a Meccan army. The Qur'ān permitted Muslims to take up arms in Q. 22:39 and then obliged them to defend themselves in 2:216.

From a specific, juristic approach, armed jihad as a duty is different from other devotional rituals and religious duties, such as alms giving, daily prayer, and fasting, in that jihad requires eligibility/legitimacy. Jihad is task oriented and based on collective [*fard kifaya*], rather than independent, individual obligation [*fard 'ain*]. The law of eligibility for war precludes old men, children, and women from participating in war. The obligatory nature of jihad exempts all eligible individuals, if the goal has already been attained or the effort has found enough volunteer participants. One exception from the above relief provisions is that those individuals who are specifically asked by the war commander to perform a task must join. Some jurists have ruled that if a government has access to professional soldiers, jihad loses its obligatory status for the public.

Jihad is also not obligatory for the blind, sick, or individuals who, barring their ability to find a sponsor, cannot afford their household expenses, the weapons needed to fight, and the costs of travelling. Some jurists include parental consent among eligibility conditions. For Shi'i jurists, an eligible individual could, in theory, hire someone to be his deputy in performing jihad, even if the mercenary is non-Muslim or nonreligious. Sunni jurists, however, do not permit duty delegation.

Targets of Jihad

Sources of jurisprudence specify three groups of people as targets of jihad: hostile nonbelievers, all categories of infidels/disbelievers, and the *dhimmī* non-Muslims [people of the book, such as Jews and Christians, who pay a special tax to Muslim governments in exchange for their protection] only if they fail to pay their taxes or fail to implement other provisions of their contracts with their Muslim protectorate. For some jurists, Muslim insurgents could also be targets of armed jihad.

Jurists from all schools maintain that the main task of jihad is to remove obstacles preventing an invitation to convert [*da'wa*]. Muslims are not allowed to initiate a battle before the actual invitation to conversion takes place [which parallels the no-first-strike principle in modern wars]. But if the enemy initiates a battle, then war becomes an obligation for Muslim fighters. Muslim commanders, based on various expediencies, can decide to end the war as they wish.

General Conditions for Armed Jihad

For Shi'i jurists [the majority of them], jihad is an obligation only when an infallible imam or his explicitly appointed deputy is present. In other words, armed jihad under an illegitimate ruler, or in cases when there is no ruler, is strictly forbidden and is, in fact, a cardinal sin, unless the war is strictly defensive. In Sunni schools, however, armed jihad is legitimate under any caliph [just or unjust]. The source of the juristic ruling for Sunni schools was a Prophetic hadith, which states that jihad is permitted under all rulers [*al-jihad ma'a kulli amir*]. For both the Sunni and Shi'i schools, military service at the borders [*murābita*] was permitted without the presence or permission of any imam because it did not necessarily lead to war. However, for the Shi'i school, the absence of the occult imam means no offensive war is legitimate. Defensive wars, however, are allowed irrespective of the legitimacy of political authorities. Importantly, some Shi'i jurists refrain from using the word jihad in relation to defensive wars. Instead, they simply refer to it as defence [*difā'*].

Armed jihad is not permitted during four specific months, unless the enemy does not observe this condition or has initiated the war [the four lunar months include *Muharram*, *Rajab*, *Dhi'l Qa'da*, and *Dhi'l Hijjah* in the Arabic calendar]. Some jurists [such as Ibn Quddāma] have stated that for the promotion or expansion of Islam, armed jihad must be performed on an annual basis. Others have commented that such a ruling was relevant in earlier periods of the Islamic advent, when the newly formed Muslim society was on the defensive. But in other periods, Islam can only be promoted within particular time cycles. Some jurists highlight details relating to the devotional rituals in battlefields, such as performing daily prayers.

A number of legal manuals focus on the laws in war, such as banning the use of fire, flood, or scorching the earth as war tactics. They also ban the destruction of sanctuaries, as well as surprise, nonchivalrous night attacks, and killing women, children, and monks – both as primary and secondary targets. There are also detailed on regulations about prisoners of war and on the treatment of the corpses of enemy fighters. Prisoners must be treated humanely and protected from harm.

Some texts pay special attention to questions relating to financing armed jihad. Many jurists, for example, state that the alms tax could be given to warriors. Some texts even detail the clothing worn by Muslim fighters: unless the martyr is naked, he does not need to be wrapped in a shroud for burial.

The ethics of war has become a subject of renewed scholarly interest in recent years, with a new trend of Muslim scholarship on the rise in the field. In the Sunni school, Zuhayr Shafiq Kibbi has written an important jihad treatise entitled *Fiqh al-jihad* [The jihad jurisprudence], which is based on the views of Ibn Taymīyya (d. 1328 CE). Muhammd Khayyir Haykal has also written a doctoral thesis titled *Al-jihad wa'l qitāl fi'l sīyāsa al-shar'īya* [Jihad and war in the politics of Islamic law]. Both authors have developed a well-structured and thorough discussion on jihad jurisprudence according to various Muslim legal schools.

Jihad in the History of Muslim Cultures

The Prophet Muhammad was associated with many wars, which were alternately called *sarīya* whenever he was present in battle and *ghazwa* whenever he was not. The venture of these battles and forays, launched mostly against the Arab polytheists and sometimes against Jewish communities, were called *ghazawāt* [Arabic plural of *ghazwa*] or *maghāzī* [literary forays or battles]. A number of Qur'ānic verses on jihad are also connected with occasions of intertribal battles. As such, many rules and regulations about war were developed during the Prophet's life and were systematized and codified later in the eighth century. These rules, echoed in Prophetic biographies [*sīyar*, Arabic plural of *sīra*] and hadith literature, eventually became sources of jurisprudence on jihad. As noted before, during the Meccan period and early years of residence at Medina, the Prophet resisted war. He never forewent possible alternatives to war, clearly preferring peaceful solutions. All of the wars he fought were either defensive or a means of pre-empting offensive wars. Nevertheless, because Prophetic wars have been subject to various interpretations on their motives, Prophetic biographies have also received a variety of scholarly treatments.

The term *ghazw* [or *ghazwa*] – and its corresponding word in Persian usage *ghazā* – had a curious relationship with the word jihad early on. Because the word jihad had a wider epistemological usage than war in Qur'ānic and biographic allusions, *ghazā*, which strictly meant war, gradually replaced the word jihad in references made to war. Historically, references to the term *ghazā* are traced to its usage by companions [*sahāba*] of the Prophet and their next generation [*tābi'īn*]. For Muslim scholars of later generations, *ghazā* was interchangeably and increasingly used for jihad. Ultimately, its usage became dominant.

The fact that the term *ghazā* did not convey any religious values during the first three Muslim centuries should be reflective of a conscious cultural development. It demonstrates that Muslim scholars together with the general public intentionally frequented the usage of the term *ghazā* to underscore that the expansionist policies of some Muslim rulers were not based on pious intentions or sacred motives. This is reflected in some of the literature produced during this period.

A well-known hadith focuses on the differences between wars waged to attain sacred goals versus wars fought for material gains. During the time of the Prophets' companions [*sahāba*] and their next generation [*tābi'īn*], scholars with a reputation for piety, such as Abdullah Ibn Abbās (d. 68 AH [687 CE]), Hasan Basrī (d. 110 AH [728 CE]), and Ibn Sīrīn (d. 110 AH [728 CE]), were asked whether fighting for corrupt rulers was legitimate. These questions may not have received clear and correct answers, but all registered answers were unequivocally intended to discourage warriors from fighting for less-than-pious rulers. Besides Ibn Abbas who was outspoken in his political criticism, another very prominent figure, Abdullah b. 'Umar [d. ca. 693 CE], openly responded to public criticism about his desire not to participate in war, emphasizing that he perceived such an act as sedition [*fitna*].

The behaviour of Abū Talha, one of the Prophet's companions, further clarifies that response. During the period that he accompanied the Prophet, Abū Talha had the reputation of never missing a chance to participate in Muslim military campaigns. After the Prophet's demise, he spent his life mostly fasting, reluctant to participate in wars.

In any case, vast conquests of non-Muslim lands under the second caliph 'Umar b. Khattāb (d. 23 AH [644 CE]) occurred around the time when many of the Prophet's close companions were still alive. This time proximity could grant some legitimacy for 'Umar's wars, from which the caliphs after him did not benefit. As a result, when vast borderlines of Muslim territories needed border guards and soldiers, Muslims themselves were reluctant to volunteer for military service. One possible solution, therefore, was to encourage scholars to write *jihadīya*s, documents that motivated the public to enter military service. As a new jurisprudential genre, these *jihadīya*s began to appear from the second Muslim century and afterwards. A number of these *jihadīya*s were hadith-based arguments. They were essentially jihad-related hadith collections, which at that time also provided rules and regulations relating to jihad. Key hadith works include *Al-jihad* by Ibn Mubārak Marvazi (d. 181 AH [797 CE]), *Al-jihad* by Ibn abī 'Āsim (d. 287 AH [900 CE]), and *Al-jihad* by Ibn Batta 'Ukburī (d. 387 AH [797 CE]). Ibn Mubārak was one scholar who actually participated in war.

Gradually, most war-stricken borders became hubs for hadith narrators, helping hadith scholarship gain a universal status and currency. The presence of some of the most prominent hadith narrators, such as Abū ʻUbaid Qāsim b. Salām, in war encouraged this trend. The *jihadīya*s produced by Shiʻi scholars with a distinct hadith approach, such as those written by Muhammad b. Masʻūd ʻAyyāshī and Muhammad Hasan Saffār Qumī, were produced at the end of the third Muslim century [ninth century CE].

The *jihadīya*s written from a jurisprudential approach and addressing various legal schools also included *Al-jihad* by Dawūd Isfāhānī (d. 270 AH [883 CE]) from the Zāhirī school, *Al-jihad* by Ibrahim b. Hammād (d. ca. end third AH [ninth CE] century) from the Maliki school, Abu'l Fadl Muhammad b. Ahmad Sābūnī (d. ca beginning fourth AH [tenth CE] century) from the Imami or Shiʻi school, and *Risala al-bishāra wa'l-nidhara wa'l-istibsār ila'l-jihad* by Ibn Junayd Eskāfī (d. 381 AH [991 CE]) from the Imami [Shiʻi] rationalist school.

Political incentives aside, asceticism and pietism were also alternative spiritual motives for some to join war fronts; it was a way to stay away from the corruption of the cities. For example, Ibrahim Adham (a renowned figure in Islamic mysticism) distanced himself from his aristocratic family and settled on the Syrian border. A number of hadith pieces narrated by the Prophet present jihad as "the monasticism of Muslims" or "tourism of Muslims." These genres of hadiths attracted the attention of prominent scholars, such as Hakīm Tarmadhī (d. ca. 255 AH [869 CE]).

In his research on the wars between Muslims and the Romans [Byzantine Empire] (fourth AH [tenth CE] century), Dhiyāb also concludes that, from the mid-fifth AH [eleventh CE] century on, a wave of jihadi movements were mobilized in western and central Africa by the Murābitūn dynasty (Murābit refers to border warriors).

From the late fifth AH [eleventh CE] century, the question of *ghazw* gained a new dimension of sacredness for Muslims, most likely because Muslim communities sensed they were being targeted by new waves of military advances, which manifested in the Crusades by the end of the eleventh century. Once again, the usage of jihad in reference to wars became dominant. From 448 AH [1095 CE], when the first of the Crusade wars began, the term Crusade-war found currency in Muslim lands. These wars were initiated by Christians and were, therefore, considered by Muslims to be wars in defence of their homeland. During the fifth to sixth AH [eleventh to twelfth CE] centuries, Muslims encountered four main Crusade conflicts. During these wars, the lands bordering and occupied by the Crusaders became jihadi regions. As had occurred before, hadith narrators once again gathered in cities near war borders.

The beginning of the seventh AH [thirteenth CE] century was tumultuous for Muslims. As the Crusades continued throughout Syria and Egypt, the Reconquista forces began to advance towards Muslim lands in Andalusia, managing to overthrow local Muslim rulers everywhere by 609 AH [1214 CE], save Granada. A few years later, in 616 AH [1219 CE], the Mongol forces from East Asia that were headed by Genghis Khan invaded the territory of Khwarazmshahs and conquered Transoxiana and Iraq. Contrary to the Crusades, during which Muslims mostly maintained the upper hand, the wars with the Mongol and Spanish invaders were devastating. Even after some Mongols converted to Islam, the net effect of the invasion was only a lull in the production of jihadi literature.

On the Andalusian side, the state of Granada served as a sanctuary for Spanish Muslims and acted as the only link between Andalusia and the Muslim world. As such, it was fertile ground for the production of *jihadīya* literature, such as *Al-arba'ūn fi'l-haththth 'ala'l-jihad* by Muhammad b. Adur Rahman Maqarrī Tajībī (d. 618 AH [1221 CE]), *Baghyat al-wiqād fi'l ta'rīf bisma al-jihad* by Qāsim b. Muhammad Qurtubī (d. 643 AH [1245 CE]), and those produced by Tilmisānī extended emerging scholarship in the following century, such as *Al-i'timād fi'l Jihad* by the Andalusian scholar resident in Fas, Morocco, Muhammad b. Sa'īd Ra'īnī (d. 778 AH [1376 CE]), *Sabī al-rishād fī fadl al-jihad* by Ahmad b. Ibrahim Ghurnātī, and *Hilyat al-fursān wa sha'ār al-shaj'ān* by 'Ali b. Abdur Rahman b. Hudhay Fazārī.

The Islamic middle lands were also still engaged with the Fifth (614–18 AH [1217–31 CE]), the Sixth (625–6 AH [1228–9 CE]), the Seventh (646–52 AH [1248–54 CE]), and the Eighth (668–9 AH [1270 CE]) Crusades, the last of which witnessed the retaking of Akka (690 AH [1291 CE]) in the heart of Muslim lands. During these years, the production of *jihadīya* literature continued actively with works by Iraqi, Syrian, and Egyptian scholars, including *Al-jihad* by 'Izz al-Din b. Athīr Jazrī (d. 630 AH [1232 CE]), *Ahkām al-jihad* or *fada'il al-jihad* by Yusif b. Rāfi' b. Shaddād Halabī (d. 632 AH [1234 CE]), *Subul al-rishād fi fadl al-jihad* by Sa'd al-Dīn b. Qarātakīn Maqarrī (d. ca. 647 AH [1249 CE]), and *A'lām al-ajnād wa'l-'ibād ahl al-ijtihad fadl al-rabāt wa'l-jihad* by Muhammad b. Musā b. Nu'mān Sufi (d. 683 AH [1284 CE]).

The vast amount of *jihadīya* literature produced during the Crusades resulted in the continuation of this literature long after the wars had ended. Examples are works of scholars such as, 'Afīf al-Dīn b. Dawālībi of Iraq (d. 728 AH [1327 CE]), Badr al-Dīn b. Jamā'a, a judge from Jerusalem (d. 733 AH [1332 CE]), 'Imād al-Dīn b. Kathīr Damashqī (d. 774 AH [1372 CE]) who produced his work at the request of Amir Munjīk to be used in defence of the Syrian seashores, Muhyī al-Dīn b. Nuhās Damashqī (d. 814 AH [1411 CE]) who was personally engaged in the Demyat defence line in Egypt, Majd al-Dīn Firūzābādī (d. 817 AH [1414 CE]) who was visiting Muslim borders in India and Syria, and Walī al-Dīn 'Arāqī (d. 828 AH [1424 CE]). In the fifteenth century CE, sea ports such as Alexandria were tourist attractions, but the inner cities of Syria such as Aleppo and Asqalān were still under threats.

With the growing power of Turks in Asia Minor during the eighth AH [fourteenth CE] century, the buffer zone between Syria and the Byzantine Empire was shattered due to Turkish battles with the Byzantine Christians. The Ottomans expanded their territories across Asia Minor. By the end of the eighth AH [fourteenth CE] century, they had conquered a considerable amount of the Byzantine Empire and were now threatening Constantinople. Though it took a half century to culminate to this point, the city was conquered in 857 AH [1453 CE], effectively ending the Byzantine Empire. The conquest of Constantinople, which had its name changed to Istanbul, was the beginning of Ottoman military campaigns in the heart of Europe. Such military advances revived the culture of *ghazā*. A number of Ottoman rulers, because of their long military engagements, earned the title *ghāzī* or sacred warrior.

All of this gave impetus for writers to produce a whole new series of *jihadīyya* treatises supporting the Ottoman-European campaigns. Some of these writers include Muhammad Ibrahim b. Khatīb Rūmī (d. 901 AH [1495 CE]), Yusif b. Hussayn Karbāstī (d. 906 AH [1500 CE]), Nazar b. 'Uthmān Khafā'ī (d. 914 AH [1508 CE]), Mullā Mihammad 'Umar Wā'iz (a contemporary of the rule of Sultan Salīm I ca. 918–26 AH [1512–19 CE]), Muhyī al-Dīn Muhammad b. 'Umar b. Hamza (d. 938 AH [1531 CE]) who was an immigrant from Transoxiana, Abū'l Sa'ūd Imādī (d. 951 AH [1544 CE]) who was an Ottoman judge. Worthy of mention are a number of Arab works produced beyond Turkish lands, including *Al-'arba'īn* by Suyūtī (d. 911 AH [1501 CE]) and the writings of Ibn Hajar Haytamī (d. 974 AH [1566 CE]). It is important to note that because the Ottoman wars were expansionist in nature, the above *jihadīya* works focused not on defence but mainly on justification, namely the need to expand Muslim lands through offensive wars.

In 897 AH [1492 CE], the downfall of Granada wiped out the history of Muslim Andalusia and was considered a serious warning to Muslims everywhere. This threat was soon coupled with another: the Atlantic revolution and the discovery of easy European-ocean access to India in 903 AH [1498 CE]. This event facilitated communication across a vast part of Muslim lands. European navies could easily move from the shores of Sabta in western Morocco to East Africa, the Sea of Oman, India, and Southeast Asia. In the beginning, these incursions were more of a commercial nature, but soon the mixture of cultures precipitated tensions along many of the borders. This was the start of European colonialist advances, specifically by the Portuguese who had already conquered several sea ports. At this time, the institution and literature of jihad reappeared, this time with the goal of strengthening narratives about defensive war. This turning point was echoed in the works of many, including in the works of scholars like Muhammad b. Ahmad Zīānī 'Ayyāshi (d. 1051 AH [1641 CE]), who focused on criticizing the Portuguese. These colonial encounters with Muslims produced new *jihadīyas*, such as *Tuhfat al-mujahidīn fī ba'di al-akhbār al-burtughāliyyīn* (The gift of warriors on some news about the Portuguese) by Malagueño scholar Zain al-'Ābīdīn Mu'abbarī and *Falak al-sa'āda* by Abdul Hādī b. Abdullah Salmājī (d. 1056 AH [1646 CE]).

Portuguese colonial advances towards the Persian Gulf region simultaneously occurred with the above developments, effectively encouraging the production of many *jihadīya*s by the Imami (Twelver-Shi'i) scholars of the region. Among these works, one can refer to *'Izza'l Islam fī bayān al-jihad* by 'Abdu'l Wahīd b. Ne'matullah Astarābādī who was the student of Shaykh Bahā'ī (d. 1030 AH [1620 CE]), Muhammad Sadiq Sarkānī's Persian translation of the chapter on jihad of Shaykh Tūsī's book *Al-Nahāya* by (written 1030 AH [1621 CE]), and *Wujūb al-jihad li'l-'aduw fī zamān al-ghayba* [the obligation of jihad against an enemy at the time of occultation of the twelfth imam] by Abdullah b. Alī Bahrānī Bilādī (d. 1148 AH [1735 CE]. In the last work, the author attempts, based on the defensive nature of jihad against the Portuguese, to demonstrate that in such a jihad [contrary to offensive or *da'wah* jihad], the presence of an infallible imam is not necessary.

From the twelfth AH [eighteenth CE] century on, European politics relating to African and Asian countries changed with the emergence of formal colonialism. As such, European invasions were no longer confined to sea ports; rather, they created a broad-regime change and established colonial governments. Such advances resulted in the domination of non-Muslim states over Muslim countries. The gradual colonization of India by Britain and Crimea by Russia, who overthrew the Muslim khanates of this region, are just two examples. Both cases took place in the thirteenth AH [nineteenth CE] century but began during the twelfth AH [eighteenth CE] century. During this period, the Muslim world experienced significant cultural changes in many aspects of life. Britain's domination in the northern parts of India and southern Iran, France's domination over Algeria and other parts of North Africa, in addition to colonial tensions between Britain and France over Egypt and Russia's expansionist policy in Central Asia and Caucasus, all represented monumental threats to the Muslim world.

Some of the rare instances of using jihad's nondefensive interpretation can be found in the approach of the Fulānī tribes of West Africa. These tribes dominated parts of sub-Saharan Africa, creating the Muslim governments of Futa Toro, Khasu, and Futa Jallon in southern Senegal. As far as Iran is concerned, the first and second Russo-Iranian wars (which took place between 1218–28 AH [1803–13 CE] and 1241–3 AH [1825–7 CE], respectively) led to the cessation of the Caucasian region of Iran from the main land and threatened inner Azerbaijan. In the East, British advances in Afghanistan resulted in Herat's cessation from Iran in 1280 AH [1863 CE]. Additionally, southern Iranian sea ports, especially Bushehr, were threatened. Even after the conclusion of colonial wars, British and Russian colonial threats mounted against Iran. The Imami [Shi'i] scholars in the region produced waves of *jihadīya*s under these circumstances. This mobilized the public towards defensive jihad for a long time as the British and the Russian threats continued.

The dominance of such a threatening space, the lack of orderly armed forces, and the resulting need for the presence of jihadi volunteers was felt across the Iranian and Iraqi religious circles connected to Iran. This led to the production of two spectra of *jihadīya*s. One type included works written entirely with a jurisprudential approach, which discussed the possibility of juristic obligations for believers participating in war. This type of work included treatises from Shaykh Ja'far Kāshif al-Ghitā' entitled *Ghāyat al-murād*; a work from Sayyid 'Alī Tabātabā'ī, the author of *Rīyād* (d. 1231 AH [1815 CE]), entitled *Al-jihadīya*; and other works sharing the same title from Mīrzā Yusef Tabātabā'ī Tabrīzī (d. 1242 AH [1826 CE]) and Sayyīd Muhammad Mujāhid (d. 1242 AH [1826 CE]), who had a significant personal participation in the Russo-Iranian wars.

The second type included works by politicians who attempted to position the politico-military activities of governments in a religious and jihadi framework based upon the *fatwas* [religious rulings] of the 'Ulamā [religious authorities]. This type of work included two minor and major *jihadīya*s by Mīrzā 'Isā Khān Wazīr, a *jihadīya* from Mirzā Abū'l Qāsim Farāhānī (d. 1251 AH [1835 CE]), a *jihadīya* written by a number of government secretaries of Fathali Shah Qajar, and a *jihadīya* from Hāj Karīm Khān Qajarī (d. 1283 AH [1866 CE]). In the same period, a scholar from Bushehr, Sayyid Abdullāh b. Abī Qāsim Mūsavī, wrote *Īqāz al-habīb fī mazālim al-salīb*, which focuses on defence against aggressors while expressing gratitude to God for having proscribed jihad as a practical principle of Islam.

During the thirteenth AH [nineteenth CE] century, the Ottomans also faced invasions by their neighbours, resulting in the production of *jihadīya*s, including ones written by Mu'adhdhin 'Uthmānī in 1222 AH [1807 CE] entitled *Risālat al- mu'adhdhin al-'uthmānī ilā ikhwānih'l mu'minīn* (Treatise of the Ottoman al-Mu'adhdhin to his Muslim bretheren). In this work, the author tried to mobilize Muslims against the Franks [i.e. French]. Ahmad b. Mustafā Kameshkhāne'ī's (d. ca. 1293 AH [1876 CE]) book *Al-'bir fī ansār wa'l muhājir* was written about the virtue of jihad. This latter work demonstrates the role of the Naqshbandi Sufi order in jihadi movements across the Muslim world. In this period, even some European Muslim scholars, like 'Alī b. Mustafā Busnawī, the author of *Fadā'il al-jihad,* tried to defend the Islamic identity of their countries.

Works related to the Ottoman colonies in Iraq and Syria include *Sufrat al-zād fī [li] safaratu'l-jihad* by Shihāb al-Dīn Muhammad Ālūsī (d. 1270 AH [1854 CE]), as well as *Tashwīqāt al-jīyād fī ghazw al-jihad* by Abdul Razzāq b. Abdul Fattāh Lādhiqi Hanafī (d. ca. 1270 AH [1854 CE]).

The thirteenth AH [nineteenth CE] century produced other types of *jihadīyas* that can be traced back to Oman, Yemen, India, Caucasia, and Morocco. In the fourteenth AH [twentieth CE] century, such productions continued, though not at the rate of previous centauries.

Jihadīya literature reemerged during the First World War, when the Ottomans were under European incursion and major parts of Muslim lands were engaged in war. During these events, although the Ottoman government was known to be the patron of Sunni Islam, Shi'i Ulamā [religious scholars and authorities] became seriously engaged in issuing *fatwa*s to mobilize the public in defence of what they called the domain of Islam.

In recent decades, following the rise of Islamist movements across various corners of the world, jihad, in its various interpretations, has once again become the focus of attention among scholars. Among important contemporary works written on the subject are: *Jihad* by the Shi'i scholar Murtazā Mutahharī (published in 1995), *Al-jihad fī sabīl Allah* by the Indian salafi scholar Abū'l A'lā Mawdūdī, *Jihad al-a'dā'* by the salafi scholar of Najd [in Saudi Arabia] Abdul Rahman b. Nāssīr Sa'dī (published in 1990), and *Al-jihad fī'l-Islam* by the Syrian scholar Muhammad Sa'īd Ramadān al-Būtī (published in 1993).[5]

Appendix II

"Jang" (war): Laws in War according to Twelver-Shi'i Jurisprudence[1]

Some Arab scholars have defined war [*qitāl*] as a "battle and defence by weapon." However, the definition of jihad as "war with the disbeliever enemy" has added confusion between these words.

First: Laws at War

Declaration of War: State constitutions and well-established international precedents have given the responsibility of war to executive powers; that is, the decision is determined by a state's highest authority, with or without the consent of a state's legislative power. In France, for example, the proclamation of war needs the consent of both parliamentary assemblies. In the Islamic Republic of Iran, according to Article 110 of the country's constitution [adopted in 1980], "the proclamation of war and peace and the mobilization of all armed forces as suggested by the Supreme Defence Council" is among the powers given to the supreme leader of this country. In a constitutional amendment adopted in 1995, the phrase "as suggested by the Supreme Defence Council" was omitted. In Islamic law, only the caliph or imam has a right to declare jihad, though he can delegate this power to a minister or army commander.

Advance Warning: Based on the Hague Convention [III] of 1907, authors of modern international law emphasize the need for a clear warning or written ultimatum prior to engaging in war. In practice, however, wars were often initiated without an official warning.

In the view of Islamic law, offensive war is strictly forbidden and a legitimate war can only come about from the following causes:

1 Punitive war [*harb al-masālih*] that aims at preventing internal insurgency [*baghy*] or sedition (dissent)

2 Absolute defensive war to repel invasion
3 Preventive war to repel an imminent threat against the country, religion, freedom of religion, or place of worship
4 War in support of friendly or allied states, usually based on an existing contract and with the aim to repel aggression, transgression, and injustice against that country

With the exception of punitive and defensive wars, all other forms of legitimate wars, according to the norms of Islamic law, require prior announcement. This is a dominant view among Muslim jurists who consider an early warning to be a preliminary step in acheiving the goals of war, particularly if it translates to solving a conflict through peaceful means. Muslim jurists maintain that a legitimate warning should include an invitation to the enemy to submit to Islam. In other words, whenever Muslims encounter non-Muslims who are not well informed about Islam, they need to invite them to accept God's unity as the foundation of rightful faith. Another alternative is asking them to accept paying a poll tax [or *jizya,* a tax imposed on non-Muslims living in Muslim communities, which compensates for their nonparticipation in Muslim conscription or defence].

The jurisprudential foundations for the above ruling are the following Qur'ānic verses:

Q. 42:15 So summon to this [unity of religion] and be steadfast.
Q. 6:125 Invite to the way of your Lord with wisdom and good advice and dispute with them in a manner that is best.
Q. 18:29 And say, "[This is] the truth from your Lord: let anyone who wishes believe it, and let anyone who wishes disbelieve it."
Q. 15:17 Whoever is guided is guided only for [the good of] his own soul, and whoever goes astray, goes astray only to his detriment. No bearer shall bear another's burden. We do not punish [any community] until we have sent [it] an apostle.

In addition to the above, the Prophetic tradition and the tradition of the early caliphs and their army commanders support the [invitation before the conflict] principle. Wars have been avoided, on many occasions, by negotiations and also by peace treaties [in the early history of Islam].

In the view of jurists, all situations in which wars begin without prior notice (specifically during early Islamic history) happened because of an extraordinary/critical social situation. Regarding this subject, the author of *Jawāhir al-kalām*, a prominent Shi'i scholar named Mohammad Hasan al-Najafī (d. ca. 1266 AH [1849 CE]) states, "War with infidels cannot be initiated, unless after they have been invited to Islam and their rejection of paying the poll tax." Ibn Faqīh, a renowned Muslim scholar and author of *al-Buldān*, written ca. 290 AH [903 CE], similarly enumerates the following four reasons for the illegitimacy of war without *da'wa* [an invitation to join Islam]:

1 A hadith narrated by Musmi' b. Abdulmalik through the authority of Imam Ja'far al-Sādiq, and he narrated through the authority of 'Alī b. Abī Tālib, stating: The Prophet once sent me to Yemen and then advised me [before departure], "Oh 'Alī, avoid war with anyone till you invite him first to Islam. I swear to God, that if he would guide one person through you, while you may also attract his kindness towards you, this is better for you than [the possession of] everything on earth that receives sunshine and sunset on them."
2 The consensus among scholars on this subject has been challenged.
3 Since the realization of all factors and preconditions legitimizing jihad depends on the lack of other peaceful solutions, an invitation to Islam before the battle becomes obligatory, given that the goal of jihad is to expand Islam.
4 Jihad, as a religious and legal obligation and by its very definition, is preconditioned on prior *da'wa*.

Given that the act of a "warning" in jurisprudence is tantamount to *da'wa*, Muslim jurists have questioned whether multiple invitations are obligatory in the case of multiple wars. There is no consensus regarding the above. Some jurists consider multiple *da'was* to be obligatory, while others recommend it [*mustahabb*] or even consider it optional [*mubāh*].

Guarantees Pertaining to the Enforcement of the Obligatory Prebattle Warning: In the view of Ibn Idris al-Shāfi'ī (d. 205 AH [820 CE]), the founder of one of the four Sunni schools of law, whenever Muslim soldiers kill enemy subjects without first inviting them to Islam, the Islamic government should pay compensation [*dīya*] for each one killed, in an equal amount, based on the scale determined by sharī'a law. Mālik b. Anas (d. 179 AH [795 CE]), the founder of another Sunni school of law, however, believed killing disbelivers did not require blood money. Moreover, the breach of *da'wa* law, according to sharī'a, is subject to legal persecution, and in the case of valid evidence, it can nullify the results or gains of war.

According to historians, when the Christian city of Samarqand was conquered by the Muslim army commander Qutaiba b. Muslim without prior warning, it went against sharī'a law, leading to the city inhabitants making a complaint to the caliph ‘Umar b. Abdul‘azīz. The caliph immediately ordered his representative in the region, Sulayman b. Abī Sarh Bājī, to take the case to a local judge for investigation. The judge picked by Sarh Jamī‘ b. Hādir ruled, “The Muslim army should leave the town at once.” The caliph accepted the ruling and ordered the verdict to be executed immediately without question.

Second: The Effects and the Results of Proclamation of War

In Islamic law, just like in modern law, the proclamation of war, in addition to its general effects, automatically annuls all bilateral contracts that are in conflict with the war’s goals.

General Impacts: A proclamation of war prohibits all citizens and officials from giving assistance, facilitation, or information to the enemy. The jurisprudential basis for this ruling is a case known as the axiom of Hātib, who was among the Prophet’s companions. Hātib, a simple-minded Muslim, was tried in court for giving information to the enemy. References are also made to a few Qur’ānic verses, including Q. 9:73, 123. Interestingly, based on humanitarian concerns, another verse (Q. 5:2) orders unconditionally: “Ill feeling for a people should not lead you, because they barred you from the Sacred Mosque, to transgress. Cooperate in piety and Godwariness, but do not cooperate in sin and aggression, and be wary of Allah.”

Impacts of War on Contracts: In Islamic law, because of the sanctity of contracts, covenants, and treaties, any breach of these legal commitments is considered treason. But if a contract cannot be fulfilled because of war, or if it goes against national interest, the proclamation of war annuls it. Needless to say, war has the potential to “cancel” friendship and harm agreements and good relations between neighbours. Surely, though, there are some types of international contracts that remain valid throughout war, such as the humane treatment of prisoners of war, the ban on severing water reserves used by the enemy, the prohibition of the destruction of occupied lands, and other humanitarian regulations. Muslim jurists have extensively commented on such cases.

Impacts of War on Commerce: War results in considering all citizens of the warring party to fall under the category of enemy. Thus, for followers of al-Shāfi‘ī’s school of law, transactions between warring citizens were prohibited. For Hanafī Muslims, however, only the transaction of weapons were prohibited. The jurisprudential basis for this Hanafī view is a Prophetic tradition. According to a particular narrative, the Prophet gifted five hundred dinars to

Abū Sufīyān [a notable figure in Mecca] while he was still a polytheist. He asked Abū Sufīyān to distribute the money among the needy and drought-stricken people of Mecca. Another story details how the Prophet sent Abū Sufīyān some dates from Medina in exchange for animal skin. The narrative holds that the business deal took place before the al-Hudaybīya peace treaty between Muslims and Meccan polytheists came to effect. The transaction, therefore, took place during the time of active hostility between the two communities. Some Hanafī jurists maintain that it is within the discretion of the Muslim government to decide which commodities are to be banned and which ones are to be free in such transactions. Some Imami [Twelver-Shi'i] jurists maintain that any weapon sales to Muslim enemies that may strengthen their military might is unconditionally and permanently banned. The predominant ruling, however, is that such transactions are to be banned only during times of war.

The Impact of War on Loans and Legal Commitments: War generally does not influence debts and loans. A few Prophetic traditions support this ruling.

1 After the Prophet immigrated to Medina to escape persecution by Meccan polytheists, he ordered his cousin 'Alī b. Abī Tālib to return all the loans given to him by hostile non-Muslims.
2 When a conflict began between the Jewish tribe Banī Nadīr of Medina and the Muslim residents of the city, the Prophet allowed them gracefully to take all of their belongings with them to their exiles. A question, however, was raised about the fate of all the loans that the Muslims owed to the Jews. The story goes on to note that the Prophet ruled that all of the loans remained valid, were still due on their deadlines, and must be paid in full. War therefore did not void financial commitments to the enemy. He added that in case Jewish lenders should voluntarily want to collect on their loans sooner than the agreed deadlines, they could do so by forming a new contract with the indebted Muslims.
3 Aswad, a slave and shepherd for a Jew, narrates that during the Khaybar War [which engaged another Jewish community] he expressed his intent to the Prophet to convert to Islam. Upon hearing his case, the Prophet ordered him to take his entire flock back to his Jewish master.

In addition to the above, jurists have also referred to Qur'ānic injunctions based on the necessity of returning all trusts (Q. 4:58 and 2:283). A number of Prophetic statements support the above view, such as "Fighting in the way of God washes away all sins but not debts" and "Whoever receives a trust from another must return it unconditionally."

Third: Obligatory Principles in War

In Islamic law, the use of all means necessary for granting victory at war has its limits. Engagement in a legitimate war, in other words, entails observing certain codes, which will be partially mentioned in this section.

1 **Principles of Compassion, Fairness, and Justice:** This principle is invoked in Qur'ānic verses 5:2 and 5:8[2] and also accords with the Prophetic hadith "Compassion and gracefulness are acts of friends of God, so if you kill, it has to be according to justice." Based on this principle, any act that is uncompassionate, unfair, and unjust is prohibited.
2 **The Ban against the Killing of Civilians Not Taking Part in War:** This principle is related to the distinction between the military and unarmed civilians. According to this principle, a Muslim fighter must make a clear distinction between armed enemy soldiers and military targets on the one hand and unarmed civilians and nonmilitary areas on the other. He can only assault military targets and personnel. As a result of the potential for indiscriminate killings, the use of all weapons of mass destruction [WMDs] is illegal in Islam.

Fourth: Prohibited Acts in War

On the basis of the two above-mentioned principles, resorting to the following acts in war is strictly forbidden:

1 **Resorting to Cruel and Perfidy-Based Killings in War:** Conventional weapons and strategies employed in early Muslim wars are all allowed by Islamic law. The permission covers the use of spears, bows and arrows, swords, shields, and siege engines, as well as the digging of ditches and the creation of buffer fences. Nevertheless, Muslim fighters had to observe certain rules and regulations as commonly ordered by their commanders, including bans on poisoned arrows and swords, which were common in pre-Islamic Arab wars. Because the latter weapons inflicted unbearable pain upon its victims, Muslim rulers banned these practices.

Shayk Tūsī, one of the major Shi'i jurisprudence authorities (d. 460 AH [1067 CE]), writes, "War with infidels is permitted through all methods except contaminating their lands with poison. This is because water contamination results in the death of innocent children, women, and insane people, whose killing are strictly banned by law." Tūsī takes a clear position against the use of weapons of mass destruction [WMDs].

A number of authors base their beliefs on *al-Bay'at al-Ridwān* [the Ridwān oath allegiance], which was formed prior to the al-Hudaybīya peace treaty between the Prophet and his companions for the purpose of war with the Meccan polytheists. These same authors argue that it is permitted to use WMDs, despite the fact that they may kill civilians. Their argument is based on the notion that the Muslim intention to launch an attack against Mecca, by default and notwithstanding the mixed population of Mecca [civilian and Muslim residents], meant that the Muslim offence could very well result in the death of unarmed civilians.

This type of reasoning, which infers the permission to use WMDs, is flawed because according to the Ridwān oath of allegiance the plan was to legally fight the Meccans, rather than to massacre them. Moreover, planning a pre-emptive assault on the Meccan polytheists with the goal of tampering their aggression against Muslims was a separate decision from deciding on the specific types of weapons to be used. These scholars attempt to interpret the Prophet's agreement to include, again by inference, an agreement to kill civilians. Such reasoning has clear tension with the Prophet's unequivocal statement in that regard. Legal opinions based on uncertain inferences are unwarranted in jurisprudential logic. The context of the alliance agreement, on the other hand, demonstrates that the purpose of the military plan was certainly to kill the aggressive polytheists, rather than to undertake a massacre that could include children, ill persons, women, and those deemed insane.

2 **Killing Civilians Unassociated with War:** In the view of Muslim jurists, only those who are physically fit may participate in war. This jurisprudential view is based on Qur'ānic verse Q. 2:190, stating, "Fight in the way of Allah those who fight you, but do not transgress. Indeed Allah does not like transgressors." The phrases "who fight you" and "do not transgress" limit the object as well as the scope of war – both of which imply that one cannot fight with someone who does not intend to fight.

This juridical inference has received support from hadith literature and also from biographies of prominent religious figures in Islam. 'Alī b. Abī Tālib, in addressing his emissary to Syria, Ma'qal b. Qais Riyahī, reportedly said, "Never fight with anyone, except only those who fight with you." According to this principle, all civilians who have not participated in war, and those unassociated with war, must be saved and immune from war. The latter groups include:

a. Women and Children: An impressive number of Prophetic statements have emphasized the ban on killing women and children in war.

Accordingly, Muslim jurists from various schools have almost unanimously banned such killings in war (e.g. Ibn Hanbal, Ibn Māja, Tabarāni, Bayhaqī, Sarakhsī [Sunni scholars]; and Kulaynī, Tūsī, Hurr al-'Āmilī, and Majlisī [Shi'i scholars]).

In the view of jurists from the four Sunni schools of law, children and women who do not help propogate war should be saved. See, for example, Mālik, Māwardī, Abu Ishāq, Sarakhsī, Samarqandī, Kāsānī, Ibn Qudāma, Nawāwī, Ibn Najīm, Haskafi b. 'Ābidīn, and Dardīr.

In the view of prominent Shi'i jurists, however, women and children are saved in war, even if they participate. The exception is when such protection becomes detrimental to the fate of that particular war. See for example rulings by Ibn Junayd, Tūsī, Ibn Barrāj, Ibn Idrīs, Muhaqqiq Hillī, Allāma Hillī, Shahid Thānī, Muhaqqiq Karakī, Shayk Bahā'i, and Mohammad Hasan Najafī.

b. **Old Men:** Certain hadith reports from the Prophet grant old men immunity during war. This is reflected in the rulings of scholars such as Malīk, Ibn Hanbal, Abu Dawūd, Kulaynī, Ibn Bābawayh, Bayhaqī, Tūsī, Muttaqī Hindī, and Majlisī. There are also conflicting rulings that do grant permission to kill old men, such as views from Ibn Hanbal, Tirmidī, and Suyūtī. In other sources, the permission is conditioned by the old men's active participation in war. See for example views by Ibn Hanbal, Bayhaqī, and Ibn Kathīr. Trying to base their view on consensus-hadith pieces, the Imami jurists, in conjuncture with the Hanafī, Hanbalī, and Malikī jurists, believe that as long as the old men are not in active support of enemy forces, they should receive amnesty (Ibn Junayd, Tūsī, Kāsānī, Ibn Quddāma, Allāma Hillī, Shahīd Thānī, Dasūqī, Muhammad Hasan Najafī, and Irāqī). Some Shāfi'ī jurists have ruled that even if old men actively support the enemy, they should be saved (al-Māwardī, Abū Ishāq, and Nawāwī).

c. **The Blind, Insane, and Crippled:** In the view of some jurists across various schools, these three categories of people should enjoy amnesty and be left alone by Muslim warriors (Sarakhsī, Abu Salāh Kāsānī, Allāma Hillī, and Muhammad Hassan Najafī).

d. **Monks, Priests, and Religious Notables:** A number of hadith reports have been used by scholars of various schools, in addition to the Qur'ānic verses, to justify amnesty for this particular group of people: Q. 2:190, 22:40, and 5:82. See for example Ibn 'Arabī, Ibn Kathīr, Qutb, Khāzim, and Zahīlī on the Qur'ānic verses; and Mālik, Ibn Hanbal, Bayhaqī, Ibn

'Abdulbirr, and Ibn Abī al-Hadīd on the hadith literature. Additionally, such precedents left by Muslim caliphs have also been used as evidence (e.g. Shaybānī and Mahmasānī). A majority of jurists have, therefore, banned the killing of this category of individuals, though a minority holds a contrary view, as works by Mālik, Māwardī, Kāsānī, Sarakhsī, Ibn Rushd, Ibn Qūdāma, Ibn Najīm, Shūkanī, and Ibn 'Ābidīn demonstrate.

Imami jurists have generally maintained that these categories, just as in the case of old men, should enjoy amnesty, except when they have active engagement in war [in which case their immunity would be annulled]. In this connection, see rulings by Ibn Junayd, Abū Salāh, Allāma Hillī, Shahīd Awwal, Shahīd Thānī, and Muhammad Hasan Najafī, and Zīyāeddīn Irāqī. Some Imami jurists (e.g. Tūsī, Fayd Kāshī, Hurr al-'Āmilī, and Majlisī) base their views exclusively on Shi'i hadith reports.

e. **Injured Army Personnel:** Injured army personnel enjoy amnesty for two juristic reasons: first, because an injured person is not considered an active fighter; and second, because a widely accepted Prophetic hadith, echoed in the Shi'i sources, unequivocally and emphatically asks Muslims to refrain from killing war-injured soldiers. Most jurists from various schools maintain that war-injured soldiers are immune and entitled to medical treatment (e.g. views by Ibn Junayd, Ibn Barrāj, Shahīd Thānī, and Khoe'ī). Some Imami jurists believe that a Muslim soldier who kills an injured enemy soldier should be punished (e.g. Muqqadas Ardabīlī and Tabātabā'ī). Regarding the injured members of insurgent Muslim soldiers, jurists hold different views (see views by Montazerī).

f. **Mutilation of Living Bodies and Corpses:** The juristic basis for a strict ban on any kind of bodily mutilation, in life or after, is found in Q. 2:190. The Qur'ānic exegetes and jurists conclude that such an act falls under the category of a "transgression" that is strictly banned by the Qur'ān, even in a just war (e.g. Zamakhsharī, Rāwandī, Baydāwī, Abū Hayyān, and Muqaddas Ardabīlī). Moreover, a number of Prophetic hadiths from both Shi'ite and the Sunni sources support the above ruling (e.g. Ibn Hanbal, Bukhārī, Abū Dawūd, Nisā'ī, Tūsī, Muttaqī Hindī, Hurr al-'Āmilī, and Nūrī). Jurists have ruled against mutilation, even if the enemy has himself engaged in the practice (e.g. Abū Salāh Ibn Barrāj and Mohammad Hasan Najafī).

g. **Wasting and Killing Animals, Cutting Trees, Destroying Houses and Farms:** The killing of domesticated animals, except when they serve as necessary food, is strictly forbidden (e.g. Sarakhsī and other sources mentioned above). The basis for this ruling rests in Shi'i jurisprudence, in addition to a number of Prophetic hadiths, including one from Jafar al-Sādiq that says: "Never kill four-legged animals except for food necessity (Kulaynī)." Based on this hadith, Allamah Hillī, a prominent Shi'i authority (d. 726 AH [1325 CE]), ruled that, just like the case of amnesty in war for women and children and in the absence of any military necessity, domesticated animals should enjoy special protection as ordered by God and his Apostle. This means domesticated animals cannot be harmed based on the claim [of the actor] that harming them will inflict damage to the enemy's property. Shahīd Thānī, a prominent Shi'i authority (d. 966 AH [1558 CE]), mentions, "Animals by nature enjoy sanctity and therefore can be subject to charitable acts. As a result, if not needed as a necessary food, they must not be killed." Based on the Qur'ānic verse 2:205,[3] as well as on a number of other hadiths, wasting environmental resources, such as unnecessarily cutting trees, destroying farms, contaminating natural waters, or killing animals in enemy lands, are forbidden by the ruling from a number of contemporary Imami jurists (Hossein Ali Montazerī, d. 2009).

h. **Raping Women:** In the view of al-Māwardī, committing such an act necessitates punishment.

i. **Killing Enemy Hostages, Even in Case They Have Killed Muslims:** According to jurists, no contract of reciprocity in this realm can be legitimate (Montazerī and Sarakhsī).

j. **Severing Enemies' Heads to Be Sent to Muslim Statesmen:** This is considered a disgusting act forbidden by some Muslim caliphs (Montazerī).

k. **Killing Parents Who Are Serving in the Enemy Army, Except in Defensive Wars:** The Apostle of Allah has strictly forbidden such acts (Montazerī).

Fifth: The Time of War

Before Islam, Arabs had forbidden war within the four lunar months of *Muharram*, *Rajab*, *Dhi'l Qa'da*, and *Dhi'l Hijjah*. The last two months of the year, followed by the first month of the Islamic calendar, were dedicated to ritual worships. The seventh month was dedicated to commerce (Shaybānī and Mahmasānī maintain that Islam adopted this custom), and subsequently the Qur'ān banned war during the four aforementioned months (Q. 2:217; 9:5, 36). The one exception, however, is if infidels want to abuse the law and attack Muslims during these months, in which case the Qur'ān grants Muslims permission to fight back. As noted in Q. 2:194, "A sacred month for a sacred month, and all sanctities require retribution. So should anyone attack you, assail him in the manner he assailed you." Based on this verse, the Prophet permitted the war of Tabūk in 630 CE. This ruling has been also used as a juristic basis for the principle of reciprocation (Ibn Qayyīm).

Sixth: Ending War

War is considered a temporary activity. The concept, therefore, conveys the expectation of an end to it, sooner or later. The means and methods of ending war in Islamic law include three elements: surrender, victory, and a negotiated ceasefire ([according to Sunni jurists] al-Māwardī and Ibn Quddāma).[4]

Appendix III

Iran's Official Position on War Crimes by Daesh[1]

Statement by the Iranian Ambassador and Permanent Representative of the Islamic Republic of Iran to the United Nations in the Open Debate in the Security Council on the Victims of Attacks and Abuses on Ethnic or Religious Grounds in the Middle East.

The following statement was delivered by Gholamali Khoshrou in the United Nations Security Council on 27 March 2015:

Mr. President,
The Islamic Republic of Iran strongly condemns widespread targeting and killing of ethnic and religious minorities by Daesh terrorists and all other extremist groups. We also condemn the destruction of mosques, holy shrines, churches, temples, as well as artifacts and archeological treasures representing the rich cultural heritage of humanity.

Violent extremism has emerged as [an] unprecedented composition of narcissistic, dogmatic, and violent entities with [a] global agenda and with the following characteristics:

1 It is a unique global terror network, active in recruiting in as many as 90 countries, all united in pursuing a policy of terror and destruction. They mobilize individuals, grow their ranks, spread their influence, and threaten places near and far. As such, this phenomenon is reminiscent of the Arab-Afghans of the 1980s and could be dubbed European-Arabs. Thus, it is indicative of failing to learn from history.
2. These like-minded extremists have consolidated their networks by sharing terror tactics and romanticizing violence and bloodshed. They continue to use the most advanced social media to reach out to the young people and

recruit new fighters from all around the world, some starting as tourists and ending up in terrorism.

3 It has committed unparalleled brutality, as it set fires to houses and schools, enslaves the free, oppresses the vulnerable, and kills the innocent with astonishing cruelty. Beheading, burning, and enslaving women and children, shamefully advertised by the group on social media, exposes the extent of the threat they pose to the global community.
4 While these terrorist groups falsely call themselves Muslims, they have killed thousands upon thousands of Muslims, which is unprecedented in human history. Killing around 140 innocent Yemeni people in two recent suicide bombings and San'a was one of the latest example in this savagery. Acting in a true Takfiri manner, they call whoever is not with them nonbeliever, thus condemning them to death. They have established an ever-expanding list of enemies, including Shiites, Christians, Yezidis, Kurds, Turkmens, as well as [the] vast majority of moderate Sunnis, subjecting them to slavery and death.

Mr. President,
Until terrorist and extremist groups are not dismantled, these extremists will continue to pose the gravest threat to the world. The international community's inconsistent, incoherent policy and strategy in combating extremist groups not only did undermine the effort to confront them, but also resulted in emboldening them.

A genuine commitment by the international community to a serious and comprehensive approach to challenge extremism is imperative. Any failure in this field will doom efforts in ridding the region of this malicious force. A comprehensive strategy against Daesh must address ideological, social, political, and economic dimensions of violent extremism.

If there is a genuine resolve to combat extremism, it must be translated into specific and effective actions. It is imperative to adopt a united front, with a clear message and a coordinated strategy. The disruption of financial and logistical support and sharing of relevant information and intelligence, as well as enforcing effective and coordinated border control, are critical to the success of this campaign. Failing to take the necessary actions to disrupt support to terrorists and destroy their networks would only lead to more bloodshed and destruction.

Mr. President,
In the 68th Session of the General Assembly, Dr. Hassan Rouhani, President of Iran, called for a World Against Violence and Extremism and backed it up in

every instance and field. We have been steadfast in our fight against extremism and have in practice demonstrated that Iran is a true partner in a sincere international fight against extremist groups.

Appendix IV

The following text was issued as religious advice to Iraqi armed forces from the office of Grand Ayatollah Sayyid ʿAlī al-Sīstānī, in the Holy City of Najaf, on 12 February 2015. The text forms a manual on the codes of ethics in war according to Shiʻa instructions and sources. It is the most comprehensive manual of its kind issued by an authority of emulation in modern Shiʻism. The English translation is reproduced from the ayatollah's official website.

Advice and Guiding to the Fighters on the Battlefields: A Shiʻi Manual[6]

In the Name of God, Ever-Merciful, Ever-Compassionate

Praise is God's, Lord of the Cosmos, and ever-lasting peace be upon the best of His creation, Muhammad and his noble and pure progeny. I call your attention to the following:

Let the dear fighters know, the ones who have been given the honour to be present in the battlefield against the transgressors, that:

1 Just as God, exalted is He, has called the believers unto Jihad [against the transgressors] and made it one of the pillars of religion, and just as God has privileged the Holy Warriors over those who do not fight [in jihad], He, noble is His name, has placed certain conditions and etiquettes [on the conduct of jihad]. Such conditions are necessitated by wisdom and mandated by the primordial nature of human beings. It is necessary, then, to learn these conditions and etiquettes thoroughly and to follow them sincerely, for the one who learns these conditions and follows them sincerely will receive his deserved reward and blessings from God, and the one who neglects these conditions will not receive [the blessings] he hoped for.

2 With regards to Jihad there are general guidelines to which one must adhere even when confronting non-Muslims. The Prophet, peace be upon him and his progeny, advised his Companions to follow these general guidelines before sending them off to battle. In an authentic tradition, it has been reported that the Imam Ja'far al-Sadiq (d. 765), peace be upon him, said: "When the Messenger of God, peace be upon him and his progeny, would want to send a fighting contingent, he would sit down with them and advise them to represent God justly and to follow the good example of the religion of the Messenger of God. He would [further] say, 'Do not indulge in acts of extremism, do not disrespect dead corpses, do not resort to deceit, do not kill an elder, do not kill a child, do not kill a woman, and do no not cut down trees unless necessity dictates otherwise.'"

3 Similarly, the fighting against those Muslims who oppress [others] and who wage war [unjustly] has its guidelines and etiquettes, too. Indeed such guidelines and etiquettes informed the actions of the Imam 'Ali (d. 661), who, when confronted with such situations, admonished his followers [to follow these guidelines and etiquettes]. The Muslim world agreed in unanimity that the actions, guidelines, and etiquettes of Imam 'Ali are a worthy example to emulate. So pay heed to the example of Imam 'Ali and follow his path. He, peace be upon him, said: "Set your sights on the Family of the Prophet. Make them proud. Follow their deeds. Verily, the Family of the Prophet will not lead you away from the path of guidance, nor will they make you return to the path of error. If they rise, so shall you; and if they stand, so shall you. Do not traverse the path ahead of them, for you shall lose your way; and do not abandon them, for you shall perish."

4 Be attentive to the sanctity of the human souls! Never should you do to them something which God has not deemed permissible. What great travesty it is to kill innocent souls, and what great honour it is to safeguard innocent souls, just as God, exalted is He, mentioned in His book [i.e. the Qur'an]. The killing of an innocent soul has dangerous consequences, both in this world and in the hereafter. History has taught us that the Commander of the Faithful [i.e. 'Ali], peace be upon him, took much caution to protect the sanctity of the human soul in his wars. During his reign [as caliph] he said to [his companion] Malik al-Ashtar, whose friendship and proximity to 'Ali is well known: "Be vigilant! Do not spill the blood of the innocent." If you [i.e. the fighters of the Popular Mobilisation Committees] find yourselves in an uncertain situation from which

you fear the divine wrath, issue a vocal warning [to those fighting you], or issue a physical warning by directing your bullets in a manner which does not strike the target or cause its destruction. Surely this is better for you than to kill innocent souls.

5 Be attentive to the sanctity of the lives of those who do not fight you, especially the weak among the elderly, the children, and women, even if they were the families of those who fight you. The property of those who fight you does not include their families, but it only includes the money those fighters possess. It was the noble habit of the Commander of the Faithful [i.e. ʿAli], peace be upon him, to prohibit [his soldiers] from attacking the properties of the families, women, and children of those against whom he fought, despite efforts by some of those who [claimed to] follow him, such as the Kharijites, who insisted on attacking the families of their enemies. To refute them, ʿAli would say: "We fought the men, but we do not inflict harm on their women, for they are Muslims. Do not inflict harm upon their women."

6 Do not condemn others to heresy. Do not accuse them of blasphemy, which could then lead to their death. Do not imitate the way of the Kharijites of the early Islamic period and their contemporary followers who are ignorant of the basic tenets of the religion. Some people today have followed the way of the Kharijites and have sought to justify their [un-Islamic] actions by recourse to some textual evidence, though in reality they have misunderstood the original texts. The Muslims of today have to live with the consequences of these misinterpretations.

Know that whosoever bears testimony that there is only one God and that Muhammad is His messenger is indeed a Muslim. That person's life and property must be safeguarded. If that person falls into the path of [theological] deviance and commits deeds not sanctioned by Islamic law, then know that not every error in judgment leads to disbelief, nor does every misdeed strip one of their faith.

7 Never inflict harm on non-Muslims, regardless of their religion and sect. The non-Muslims [who live in predominantly Muslim lands] are under the protection of the Muslims in those lands. Whosoever attacks non-Muslims is a coward. And rest assured that such an act of cowardice is one of the most repugnant in the eyes of God. In fact the Muslim must protect his non-Muslim neighbours in the same manner and vigour as he would when he protects his own family.

8 Do not steal the money of others. Those who steal from others will find themselves seated in the flames of the fires of hell.

9 Do not violate things sacred. Do not violate things sacred with your tongues and actions. It has been reported that the Commander of the Faithful said: "Do not disrespect the corpse of the dead, and if you defeat the men of your enemies do not violate the sanctity of their women and their houses. Do not enter their houses. Do not take anything from their houses. Take only what you find in their military encampments. Do not verbally abuse their women. Do not insult their honour, even if your enemies abuse your women and insult your honour.

10 Do not deprive any people, who do not fight you, of their rights even if they made you angry.

11 Know that most of those who fight you are victims who have been led astray by others. Do not let those who lead others astray be better than you. Let your righteous actions, your just conduct, and your sound admonition, serve as an example for them. Do not resort to oppression. Do not insult others. Whosoever helps misguided souls find the path of righteousness is like the one who saves a soul from perdition. And whosoever misguides a person knowingly it is as if he has killed him.

12 Corruption can only be cured by justice.

13 It may be the case sometimes that when you adhere to good conduct and remain disciplined, you suffer [military] losses; this, nevertheless, is more spiritually rewarding. The example set by the Imams serves as a case in point. They did not wage war unless they were attacked, even if such actions caused them temporary losses.

14 Be the guardians and admonishers of those who accept you, so that in the end they will support you against your enemies. Help the weak among them in whatever you can. They are your brothers and your family. Show compassion towards them just as you show compassion towards your own. Know that you are within God's sight, and that He knows your actions, intents, and your inner dispositions.

15 Do not let anything take precedence over your obligatory prayers. Prayer is the means through which man humbles himself before God. It is the

foundation of religion and the criterion through which actions are judged. But in times of war God does not want to overburden you. During fighting and when in fear one may simply proclaim, “God is Great.”

16 Remember God at all times. Recite passages from the Qur’an. Remember that one day you will stand before Him.

17 Strive to act in the same righteous manner as the Prophet and his progeny, peace be upon them, in times of war and peace did. Be the good example that Islam deserves. This is the religion that was built on illumination, reason, and good manners.

18 Do not be in haste in situations where caution is required. Do not undergo an action which will be the cause of your spiritual perdition. Hold your lines and keep a united front.

19 Advise each other. You will not find better advice than that which you offer to each other. Unite, come together, and overlook your differences.

20 Everyone must let go of those sentiments which carry hatred and bigotry. Follow the noble manners. God has made people into different tribes and races so that they may know each other. Do not be overcome by narrow-minded views. Do you not see how the majority of Muslims today are engaged in self-destruction where they spend their resources, energy, and wealth on killing and destruction? They should instead spend their resources and wealth on the advancement of knowledge and in order to improve the welfare of the people. Avoid internal strife. And if internal strife occurs, try your best to put it down. Hold on to the rope of God and do not disunite. Know that God knows whatever is in your hearts. Indeed nothing is beyond the remit of God.

Notes

Preface

1 Prince Turki al-Faisal, the former head of Saudi intelligence and the former ambassador to the United Kingdom and the United States, notwithstanding that Daesh is ideologically and financially a Saudi product, has defined this group eloquently:

> I have given the group a different name, however: "/Fahesh/." I believe it is the more appropriate one, as the word derives from an Arabic root meaning, "obscene." When we refer to someone using this word it means they commit obscenities, whether through words or deeds. For what could be more obscene than killing innocent people, enslaving women, declaring countless Muslims as infidels, driving people from their homes, brazenly exhibiting the heads of those you have decapitated, legitimizing the killing of those who say, "There is no god but God, and Muhammad is His Prophet," plundering banks, selling captives like chattel, and extorting those in areas under your control?
>
> Moreover, the group's styling itself as "Islamic State" shows it is completely out of touch with reality and ignorant of international laws, since the dictionary definition of the word "state" is: "a politically organized body of people usually occupying a definite sovereign territory, overseen by a group of permanent institutions." The essential components of any state are, therefore, a government, a people, a defined physical territory, and sovereignty, as well as the international and legal recognition of its statehood. Neither Iraq nor Syria totally fall under the control of this group, neither does it practice its authority via permanent institutions – and, of course, there is no international recognition of any kind for this so-called

state. As for its "Islamic" credentials, these are completely bogus. The members of this group are indeed the new Kharijites of the Muslim world (a 7th-century group that left the fold of Islam and was notorious for its barbarity and cruelty). ISIS's crimes testify to the appropriateness of this particular appellation.

For full article published as Op-Ed, see Prince Turki al-Faisal, "Opinion: A New Name for ISIS," *Asharq Al-Awsat*, 15 November 2014, accessed 21 January 2015, http://www.aawsat.net/2015/01/article55340407.

Introduction

1 Machiavelli, *Art of War*, 4.
2 See Albright's statement in Barbara Crossette, "Albright, in Overture to Iran, Seeks a 'Road Map' to Amity," *New York Times*, 18 June 1998, accessed 23 October 2013, http://www.nytimes.com/1998/06/18/world/albright-in-overture-to-iran-seeks-a-road-map-to-amity.html.
3 PressTV, "Zarif, Ashton Meet after Nuclear Talks in Geneva," 15 October 2013, http://www.presstv.ir/detail/2013/10/15/329563/zarif-ashton-meet-after-geneva-talks/.
4 For the image of the UN Persian rug, see Payvand Iran News, "Oneness of Mankind: A Precious Persian Carpet Decorates UN Headquarters in New York," 24 August 2005, http://www.payvand.com/news/05/aug/1234.html.
5 Iraj Bashiri, trans., "A Brief Note on the Life of Shaykh Muslih al-Din Sa'di Shirazi," accessed 6 November 6, 2014, http://www.angelfire.com/rnb/bashiri/Poets/Sadi.html.
6 See Joe Klein, "Forgotten Fact: Night of 9/11, Iran: Spontaneous Candlelight Vigil to Express Sympathy and Support for the American People," Liveleak, accessed 20 December 2013, http://www.liveleak.com/view?i=44b_1359356589&comments=1#DvqyJc0Hgia6MUqF.99.
7 See the image of the American flag burning on 4 November 2013 reported by RT.com: "Death to America? Iran Divided on Anniversary of US Embassy Takeover," 4 November 2013, http://rt.com/news/iran-us-embassy-anniversary-192/.
8 Barks, *Essential Rumi*, 36.
9 For a succinct overview of the genealogy, various modern factions, and ideological orietations of jihadi-salafi groups, see Haim Malka, "Jihadi-Salafi Rebellion and the Crisis of Authority," *Religious Radicalism after the Arab Uprising,* Center for Strategic and International Studies, 2014, accessed 14 January 2015, http://csis.org/files/publication/Malka_ReligiousRadicalism_Chapter2.pdf.
10 Frost, *History*, 703.

11 Ibid.

12 On the question of whether, during the course of the last thirty years, it was religion that fashioned Iranian politics or the other way around, I fully agree with Robert Lee who maintains that "political decisions and opportunities have recast a version of Islam (Twelver-Shiʿism) from a pacifist, minority stance into a badge of national identity, a religious establishment like no other in the Muslim world, a set of competing political ideologies, and an authoritarian effort to promote religion." See Lee, *Religion and Politics*, 169.

13 Walzer, *Just and Unjust Wars*, xxxi and 4.

14 From the text of the undelivered address that Roosevelt was supposed to read on Jefferson Day, 13 April 1945. For the full text, accessed 5 February 2016, see http://www.presidency.ucsb.edu/ws/?pid=16602.

15 From the text of King's acceptance speech on the occasion of the award of the Nobel Peace Prize in Oslo, 10 December 1964. For the full text, accessed on 5 February 2016, see http://www.nobelprize.org/nobel_prizes/peace/laureates/1964/king-acceptance_en.html.

Chapter 1

A version of this chapter is published as "Ethics of War and Peace in *Shahnameh* Ferdowsi," *Journal of Iranian Studies* 48 (6 November 2015), 905–31.

1 Doostkhāh, *Avesta*, 1:275.

2 Among many editions of the *Shahnameh*, I have used the latest critical edition by Djalal Khaleghi-Motlagh; Ferdowsi, *Shahnameh*, ed. Khaleghi, 8 vols.

3 Unless referenced, all poetry translations here are those of the author and are intended to give an accurate interpretation of the original, without being overly literal. I have, however, consulted the translations of *Shahnameh* by Arthur George and Edmond Warner (George and Warner, *Warriors of the World*). In the understanding of *Shahnameh's* specific terms and concepts as used in this book, I have also benefited from Mehri Behfar, who has provided excellent commentaries, annotations, and a rich glossary for difficult words in the *Shahnameh* (Behfar, *Shahnameh Ferdowsi*).

4 Anonymous translation of the poem provided in the text of President Hassan Rouhani's speech at the United Nations. For the full text of the speech, see "Statement by H.E.Dr. Hassan Rouhani President of the Islamic Republic of Iran at the Sixty-Eighth Session of the United Nations General Assembly," delivered on 24 September 2013, gadebate.un.org, accessed 29 May 2014, http://gadebate.un.org/sites/default/files/gastatements/68/IR_en.pdf.

5 Davis, "Iran and *Aniran*," 38.

6 Heravī, *Samanid History*, 61.

7 Ong, *Orality and Literacy*, 43.

8 Several sources report how Mahmud massacred more than fifty thousand Shi'ites (called *rāfezī* at the time) in the central Iranian town of Ray in order to rid his Sunni state of religious dissidents and to curry favour with the Abbasid caliph. Gardizi reports that many of the Shi'i prisoners of war died of torture; see Gardizi, *Tarikh-e Gardizi*, 418.

9 See *Encyclopaedia Iranica,* s.v. "ADAB i. Adab in Iran," by Djalal Khaleghi-Motlagh, 1982, accessed 23 March 2016, http://www.iranicaonline.org/articles/adab-i-iran.

10 See Lambton, "Justice."

11 See ibid., 102. According to Lambton, the medieval political theory predominant in Muslim lands is well reflected in the words of the Seljuq minister Nizam al-Mulk in his *Siyasatnameh*: "The object of temporal rule was to fill the earth with justice. This is illustrated by a long anecdote of Anushirvan, in which he is made to say that he would answer the tyrannical with the sword, protect the ewe and the lamb from the wolf, shorten the hands of tyrants, root out from the earth the corrupt, and make the world prosperous by equity, justice, and security, for which purpose he had been created." Nizam al-Mulk adds, "The way in which the world was to be filled with justice was by the maintenance of each in his rightful place so that stability would be preserved." Lambton stresses that "the theory of Nizam al-Mulk conservatism, deriving in part from the theocratic nature of Islamic society, was reinforced by the memory of the pre-Islamic Persian theory of government and the hierarchical organization of Persian society."

12 In mythical Persian history, Iraj is the founder of the Kayanian dynasty and the first ruler of Iran proper. See Daryaee, *Sasanian Persia*, 34. As Daryaee maintains, the Kayanid ideology, well reflected later on in the *Shahnameh*, became the ideal political standard for the Sassanian dynasty from the fourth to sixth centuries. Among the major concepts of this ideology was the Kayani charisma, a divine prerequisite for monarchs in the Sassanian era.

13 See Sarami, *Az Rang-e Gol*, 444. According to Sarami, of the approximately two hundred wars reflected in the *Shahnameh*, 137 are international, eighty-four of which are prehistoric Iranian-Turkish (Turani) wars. It contains ten apiece of the Iranian-Roman (reflecting historic wars) and Iranian-Arab wars.

14 Meisami, *Persian Historiography,* 38.

15 Aghriras saves the lives of hundreds of Iranian prisoners of war captured by his brother Afrasiyab.

16 Amanat, "Iranian Identity Boundaries," 11.

17 Davis, "Iran and *Aniran*," 38.

18 Ibid., 39.

19 See Ferdowsi, *Shahnameh*, ed. Khaleghi, 1:157. Rostam's father Zal was a descendent of the Arab Zahhak and married Rudabeh, the daughter of Mehrab

the king of Kabul. Kaykhosrow's mother was Farangis, the daughter of Afrasiyab the king of Turan.

20 See Sarami, *Az Rang-e Gol*, 774, 775. Sarami points out that, from time to time, some of the most praised heroes of the *Shahnameh,* including Iraj, Siyavash, Forud, Esfandiyar, and even sacred figures like Zoroaster, Mazdak, and Mani, commit acts that do not follow a moral logic. He concludes that there is no perfect human being in the *Shahnameh* world.

21 See *Encyclopaedia of Islam,* 3rd ed., s.v. "Harb, v. Persia," by C.E. Bosworth (Leiden: Brill, 2007). According to Bosworth, with the decline of the caliph's power from the ninth century on, maintaining multinational professional armies, as during the pre-Islamic imperial eras, once again became a norm for the emerging monarchic dynasties. He also adds that "the deployment and tactics of cavalrymen during early years of the Islamic conquest wars … must have been similar to the type of heroic warfare depicted by the *Shah-nameh*."

22 Ferdowsi, *Shahnameh*, ed. Khaleghi, 3:182.

23 All translations of *Shahnameh* verses in this chapter are mine. I need, however, to thank Shirin Radjavi, who read all lines with me and suggested important improvements to my translations.

24 Ferdowsi, *Shahnameh*, ed. Khaleghi, 3:182.

25 Shambyati, *Glossary of Terms*, s.v. *daliri*; I have used this volume for definitions of all key *Shahnameh* terminologies.

26 Ferdowsi, *Shahnameh*, ed. Khaleghi, 4:11. "Keeping a cow in its skin" is an idiom used only in the *Shahnameh*, meaning roughly that one's positive and negative will remain hidden in peace. War on the other hand reveals one's weaknesses.

27 See Pourshariati, *Decline*, 352. Pourshariati mentions that among the great triad of gods in ancient Iran, Mithra appears as the lord of contracts and as a warrior god who punishes those who break contracts. Punitive justice as a justified cause of war therefore has deep roots in ancient Iranian ideology.

28 Rostam vehemently protested the unprovoked invasion of Mazandaran by Kayqubad.

29 Ferdowsi, *Shahnameh,* ed. Khaleghi, 7:290.

30 Ibid., 4:210.

31 Sarami, *Az Rang-e Gol*, 650. Sarami points out that the main cause of war in the *Shahnameh* is revenge (*kin*) to establish justice. However, he asserts that such revenge is asked for and sanctioned by the Divine. He maintains, "The first act of revenge in the epic is directly ordered by God (Ahura Mazda)."

32 Ferdowsi, *Shahnameh,* ed. Khaleghi, 4:233. Similar prebattle prayers can be traced in 4:217–18, 984, and also in 3:9.

33 See Daryaee, *Sasanian Persia*, 15. Daryaee points out that the "alliance between the priests and the warriors was of paramount importance since the idea of *Iranshahr* (Iranian state), which had manifested itself under the Sasanian as a set

territory and ruled by the warrior aristocracy, conceptually had been developed and revived by the priests. This alliance was very important in the survival of the state at the beginning of the Sasanian Empire, and it became part of the idyllic axiom of the Zoroastrian religion, where religion and the state were seen as two pillars, which were inseparable from each other. It was believed that the one would not be able to survive without the other. In reality, both groups attempted to impose their will on the other and this long battle caused the final fragmentation and the weakening of the empire." He adds, "The function of warriors who were in effect the largest part of nobility was to protect the empire, and to deal with people with gentility and keep their oath."

34 Ferdowsi, *Shahnameh*, ed. Khaleghi, 1:162.

35 The nature and definition of justice as a cardinal divine virtue has been the subject of continuous theological debate in Muslim history. Two opposing Mu'tazilī and Ash'arī theological schools have been in total disagreement over whether justice is a universal and an extrareligious virtue or if it can only be defined by scripture. The Shi'i and Mu'tazilī theologies support the former notion of justice.

36 *dād* (justice) and *kherad* (wisdom) are the twin foundational moral factors in the *Shahnameh* world view. See Shambyati, *Glossary of Terms*, s.v. *dād*; Shambayati defines *dād* as justice, truth, good, and bounty.

37 Ferdowsi, *Shahnameh*, ed. Khaleghi, 1:11.

38 See Chubineh, *Hekmat-e Nazari*, 223–5. Chubineh maintains that Ferdowsi's ethics of war and peace are highly influenced by views of the first Shi'i imam 'Alī b. Abī Tālib. Also, see a similar assertion by Hosseini, *Shahnameh*, 63.

39 Ferdowsi, *Shahnameh*, ed. Khaleghi, 2:10.

40 Hosseini, *Shahnameh*, 56.

41 Ferdowsi, *Shahnameh*, ed. Khaleghi, 7:131.

42 Ibid., 4:62.

43 Hosseini, *Shahnameh*, 67.

44 Ferdowsi, *Shahnameh*, ed. Khaleghi, 3:209.

45 Ibid., 3:59.

46 Ibid., 4:169–74.

47 Ibid., 6:217–20.

48 Ibid., 2:82.

49 Ibid., 7:392.

50 Ibid., 4:160–1.

51 Ibid., 4:263–4.

52 Ibid., 4:230.

53 See Shambayati, *Glossary of Terms*, s.v. *mardi*. Shambayati defines *mardi* in the context of the *Shahnameh* as heroism, courage, steadfastness, chivalry, piety, and truthfulness.

54 These institutions are addressed in ch. 3 of this volume.

55 See Tor, *Violent Order*, 263; *Encyclopaedia Iranica Online*, 2012, http://www.iranicaonline.org/articles/javanmardi. According to Zakeri, *javānmardī* with a more abstract meaning of moral and spiritual nobility is probably the Persian root of the Islamic institution of *fotowwa*, which in his view "was the social and ethical code practiced by *āzādān*, a class of Persian nobility which consisted of small landholders and warriors who served as military commanders, administrators, and court bodyguards. Their ethos is said varyingly to have been designated as *āzādagī*, implying bravery and readiness to help actively the defenseless."

56 In addition to the *Shahnameh* of Ferdowsi, the *Qabusnameh* (a mirror for princes written by 'Unsor al-Ma'ali Kaykavus b. Eskandar in 1082), one of the most important sources of *adab* literature in Persian, associates the *'ayyari-javānmardī* with wealth, generosity, magnanimity, and courage. The three cardinal principles of *javānmardī* are: fulfilling one's promises, refraining from untruthfulness, and having fortitude in all affairs. *Qabusnameh* is also rich in humanitarian codes of war, such as the good treatment of prisoners of war and the avoidance of revenge. See Levy, ed., *Mirror for Princes*, 247. See also Tor, *Violent Order*, 262, 263 on *Shahnameh's* reference to *'ayyari* in the story of a figure named Shahooy.

57 Tha'alebi, *Tarikh-e Tha'alebi*, 157–8.

58 Ferdowsi, *Shahnameh*, ed. Khaleghi, 4:295–6.

59 Ibid., 4:249.

60 Ibid., 4:157.

61 Ibid., 5:401.

62 Ibid., 6:226.

63 Ibid., 2:30.

64 Davidson, *Poet and Hero*, 164.

65 Ferdowsi, *Shahnameh*, ed. Khaleghi, 5:237.

66 Davidson, *Poet and Hero*, 165.

67 Ferdowsi, *Shahnameh*, ed. Khaleghi, 1:184.

68 Ibid., 2:171.

69 Ibid., 3:97.

70 Ibid., 2:171.

71 Ibid., 4:259.

Chapter 2

1 Dao De Jing, "24 ways of looking at Dao De Jing 33," transl. James Legge, accessed 5 March 2016, http://home.ccil.org/~cowan/chap33.html.

2 Tūsī, *Nasirean Ethics,* 237.

3 The Aristotelian-Avicennian classification of philosophical sciences adopted by most of the classical and medieval Muslim authors divides philosophy into two main branches: 1) speculative wisdom (*al-hikmat al-nazariyya*), including

mathematics, theology, and natural sciences; and 2) practical wisdom (*al-hikmat al-ʻamalīya*), including ethics, politics, and household management or economics. See classifications by Nasīr al-Dīn Tūsī in Fakhry, *Ethical Theories in Islam*, 131; and by al-Ghazālī in Sherif, *Ghazālī's Theory of Virtue*, 3, 4.

4 Snouck Hurgronje, quoted in Masud, "Scope of Pluralism," 139.

5 Within the Western ethical discourse, such a distinction exists between the Aristotelian character-based ethics versus the principle-based deontological and teleological ethics. See Mayo, "Ethics and the Moral Life," 151–4.

6 Izutsu, *Ethico-Religious Concepts*, 20. Notions of good (*khayr*) and evil (*sharr*) are examples of evaluative Qur'ānic words, different from such descriptors as "do-gooder" (*sālīh*).

7 Ibid., 21, 23.

8 Ibid., 22.

9 Kadivar, "Religious Intellectualism," 47–74. For the online version of the article, see "Human Rights and Intellectual Islam," Kadivar.com, accessed 24 August 2013, http://en.kadivar.com/human-rights-and-intellectual-islam. Kadivar's proposal for the moral reconstruction of Islam law is discussed below in ch. 4, 96.

10 Kadivar, "Religious Intellectualism," 34.

11 Gratian, *Decretum*, 4.

12 Rahman, "Law and Ethics," 8.

13 Ibid., 12.

14 Hashmi, "Islamic Ethics," 170.

15 Goodman, *Islamic Humanism*, 88.

16 Coulson, *Conflicts and Tension*, 79, 80.

17 George Makdisi holds that it was al-Shāfiʻī who, for the first time, separated *kalām* (theology) from *fiqh* (jurisprudence). See Makdisi, "Ethics," 54.

18 According to Kant, the "moral value [of an action], therefore, does not depend on the realization of the object of the action, but merely on the principle of volition by which the action is done, without any regard to the objects of the faculty of desire." See Kant, "The Good Will," 119.

19 See Coulson, *Conflicts and Tension*, 77.

20 Abdolkarim Soroush maintains that "law contains the minimal morality for the society, but the society's moral needs go far beyond and above that level." See Soroush's interview with the BBC: "The Perfect Islamic Society in the View of Abdolkarim Soroush," interview by Masoud Behnood, BBC, 8 January 2006, http://www.bbc.co.uk/persian/iran/story/2006/01/060108_sm-mb-soroush.shtml.

21 See Aristotle, *Nicomachean Ethics* 1155a.

22 For a concise account of these theories, see Coleman and Murphy, *Philosophy of Law*. For formalist theory, see the works of R.M. Hare; for content theory, see the works of H.L.A. Hart; for "positive" ethics, see the works of G.H. Warnock.

23 Kraemer, "*Jihad* of the *Falāsifa*," 312 n74; Butterworth, "Al-Fārābī's Statecraft," 97. Kraemer maintains that the issue of just war is amply addressed by Western theologians, political philosophers, and theorists of international law; however, it is not a relevant topic for Islamic political doctrine, for which the concept of just (or justified) war is comprehended by jihad. Butterworth rejects Kraemer's contention by examining Ibn Khaldūn's views on war, which prove, as Butterworth believes, that Muslim philosophers observed a clear distinction between jihad and just war. Ibn Khaldūn describes four kinds of war: 1) tribal warfare, such as that which existed in the Arabian desert, caused by "jealousy and envy"; 2) feuds and raids, which are characteristic of primitive people, caused by "hostility"; 3) wars prescribed by the sacred law, caused by "zeal on behalf of God and His religion"; and 4) wars against rebels and dissenters, caused by "zeal on behalf of royal authority and the effort to found a kingdom." In reference to the last category, Butterworth concludes that "contrary to Kraemer's assertion, then, Ibn Khaldūn distinguishes just war from jihad and allows neither to encompass the other." See Ibn Khaldūn, *Al-Muqaddima,* ed. de Slane, 65–88.

24 Butterworth, "Al-Fārābī's Statecraft," 80.

25 Ibid., 70.

26 al-Fārābī, *On Civil Government*, 168. Al-Fārābī uses the term *al-mudun al-fādila* in the plural (the perfect states); see al-Fārābī, *On the Perfect State*, 257–8.

27 For more details, see Khadduri, *War and Peace*, 52, 53. It is al-Shāfi'ī (d. 820) who adds the third category (*dār al-'ahd*).

28 Many authors have attributed the lack of development of an Islamic international law to this factor. See Tibi, "War and Peace in Islam," 15.

29 al-Fārābī, *On Civil Government*, 155.

30 al-Fārābī, *On the Perfect State*, 497. For details on Plato's view of the ethics of war, see his chapter on "Usages of War," wherein the whole world beyond the Greek borders of *Hellas* is considered to be "enemy"; Plato, *Republic* 466d–471c.

31 al-Fārābī, *On the Perfect State*, 430.

32 Ibid., 281.

33 al-Fārābī, *On Civil Government*, 163.

34 Goodman, *Islamic Humanism*, 9.

35 al-Fārābī in *Fī Tahsīl al-Sa'āda*, quoted in Goodman, *Islamic Humanism*, 37. Majid Fakhri also asserts that, for al-Fārābī, "justice is identified with conquest, and the duty of the just man is said to consist, as Thraysymachos has put it in *Republic I,* 337D, in 'doing what is most advantageous to the conqueror' so that the subjugation (*isti'bād*) of the conquered by the conqueror is regarded as eminently just." See Fakhry, *Ethical Theories in Islam*, 84.

36 al-Fārābī, *Fusūl al-madanī*, quoted in Butterworth, "Al-Fārābī's Statecraft," 85–7.

37 Goodman, *Islamic Humanism*, 9.

38 Butterworth, "Al-Fārābī's Statecraft," 94.

39 al-Fārābī, *On Civil Government*, 169.
40 Ibid., 170. See also al-Fārābī, *On the Perfect State*, 454.
41 al-Fārābī, *On Civil Government*, 181.
42 Ibid.
43 Ibid., 182–3.
44 al-Fārābī, *On the Perfect State*, 451.
45 Aristotle, *Nicomachean Ethics* 1129b–1130a.
46 Fakhry, *Ethical Theories in Islam*, 83.
47 This point is also well developed in Aristotle, *Nicomachean Ethics* 1155a.26–7.
48 This point was also mentioned by Abū Bakr al-Rāzī (d. ca. 925), an outstanding Islamic Platonist, in reference to Alexander the Great. According to Fakhry, in his work *Rasāil Falsafiyya* al-Rāzī maintained that "the defect of the irascible is to fail to curb the appetitive soul (concupiscence), whereas its excess is to be puffed up by pride and the lust for conquest, as illustrated by the case of Alexander the Great." Fakhry, *Ethical Theories in Islam*, 83.
49 al-Fārābī, *On Civil Government*, 194.
50 Fakhry, *Ethical Theories in Islam*, 84–5.
51 Ibid., 89.
52 Butterworth, "Al-Fārābī's Statecraft," 87.
53 According to most of the Islamic philosophers such as Ibn Sīnā and others, evil is the lack of good or perfection, or in Fakhry's words, "Evil, as a 'cosmic' entity, is entirely non-existent." See Fakhry, *Ethical Theories in Islam*, 85; also *Great Islamic Encyclopedia*, 1st ed., s.v. "Ibn Sīnā," by Sharafuddīn Khorāsānī (Tehran: *Great Islamic Encyclopedia*, 1989).
54 Butterworth, "Al-Fārābī's Statecraft," 92–3.
55 Goodman, *Islamic Humanism*, 102.
56 To the best of my knowledge, Ibn 'Adī's works do not contain much that relates to war.
57 Goodman, *Islamic Humanism*, 105; cf. al-Fārābī, *On Civil Government*, 77–80; cf. Walzer, *Greek into Arabic*, 33, 222; cf. al-Fārābī, *On the Perfect State*, 482–4.
58 Goodman, *Islamic Humanism*, 105.
59 Fakhry, *Ethical Theories in Islam*, 118.
60 Ibid.
61 Goodman, *Islamic Humanism*, 111.
62 Quotations from *Tahdhīb al-Akhlāq wa taḥārat al-a'rāq* in Fakhry, *Ethical Theories in Islam*, 126.
63 Ibn Miskawayh, *Tahdhīb* Q. 91:7, 8, in Fakhry, *Ethical Theories in Islam*.
64 Goodman, *Islamic Humanism*, 108.
65 Ibid., 110.
66 Ibid.

67 Ibid., 88.

68 al-Rāzī, *Tahdhīb al-Akhlāq*, 138. See Ibn Miskawayh, *Refinement of Character*, 139.

69 Ibn Miskawayh, *Tahdhīb*, 147 and *Refinement of Character*, 150.

70 Ibn Miskawayh, *Tahdhīb*, 122 and *Refinement of Character*, 116.

71 Ibn Miskawayh, *Tahdhīb*, 128 and *Refinement of Character*, 128.

72 Ibn Miskawayh, *Tahdhīb*, 129 and *Refinement of Character*, 128.

73 Ibn Miskawayh, *Javidan Khirad*, 15.

74 Ibid., 19.

75 Ibid., 51.

76 For example, courage as a virtue is the moral mean between the two extremes of this virtue, namely recklessness and cowardice.

77 Fakhry, *Ethical Theories in Islam*, 199.

78 See al-Ghazālī, *Ghazālī's Book of Counsel.*

79 Fakhry, *Ethical Theories in Islam*, 201. These pleasures are eating, drinking, sex, attire, habitation, smell, hearing, and sight.

80 Ibid., 201; al-Ghazālī's views on positive law are reflected in his monumental book *Ihyā' 'Ulūm al-Dīn*. His philosophic views on the theory of ethics are mostly written in his work *Mīzan al-'Amal*.

81 Hourani, *Reason and Tradition*, 155.

82 al-Ghazālī, *Ihyā'*, 383.

83 Ibid., 363.

84 Goodman, *Islamic Humanism*, 117; see also al-Ghazālī, *Ihyā'*, 363–70.

85 al-Ghazālī, *Ihyā'*, 375.

86 Paraphrased from Fouchécour, *Moralia*, 552–3.

87 Ibid., 553.

88 Hodgson, *Venture of Islam*, 184–5. Hodgson maintains that al-Ghazālī refuted the Ismā'īlīs repeatedly because "he found something in their position to be persuasive." In Hodgson's view, the role of the Sufi in validating a kerygmatic, historical vision and his mystical role is not far from the role of imam in Isma'īlī theology.

89 See al-Ghazālī, *Al-Mustazharī*, 146–68. The range of sects that al-Ghazālī condemns to heresy or unbelief includes Batinīya, Qarāmita, Qarmatīya, Khorramīya, Khorramdīnīya, Bābakīya, Ismā'īlīya, Shī'īya, Ta'līmīya, and 'Amara.

90 al-Ghazālī, *On the Boundaries*.

91 Ibid., 125.

92 Ibid., 112.

93 Ibid., 120.

94 Ibid., 89.

95 Ibid., 126.

96 Ibid., 120; cited also in Jahānbegloo, *Introduction to Nonviolence*, 45.

97 Goodman, *Islamic Humanism*, 16.

98 Tūsī, *Akhlāq-e Nāsirī,* 310; Tūsī, *Nasirean Ethics*, 196. See also Fakhry, *Ethical Theories in Islam*, 138.

99 Fakhry, *Ethical Theories in Islam*, 139.

100 Ibid.; also Tūsī, *Nasirean Ethics*, 235.

101 Fakhry, *Ethical Theories in Islam*, 142.

102 Tūsī, *Akhlāq-e Nāsirī,* 376; idem, *Nasirean Ethics*, 236.

103 Tūsī, *Akhlāq-e Nāsirī,* 376–7; idem, *Nasirean Ethics*, 236.

104 Tūsī, *Akhlāq-e Nāsirī,* 334.

105 Tūsī, *Nasirean Ethics*, 236–7.

106 The original Persian text is acquired from the following website: moridemolana .com, accessed 5 June 2014, http://www.moridemolana.com/Masnavi%20e% 20Manavi.htm.

107 Between the two fingers of God refers to the hadith, or saying of the prophet Muhammad: "The true believer's heart is between two fingers of the Merciful God." For various sources of this hadith, see Sunan Ibn Majah, sunnah.com, http://sunnah.com/search/?q=+مَا+مِنْ+قَلْبٍ+إِلا+بَيْنَ+أُصْبُعَيْنِ+مِنْ+أَصَابِعِ+الرَّحْمَنِ. Nicholson explains that the "two fingers are the Divine attributes of Majesty (*Jalāl*) and Beauty (*Jamāl*). Accordingly as God reveals Himself in one or other of these aspects, the mystic's heart contracts with grief (*qabd*) or expands with joy (*bast*)"; quoted by Ibrahim Gamard, accessed 26 March 2016, http://www .dar-al-masnavi.org/n-V-1675.html.

108 These selected couplets are from the prelude to ch. 6, Jalaluddin Rumi, *Maṭhnavī-e Ma'navī* transl. Ibrahim Gamard, dar-al-masnavi.org, accessed 25 August 2013, http://www.dar-al-masnavi.org/n.a-VI-0045.html.

109 The extension of this argument into biology has led to the chronic misperception that "war is in the blood." According to primatological findings of Sapolsky, "some primate species, it turns out, are indeed simply violent or peaceful, with their behavior driven by their social structures and ecological settings. More important, however, some primate species can make peace despite violent traits that seem built into their natures." He further asserts, "Contrary to what was believed just a few decades ago, humans are not 'killer apes' destined for violent conflict, but can make their own history." See Sapolsky, "Natural History of Peace"; for the online version of this article, see Robert Sapolsky, "A Natural History of Peace," *New York Times*, 2 January 2006, accessed 24 March 2016, http://www.nytimes.com/cfr/international/20060101faessay_v85n1_sapolsky .html?pagewanted=print.

110 *Great Islamic Encyclopedia*, 1st ed., s.v. "Ibn Sina," by Fathollāh Mojtabā'ī.

111 See Rumi, *Mathnavī-e Ma'navī*, ed. Sobhani, Q. 2:251: "And if God had not repelled some men by others, the Earth would have been corrupted."
112 Rumi, *Mathnavī-e Ma'navī*, ed. Sobhani, 5:787–8.
113 Ibid.
114 Ibid., 5:151–3. This story is mentioned in detail in part 2 below, ch. 5, 129–30.
115 Ibid., 4:542.
116 Ibid., 1:159.
117 Rumi, *Mathnawī*, trans. Nicholson, 1:1373–4. These lines are based on a Prophetic hadith. See al-'Āmilī, *Jahād bā Nafs,* vol. 6., sec. 2, hadith 1 (8).
118 Rumi, *Mathnavī-e Ma'navī*, ed. Sobhani, 1:159.
119 Ibid.
120 Though Sufi determinism and pacifism are compatible, Abdolkarim Soroush, one of the top Rumi scholars in the world, argues that because Sufism does not recognize any inherent rights for human beings, it becomes very dangerous if mixed with politics. He points out that the denial of any rights for a human can help a suppressive and despotic regime with a leader ruling in the name of God. See Soroush, *Akhlāq-e Khodāyān*, 180–2.
121 "Here, the remedy against the irreversibility and unpredictability of the process started by acting does not arise out of another and possibly higher faculty, but is one of the potentialities of action itself. The possible redemption from the predicament or irreversibility – of being unable to undo what one has done though one did not, and could not, have known what he was doing – is the faculty of forgiving … Without being forgiven, released from the consequences of what we have done, our capacity to act would, as it were, be confined to one single deed from which we could never recover; we would remain the victims of its consequences forever." Arendt, *Human Condition*, 236, 237.

Chapter 3

1 In this line of *Mathnavī,* Rumi refers to a few of the most important principles of *futūwwa*, that is, to be characteristically charitable for no ulterior motive; quoted in Gowharīn, "Maktab-e Fetyān," 219.
2 "Commemoration of Pahlavani Culture Day with Hasan Khomeini," Hasan Khomeini official website, 27 August 2013, accessed 24 March 2016, http://www.hasankhomeini.ir/?persian=content&categoryID=455&nodeID=2341.
3 Ridgeon, *Morals and Mysticism*, 167. For an elaborate introduction to the contemporary institution of *zurkhaneh*, see ch. 6 of this volume, "Futuwwat in the modern era: the *zurkhana* between tradition and change."
4 "Moral sports" refer to exercises in which the goal is not only to be physically fit but also to strengthen the power of the body with solid moral traits, such as

forgiveness, magnanimity, etc. There are many *zurkhaneh* narratives that explore cases in which a senior wrestler deliberately lost to his counterpart out of compassion and simply to preserve his opponent's honour.

5 Ya'qūb Layth Saffār was a Persian coppersmith who reigned over a large territory encompassing modern-day Afghanistan, Iran, and Pakistan. As Marina Gaillard has mentioned, Samak-e 'Ayyār is a legendary figure from "a prose narrative originating in the milieu of professional storytellers, transmitted orally and written down around the 12th century. The only extant manuscript is in the Bodleian Library in Oxford. *Samak-e ʿayyār* is a mine of cultural and social information." William L. Hanaway has pointed out, "The popular romances are a rich source for reconstruction of the social history of medieval Persia, a source only beginning to be investigated." Quoted in *Encyclopaedia Iranica,* s.v. *Samak-e ʿayyār*, by Marina Gaillard.

6 In recent years the question of the sources of Iranian social identity has received unprecedented attention in Iran. One reason is a mounting dialogue and tension between the Iranian and Islamic identities. As a result, many new books and articles have been published, in addition to an increase in student research on *javānmardī*, itself containing a significant portion of the pre-Islamic Iranian codes of social ethics that were later mixed with Islamic ethics. An increasing number of articles have also been published in Iranian academic periodicals, some of which are available on the web. A cursory review of the entries on *javānmardī* or *futūwwa* on Persian sites is telling. See Akram Nūrī, "The Bibliography of *Futuwwat-nāmeh*s and *Javanmardān*" (*ma'khaz shenāsī-e futūwwat-nāmehā wa javānmardān* in Persian), accessed 28 December 2013, http://www.anthropology.ir. In this work, the author lists ninety-one entries, including books and articles, available in the Persian language.

7 Zakeri, *Sasanid Soldiers*; Afshari, *Chahardah*; see also Afshari, *Āyīn-e javānmardī*; Tor, *Religious Warfare*; Ridgeon, *Jawanmardi*.

8 *Encyclopaedia of Islam,* new ed., s.v. *Futūwa*, by Cl. Cahen and Fr. Taeschner.

9 Ibid.

10 Zakeri, *Sasanid Soldiers*, 3, 6.

11 Ibid., 6–7.

12 Ibid., 11. According to Zakeri (45), *dihqān* is a name that covers an entire gamut of people, from simple cultivators scarcely better off than their neighbours and subordinates, to higher-than-ordinary peasants, to true village lords.

13 Ibid., 61. Zakeri explains how *asbārān*, as a group of cavalrymen in the time of the Sassanian king Anushīravān, was under the influence of Mazdak's socialist revolutionary teachings, which led to moral discontent with the Sassanian monarchs.

14 Ibid., 115. Zakeri refers to information provided by al-Balādhurī's *Futūh* and concludes: "These defectors indeed proved useful allies and served the Muslims

at Qādisīya, Jalūlā', and Khuzistan … The caliph 'Umar I instructed them to call in more of their kind, and they were exempted, at first from paying *jizya* ... They participated in the conquest of Fārs, Kirmān, and Khurāsān," thus their easy and much welcomed settlement early on in Basra and Kūfa.

15 Zakeri, *Sasanid Soldiers,* 192.

16 The Abbasid Revolution refers to an Iranian-led Muslim insurgency, which mobilized a force in northeastern Iran and ultimately defeated the Umayyad dynasty in 750, bringing the Abbasid caliphate to power.

17 According to Izutsu, "The *murūwah* represents the highest idea of morality among the Arab Bedouin, the virtue of virtues ... man-ness." He adds, "It includes various virtues as generosity, bravery and courage, patience, trustworthiness, and trustfulness." These virtues, Izutsu maintains, were not abolished by Islam but reoriented into a new moral system and trimmed of their excesses. See Izutsu, *Ethico Religious Concepts*, 27, 75.

18 Afshari, *Āyīn-e javānmardī*, 94–5, quoted in Ridgeon, *Morals and Mysticism*, 8.

19 See Tor, *Religious Warfare,* 85.

20 Ridgeon, *Morals and Mysticism*, 15.

21 Well documented by declassified political documents in the United States and Britain, these states cooperated in organizing a successful coup d'etat against the government of Mohammad Mosaddeq in 1953 and paid some pro-Shah elements, including some *zurkhaneh* members, to use their force and influence in the process.

22 Corbin, *Āyīn-e Javānmardī*, 8.

23 Zakeri, *Sasanid Soldiers,* 318.

24 The Prophet is reported to have praised Alī with the following: *anta fatā hādhihi al-umma* (lit. You are the [courageous, well-mannered] young man of this community). See Corbin, *Āyīn-e Javānmardī,* 21. The detailed story of the inception and the rituals of the *futūwwa* order, and their symbolic significance, are well covered by Corbin, introduction to *Rasāel-e Javānmardān*; see also *Encyclopaedia of Islam*, new ed., s.v. *Futūwa*, by Cl. Cahen and Fr. Taeschner.

25 Corbin, *Āyīn-e Javānmardī,* 21.

26 Alī's legacy to the ethics of war is further detailed in part 2. For now, it is important to pay close attention to the forgiveness-justice balance that constitutes the foundation of a normative system of chivalry in Iranian culture. It is unfortunate that the appearance of the sword in Alī's or the prophet Muhammad's hand in their images across Shi'i culture and beyond is misinterpreted. The sword has mistakenly been used to legitimize the use of force in expanding Islam. However, in the Islamic context that sword is a symbol of justice, just as the image of the scale in modern, universal cultures represents justice.

27 "O you who have believed, prescribed for you is legal retribution for those murdered – the free for free, the slave for the slave, and the female for the female.

But whoever overlooks from his brother anything, then there should be a suitable follow-up and payment to him with good conduct. This is alleviation from your Lord and a mercy. But whoever transgresses after that will have a painful punishment" (2:178).

28 Suhravardī in Persian, or Suhrawardī in Arabic sources, is one of the most important Sufis in Sunni Islam, responsible for bringing *futūwwa* and *tasawwūf* closer to each other. See *Encyclopaedia of Islam*, new ed., s.v. "Suhrawardī," by Angelika Hartmann.
29 Corbin, "*Futūwatnāme-ye* Shihabaddīn Suhrawardī," 50.
30 Ibid., 50.
31 Ridgeon, *Morals and Mysticism*, 3.
32 Natel-Khanlari, "Ayīn-e 'Ayyārī," 173–4; Natel-Khanlari argues that this principle is clearly reflected in the oath of allegiance all new *'ayyārs* must take.
33 *Encyclopaedia of Islam,* new ed., s.v. "Ghāzī," by I. Melikoff.
34 Ibid., quoting the Turkish poet Ahmadī.
35 Ibid. Melikoff refers to one case in which Sultan Mahmūd took some twenty thousand *ghāzi* troops to India.
36 *Encyclopaedia of Islam,* new ed., s.v. *Futūwa*, by Cl. Cahen and Fr. Taeschner. The authors maintain that "the study of these movements is made difficult by the fact that, in the course of history, they have assumed very diverse forms."
37 See *Encyclopaedia of Islam,* 3rd ed., s.v. "Ya'qūb b. al-Layth al-Saffār," by C.E. Bosworth. Bosworth maintains that Ya'qūb, in establishing the first independent provincial dynasty (861–1003), repudiated the caliphal claims to supreme authority and breached the fabric of Abbasid rule; he was also known for fighting the Kharijite insurgence in Sīstān.
38 Sadeqi, *Tārikh-e Sīstān*, 142; see also Bosworth, *Sīstān under the Arabs*.
39 Gowharīn, "Social Roots," 131.
40 Sadeqi, *Tārikh-e Sīstān*, 142.
41 Ibid., 142.
42 Ibid., 143.
43 Khanlari, *Shahr-e Samak*, 64.
44 Ibid., 73.
45 Ibid., 76; cf. *Encyclopaedia Iranica,* s.v. *'Ayyār*, by Cl. Cahen and W.L. Hanaway Jr.
46 Khanlari, *Shahr-e Samak*, 34.
47 Ibid., 98.
48 *Encyclopaedia Iranica,* s.v. *'Ayyār*, by Cl. Cahen and W.L. Hanaway Jr.
49 Ibid.
50 Ibid.
51 *Encyclopaedia of Islam*, new ed., s.v. *Futūwa*, by Cl. Cahen and Fr. Taeschner.
52 Ibid.

53 *Encyclopaedia Iranica,* s.v. "*'Ayyār*," by Cl. Cahen and W. L. Hanaway Jr.

54 Kraemer, *Humanism in the Renaissance*, 51.

55 *Encyclopaedia of Islam*, new ed., s.v. *Futūwa*, by Cl. Cahen and Fr. Taeschner.

56 Tor points out, "In the ideological conflict between these two views – i.e. do political leaders have religious control over the Jihad or is it, rather, a religious obligation incumbent upon all believers, irrespective of political authority – it was the latter view, the view of the *mutatawwi'a* [free warriors], which won (at least in Iraq), and was adopted by both the Shafi'ite and Hanbalite schools." See Tor, *Violent Order,* 45.

57 *Encyclopaedia of Islam,* new ed., s.v. "al-Ma'mūn," by M. Rekaya.

58 Hodgson, *Venture of Islam*, 2:128.

59 *Encyclopaedia of Islam,* new ed., s.v. "al-Nāsir Li-Dīn Allāh," by Angelika Hartmann.

60 Ibid. See Zarinkoob, "Ahl-e Malāmat wa Fityān," 201; Zarinkoob maintains that al-Nāsir used the *futūwwa* association much like a political party in the modern sense.

61 *Encyclopaedia of Islam*, new ed., s.v. "al-Nāsir Li-Dīn Allāh," by Angelika Hartmann.

62 See ch. 3, 114 above on Gratian's *Decretum* and ch. 5, 134.

63 Zakeri, *Sasanid Soldiers*, 2; cf. *Encyclopaedia of Islam*, new ed., s.v. *Futūwa*, by Cl. Cahen and Fr. Taeschner.

64 Zakeri, *Sasanid Soldiers*, 14. Frye argues that feudalism is a political entity, rather than an economic one, based on the mutual obligation between the lord and his serf, something that did not exist in the pre-Islamic Near East.

65 Ibid., 13.

66 A. Christensen, quoted in ibid., 59.

67 Mahjoub, *Āyīn-e-Javānmardī*, 66. See similar views expressed by other prominent Iranian scholars, such as Sa'id Nafīsī (d. 1966) and Muhammad Taqī Bahār (d. 1951), in Corbin, *Āyīn-e Javānmardī*, 109, 110.

68 Hākemī, "Āyīn-e Futūwat wa 'Ayyārī,"167.

69 Corbin, *Āyīn-e Javānmardī*, 8.

70 Compare the main commandments as stipulated in Ibn Eskandar, *Qābūs Nāma* and in Gautier, *Chivalry*, 24, 45, 61.

71 Hay "Collateral Damage," 9, 10.

72 Ibid., 13.

73 Housley, "Crusades Against Christians," 23. Housely identifies the period between 1148 and 1153 as when "the most detailed justification for directing Christian arms against other Christians instead of pagans" was formulated. He discusses how in 1199 Pope Innocent III proposed crusades against the German adventurer Markward of Anweiler, and again in 1208 against Cathars and their protectors.

74 Riley-Smith, *History, Crusades, the Latin East*, 56.

75 France, "Thinking about Crusader Strategy," 80.

76 Ibid., 84–7.

77 *Encyclopaedia of Islam,* new ed., s.v. "Crusades," by Cl. Cahen; Cahen believes that the deterioration of the situations of the Christian Maronites and Armenians under the Mamlūks resulted directly from these confrontations.

78 Ibid.

79 Ibid. In other words, the Crusades, according to Cahen, were responsible for the radicalization of the Muslim culture across a large area with lasting effects.

80 See *Encyclopaedia of Islam*, new ed., s.v. "Salāh al-Dīn," by D.S. Richards. Richards draws attention to an exception to the general attitude suggested by Cahen; he contends that the Sinjārs and Zangīs, who frequently helped Salāh al-Dīn, did not have any other motive in their support of the political rival except a common Islamic cause.

81 Runciman, *History of Crusades*, 3:560.

82 English translation, Richards, *Rare and Excellent History*, 35. Bahā' al-Dīn Ibn Shaddād wrote an authentic chronicle of inside information about Salāh al-Dīn's war campaigns and day-to-day activities. Here, the author narrates how Salāh al-Dīn generously gave the lord of Antioch (a Christian) a territory that he had lost before the final peace treaty of 1192.

83 See "The Massacre of Shi'ites in Allepo by Salāh al-Dīn Ayyoubī," accessed 16 December 2014, http://www.askdin.com/thread16159.html.

84 The Persian founder of the illuminationist school of philosophy.

85 See "Salāh al-Dīn Ayyoubī," accessed 16 December 2014, http://hajj.ir/99/4096.

86 Richards, *Rare and Excellent History*, 38.

87 After capturing Prince Guy and his brother, the notorious Prince Reynald, during the 1187 battle of Hattin, Salāh al-Dīn offered the former a drink, which he passed to Prince Reynald. Salāh al-Dīn then instructed his interpreter, "Tell the king, you are the one giving him a drink. I have not given him any drink." According to the customs of the Arabs, whoever gave a prisoner food or drink extended to him a promise to spare his life. Salāh al-Dīn's intention was to strictly observe these customs. He disavowed any generosity toward Reynald, because he wished to execute him for numerous treacherous attacks against the Muslims. See Richards, *Rare and Excellent History*, 75.

88 Ibid., 211.

89 Finally, as Cahen mentions, he succeeded in establishing a policy of détente with the Franks. See *Encyclopaedia of Islam*, new ed., s.v. "Ayyūbids," by Cl. Cahen.

90 This matter is stressed both by Ibn Shaddād and Richards, *Rare and Excellent History*.

91 Many medieval historiographical accounts (including that of Ibn Shaddād) stress that he was forced to accompany his uncle to Egypt on a military mission.

92 Richards, *Rare and Excellent History*, 17.

93 *Encyclopaedia of Islam,* 3rd new ed., s.v. "Shaddādīds," by C.E. Bosworth.

94 The *Ashāb-e Kahf,* who are referred to as the "Seven Sleepers of Ephesus" in Christian Occident literature, were a group of young people who resisted the idolatrous ideology of the emperor Decius (240–51 BCE) and his persecution. They sought refuge in a cave, sank into a miraculous sleep for some 309 years, and then awoke under the Christian emperor Theodosius. They became symbols of youthful resistance to injustice in the constitutions of many *futūwwa* institutions; see Corbin, introduction to *Rasāel-e Javānmardān*. For more, see also *Encyclopaedia of Islam*, new ed., s.v. "Ashāb al-Kahf," by R. Paret.

95 See Ferdowsi discussion above, ch. 1, 37; Levy, *Mirror for Princes*, 247.

96 *Encyclopaedia Iranica,* s.v. "'*Ayyār*," by Cl. Cahen and W. L. Hanaway Jr.

97 Ibid.

98 Ibn Eskandar, *Qabusnameh*, 247.

99 This rule of chivalry is mentioned in some other sources such as the *Tārīkh-e Gozīdeh* of Mustawfi Qazwini: "*Jawānmardī* consists of giving justice [*ensāf dādan* in Persian], but not soliciting justice [for oneself]." Similar notions are mentioned in *Risāla* of al-Qushyrī and *Tabaqāt-e Sufiyya* of al-Sumāmī, cited in Tor, *Violent Order*, 244.

100 Husayn Gārzagāhi lived towards the end of the fifteenth century.

101 Quoted in Ridgeon, *Morals and Mysticism*, 195.

102 Rumi, *Mathnawī*, trans. Nicholson, 6:776.

103 Tor, *Violent Order*, 266. Tor cites Muslim works such as Shahāb al-Dīn Ahmad al-Tifāshī's *Nuzhat al-albāb* or Ibn Miskawayh's *Tajārib al-umam*.

104 The traditional Twelver-Shi'i political philosophy maintains that since the postponement of the religio-political leadership of the charismatic twelfth imam in time of his divine occultation in 873, no political leader has legitimacy. It was primarily during the Safavid era (sixteenth century) that Shi'i jurists devised an alternative theory that Shi'i jurists, as legitimate representatives of the occult imam, have the authority to delegate their power to de facto rulers. This activist political philosophy reached its theoretical and practical culmination with Ayatollah Khomeini in the 1970s. The establishment of the Islamic Republic of Iran headed by a jurist was in effect a monumental turning point in Shi'i political philosophy. According to Ayatollah Khomeini in his *Wilāyat-e Faqīh* (Rule of jurisconsult), a knowledgeable and just jurist can establish a fully legitimate political rule.

105 According to the war historian David Nicolle, "The complications implicit in the concept of *courtly love* hardly applied [in Western chivalry] since women were still all but excluded from the ideals of *knighthood. Courtly love,* in which a *knight* or *squire* was duty bound to honor and pursue the fair sex in a stylized yet

still very real manner, developed separately under the influence of Arab-Islamic concepts of romantic love; only being integrated into the ideals of *chivalry* during the 13th and 14th century." See Nicollc, *Medieval Warfare*, 260.

106 See *Encyclopaedia of Islam*, new ed., s.v. "al-Nāsir Li-Dīn Allāh," by Angelika Hartmann.

107 Unfortunately it is not difficult to provide evidence of these atrocities, which in the summer and fall of 2014 reached an unprecedented scale. The infamous massacre of Iraqi and Syrian civilians by Daesh, the mass murder of Palestinian children by the Israeli army in Gaza, and the massacre of school children by Pakistani Taliban in Pishavar on 16 December 2014 are unfortunately not isolated acts.

Chapter 4

1 Khwāja Shamsuddīn Mohammad Hafez is the most renowned Persian poet of the fourteenth century and one of the most influential poets in Persian literature.

2 Coates, "Culture," 215.

3 Ibid., 215, 217.

4 Seyyed Hossein Nasr, "Reply to Sallie B. King," in *The Philosophy of Seyyed Hossein Nasr,* 231, quoted in Shah-Kazemi, "Nasr's Universalism vs. Hick's Pluralism," 255.

5 Ibid., 251.

6 Ibid., 254.

7 For further enquiry into Nasr's philosophy, see Nasr, *Islamic Philosophy*.

8 See Nasr, *Traditional Islam*.

9 For an accurate and concise history of Wahhabism, see Algar, *Wahhabism*.

10 For the full account of Nasr's arguments on these civilizational ironies, see the introduction to Nasr, *Islam*, xi–xxv.

11 Seyyer Hossein Nasr, "The Spiritual Significance of Jihad," in Chittick, *Inner Journey*, 46.

12 Seyyed Hossein Nasr, "Justice to the Enemy," in Chittick, *Inner Journey*, 49. The original proverbial hadith contends that on Judgment Day the blood of all martyrs will be weighed against the ink of scholars that will be revealed as the more weighty ink.

13 Ibid., 51.

14 Ibid., 54.

15 Shabestarī, "Hermeneutics and the Religious Interpretation." Rahesabz.net, accessed 24 October 2013, http://www.rahesabz.net/story/34350/.

16 Ibid.

17 Shabestarī, *Imān va Āzādī*, 78–9.

18 See "ISIS commits mass murder, advertises it': Iraq executions detailed," accessed 14 June 2014, http://rt.com/news/168916-isis-iraq-war-crimes/.

19 Mohammad Mojtahed Shabestarī, "If Daesh (Persian abbreviation for ISIS) Asks Jurists (agar daesh az faqihan beporsad)," accessed 30 November 2014, http://mohammadmojtahedshabestari.com/articles.php?id=354&title=%اگر20«داعِش»فقر 20%از%20بی20%بپرسدهان.

20 A student of Ayatollah Montazerī and himself a jurist, Mohsen Kadivar was dismissed from Tehran University because of his bold critical views. Presently, he teaches Islamic law at Duke University. He is one of the leading Iranian jurists trying to reconstruct and modernize Shi'i jurisprudence both from within and outside of the boundaries of the seminarian methodologies.

21 See Kadivar, "Religious Intellectualism," 28. See "Human Rights and Intellectual Islam," Kadivar.com, accessed 24 August 2013, http://en.kadivar.com/human-rights-and-intellectual-islam.

22 Kadivar, "Religious Intellectualism," 34.

23 Ibid.

24 Mostafā Malekīān, "Lets Posit Ethics on the Top," published online in Persian, Fararu.com, accessed 25 October 2013, http://fararu.com/fa/news/164649/.

25 Malekīān, "Honar va Sulh," 27–9.

26 Fanā'ī, *Aklāq-e dīn shenāsī* , 273.

27 Ibid., 285.

28 Ibid., 492.

29 Soroush, "More Robust than Ideology [*Farbehtar az ideology*]," 81–126. The periodical is published by the Iranian *Center for Research and Middle East Strategic Studies* and available online at http://en.cmess.ir/Default.aspx?tabid=73&articleid=40&dnnprintmode=true&mid=422&SkinSrc=%5BG%5DSkins%2F_default%2FNo+Skin&ContainerSrc=%5BG%5DContainers%2F_default%2FNo+Container (accessed 21 February 2016).

30 Ibid., 107, 109.

31 Ibid., 87, 88, 95, 97, 105, 108, 110, 111, 116, 117.

32 Ibid., 102.

33 Ibid., 104.

34 Sa'di, *Gulestan and Bustan*, 348.

35 This is my rough translation of the proverbial couplet from Sa'di, known as one of the greatest gnostic poets of the Persian language.

36 Hafiz, *Divan Hafiz*, ed. Khorramshahi, 326.

37 Hafiz, *Collected Lyrics*, 39.

38 Abdolkarim Soroush, "The Virtue of Weakness," (lecture, University of Waterloo, Waterloo, ON, May 2013), accessed 31 October 2013, http://lectures.drsoroush.com/Persian/Lectures/2013/andar%20fazilate%20natavani.mp3.

39 For news details about the incident, see "Gunmen attack Paris magazine Charlie Hebdo's offices killing at least twelve," *Guardian*, accessed 8 February 2015, http://www.theguardian.com/world/2015/jan/07/satirical-french-magazine-charlie-hebdo-attacked-by-gunmen.

40 For the full text of the article published in Persian, see Abdolkarim Soroush, "*hele bar khiz ke andishe degar bayad kard* (*Wakeup to Rethink*)," drsoroush.com, 2 February 2015, accessed 8 February 2015, http://drsoroush.com/fa/هله-بر-خیز-که-اندیشه-دیگر-باید-کرد/.

41 Ibid.

42 In the authoritative Sunni hadith source Sunan Abi Dawud, Abu Sirmah narrates that "the Prophet said: If anyone harms (others), Allah will harm him, and if anyone shows hostility to others, Allah will show hostility to him." See Sunan Abī Dawud, book 25, hadith 65, *Sunnah.com*, accessed 22 February 2014, http://sunnah.com/abudawud/25/65.

43 See the website Maqsoud Farāsatkhāh, accessed 2 December 2014, http://farasatkhah.blogsky.com.

44 Maqsood Farāsatkhāh, "Critical Shi'a Studies," section 3, Maqsoud Farāsatkhāh website, accessed 2 December 2014, http://farasatkhah.blogsky.com/1393/02/05/post-226/F.

45 Ibid.

46 "Religion Against Religion" is the title of a book by Ali Sharī'atī, published in English translation as *Religion vs. Religion*; this volume comprises a short discussion of the thesis that throughout the history of mankind, religion has fought against religion rather than against nonreligion. See Maqsood Farāsatkhāh, "Critical Shi'a Studies," section 3, Maqsoud Farāsatkhāh website, accessed 2 December 2014, http://farasatkhah.blogsky.com/1393/02/05/post-226/.

47 Farāsatkhāh, *We Iranians*, 130.

48 Ibid.

49 This line was translated by Mohsen Ashtiani.

50 Farāsatkhāh, *We Iranians*, 130.

51 See Maqsood Farāsatkhāh, "Ethical Turning Points in Iran and the Responsibility of Intellectuals," *Sharq* newspaper, 7 December 2014, accessed 24 March 2016, http://www.pishkhaan.net/Archive/1393/09/13930916/Shargh8310410311497495754152458.pdf.

52 Ibid.

53 Ibid.

54 See this chapter, 117 below.

55 See Katouzian, "Short-Term Society," 1.

56 Milani, *Words, Not Swords*, 156.

57 Ibid., 158.

58 Ibid., 173; from "Our Tears are Sweet," previously published and translated in Behbahānī, *A Cup of Sin*, 173.
59 Ibid., 171.
60 Ibid.
61 Ibid.
62 Behbahānī, *A Cup of Sin*, 31.
63 Milani, *Words, Not Swords*, 173.
64 Ibid. ; from "My Country, I Will Build You Again," previously published and translated in Behbahānī, *A Cup of Sin*, 155–6.
65 "Lay Down Your Rifle" was copied here from a blog titled *goodread*, accessed 22 February 2016, http://www.goodreads.com/quotes/227454.
66 "Iran: Famous Singer Shajarian decries, 'Language of Fire,'" trans. Ramin Mostaghim and Borzu Daragahi, *Los Angeles Times*, 6 September 2009, accessed 29 December 2014, http://latimesblogs.latimes.com/babylonbeyond/2009/09/iran-famous-singer-shajarian-decries-language-of-fire.html.
67 Moshiri, *Selected Poems*, 196, 197.
68 These lines are from a longer poem titled "Naseemi az diyar-e ashti" (A breeze from the land of reconciliation) published in Moshiri, *Az Diyar-e Ashti*, n.p.
69 Tapper, *New Iranian Cinema*, 13.
70 For an eloquent review of the film, see David Shasha, "Gilaneh," The American Muslim website, accessed 15 December 2014, http://theamericanmuslim.org/tam.php/features/articles/movie_review_gilaneh_rakhshan_bani_etemad_and_mohsen_abdolvahhab_2005.
71 Directed by Bahrām Beyzā'ī and released in 1989, this film presents the miserable life of a young orphan boy who lost his parents during the Iran-Iraq war and who struggles to be adopted by another family.
72 Directed by Ebrahim Hātamikīā, this film, screened in 1992, depicts the tragic life story of an disabled Iranian war veteran who has been harmed by Iraqi chemical weapons and endures a torturous life.
73 For the entire article in Persian, see Elaheh Najafī, "Sparrow's Chirping and the Controversy about the Prophet," *Radio Zamaneh*, accessed 21 December 2014, http://www.radiozamaneh.com/194005.
74 For details, see "Fatwa against AR Rahman, Majīd Majīdī," Zeenews, 13 September 2015, accessed 24 March 2016, http://zeenews.india.com/entertainment/celebrity/fatwa-against-ar-rahman-majid-majidi_1795112.html.
75 Jahānbegloo, *Introduction to Nonviolence*, 43.
76 Ibid.
77 Jahānbegloo was detained in Iran in late April 2006 after being accused by Iranian intelligence of attempting to aid a 'velvet revolution' in Iran.
78 Jahānbegloo, *Introduction to Nonviolence*, 43.

79 Ibid., 48.
80 Ibid., 51.
81 Ibid., 160.
82 Ibid., 162.
83 Ibid., 163.

Chapter 5

1 Radī, *Nahju'l-balāgha*, 235. See also Ibn A'tham, *al-Futūh*, 753. Another Prophetic hadith goes further: "Said the Apostle of God: Indeed remembrance of God in mornings and at nights is better than breaking the swords in the way of God" (قال رسول الله: لذكرالله بلغدو و الآصال خير من حطم السيوف فى سبيل الله عز و جل). See Ibn al-Hassan, *Wasā'il al-shī'a*, 351.

2 Radī, *Nahju'l-balāgha*, 248–9.

3 These wars were guided by the person of the Prophet Muhammad, some of which he directly participated in. Questions and responses abound regarding possible ideological, defensive, pre-emptive, economic, punitive, liberating, and other incentives for these wars, but there is little controversy about the fact that the Prophet did not seek to establish his rule beyond the Arabian Peninsula.

4 There may be some exaggerations in the war chronicles reporting the miracles of Muslim military victories, but given the rather fast pace of conquests, there could be no other term to explain the phenomenal military triumphs. Ibn A'tham reports in *al-Futūh* that in a conflict with the Roman forces, twenty thousand Muslims fought sixty thousand Romans, resulting in the deaths of fourteen thousand Romans – a stark contrast to the seventeen Muslims killed. To elaborate on this figure, consider Ibn A'tham's reports on other battles: Persian commander Mehrān had eighty thousand troops and fought against Abū 'Ubaida, who only had five thousand troops. He also fought against Rostam, who only had 150 thousand, against Mehrān's forty thousand. See Ibn A'tham, *al-Futūh*, 91, 96, 105.

5 One statement by Hormozān, a Persian army commander (captured in 640) who was brought before the caliph 'Umar, reveals how non-Muslims perceived such thunderous Muslim victories. Hormozān says to 'Umar: "In the past, God was neutral in wars, and had given us a free hand, thus our dominance upon you." To this 'Umar responds: "No, the reason was that you were united and we were not." See Khadduri, *War and Peace,* 196.

6 Perhaps the most succinct and all-encompassing Prophetic advice on the ethics of war is reflected in the following passage: "I advise you to be pious to God, and have goodwill towards your fellow Muslim; fight in the name of God, and in His way; fight only against those who disbelieve God; avoid deceit and treachery; do not kill women and children; before engaging in battle, invite your enemy

to the three options of accepting Islam in which case the conflict terminates, ask them to leave their land in which case their [other] rights will be observed, ask them to pay poll tax [*jizya*] in which case there is no cause for conflict; and prepare for the battle only if these first three options fail." Ibn 'Umar al Wāqidī, *Tārikh-e janghāy-e payāmbar*, 2:577. The Prophet, in deciding to appoint an army commander, says the following: "Fight in the name of God, and in the way of God. Fight whoever denied Allah. And do not resort to treachery [breaking a covenant], nor exceed the bounds. Do not mutilate. Do not kill children or the monks in their monasteries. Do not set palm trees afire, nor destroy them by flood. Do not cut any fruit trees, nor set the farms afire, for you never know you might need them. Do not kill eatable animals unless you have no other choice for food. And whenever you encounter your enemy from among the polytheists, invite them to the three options. If they accepted, you should accept peace and provide for them full security." al-Tūsī, *Tahdhīb al-ahkām*, 6:138, 139. See also al-Zurbāttī, *Aklāq al-harb*, 69.

7 See Abū Bakr's moral advice to his commander Yazīd b. Abī Sufyān on his way to a Syrian conquest: "O Yazīd, stay firm in jihad ... be cognizant that you are on your way to a land which is full of enemies and blessings too. Do not be distracted, under any circumstances, from remembering Allāh, and make your heart always available in his domain, never seek killing of women and children, do not uproot or cut palm and fruit trees; do not try to kill children and the elderly; and do not kill anybody in vain. Stay away from destroying buildings and developments, and be attentive to all this so that God may grant you victory as He is the Omnipotent." Ibn A'tham, *al-Futūh*, 57.

8 See appendix 2 below. *Great Islamic Encyclopedia*, 1st ed., s.v. "Jang (war)," by Mohammad Qārī Sayyed Fatemi and Mostafā Mohaqqeq Dāmād.

9 The standard Sunni Muslim view defines the five cardinal pillars of faith (which do not include jihad), encompassing *shahada, salat*, *zakat*, *hajj*, and *sawm* (professing on the unity of God and the prophecy of Muhammad, daily prayer, almsgiving, pilgrimage, and fasting).

10 The beheading of Egypt's ambassador to Iraq by Iraqi militants in July 2005 is a demonstrative case wherein a noncombatant Sunni Muslim emissary was beheaded by his coreligionists (Sunni Iraqis) in direct contravention to all Islamic laws and ethics of war. The mass execution of hundreds of Iraqi Shi'is by Daesh (ISIS) rebels in June 2014 represents a large-scale cross-sectarian case of crime against humanity.

11 Ibn A'tham, *al-Futūh*, 428.

12 Elaborate accounts of laws of war against *bughāt* (rebels) by Shi'i jurists are provided by Sālehī-Najafābādī, *Jihad in Islam*, 113–55.

13 It is important to note that because theocracy is the authoritative system of government in Iran, the historic Shi'i master narratives are used officially day

to day for various political agendas. For example, the controversy over Iran's contentious 2009 presidential election continues to be framed as "sedition" – a term that references 'Alī's enemies who challenged his caliphate and waged war against him. After Iran's most recent presidential race, which resulted in the election of Hassan Rouhani, some of the new president's cabinet choices were subject to severe criticism by radical members of the Iranian parliament, who claimed that Rouhani had collaborated with the 2009 "seditionists." Some of the cabinet members compared the situation to the general amnesty given to Meccan polytheists by the Prophet Mohammad and ended up asking for political forgiveness. A number of radical critics instead compared the situation to the dissent against 'Alī, which resulted in three wars. A few days after three cabinet choices were rejected for the positions, an outspoken cleric from the radical faction, Panahian, invited parliament's members to study the history of the civil wars during 'Alī's short caliphate. For additional details, see rajanews, http://rajanews.com, a website that voices the views of most militant ideologues active in Iranian politics. Panahian's talk can be found at "Today More Than Ever, We Need to Learn about Early History of Islam," rajanews, accessed 18 August 2013, http://rajanews.com/detail.asp?id=165299.

14 Ch. 4, 72.

15 al-Minqarī, *Waq'at siffin,* 317.

16 One should not expect that 'Alī's ethics of war were followed precisely by his camp. Ibn 'Atham, for example, narrates that a specific soldier in 'Alī's camp, during the time of the Siffīn battle, defied 'Alī's order and did finish off some of the wounded, probably acting on the pre-Islamic standards. Ibn A'tham, *Al-Futūh*, 528.

17 al-Minqarī, *Waq'at siffin,* 174–5, 212, 278–9. See also Radī, *Nahju'l-balāgha,* 207, military instruction 14.

18 al-Minqarī, *Waq'at siffin,* 145, 171, 303, 322, 641. In fact, immediately after the end of the war, 'Alī, unilaterally and unconditionally, released all the captives; ibid., 718.

19 Radī, *Nahju'l-balāgha*, 206. The English translation is taken from "Peace and Treatise," Al-Islam, accessed 1 May 2015, http://www.al-islam.org/richest-treasure-imam-ali/peace-and-treaties.

20 Modern theories of ethics in war (just war) revolve mainly around the two domains of *jus ad bellum* and *jus in bello*. The first addresses the causes and goals of war, which themselves are comprised of six main categories: just cause, right authority (who decides for war), proportionality (between the inflicted damage and war's ultimate goals), last resort (war is used only after all other means of conflict resolution have failed), the reasonable hope of success, and the right intention. The rubric *jus in bello* addresses the conduct of war and consequently is concerned with the boundaries or limits of war, the legitimate extension of war

to combatants or noncombatants, the types of weapons used (concerning intended, impact, and level of destruction, known as the principle of discrimination), the treatment of wounded and prisoners of war, and so forth.

21 Radī, *Nahju'l-balāgha*, 248–9. See the full text of the letter translated into English, "Peace and Treatise," Al-Islam, accessed 1 May 2015, http://www.al-islam.org/richest-treasure-imam-ali/peace-and-treaties.

22 For a more detailed view of Arendt, see "Hannah Arendt and Collective Forgiving," *Academia.edu,* accessed 1 May 2015, http://www.academia.edu/750007/HannahArendtandCollectiveForgiving.

23 Rumi, *Mathnavī-e Ma'navī*, ed. Sobhani, 1:151–3.

24 Rumi, *Mathnavi, Book One*, trans. Mojaddedi, 227–42.

25 Rumi, *Mathnavī-e Ma'navī*, ed. Sobhani, 1:156.

26 Rumi, *Mathnavi, Book One*, trans. Mojaddedi, 235.

27 Lut Ibn Mikhnaf (d. 757/774) is the oldest biographer detailing al-Husayn's martyrdom. He systematically reported details regarding one of the most tragic events in Shi'a history, which reached the world by way of his student Hisham b. Muhammad Kalbī. Ibn Mikhnaf's book, written in Arabic, is found in several publications in Iran and Beirut, such as in *Maqtal al-Husayn*. Hamid Mavani provided a very good English translation entitled *Reconstructing the Episode of Karbala*, cicm.org, accessed 18 August 2013, http://www.sicm.org.uk/index.php?page=downloads.

28 'Askarī, *Martyr*, 94.

29 For the full story of al-Husayn's tragedy as narrated by al-Tabari, see Chaliand, *The Art of War*, 395–9.

30 Abu Mikhnaf, *Reconstructing the Episode of Kerbala*, trans. Hamid Mavani, 167, cicm.org, accessed 18 August 2013, http://www.sicm.org.uk/index.php?page=downloads.

31 Walzer, *Just and Unjust Wars*, xxxi and 4.

32 *Kullu yawmin 'Ashūrā wa kullu ardin Karbalā*. 'Āshūrā is the tenth of *Muharram*, the first month of the Arabic calendar, during which Husayn and all of his small camp were martyred.

33 This proverbial hadith maintains that jihad targeted at infidels (known as *jihad asghar* or "the minor jihad") is less important and difficult for a Muslim than jihad with one's own carnal soul (known as *jihad akbar* or "the greater jihad"). The Prophet reportedly noted this after he and his companions victoriously returned from one of their forays. References to this hadith are abundant in all Sunni and Shi'i hadith sources, such as by the hadith collections of Bukhari and Kulayni.

34 A 2011 report published by Iraq Body Count reveals that between 2003 and 2010 at least 12,284 civilians were killed in some 1003 suicide bombings in Iraq. The study shows that suicide bombings kill sixty times as many civilians

as soldiers. The savagery of these bombings, which are mostly conducted by al-Qaeda affiliates, culminated in a dozen incidents across Iraq, at the end of Ramadan in August 2013, that killed more than seventy people during the sacred Muslim festival of Eid al-Fitr. For both reports, see "Casualties of Suicide Bombings in Iraq, 2003–2010," Iraqibodycount.org, accessed 26 March 2016, http://www.iraqbodycount.org/analysis/numbers/lancet-2011/; "Al Qaeda Claims Eid al-Fitr Bomb Attacks across Iraq," Globalpost.com,, accessed 20 July 2014, http://www.globalpost.com/dispatch/news/regions/middle-east/iraq/130810/eid-al-fitr-iraq-sees-scores-killed-bomb-attacks.

35 Chaliand, *The Art of War*, 393–4.

36 For an elaborate account of this historic development, see Haider, *Shi'i Islam*, ch. 10.

37 Shaybānī, *Islamic Law of Nations*. Shaybānī's *Kitāb al-siyar al-kabīr* received an elaborate commentary by Muhammad b. Ahmad Sarakhsī (d. 1090) entitled *Sharh al-sīyar al-kabir*.

38 According to Khadduri, Shaybānī was responsible for the most important jurist writing on *Sīyar*, but it was not the first one. Among the first authors, he mentions Ibrāhīm al-Nakha'ī (d. 714), Hammad b. Sulaymān (d. 738), al-Sha'bī (d. 723), Sufyān al-Thawrī (d. 738), Mālik b. Anas (d. 796), Zuhrī (d. 742), Rabī'a (d. 754), 'Abd al-Rahman al-Awzā'ī (d. 774), and Shaybānī's teacher, Abu Hanīfa (d. 768). See Shaybānī, *Islamic Law of Nations,* 22. Note that Abu Hanīfa was a student of Ja'far al-Sādiq (d. 765), who was known as the founder of Twelver Shi'i jurisprudence.

39 Shaybānī, *Islamic Law of Nations,* vii.

40 Kelsay, "Islam and the Distinction," 199.

41 Khadduri, *War and Peace*, 53, 58.

42 Ibid., 58. See also Mohaqqeq Dāmād, *Protection of Individuals*, 92.

43 Ibid., 58.

44 Paraphrased by Khadduri, *War and Peace*, 59, from Taqī al-Dīn Ibn Taymīya, "Qā'ida fī qitāl al-kuffār," in *Majmū'at rasālāt,* ed. M. Hamīd al-Fiqqī (Cairo: n.p., 1949), 123. Note should be taken that Ibn Taymīya issued a *fatwa* calling for jihad against various Shi'i sects, including the Nusairīya (a group of extremist Shi'as that elevated 'Alī's status to divination), and ruled that this is the most obligatory of all sharī'a rulings, even more important than jihad with disbelievers. See Badawī, *Madhāhib al-Islamīyīn*, 421. Since being issued, and through today, this *fatwa*, has caused many extremist attempts to wipeout Shi'i communities in various regions.

45 Ibn Taymīya, *Risāla al-qitāl*, quoted in Mohaqqeq Dāmād, *Protection of Individuals*, 92.

46 Al-Sādiq is frequently referred to in Shi'i hadith literature by his alternative name Abā 'Abd Allāh.

47 The significance of *Wasā'il* is that it includes all hadith reports presented in the four original authoritative sources of Shi'i jurisprudence, namely *al-Kāfī* by Muhammad Ibn Ya'qub Kulainī (d. 940), *Man lā yahduruhu'l-faqīh* by Muhammad b. 'Alī b. Bābawayh Qummī, who was also known as Shaykh Sadūq (d. 991), and *Tahdhīb al-ahkām* and *al-Istibsār* both by Muhammad Ibn Hasan al-Tūsī, who was also known as Shaykh al-Tā'ifa (d. 1067).

48 al-'Āmilī, *Wasā'il al-shī'a*, vol. 6.

49 Ibid., 6:32.

50 Ibid., 6:33.

51 The reference to the pre-Islamic Arab culture as *jāhilī* in Islamic literature addresses negative attributes of this culture, such as its impulsiveness and polytheism that amounted to general ignorance; this, however, does not have an absolutist connotation.

52 al-'Āmilī, *Wasā'il al-shī'a*, 6:32.

53 Cited in Legenhausen, "Islam and Just War Theory," 21.

54 "Lo! Allāh hath bought from the believers their lives and their wealth because the Garden (heaven) will be theirs: they shall fight in the way of Allāh and shall slay and be slain. It is a promise, which is binding on Him in the Torah and the Gospel and the Qur'ān. Who fulfilled his covenant better than Allāh? Rejoice then in your bargain that ye have made, for that is the supreme triumph" (9:111). Pickthall, *Meaning of the Glorious Qur'ān*.

55 "(Triumphant) are those who turn repentant (to Allāh), those who serve (Him), those who praise (Him), those who fast, those who bow down, those who fall prostrate (in worship), those who enjoin the right and those who forbid the wrong and those who keep the limits (ordained) of Allāh – and give glad tidings to believers" (9:122). Pickthall, *Meaning of the Glorious Qur'ān.*

56 al-'Āmilī, *Wasā'il al-shī'a*, 6:34.

57 Ibid., 6:36.

58 Ibid., 6:37.

59 This hadith is referred to by many authoritative Shi'i and Sunni sources. For an elaborate analysis of the subject, see Tabātabā'ī , *Shi'ite Islam*, 210–11. Abdulaziz Sachedina has also provided a thorough treatment of the subject in Sachedina, *Islamic Messianism*. For references to the hadith in most authoritative Sunni sources, see "Identification of the Prophesied Imam Mahdi," Irshad.com, accessed 7 March 2016, http://www.irshad.org/islam/prophecy/mahdi.htm.

60 Ayoub, *Crisis of Muslim History*, 147.

61 See ch. 8, 197–200 below.

62 This notion reflects the Platonic sense of the inner enemy.

63 al-'Āmilī, *Wasā'il al-shī'a*, 6:102. It is important to note that, according to Mohaqqeq Dāmād, a legal distinction between ruse and perfidy, i.e. acceptance

of the former and rejection of the latter, is stipulated in the Hague Convention of 1907, as well as in other modern international protocols. See Mohaqqeq Dāmād, *Protection of Individuals*, 405.

64 al-'Āmilī, *Wasā'il al-shī'a*, 6:63–4.
65 Ibid., 6:113.
66 Ibid., 6:56.
67 Ibid., 6:58–9.
68 Ibid., 6:57.
69 Ibid., 6:96.
70 Ibid., 6:68.
71 Ibid., 6:35.
72 McDermott, *Theology of al-Shaikh al-Mufid*, 327.
73 *Al-Jamal,* literally the Camel, denotes one of the three civil wars in which 'Alī engaged.
74 McDermott, *Theology of al-Shaikh al-Mufid*, 328.
75 In a hadith from 'Alī b. Abī Tālib transmitted through a chain of authorities and narrated by Ibn Bābawayh (d. 991), known as Shaykh Sadūq (one of the most prominent and earliest Shi'i scholars), 'Alī asserts that jihad has four forms: commanding right, forbidding wrong, truthfulness (*al-sidq*) everywhere, and enmity with conscious sinners (*al-fāsiqīn*). The same source refers to another hadith from al-Sādiq who determines other branches of jihad, such as: jihad with one's own carnal soul (*al-nafs*), establishing or reviving a charity, and fighting with unbelievers. See Ibn Bābawayh, *Al-Khisāl*, 1:337, 349.
76 Cook, *Commanding Right*, 254.
77 Cook, *Commanding Right*, 276.

Chapter 6

1 Tabātabā'ī, *Shī'ah*, 85, 155.
2 Nicolle maintains, for example, that the Muslim distinction between combatants and noncombatants may also have influenced European practices. See Nicolle, *Medieval Warfare*, 242.
3 Mohammad b. Hassan Tūsī (d. 1067) was a prominent Shi'i scholar, known as the first jurist to adopt a part of Sunni jurisprudence into the Shi'i school. Abū Abdallāh Muhammad b. Idris al-Shāfi'ī (d. 820) was a prominent Sunni scholar, known as the first author of *'usūl al-fiqh* (methodology in Islamic jurisprudence). For Tūsī's import of Sunni jurisprudence into Shi'i law, see also Modarressi, *Introduction to Shī'ī Law*, 44; Modarressi contends that it was through Tūsī that "non-Shi'i concepts, which were alien to traditional Shi'i thought, also crept into Shi'i law and created some inconsistencies in it."

4 al-Shāfi'ī, *Al-Umm*, 4:168.

5 Tūsī, *Al-Mabsūt*, 2:13.

6 Muhaqqiq Hillī, *Sharāye' al-Islam*, 1:235; Ibn Mutahhar Hilli, *Tadhkirtu'l fuqaha'*, 9:44; Karakī, *Jami' al-maqasid*, 9:44; Najafi, *Jawāhir al-kalām*, 21:10–11.

7 Najafi, *Jawāhir al-kalam*, 21:13.

8 This view granting importance to the cause of war is a double-edged sword, for it can instigate an unlimited war (a war beyond conventional objective results) or a limited war (a war that ends before attaining an objective result). Tabātabā'ī, *Tafsīr al-mīzān*, 1:80.

9 Some similar traces of thought can be observed in the views of Tabātabā'ī's student Mutahharī, justifying war on the grounds of defending "human rights." Ibid.

10 Ibid., 1:95.

11 Ibid., 1:430–1.

12 Ibid., 1:89.

13 Ibid., 1:415.

14 "Fight in the way of Allah those who fight you, but do not transgress. Indeed Allah does not like transgressors. And kill them wherever you find them, and expel them from where they expelled you, for faithlessness [sedition] is graver than killing. But do not fight them near the Holy Mosque unless they fight you therein; but if they fight you, kill them; such is the requital of the faithless. But if they relinquish, then Allah is indeed all-forgiving, all-merciful. Fight them until faithlessness is no more and religion becomes [exclusively] for Allah. Then if they relinquish, there shall be no reprisal except against the wrongdoers." Qara'i, *Qur'ān*, Q. 2:190–4.

15 Tabātabā'ī, *Tafsīr al-mīzān*, 2:415.

16 "And how many a prophet [fought and] with him fought many religious scholars. But they never lost assurance due to what afflicted them in the cause of Allāh, nor did they weaken or submit. And Allāh loves the steadfast" (3:146). "They said, 'O Moses, indeed we will not enter it, ever, as long as they are within it; so go, you and your Lord, and fight. Indeed, we are remaining right here'" (5:24). "Return to them, for we [Solomon] will surely come to them with soldiers that they will be powerless to encounter, and we will surely expel them therefrom in humiliation, and they will be debased" (27:37). See Tabātabā'ī, *Tafsīr al-mīzān*, 1:92–3.

17 Mill, "The Contest in America," quoted in Reichberg, Syse, and Begby, *Ethics of War*, 585.

18 Reichberg, Syse, and Begby, *Ethics of War*, 582–3.

19 "There shall be no compulsion in [acceptance of] the religion. The right course has become clear from the wrong" (2:256).

20 James Turner Johnson addresses this question and some of its responses; see Johnson, "Contemporary Just War," 660–9.

21 Tabātabā'ī, *Shī'ah*, 220.

22 Ibid., 220–1.

23 Ibid., 216.

24 Ibid., 212.

25 "Mankind was one community; then Allāh sent the prophets as bringers of good tidings and warnings and sent down with them the scripture in truth to judge between the people concerning that in which they differed" (2:213). "Say, 'O people of the scripture, come to a word that is equitable between us and you – that we will not worship except Allāh and not worship except Allāh and not associate anything with him and take one another as lords instead of Allāh.' But if they turn away, then say, 'Bear witness that we are Muslims (submitting to him)'" (3:64). Qarā'ī, *Qur'ān*; Tabātabā'ī, *Shī'ah,* 85, 155.

26 Ibid., 227.

27 For Shahrūr's highly controversial but novel exegetical methodology and its application, see Shahrūr and Christmann, *The Qur'ān*.

28 Motahharī, "Jihad in the Qur'ān," 88.

29 Ibid., 97.

30 Ibid.

31 Ibid.,104.

32 Ibid.

33 Ibid., 105.

34 Ibid., 103.

35 There is an impressive amount of literature criticizing war for democracy. For an interesting prediction of the failure of such policies, written before these wars, see Paul Starr, "A War for Democracy?" *The American Prospect*, 13 March 2003, accessed 21 August 2013, http://prospect.org/article/war-democracy.

36 Motahharī, "Jihad in the Qur'ān," 113.

37 See Qārī and Mohaqqeq Dāmād's views on Motahharī in *Great Islamic Encyclopedia*, 1st ed., s.v. "Jang (war)," by Muhammad Qārī Sayyid Fatemi and Mostafa Mohaqqeq Dāmād, translated from Persian in appendix 2 below.

38 Vacek, "Divine-Command," 639; also available at, theologicalstudies.net, accessed 25 March 2016, http://www.ts.mu.edu/readers/content/pdf/57/57.4/57.4.3.pdf.

39 Emon, "On Islam and Islamic Natural Law: A Response to the International Theological Commission's 'Look at Natural Law,'" in John Berkman, William C. Mattison, eds., *Searching for a Universal Ethic*, SSRN, 9 February 2011, accessed 22 July 2014, http://ssrn.com/abstract=1758968 or http://dx.doi.org/10.2139/ssrn.1758968.

40 Reichberg, Syse, and Begby, *Ethics of War*, 469.

41 Shabestarī, *Jihad in Islam*, n.p.; this article was an independent volume separate from the Association of Muslim Students' periodical. Raosul Ja'farian, a

contemporary clerical historian, has written an article on this volume in which he highlights the remarkable evolution of Shabestarī's thought; see Rasoul Ja'farian, "Learning Lessons from a 180 Turn of Opinion," Tabnak, 9 July 2008, http://www.tabnak.ir/fa/news/13561/عبرت-گرفتن-از-يك-چرخش-180-درجه-فكري.

42 Although I have not read any recent articles by Shabestarī revoking his previous ideological stance on jihad, his postrevolution work suggests that he does not maintain his previous views, due mainly to his hermeneutical approach to religion, as Ja'farian has noted. Ja'farian quotes Shabestarī as saying, "Jihad in Islam is armed defence for the expansion of revolution"; see Ja'farian, "Learning Lessons."

43 His latest ideas were explored above, ch. 4, 94–5.

44 This will be discussed further in ch. 7 below.

Chapter 7

1 Nielsen, "God and the Basis," 345.

2 See Chubin and Tripp, *Iran and Iraq*, 50.

3 Even today, this subject is still heavily sensitive and passionately disputed among Iran's political and military leadership. Iranian authorities deny that they ever received a concrete, compensatory peace proposal from regional countries.

4 See Montazerī's statement in *Khaterat* (Memires), amontazeri.com, accessed 23 August 2013, https://amontazeri.com/book/khaterat/volume-1/593.

5 On Mahdi Bazargan's position on war, see Jahanbakhsh, *Islam, Democracy*, 111. A pamphlet of the Freedom Movement of Iran headed by Mahdi Bazargan, the first prime minister of the Islamic Republic, criticizes Iran's war policies. It provides an elaborate historical and scholarly account of war in Islam and criticizes the official policy of continuing war and rejecting peace mediations, thus denying the Islamic Republic a universal mission to pursue through the war and prompting the government to end the war as soon as possible.

6 See Jonathan C. Randal, "Iran-Iraq War," *War Crimes, A to Z Guide,* accessed 23 August 2013, http://www.crimesofwar.org/thebook/iran-iraq-war.html. The following report from Jonathan Randal shows both the extensive use of chemical weapons by Iraq and the UN Security Council's passive response to Iraq's grave violations of the 1925 Geneva Protocol:

> Halabjah should not have come as the surprise it did. In November 1983 Tehran lodged the first of several complaints with the UN charging Baghdad with using chemical weapons to stop Iranian human-wave infantry attacks. Iraq refused a UN proposal to send experts to both belligerent countries for on-site investigations. The 1984 UN report dealing solely with findings on

Iranian soil agreed that Iraq had used mustard gas and tabun. But without film and photographic illustration it had little impact. The Security Council issued a wishy-washy resolution that refrained from naming Iraq. The council's rotating chairman condemned the use of chemical weapons in a separate, little-noticed declaration issued in his own name. The council scarcely could have done less … Indeed Halabjah was not an isolated case. Iraqi documents among millions captured by the Kurds in 1991 establish that in 1987 and 1988 Saddam, in a campaign code-named Al Anfal, used chemical weapons at least sixty times against Kurdish villages.

7 Serious Western sanctions against selling military equipment to Iran forced Iran's defence strategy to be heavily dependent on manpower and its basis on irregular war. This strategy, as the top commanders of the Revolutionary Guard believed, could only protect Iranian territory if the military kept up an offensive rather than a defensive position. Most political reports detailing these wartime decisions, including assertions by Ayatollah Montazerī, show that it was by the above technical argument that they convinced Ayatollah Khomeini to push the war into Iraqi territory. See statements by Ayatollah Montazerī on war in *Khaterat* (Memires), amontazeri.com, accessed 23 August 2013, https://amontazeri.com/book/khaterat/volume-1/593.

8 The phrase "the chalice of poison" used by Ayatollah Khomeini could be predicated on several factors. He had to take full responsibility for the unfulfilment of many costly declared goals of war. But he probably also remembered that on occasion he had to throw his full spiritual weight in justifying the problem of unproportional human loss on the Iranian side. Proportionality is of course an important factor among the six standard conditions for *jus ad bellum.* But because of the lack of relations with the industrial world and the shortage of military logistics, Iran had to rely strategically on manpower. This, nevertheless caused many questions and emotional-humanitarian concerns among the rank and file of fighters. The following example is telling: According to a statement by Rahim Safavi, a former Revolutionary Guard commander, during the early years of war and as a new offensive operation was in the making, three commanders approached Safavi and said, "Because of the very high human toll on soldiers under our command and with our responsibility in every operation, we have decided to resign as commanders and just want to be single shooters with no responsibility for other lives." Safavi states that since he and Mohsen Reza'i, the chief commander of the Revolutionary Guards, could not convince them to alter their decision, they had to take them for a meeting with Imam Khomeini, who convinced them through following statement: "You should be thankful that God brought you to life at this juncture. Since the names of all martyrs are

registered in the protected Divine Tablet [*lowh-e Mahfouz-e elahi* or Book of Destinies], you need to manage your tasks well, but do not worry about who among you will be martyred and how many you will kill." Perhaps Ayatollah Khomeini did not expect that his mystical approach to the life and death of hundreds of thousands of his compatriots would result in a less-than-decisive military victory. For the full text of Safavi's statement, see "We Did Not Fear from War," Tabnak, 21 September 2015, accessed 21 October 2015, https://www.tabnak.ir/fa/news/533185/%D8%B1%D8%AD%DB%8C%D9%85-%D8%B5%D9%81%D9%88%DB%8C-%D9%85%D8%A7-%D8%A7%D8%B2-%D8%AC%D9%86%DA%AF-%D9%86%D8%AA%D8%B1%D8%B3%DB%8C%D8%AF%DB%8C%D9%85.

9 Sālehī-Najafābādī begins the introduction to his book with the following: "In the time when the Iraqi-imposed war on Iran went on, I visited the war front, and by witnessing the horrible scenes of martyred and injured soldiers being carried away, I felt the bitterness and the burning side of war with all my senses. It was then that the idea of having a comprehensive research about jihad in the Qur'ān, hadith, and jurisprudential texts sparkled in my mind. I thought we must know the truth about jihad ... My enquiries proved that the Qur'ānic and the *sīra* [biography of the Prophet] literature on jihad is diagonally opposed to the conclusions reached in the jurisprudential texts." Sālehī-Najafābādī, *Jahād dar Islām*, 1. Recently, Hamid Mavani provided an excellent translation of select chapters of this book; I am thankful that he sent me a copy. See Sālehī -Najafābādī, *Jihad in Islam*.

10 Qarā'ī, *Qur'ān.*

11 The two hadith pieces are narrated by Muhammad b. Ya'qūb and Muhammad b. 'Alī al-Husayn; see Eskandarī, *Qā'edey-e moqābele*, 157.

12 Paraphrased by Eskandarī from Muhammad Rashid Ridā's Qur'ānic exegesis *al-Minār*; ibid., 139.

13 Ibid., 155.

14 Ibid., 98, 147.

15 Ibid., 163, 164.

16 Ibid., 281.

17 Ibid., 175.

18 Ibid., 233.

19 Mohaqqeq Dāmād's father was a prominent professor of Islamic law at Qom Seminary and the son-in-law of Shaykh Abdolkarim Hāerī (d. 1937), founder of the Qom Seminary in the early twentieth century. In the early years after the Iranian Revolution, Mohaqqeq Dāmād became Iran's official Inspector General and had a wide authority to audit and inspect any governmental organization suspect of misconduct. After finishing his seminarian education, Mohaqqeq Dāmād continued his study of law in Belgium, eventually earning his PhD with a thesis on the Islamic

ethics of war, published later under the title *Protection of Individuals in Times of Armed Conflict under International and Islamic Laws*. In this book, Mohaqqeq Dāmād takes a rational and somewhat apologetic approach to the ethics of war in Islam. A few years later, after writing occasional articles on the same subject in Persian, he became a staunch critic of the writings and views of some of the most prominent contemporary figures in Shi'i jurisprudence; these critical views appear in Mohaqqeq Dāmād, *Rowshangarī Dīnī*.

20 Mohaqqeq Dāmād, *Protection of Individuals*.

21 Ibid., 91.

22 Ibid., 91, 92.

23 Ibid., 325. The sources for the minority views mentioned are Ibn Quddāmah, *Mughnī al-muhtāj*, 4:223; Ibn Rushd, *Bidāyat al-mujtahid,* 371; al-Kho'ī, *Minhāj al-sālihīn*, 1:296.

24 Mohaqqeq Dāmād, *Protection of Individuals*, 92.

25 Ibid., 92, 93, 325–9. "And when the sacred months have passed, then kill the polytheists wherever you find them and capture them and besiege them and sit in wait for them at every place of ambush. But if they should repent, establish prayer, and give zakāh, let them on their way. Indeed, Allāh is Forgiving and merciful" (9:5).

26 Mohaqqeq Dāmād, *Protection of Individuals*, 96.

27 Ibid., 113.

28 Ibid., 356. Mohaqqeq Dāmād refers to Muhaqqiq Hillī, Shaykh Tūsī, Ibn Idrīs, and Mohammad Hasan Najafī as the prominent Shi'i jurists strongly opposed to killing women and children. The only exception proposed by one of these jurists, Shaykh Tūsī, is if women and children are used as human shields against Muslim forces, in which case they may be targeted.

29 Ibid., 335, 336.

30 Ibid., 395.

31 It should be noted that one senior Shi'i jurist, Hosseinali Montazerī, issued a *fatwā* precluding mere religious conversion from the laws of apostasy. He asserts that the very few apostates subjected to severe punishment in the early history of Islam were punished for conspiracy against the state rather than for converting. The *fatwa* was issued in February 2005. See Reza Ahmadi, "The Evolution of Ayatollah Montazerī's *fatwa* on Apostasy (*irtidād*)," Rahesabz, accessed 25 March 2016, http://www.rahesabz.net/story/77707/.

32 For further details, see Johnson, "Historical Roots," 3–31.

33 As discussed at the end of this chapter, Mohaqqeq Dāmād's later writings fill the gap by launching bold criticisms regarding the traditional minority view.

34 Muhammad Ibn al-Hasan al-Tūsī was a prominent Shi'i scholar known as the first jurist to adopt part of the Sunni jurisprudence for the Shi'i school (ch. 7,

168 above). Abū Abdallāh Muhammad Ibn Idris al-Shāfi'ī, a prominent Sunni scholar, was known as the first author of '*Usūl al-fiqh* (methodology in Islamic jurisprudence (ch. 7, 168 above). Sālehī-Najafābādī maintains that the root cause of militant views on war is the sanctification of several unauthentic hadiths that came from Abū Hurayra, Ibn 'Umar, and Talhat Ibn Zaid. "Once such radical views were expressed by some of [the] Prophet's companions and the second generation [*tābi'īn*] and established without any critical challenge within the first two centuries, they were sanctified and hard to change by later generations." Sālehī-Najafābādī, *Jihad in Islam*, 158.

35 Ibid., 76.

36 Ibid., 76, 83–5.

37 "Fight them until there is no [more] fitnah and [until] worship is [acknowledged to be] for Allah. But if they cease, then there is to be no aggression except against the oppressors" (2:193).

38 Sālehī-Najafābādī, *Jihad in Islam*, 12.

39 Ibid., 18.

40 Ibid., 97.

41 Ibid., 98.

42 "O Prophet, tell the captives you have taken: 'If God finds some good in your heart, He will reward you with something better than was taken away from you, and forgive your sins, for God is forgiving and kind" (8:70).

43 "So, when you clash with the unbelievers, smite their necks until you overpower them, then hold them in bondage. Then either free them graciously or with ransom, until war shall have come to end" (47:4).

44 Sālehī-Najafābādī, *Jihad in Islam*, 149.

45 Ibid., 156.

46 Ibid., 180.

47 Ibid., 222–6.

48 Ibid., 133.

49 Ibid., 178.

50 Feirahī, *Power, Knowledge, and Legitimacy*, 231.

51 al-Māwardī, *Al-Ahkam al-Sultaniyya*, quoted in ibid., 275.

52 Ibid.

53 Ibn Bābawayh, *Al-Muqni 'fi'l fiqh*, quoted in Feirahī, *Power, Knowledge, and Legitimacy*, 316.

54 Feirahī quotes Ibn Taqtaqī (d. 1309), saying that all societies are established upon three theories of the relationship between sword and pen: One group believes that the sword is the guardian and in the service of pen; another group conversely believes that the pen is in the service of sword; and a minority group believes that the sword and pen are mutually dependent on one another, with neither having

a higher status. See Feirahī, *Power, Knowledge, and Legitimacy*, 375; also Ibn Taqtaqī, *Al-Fakhrī*, (*Tarikh-e Fakhri*), 66, cited by Feirahī.

55 See ch. 6, 149 above.

56 Davoud Feirahī, "Conditional Defense, Terror and Suicidal Attack in Shi'i Tradition," feirahi.ir, accessed 23 August 2013, http://www.feirahi.ir/?article=8.

57 Note that this assertion does not agree with Mohaqqeq Dāmād's view, as mentioned above (ch. 7, 165).

58 Feirahī, "Conditional Defense."

59 Mohammad Hasan Najafī, *Jawāhir al-kalām*, quoted in ibid.

60 الايمانُ قَيّد الفتكَ، فلا يَفتكُ مؤمن

61 Feirahī, "Conditional Defense,"

62 Ibid.

63 لايَنبغى للمسلمينَ الغدرُ، ولا يَأمروا بالغدرِ، ولايُقاتِلوا معَ الذينَ غَدروا

64 Feirahī, "Conditional Defense."

65 Davoud Feirahī, "*Nabayad-hay-e Jang* (Forbidden Acts in War)," feirahi.ir, accessed 2 August 2013, http://www.feirahi.ir/?article=64. Feirahī substantiates all the mentioned provisions by referring to a number of hadiths quoted from an encyclopedia of Shi'a hadiths: Mohammad Baqir Majlesī, *Bahār al-Anvār fi Akhbār al-A'imma*.

66 For the full text of the roundtable dated 31 January 2015, see "Roundtable on Salafism," Center for Great Islamic Encylopedia, accessed 30 October 2015, http://www.cgie.org.ir/fa/news/60812.

67 Hoseinali Montazerī, "Wilāyat-e Faqīh," chapter on *jihad va defā'* (jihad and defence), amontazeri.com, accessed 23 August 2013, https://amontazeri.com/book/khaterat/volume-1/642.

68 Ibid.

69 Hoseinali Montazerī, "The Sanctity of International Treaties," amontazeri.com, accessed 26 March 2016, https://amontazeri.com/book/hoghogh/120.

70 Hoseinali Montazerī, "On the Primacy of Peace," amontazeri.com, accessed 26 March 2016, https://amontazeri.com/book/hoghogh/117.

71 Hoseinali Montazerī, "On Good Relations with All Countries," amontazeri.com, accessed 26 March 2016, https://amontazeri.com/book/hoghogh/119.

72 Hoseinali Montazerī, "On the Rights of Prisoners of War," amontazeri.com, accessed 26 March 2016, https://amontazeri.com/book/hoghogh/122.

73 It should be noted that according to Provision 110 of the Constitution of the Islamic Republic of Iran, which was adopted in 1980, entering war, engaging in peace, and mobilizing armed forces are based on the authority of the state's supreme leader, after he receives recommendations on such matters from the Supreme National Defense Council. In an amendment ratified in 1990, the last phrase was deleted, giving the supreme leader absolute power on such matters. Montazerī's criticism works against the original provision of the constitution, and

even more so against the amended one. See *Great Islamic Encyclopedia*, 1st ed., s.v. “Jang (war),” by Mostafā Mohaqqeq Dāmād and Mohammad Qārī Sayyid Fatemī (in appendix 2 below).

74 Mūsavī Tabrīzi, “Imam [Ayatollah Khomeini] Did Not Want to Make War with America,” interview by a group of Qom reformists, Kalemeh, 15 February 2014, http://www.kaleme.com/1392/11/25/klm-174383/.

75 Ibid.

76 The same assertions came from Masoud Roughani Zanjani, who was minister of budget and planning during the 1980s. In an interview published by the Persian periodical *Andishey-e Pouya*, Zanjani argues that the decision-making impasse on war responsible for its prolongation resulted from the insufficient flow of information to Imam Khomeini on the economy and finances of the war. Zanjani adds, “I do not deny that among cabinet members, some had an emotional posture on war.” For the full text of the interview, see Zanjani, interview by Ali Malihi, 72, 73.

77 See 165–7 above.

78 Mohaqqeq Dāmād, *Rowshangarī-e Dīnī*, 2:186.

79 Ibid., 2:183.

80 Ibid., 2:76, 77. Ayatollah Kho’ī discusses his juridical views, including views on armed jihad, in *Minhāj al-sālihīn*. Ayatollah Kho’ī receives additional criticism, for unlike the majority of Shi‘i scholars, he does not base the legitimacy of offensive wars on the presence and authority of an infallible imam.

81 Mohaqqeq Dāmād, *Rowshangarī-e Dīnī*, 1:78.

82 Adāk, *Rahmat-e nabavī*, 19.

83 Ibid., 20.

84 Ibid., 21.

85 Ibid., 25.

86 Ibid., 66.

87 Ibid., 220.

88 Ibid., 170, 172.

89 Ibid., 166–70.

90 Ibid., 220.

91 There are five standard pillars of Islam, which for most mainstream jurists do not include jihad. In Shi‘i jurisprudence, however, the number of pillars amount to ten, including jihad, commanding right, forbidding wrong, liking the good (*tavallā*), and despising the evil (*tabarrā*).

92 See Hasan Yousufī Ashkevarī, “*Amr-e be ma‘rūf, nahy az munkar wa jihad*,” Rahesabz, accessed 17 November 2013, http://www.rahesabz.net/story/77329/.

93 Soodmandī, *War and Peace*, 117.

94 Meybodī, “Essence of War”, 5–13.

95 Saqafī, “Invitation to Islam,” 35–41.

Chapter 8

1 Coates, "Culture," 217.
2 See Debra Kelly, "The Ancient Christian Cult of Suicidal, Daredevil Martyrs," KnowledgeNuts, accessed 29 November 2015, http://knowledgenuts.com/2014/03/26/the-ancient-christian-cult-of-suicidal-daredevil-martyrs/.
3 "Indeed God has created human being in the best mould" (95:4); "Blessed is the best of all creators" (23:14).
4 Todenhofer, the only Western journalist who has visited the Daesh territory, has offered deep insights about the root causes of this terrorist organization, which he believes is fallout of two centuries of Western violent intervention in the Muslim world. He is the author of *Thou Shalt Not Kill* (*Du sollst nicht toten*, originally published in German in 2013), Juergentodenhoefer, accessed 9 February 2015, http://juergentodenhoefer.de/terrorism-has-much-to-do-with-islam/?lang=en.
5 Asad, *On Suicide Bombing*, 17.
6 Although, since the establishment of Daesh's power in Syria and Iraq early on, the international and United Nations' observers identified many of Daesh's acts as crimes against humanity, the increasing scale and scope of these crimes surpass any evil imagination. According to one report published online by *Alarabiya*, "the U.N. Commission of Inquiry on Syria presented a horrific picture of what life is like in areas controlled by ISIS militants in its first report on the group. Based on more than 300 interviews with people who have fled areas controlled by ISIS, the U.N. panel said civilians were subjected to a 'rule of terror' under the group, including massacres, beheadings, sexual enslavement and forced pregnancy." "The commanders of ISIS have acted willfully, perpetrating these war crimes and crimes against humanity with clear intent of attacking persons with awareness of their civilian or 'hors de combat' (non-combat) status," the report said, as quoted by Agence France-Presse. For the full article, see "ISIS is Accused of Crime against Humanity," Alarabiya, 14 November 2014, accessed on 15 January 2015, http://english.alarabiya.net/en/News/middle-east/2014/11/14/ISIS-commits-crimes-against-humanity-in-Syria.html.
7 On 16 December 2014, a group from the Pakistani branch of Taliban called "Tehreek e Taliban Pakistan," or TTP, attacked an elementary school in Peshawar and massacred 142 people including 132 children who where deliberately targeted as revenge for the Pakistan army's earlier operation against Taliban. As reported by the *Wall Street Journal*, according to Qasim Nauman and Safdar Dawar of Peshawar, Pakistan, and Saeed Shah of Islamabad, Pakistan, one of the students "Amir Ameen, 18 years old, said he and 11 other students were taking an exam when two gunmen entered their classroom. They shot students one by one, mostly in the head, he said from his bed at Peshawar's Lady Reading Hospital."

The report adds, "The attackers shouted *Allahu akbar* or 'God is great' over and over as they shot each student, Mr. Ameen said. They spoke Pashto – the language of Pakistan's Pashtun ethnic majority in northwest Pakistan and southern Afghanistan. The gunmen shot the teacher in his classroom and her 2-year-old daughter, who she was cradling in her arms, Mr. Ameen said." For the full report, see Qasim Nauman, "Taliban Militants Attack Pakistan School," *Wall Street Journal*, 17 December 2014, accessed 15 January 2015, http://www.wsj.com/articles/taliban-militants-attack-pakistan-school-1418716418.

8 On 15 January 2015, according to a report by Phil Hazlewood of the American Foreign Press, Amnesty International reported massacres in two Nigerian cities. "Hundreds of people, if not more, are reported to have been killed in attacks on the towns of Baga and Doron Baga on the shores of Lake Chad in Borno state, according to Amnesty International." The report depicts a crime scene from an eyewitness as follows: "Amnesty said on Thursday it had received accounts from survivors of Boko Haram fighters killing a woman as she was giving birth, during indiscriminate fire that also cut down small children … Half of the baby boy (was) out and she died like this," the unnamed witness was quoted as saying." Earlier reports attested that "some 300 women were said to have been rounded up and detained at a school, witnesses told Amnesty, adding that older women, mothers and children were released after four days but younger women kept." For the full report see Phil Hazlewood, "Boko Haram Accused of 'Crime against Humanity' as Massacre Images Emerge," modernghana.com, accessed 15 January 2015, https://www.modernghana.com/news/592322/boko-haram-accused-of-crime-against-humanity-as-massacre-i.html.

9 On 7 January 2015, two Muslim gunmen attacked the office of the French satirical weekly newspaper *Charlie Hebdo* and killed twelve cartoonists, including the editor of the paper. The incident mobilized an international chain reaction of sympathy for the paper's surviving staff. Pursuant to the incident, the French president François Hollande declared on 14 January, "France will not dispatch its only aircraft carrier, the nuclear-powered Charles de Gaulle, to reinforce the campaign against Isil." For the full report, see David Blair and Henry Samuel, "Charlie Hebdo: 'France will send aircraft carrier to Middle East,'" *Telegraph*, accessed 15 January 2015, http://www.telegraph.co.uk/news/worldnews/europe/france/11346285/Charlie-Hebdo-France-will-send-aircraft-carrier-to-Middle-East.html.

10 On 15 February 2015, Daesh terrorists beheaded twenty-one Egyptian Christian labourers in Libya. On 19 April 2015, they beheaded thirty Ethiopian Christians again in Libya. For details, see Ahmed Tolba and Michael Georgy, "Sisi Warns of Response after Islamic State Kills 21 Egyptians in Libya," Reuter, accessed 20 April 2015, http://www.reuters.com/article/2015/02/15/us-mideast-crisis-libya-egypt-idUSKBN0LJ10D20150215.

11 On 10 October 2015, two suicide bombs exploded at a peace rally near the main train station in Ankara; ISIS was the main suspect for the explosion. CNN reported that, according to the Turkish Medical Association, ninety-seven people had died and more than four hundred were wounded. For more details, see Don Melvin, "Turkey Train Station Bombings Kill Dozens in Ankara," CNN, accessed 29 October 2015, http://edition.cnn.com/2015/10/10/middleeast/turkey-ankara-bomb-blast/index.html.
12 See ch. 7, 176 above.
13 Ibid.
14 See ch. 8, 191 below.
15 See 'Askarī, *Martyr*, 98.
16 See also introduction, 7 and ch.7, 176 above.
17 Sālehī-Najafābādī's *Shahīd-e Jāvīd* was originally published in Qom-Iran in 1972 and, according to Ahmad Naraqi, "brought a turning point in the historiography of 'Āshūrā." See Sālehī-Najafābādī, "Shahīd-e Jāvīd, Abstract," Alseraj, accessed, 9 April 2016, http://www.alseraj.net/maktaba/kotob/english/FourteenInfallibles/ImamKhomeiniAndtheCultureofAshura/english/imam/imam-books/ashura/index.html. See also an elaborate book review, Evan J. Siegel, "The Politics of *Shahid-e Javid*," webcitation.org, accessed 21 August 2013, http://www.webcitation.org/query?url=http://www.geocities.com/evan_j_siegel/ShahidJavid/SHFrames.htm; originally published in Rainer Brunner and Werner Ende, eds., *The Twelver Shia in Modern Times*, Social, Economic, and Political Studies of the Middle East and Asia 72 (Leiden: Brill, 2001), n.p.
18 Sālehī-Najafābādī, *Shahīd-e Jāvīd*, 159.
19 Ibid., 336.
20 Ibid., 45.
21 The traditional law dictates that if enemy forces are twice as many as Muslim forces, then Muslims are under no obligation to enter battle.
22 This question has turned into a very heated public debate in Iranian political circles, especially after the election controversy of 2009.
23 Ali Sharī'atī, *Husain Wāreth-e Ādam* [Husain, Adam's heir], quoted in Evan J. Siegel, "The Politics of *Shahid-e Javid*," webcitation.org, accessed 21 August 2013, http://www.webcitation.org/query?url=http://www.geocities.com/evan_j_siegel/ShahidJavid/SHFrames.htm.
24 For the voice recording of Soroush's talk in Persian, see his official website, "The Problem of Religion as Identity," drsoroush.com, accessed 7 January 2014, http://drsoroush.com/fa/category/speech/.
25 Ibid.
26 Abdolhamid Zīyā'i, *Jame-eh shenasi-e tahrifat-e ashura* [The sociology of Ashura distortion], 22, 23, accessed 21 March 2016, http://dl.irpdf.com/ebooks/Part20/www.irpdf.com(6849).pdf.

27 Ibid., 24.

28 Ibid., 21.

29 See Mohammed Sawaf, "Iraq Says Record 17 million Shiite Pilgrims in Karbala," *Daily Mail*, 25 December 2014, http://www.dailymail.co.uk/wires/afp/article-2870635/Iraq-says-record-17-million-Shiite-pilgrims-Karbala.html.

30 Cf. Mohsen Kadivar, "The Husayni Uprising: Two Different Perspectives," voice file on Rahesabz, November 2014, accessed 25 December 2014, http://www.rahesabz.net/story/87502/.

31 Founded by Abu'l Hasan al-'Ash'arī (d. 936), the 'Ash'arī theological school opposes the earlier Mu'tazili school that believed in the universal sense of objective ethics. Although believing in the rational understanding of religion on the basis of the Qur'ān and the Prophetic tradition, the 'Ash'arī school does not support an intrinsic sense of ethics in human beings and therefore does not recognize any source of normative values outside the Islamic tradition. See Neal Robinson, "Ah'ariyya and Mu'tazila," muslimphilosophy.com, accessed 26 March 2016, http://www.muslimphilosophy.com/ip/rep/H052.

32 See Mohammad Soroush-Mahallati, "How a Religious Person Commits Crime," Rahesabz, 16 November 2014, accessed 25 December 2014, http://www.rahesabz.net/story/87754/.

33 Ibid.

34 Esfandīārī, *Hamey-e mā barādarīm*, 19.

35 Ibid.

36 Ibid., 20.

37 Ibid., 22–5.

38 Esfandīāri published this summary report on his book: "With What Goals Did Imam Husayn Go to Karbala," Iran Book News Agency, 17 November 2014, accessed 22 March, 2016, http://www.ibna.ir/fa/doc/report/211110.

39 Ibid.

40 For the full text of the conference's final resolution, see International Congress on Extremism and Takfiri Threats, Qom, Iran, November 2014, abna.ir, accessed 25 December 2014, http://www.abna.ir/english/653915/print.html.

41 For the full text of the resolution, visit the conference website: First International Conference on World Against Violence and Extremism, Tehran, December 2014, abna.ir, accessed 25 December 2014, http://www.conferenceonwave.ir/en/declaration/.

42 For the full text of the speech, see Times of Israel.com, accessed 19 October 2015, http://www.timesofisrael.com/full-text-of-rouhanis-2015-address-to-the-un-general-assembly/.

43 See appendix 3, article 3, 260 below. The full text of the ambassador's statement appears in appendix 3, 259–62.

44 Cook, *Martyrdom in Islam*, 58, 59.

45 Ibid., 59.

46 Ibid., 61.

47 In addition to the three standard principles of faith for every Muslim are unity of God (*tawhid*), the prophecy of Muhammad (*nabuwwa*), and afterlife (*mu'ād*). The two additional standard principles for every Twelver Shi'a are justice (*'adl*) and the charismatic leadership of imams (*imama*).

48 For a full report of the Bentley story, see "The Saudi Prince Who Offered Bentley to Bombers, BBC, 23 April 2015, accessed 25 April 2015, http://www.bbc.com/news/blogs-trending-32417773. For a report on the civilian casualties resulting from the Saudi bombing of Yemen, see Ahmed Al-Haj and Maggie Michael, "UN Says Fighting in Yemen Had Killed 550 Civilians Including 115 Children," BBC, accessed 25 April 2015, http://www.usnews.com/news/world/articles/2015/04/24/115-children-killed-since-start-of-saudi-led-yemen-offensive.

49 "Saudi Prince," http://www.bbc.com/news/blogs-trending-32417773.

50 Johnson, "Historical Roots," 12.

51 For a full report of the incident, see "Jordan Pilot Hostage Moaz al-Kasasbeh Burned Alive," BBC, 3 February 2015, accessed 20 April 2015, http://www.bbc.com/news/world-middle-east-31121160.

52 For a full report of the incident, see "Islamic State Militants 'Burn to Death 45 in Iraq,'" BBC, 17 February 2015, accessed 20 April 2015, http://www.bbc.com/news/world-middle-east-31502863.

53 For a full report of the incident, see "Sisi Warns of Response after Islamic State Kills 21 Egyptians in Libya," Reuters news agency, 15 February 2015, accessed 20 April 2015, http://www.reuters.com/article/2015/02/15/us-mideast-crisis-libya-egypt-idUSKBN0LJ10D20150215.

54 For a full report of the incident, see "Islamic State Shoots and Beheads 30 Ethiopian Christians in Libya," video, Reuters news agency, 19 April 2015, accessed 20 April 2015, http://www.reuters.com/article/2015/04/19/us-mideast-crisis-islamicstate-killings-idUSKBN0NA0IE20150419.

55 A report about the new style of Daesh excecution was published by the Persian news website Tabnak, 1 May 2015, http://www.tabnak.ir/fa/news/496434/وهیش-
داعش-جلادان-توسط-اعدام-دیدج.

56 For a full report about the *fatwa*, see "Top Islamic Authority Calls for Killing, Crucifixion, and Dismemberment of ISIS Terrorists," Egyptianstreets website, 4 February 2015, accessed 20 April 2015, http://egyptianstreets.com/2015/02/04/top-islamic-authority-calls-for-killing-crucifixion-and-dismemberment-of-isis-terrorists/.

57 See the previous discussion of Ferdowsi, ch. 1, 37 above.

58 Carol Giacomo, "Interview with an Ayatollah," *New York Times*, 16 December 2013, accessed 18 December 2013, http://takingnote.blogs.nytimes.com/2013/12/16/

interview-with-an-ayatollah/?_r=0. See also Ayatollah's official site, accessed 15 December 2013, http://saanei4.tk/?view=01,00,00,00,0#01,01,02,144,0.

59 See the discussions of Montazerī and Feirahī above, ch. 7, 178–9.

60 Davoud Feirahī, "Forgiveness Is Above Justice," kaleme.com, 3 February 2015, accessed 4 February 2015, http://www.kaleme.com/1393/11/14/klm-209074/ (full text of the article in Persian).

Chapter 9

1 See a summary of this saga in Jeff Weintraub, "Who Supported Saddam Hussein During the Iran-Iraq War?" Gulf 2000 website, 10 April 2013, accessed 24 August 2013, http://jeffweintraub.blogspot.com/2003/03/who-armed-saddam-some-reality-checks.html: "That intense and widely pervasive fear of an Iranian victory helps explain why the so-called 'international community' quite shamefully allowed Saddam Hussein to get away with the extensive use of poison gas against the Iranians, on a scale not seen since World War I (that was before he started gassing Kurdish civilians in 1988). Tolerating this massive war crime no doubt looked like hardheaded realpolitik at the time, but in retrospect it looks not just immoral but also extremely dangerous and unwise. The US government was complicit in that scandal – but, again, so was almost every other government of any significance. And the vast bulk of Saddam's arms and funding came, not from the US, but from France, the Soviet bloc, China, the Arab world, and a number of other countries." Weintraub incluldes a chart of countries that helped Saddam.

2 Mayer, "War and Peace," 195.

3 Ibid., 200, 201. For a thorough examination of Mayer's view on Islam and human rights, see Mayer, *Islam and Human Rights*, 195–226.

4 "Iran's Statement at IAEA Emergency Meeting," fas.org, accessed 24 August 2013, http://www.fas.org/nuke/guide/iran/nuke/mehr080905.html.

5 Quoted from an official statement by the Iranian supreme leader and distributed at a conference titled "International Disarmament and Non-proliferation: World Security without Weapons of Mass Destruction" (Tehran, 17–18 April 2010), *Los Angeles Times*, accessed 6 August 2013, http://articles.latimes.com/2010/apr/18/world/la-fg-iran-nukes18-2010apr18.

6 Discussing the significance of Khamenei's *fatwa*, former Iranian chief nuclear negotiator Hossein Mousavian maintains that, in its secularization, the *fatwa* "would facilitate and expedite a final nuclear deal between Iran and the world powers." He adds, "With its strong roots in Islamic belief [it] could also play a constructive role far beyond resolving the Iranian nuclear crisis." A first step could encompass "efforts to have prominent Islamic leaders from both the Sunni and Shi'a sects speak in unison on the issue of banning weapons of mass destruction."

For the full article, see Hossein Mousavian, "Opinion: Khamenei's Nuclear Fatwa Shows the Way Forward," *Asharq Al-Awsat*, 10 May 2014, accessed 2 June 2014, http://www.aawsat.net/2014/05/article55332038.

7 See Ayatollah Montazerī's statement on weapons of mass destruction issued in October 2010 in Persian on his website Amontazeri, accessed 7 August 2013, https://amontazeri.com/book/didgaha/volume-3/155.

8 For the full text of Ahmadinejad's statement, see "The Nuclear Bomb Is a Fire against Humanity Rather Than a Weapon for Defense," Globalresearch, 3 May 2010, http://www.globalresearch.ca/the-nuclear-bomb-is-a-fire-against-humanity-rather-than-a-weapon-for-defense/18982.

9 See "Rouhani Calls for Nuke-Free World," iranprimer.usip.org, accessed 26 September 2013, http://iranprimer.usip.org/blog/2013/sep/26/rouhani-calls-nuke-free-world.

10 For further details, see the official website of the Grand Ayatollah Makārem Shirazi: MakaremShirazi, 19 December 2013, http://makarem.ir/news/?typeinfo=4&lid=0&mid=318197&catid=0&start=1&PageIndex=0.

11 Quoted in Ayatollah Abolqāsem Alīdoost, "The Religious Foundations of Edicts (*fatwa*) by Shi'ite Jurists Prohibiting Weapons of Mass Destruction," (paper presented at the Nuclear Jurisprudence Conference, Tehran, March 2014), accessed 29 July 2014, http://nuclearenergy.ir/wp-content/uploads/2014/06/fatawa-text.pdf.

12 Ibid.

13 Ibid.

14 Sane'i, "Selective Interviews," 45.

15 See excerpts of Rouhani's talk on the website of Ana News Agency, accessed 12 February 2014, http://www.ana.ir/Home/Single/57290; and "The Production of WMD Does Not Serve Our National Interest," BBC, accessed 16 December 2013, http://www.bbc.co.uk/persian/iran/2013/12/131216_me_rouhani_no_plans_to_develop_wmd.shtml.

16 Abolqāsem Alidoost, "The Religious Foundation of Edicts," Fars News Agency, 17 March 2014, accessed 4 April 2016, http://en.farsnews.com/print.aspx?nn=13930327001534.

17 Quoted in ibid.

18 Ibid.

19 For more excerpts of 'Alī's letter, see ch. 6, 128 above.

20 Hashmi and Lee, *Ethics and Weapons*, 343.

21 Ibid., 340.

22 See Garrett Nada and Helia Ighani, "Old War Haunts New Election," US Institute of Peace, 11 June 2013, accessed 6 August 2013, http://iranprimer.usip.org/blog/2013/jun/11/old-war-haunts-new-election.

23 A striking example is the appearance of the following news: The website of Iran's official news agency, Fars, referenced Arash Karami of *Al-Monitor* on 13 February 2014 as saying, "According to an Iranian member of parliament, the pressure of not being able to sell Iranian oil due to economic sanctions brought former President Mahmoud Ahmadinejad's ministers to tears." Mohammad Nabavian, a conservative member of parliament representing Tehran, said of the former president's difficulties in selling Iranian oil, "Toward the end of Ahmadinejad's administration, some of the ministers in closed meetings would shed tears and say to members of parliament, 'You know our situation; why do you speak like this in open sessions?'" This is the first statement from an Iranian official that suggests Ahmadinejad's administration understood the severity of the sanctions. Ahmadinejad himself was flippant in his public statements about the effects of international sanctions on Iran's economy. He called them "torn pieces of paper" and taunted Western officials to pass more sanctions to the point that they "become tired." For the full translation of this piece, see *Al-Monitor*, accessed 14 February 2014, http://iranpulse.al-monitor.com/index.php/2014/02/3911.

24 The current foreign minister Javad Zarif does not miss a chance in his public addresses to speak about the vast possibilities for win-win political deals with international counterparts. As the key Iranian diplomat in nuclear negotiations, Zarif defines his approach in the following terms, as quoted by Iran's Press TV: "We should not shoot for concessions, either getting concessions or giving concessions; we should aim for finding solutions [to Iran's nuclear issue]." For the full article, see "Iran Responds to US Actions by Boosting Missile Power: Zarif," Press TV, 12 February 2014, http://www.presstv.ir/detail/2013/10/15/329583/ntalks-must-seek-winwin-solution/. Rouhani's political advisor Mahmud Sario'lqalam also does not miss a chance to emphasize the fact that political decision making is a serious matter that should be performed only by professionals, rather than by the feelings and emotions of the lay public. See his full interview with the website Entekhab.ir, accessed 12 February 2014, http://www.entekhab.ir/fa/news/140611/.

25 See Sharam Chubin, "Is Iran a Military Threat?" *Survival, Global Politics and Strategy* 56 (April/May 2014), reprinted as an op-ed on Carnegie Endowment for International Peace website, 1 April 2014, accessed 2 June 2014, http://carnegieendowment.org/2014/04/01/is-iran-military-threat/h6id.

26 Ibid.

27 According to Richard Spencer, a reporter for the British daily paper *The Telegraph*, "Navi Pillay, the UN High Commissioner for Refugees, voiced shock over the bloodshed. Isis claims to have executed 1,700 people after capturing the Iraqi city of Tikrit. Ms Pillay said the figure could not be verified, but added: 'This apparently systematic series of cold-blooded executions, mostly conducted in various locations in the Tikrit area, almost certainly amounts to war crimes.'"

See Richard Spencer, "Iraq Crisis: UN Condemns 'War Crimes' as Another Town Falls to Isis," *Telegraph*, 16 June 2014, accessed 7 July 2014, http://www.telegraph.co.uk/news/worldnews/middleeast/iraq/10904414/Iraq-crisis-UN-condemns-war-crimes-as-another-town-falls-to-Isis.html.

28 English translation from Arabic is provided by Ahab Bdaiwi (St Andrews University), 12 February 2015, accessed 26 March 2016, https://www.reddit.com/r/islam/comments/2vxjrf/the_most_inspiring_soulawakening_advice_from/.

29 For the views of Ayatollahs Ruhollah Khomeini and Seyyed Mohammad Shirazi on jihad, see Khomeini, *Wilāyat-e faqīh*, 135–6; Shirazi, *Aqsāmu'l-jihad*, 19.

30 See Seyyed Hādī Tabātabā'ī, *Ayatollah 'Uzma Sistani and Hokm-e jihad* (The Grand Ayatollah Sīstānī and the jihad dictum), accessed 6 July 2014, http://www.rahesabz.net/story/84146/; see also the seminarian website Mobahesat, accessed 7 July 2014, http://mobahesat.ir/1393/04/3720.html.

31 The infamous case of the arrest of the economic tycoon Babak Zanjani is one example. His assets were estimated to be over $10 billion (US) and his debts to the Iranian government totaled more than $2.7 billion. For a full report on his case, see "Arrest of Billionaire Babak Zanjani Shows Political Divisions," Gulfnews, accessed 14 February 2014, http://gulfnews.com/news/region/iran/arrest-of-billionaire-babak-zanjani-shows-political-divisions-1.1284146).

Conclusion

1 Shriver, *Forgiveness in Politics*, 12.

2 Abu 'Abd Allah Muhammad b. Numan, known as Shaykh Mufīd, is a leading Shi'a theologian of Islam's Golden Age. His major treatise on Shi'a theology was recently translated into English: *Tashihu'l i'tiqād: The Emendation of a Shi'ite Creed* (Tehran: n.p. 2013).

3 Mu'tazila, an early school of theology based on rational thought, reason, and objective ethics, flourished in Basra and Baghdad between the eighth and tenth centuries.

4 Ash'arī, a school of early Muslim speculative theology, gradually became the mainstream school of thought in the Muslim world around the mid-tenth century. As opposed to Mu'tazila, Ash'arīs believed that the only source of moral value was revelation.

5 A good, modern account of historic Shi'i political suppression is provided in Nasr, *Shia Revival*.

6 Rouhani's response to Mohammad Bāqer Qālibāf, another presidential candidate who was a military veteran, on 15 June 2013.

7 Zarif's statement was given in his talk on the occasion of the parliamentary vote of confidence for him on 13 August 2013.

8 For the full text in Persian, see "Zarif's Talk at Army University," Iraneconomist, accessed 21 October 2015, http://iraneconomist.com/fa/news/90353.

9 In her short but excellent article, the late Yale professor Menocal argues convincingly that the poetic culture of Andalusia played an essential role in creating political and religious tolerance in that civilization. See Maria Rosa Menocal, "Culture in the Time of Tolerance: Al-Andalus as a Model for Our Time," published as Occasional Papers by Yale Law School, 2000, accessed 23 February 2014, http://digitalcommons.law.yale.edu/ylsop_papers/1.

10 Dabashi, *Shi'ism*, 310.

11 Ibid., 315.

12 Ibid., 321.

13 Ibid.

14 See statements by Soroush, ch. 8, 192 above.

15 Louer, *Shiism and Politics*, 125.

16 Created ca. 539 BC by Cyrus, the cylinder contains a declaration pronouncing that Cyrus has sought to help a vast number of people and cultures to live in peace.

17 See Philpott and Powers, *Strategies of Peace*.

18 Ibn Miskawayh, *Tahdhīb*, 138; and its English translation, Ibn Miskawayh, *Refinement of Character*.

19 Rezā'ī, *Jang va Tamaddon* (translation of *Arnold J. Toynbee's Views on War*), 125.

20 Walzer, *Just and Unjust Wars*, xxxi and 4.

21 A proverbial couplet from Hafez reads: "Engage in love [of humanity] before it is too late; or the life-purpose given to you by the world will be wasted." This English translation is from Jamasb Madani, "Reflections on Obama's Nowruz Address as Hafez Rolls Over in His Grave," Muftah, 3 April 2013, accessed 23 March 2016, http://muftah.org/reflections-on-obamas-nowruz-address-as-hafez-rolls-over-in-his-grave/#.VvLMp1KFFzA.

22 Martin Buber (d. 1965) in his seminal work *I and Thou* (English translation of the original title in German *Ich und Du*) contends, "The primary word *I-you* can be spoken only with the whole being" and "establishes the world of religion."

23 Salami, *Divan of Hafez*, 208; English translation by H. Wilberforce Clarke.

24 Nielsen, "God and the Basis," 345.

Appendix I

1 My English translation of *Great Islamic Encyclopaedia*, 1st ed., s.v. "Jihad in the Qu'rān and Hadith," by Mahdi Ghaffari. Note that all source references in the following translated summaries have been omitted. Those interested in the references can access the Persian text online at cgie.org.ir, accessed 4 January 2014, http://www.cgie.org.ir/fa/publication/entries/183.

2 Q. 7:45 and 11:19.
3 Q. 15:49.
4 *Great Islamic Encyclopedia*, 1st ed., s.v. "Jihad in Islamic Jurisprudence," by Ahmad Pakatchi.
5 Ibid.

Appendix II

1 My English translation of *Great Islamic Encyclopedia*, 1st ed., s.v. "Jang (war)," by Mohammad Qārī Sayyed Fatemī and Mostafa Mohaqqeq Dāmād. The bibliography provided at the end of this volume includes references used in both entry pieces.
2 "O you who have faith! Do not violate Allah's sacraments, neither the sacred month, nor the offering, nor the necklaces, nor those bound for the Sacred House who seek their Lord's grace and [his] pleasure. But when you emerge from pilgrim sanctity, you may hunt for game. Ill feeling for a people should not lead you, because they barred you from [entering] the Sacred Mosque, to transgress. Cooperate in piety and Godwariness, but do not cooperate in sin and aggression, and be wary of Allah. Indeed Allah is severe in retribution" (Q. 5:2). "O you who have faith! Be maintainers, as witnesses for the sake of Allah, of justice, and ill feeling for a people should never lead you to be unfair. Be fair; that is nearer to Godwariness, and be wary of Allah. Allah is indeed well aware of what you do" (Q. 5:8).
3 "And if he were to wield authority, he would try to cause corruption in the land, and to ruin the crop and the stock, and Allah does not like corruption" (Q. 2:205).
4 The seventh rule of war, the treatment of prisoners of war, is discussed in a later, separate entry in the encylopedia. The eighth rule on war spoils has not yet been published.

Appendix III

1 Published on the official website of the Iranian Mission at the United Nations, accessed 19 April 2015, http://iran-un.org/en/.

Appendix IV

1 Published on the official website of Grand Ayatollah Seyed 'Alī Sīstānī, accessed 16 February 2015, http://www.sistani.org/english/archive/25036/.

Bibliography

Abedi, Mehdi, and Gary Legenhausen, eds. *Jihad and Shahādat: Struggle and Martyrdom in Islam*. Houston, TX: Institute for Research and Islamic Studies, 1986.

Abou El Fadl, Khaled. "*Ahkām al-bughāt*: Irregular Warfare and the Laws of Rebellion in Islam." In Johnson and Kelsay, *Cross, Crescent, and Sword*, 149–76.

Adāk, Sāber. *Rahmat-e nabavī, khoshūnat-e jāhelī* [The Prophetic compassion and the Jahili violence: a new approach to the Prophet's treatment of others]. Tehran: Entesharat Kavir, 2010.

Afshari, Mehran. *Āyīn-e javānmardī.* 2nd ed. Tehran: Daftar-e Pazhuheshhay-e Farhangi, 2013.

– *Chahardah risalah dar bab-e futuwwat wa asnaf.* Tehran: Nashr-e Cheshmeh, 2002.

Algar, Hamid. *Wahhabism: A Critical Essay.* New York: Islamic Publication International, 2002.

Amanat, Abbas. "Iranian Identity Boundaries: A Historical Overview." In Amanat and Vejdani, *Iran Facing Others*, 1–39.

Amanat, Abbas, and Farzin Vejdani, eds. *Iran Facing Others: Identity Boundaries in a Historical Perspective*. New York: Palgrave Macmillan, 2012.

'Āmilī, Muhammad Ibn al-Hasan al-Hurr al-. *Jahād bā nafs, of wasā'il al-shī'a ilā tahsīl masā'il al-sharī'a.* Translated by Ali Afrasiyabi. Vol. 6, section II, hadith 1. Tehran: Nahavandi, 2001.

– *Wasā'il al-shī'a ilā tahsīl masā'il al-sharī'a.* Edited by Shaykh Muhammad Shirazi. 6 vols. Beirut: Dār Ihyā' at-Turāth al-'Arabī, 1962.

Amoozegar, Jaleh. *Mythical History of Iran* [Persian]. Tehran: SAMT Publishers, 2001.

Anousheh, Hasan. *The Ghaznavids: Their Empire in Afghanistan and Eastern Iran, 994–1040*. Translated by Clifford E. Bosworth. Tehran: Entesharat-e Amir Kabir, 1999.

Ansārī, Abd Allāh al-. *Tafsīr-e Adabī va Erfānī Qur'ān-e Majīd, with Commentary by Imam Ahmad Maybūdī.* 6th ed. Edited by Habīb Allāh Amūzegār. Tehran: Entesharat-e Eqbal, 1990.

Arberry, A.J., ed. *The Koran Interpreted: A Translation.* New York: Simon & Schuster, 1996.

Arendt, Hannah. *The Human Condition.* 2nd ed. London and Chicago: University of Chicago Press, 1958.

Aristotle. *The Nicomachean Ethics.* 2nd ed. Translated by Terence Irwin. Indianapolis: Hackett, 1999.

Armstrong, Karen. *Muhammad: A Biography of the Prophet.* New York: Harper, 2001.

Asad, Talal. *On Suicide Bombing.* New York: Columbia University Press, 2007.

'Askarī, Mortezā. *The Martyr of the Revival of the Faith.* Tehran: Nashre Congereh, 2001.

Augustine. *De civitate Dei.* Edited and translated by P.G. Walsh. Oxford: Oxbow Books, 2005.

Ayoub, Mahmoud M. *The Crisis of Muslim History: Religion and Politics in Early Islam*, Oxford: Oneworld, 2005.

Badawī, 'Abd-ur-Rahmān. *The History of Islamic Theological Speculations* [*Madhāhib al-Ismamiyin*]. Translated by Husayn Sāberī. Mashhad: Āstān-e Quds-e Radawī, 1994.

Baladhurī, Abu-l Abbas Ahmad al-. *Futūh al-Buldān.* Translated to Persian by Azartash Azarnoosh. Tehran: Soroush Press, 1985.

– *The Origin of the Islamic State* [*Kitāb Futūh al-Buldān*]. Translated by Philip Khuri Hitti. Piscataway, NJ: Philip K. Gorgias Press, 2002.

Balkhī, Ahmad Ibn Sahl. *Al-Bad' wa al-Tārikh.* 6 vols. Paris: Leroux, 1899.

Barks, Coleman. *The Essential Rumi.* San Francisco: Harper, 1995.

Barzangī, Muhammad Ibn Rasūl. *Al-Ishā'a li Ishrāt al-Sā'a.* 2nd ed. Damascus: Dar al-Namir 1995.

Batty, John. *The Spirit and Influence of Chivalry.* London: Kegan Paul, 2004.

Baydāwī, Nāsir al-Dīn Abū Said al-. *Anwār al-tanzīl wa asrār al-ta'wīl.* Gesamtherstellung: Proff, n.d.

Bayhaqī, Abū'l Fadl Muhammad Ibn Husayn. *Tārīkh-e Bayhaqī.* 8th ed. Edited by Qasem Ghani and Ali Akbar Fayyād. Tehran: Arghavan, 2002.

Beauchamp, Tom L. *Philosophical Ethics: An Introduction to Moral Philosophy.* New York: Macgraw-Hill, 1982.

Behbahānī, Simin. *A Cup of Sin.* Translated by Farzaneh Milani and Kaveh Safa. Syracuse, NY: Syracuse University Press, 1998.

Behfar, Mehri. *The Shahnameh Ferdowsi: Detailed Interpretation, Definition of Difficult Words and Etymology of Persian Words.* Vol. 1. Tehran: Hirmand, 2001.

Black, Antony. *The History of Islamic Political Thought from the Prophet to the Present*. New York: Rutledge, 2001.

Bostom, Andrew G., ed. *Islamic Holy War and the Fate of Non-Muslims*. Amherst, NY: Prometheus Books, 2005.

Bosworth, Clifford E. *Sīstān under the Arabs: From the Islamic Conquest to the Rise of the Saffārids (30–250/651–864)*. Rome: ISMEO, 1968.

Buber, Martin. *I and Thou*. New York: Scribner, 1958.

Butterworth, Charles. "Al-Fārābī's Statecraft: War and the Well-Ordered Regime." In Johnson and Kelsay, *Cross, Crescent, and Sword*, 79–100. New York: Greenwood Press, 1990.

Chaliand, Gérard, ed. *The Art of War in World History*. Berkeley: University of California Press, 1994.

Chittick, William. *The Imaginal Worlds: Ibn al-'Arabī and the Problem of Religious Diversity*. Albany: State University of New York Press, 1994.

– ed. *The Inner Journey: Views from the Islamic Tradition*. Sandpoint, ID: Morning Light Press, 2007.

Christie, Niall, and Maya Yazigi, eds. *Noble Ideals and Bloody Realities: Warfare in the Middle Ages*. Leiden: Brill, 2006.

Chubin, Shahram, and Charles Tripp. *Iran and Iraq at War*. London: I.B. Tauris, 1988.

Chubineh, Sajjad. *Hekmat-e Nazari va 'Amali dar Shahnameh Ferdowsi* [The practical and theoretical wisdom in Shahnameh Ferdowsi]. Shiraz: Entesharat-e Navid, 1998.

Clausewitz, Karl von. *On War*. Edited by Michael Howard and Peter Paret. Princeton, NJ: Princeton University Press, 1976.

Coates, Anthony. "Culture, the Enemy and the Moral Restraint of War." In Sorabji and Rodin, *Ethics of War*, 208–22.

Coleman, Jules L. and Jeffrie G. Murphy. *Philosophy of Law: An Introduction to Jurisprudence*. Boulder, CO: Westview Press, 1990.

Constable, Giles. "The Historiography of the Crusades." In Laiou and Mottahedeh, *Crusades from the Perspective*, 1–22.

Cook, David. *Martyrdom in Islam*. Cambridge: Cambridge University Press, 2007.

Cook, Michael. *Commanding Right and Forbidding Wrong in Islamic Thought*. Cambridge: Cambridge University Press, 2000.

– "Comments on Garcin." In *Europe and the Rise of Capitalism*, edited by Jean Baechler, John A. Hall, and Michael Mann, 133ff. Oxford: B. Blackwell, 1988.

Corbin, Henry, ed. *Āyīn-e Javānmardī*. Translated by Ehsan Naraqi. Tehran: Nashr-e Ney, 1984.

– "*Futūwatname-ye* Shihabaddīn Suhrawardī." In Corbin, *Āyīn-e Javānmardī*, 40–59.

– Introduction to *Rasāel-e Javānmardān*, 1–109. Edited by Morteza Sarraf. Tehran: French Institute of Persian Studies, 1973.

Cornish, F. Warre. *Chivalry*. New York: Macmillan, 1908.

Coulson, Noel J. *Conflicts and Tension in Islamic Jurisprudence*. Chicago: University of Chicago Press, 1969.

Dabashi, Hamid. *Shi'ism*. Cambridge: Belknap Press of Harvard University Press, 2011.

Damghani, Ahmad Mahdavi. *Hāsel-e owqāt*. Tehran: Sorūsh Press, 1999.

Daneshpazhooh, Manouchehr. *Divān-e Rūdakī* [Poetry collection]. Tehran: Tus, 1984.

Daryaee, Touraj. *Sasanian Persia: The Rise and Fall of an Empire*. London: I.B. Tauris in association with the Iran Heritage Foundation, 2009.

Davidson, Olga M. *Poet and Hero in the Persian Book of Kings*. Ithaca, NY: Cornell University Press, 1994.

Davis, Dick. "Iran and *Aniran*: The Shaping of a Legend." In Amanat and Vejdani, *Iran Facing Others*, 39–51.

Donner, Fred M. "The Sources of Islamic Conception of War." In Kelsay and Johnson, *Just War and Jihād*, 31–71. New York: Greenwood Press, 1991.

Doostkhāh, Jalil. *Avesta: The Oldest Persian Psalms.* 2nd ed. Tehran: Murvarid Publications, 1995.

Edbury, P.W. "Crusades against Christians: Their Origins and Early Development, c. 1000–1216." In Housley, *Crusading and Warfare*, 25–6.

Esfandīārī, Mohammad. *Hamey-e mā barādarīm: sīmay-e ensanī va akhlāqī-e Qurān* [We are all brothers: the humane and moral visage of Islam]. 7th ed. Tehran: Nashr-e Negah-e Moaser, 2015.

Eskandarī, Mohammad Hossein. *Qā'edey-e moqābele be methl dar hoqūq-e beyn al-melal az did-e Islām* [Retaliation rule in international law from Islam's viewpoint]. Qom: Center of Publication, Islamic Seminary of Qom, 1991.

Fadl, Khaled Abou El-. "*Ahkām al-Bughāt*: Irregular Warfare and the Laws of Rebellion Islam." In Johnson and Kelsay, *Cross, Crescent, and Sword*, 149–76.

Fakhry, Majid. *Ethical Theories in Islam*. Leiden: Brill, 1991.

Faqihi, Asghar. *Āl-e Būy-e va Owzā '-e Zamān-e Ishān (The Būyids and the Situations of their Era)*. Tehran: Gilan Publishing, n.d.

– *Shāhanshāhī-e* [The kingdom of] *Adud al-Dawla*. Tehran: Suleiman, 1968.

Fārābī, Abu Nasr Mohammad al-. *On Civil Government*. Translated by Sayid Jafar Sajjadi. Tehran: Anjoman-e Falsafe-ye Iran, 1979.

– *On the Perfect State* (*Mabānī Ārā'i Ahli Madīnat al-Fadila*). Revised ed., translated and commentary by Richard Walzer. Chicago: Great Books of the Islamic World, 1998.

Farāsatkhāh, Maqsoud. *We Iranians: A Historic and Social Contextextualizing of Iranian Ethos*. Tehran: Nash-e Ney, 2015.

Feirahī, Davoud. "Legitimate Defense, Terror, and Martyrdom-Seeking in Shiism." *The Iranian Journal of International Affairs*, 34 (August 2007): 47–64.

– *Power, Knowledge, and Legitimacy in Medieval Islam*. 5th ed. Tehran: Nashr Ney, 2006.

Ferdowsi, Abulqasim. *The Shahnameh*. Edited by Djalal Khaleghi-Motlagh. 4th ed. 8 vols. Tehran: Center for the Great Encyclopedia of Islam, 2012.

– *Shahnameh: A Critical Edition*. Edited by A.E. Bertles, M.N. Othmanof, and O. Smirano. 12 vols. Moscow: Soviet Union Academy of Sciences, 1966.

– *The Shah-Nameh*. Translated by Alexander Roger. London: Chapman and Hall, 1907.

Finnis, John. "The Ethics of War and Peace in the Catholic Natural Law Tradition." In *The Ethics of War and Peace, Religious and Secular Perspectives*, edited by Terry Nardin,15–40. Princeton, NJ: Princeton University Press, 1996.

Firestone, Reuven. "Islam Hijacked." *The Jewish Journal of Greater Los Angeles*, 28 (September 2001).

– *Jihād: The Origin of Holy War in Islam*. New York: Oxford University Press, 1999.

Fouchécour, Charles-Henri de. *Moralia: Les notions morales dans la littérature persan*. Translated [French to Persian] by Mohammad Ali Amirmoezzi. Tehran: Markeze Nashr-e Daneshgahi, 1998.

France, John. "Thinking about Crusader Strategy." In Christie and Yazigi, *Noble Ideals and Bloody Realities*, 75–96.

Frost, J. William. *A History of Christian, Jewish, Buddhist, and Muslim Perspectives on War and Peace*. Vol. 2, *A Century of Wars*. Lewiston, NY: Edwin Mellen Press, 2004.

Gardīzī, Abū Sa'īd. *Tārīkh-e Gardīzī*. Edited by 'Abdulhayy Habībī. Tehran: Donyāy-e Ketab, 1985.

Gass, William. "The Case of the Obliging Stranger." *Philosophical Review* 66 (1957): 193–204.

Gautier, Leon. *Chivalry*. Translated by Henry Frith. London: George Rutledge and Sons, 1891.

George, Artur, and Edmond Warner. *Warriors of the World: The Life and Feats of Rostam*. Edited by Hushang Rahnama. Tehran: Hermes, 2012.

Ghazālī, Abu Hamid al-. *Al-Mustazharī fi Fadā'ih al-Bātiniyya wa Fadā'il al-Mustazhariya*. Leiden: Brill, 1916.

– *Ghazālī's Book of Counsel for Kings*. Translated by F.R.C. Bagley. Persian text edited by Jalāl Humā'i. Bodelian Arabic text edited by H.D. Isaacs. University of Durham Publications 74. London: Oxford University Press, 1964.

– *Ihyā' 'Ulūm al-Dīn, Rub'i Muhlikāt*. Translated by Mo'ayyid al-Din Khwārazmī. Edited by Husayn Khadīv Jam. Tehran: Sherkat-e Entesharat-e Elmi va Farhangi, 1973.

– *On the Boundaries of Theological Tolerance in Islam* (*Faysal al-Tafriqah bayn al-Islam wa'l-Zandaqah*). Translated by Sherman A. Jackson. Abu Hamid Al Ghazālī Studies in Islamic Philosophy. Oxford: Oxford University Press, 2002.

Gibb, H.A.R. "Al-Māwardī's Theory of the Khilāfah." *Islamic Culture* 12 (1937): 291–302.

Goitein, Shlomo D. "The Community." In *A Mediterranean Society*, 287–8. Vol. 2. Berkeley: University of California Press, 1971.

Goodman, Lenn E. *Islamic Humanism*. Oxford: Oxford University Press, 2003.

Gowharīn, Sayyed Sādeq. "Maktab-e Fetyān." In Corbin, *Āyīn-e Javānmardī*, 218–23.

– "The Social Roots of *Fityān* and *'Ayyarān*." In Corbin, *Āyīn-e Javānmardī*, 127–32

Gratian. *The Treatise on Laws, Decretum DD. 1–20*. Translated by Augustine Thompson, OP. Washington, DC: Catholic University of America Press, 1993.

Grotius, Hugo. *The Law of War and Peace: De jure belli ac pacis libri tres*. Translated by Francis W. Kelsey. Oxford: Clarendon Press, 1925.

Hafez, Khawjah Shamseddin Muhammad. *Collected Lyrics of Hafiz of Shiraz*. Translated by Peter Avery. Cambridge: Archetype, 2007.

– *Divan Hafiz*. Edited by Baghaeddin Khorramshahi. Tehran: Negar Books, 2008.

– *The Divan of Hafez*. Edited by Ismail Salami. Tehran: Gooya Art House, 2007.

Haider, Najam. *Shi'i Islam: An Introduction*. Cambridge: Cambridge University Press, 2014.

Hākemī, Esmā'īl. "Āyin-e Futūwat wa 'Ayyārī." In Corbin, *Āyīn-e Javānmardī*, 166–9.

Hallaq, Wael. "Was the Door of *Ijtihād* Ever Closed?" In *Law and Legal Theory in Classical and Medieval Islam*, 3–41. Aldershot: Variorum, 1995.

Hamedānī, Rafī' al-Dīn Ishaq Ibn Muhammad, trans. *Sirat-e Rasūlullah*. Tehran: Nashr-e Markaz, 1985.

Hashmi, Sohail H., "Interpreting the Islamic Ethics of War and Peace." In Nardin, *Ethics of War and Peace*, 146–69.

– "Islamic Ethics in International Society." In *Islamic Political Ethics*, 148–73.

– ed. *Islamic Political Ethics: Civil Society, Pluralism, and Conflict*. Princeton, NJ: Princeton University Press, 2002.

Hashmi, Sohail H., and Steven P. Lee. *Ethics and Weapons of Mass Destruction: Religious and Secular Perspectives*. Cambridge: Cambridge University Press, 2004.

Hay, David J. "Collateral Damage, Civilian Casualties in the Early Ideologies of Chivalry and Crusade." In Christie and Yazigi, *Noble Ideals and Bloody Realities*, 3–25.

Heravī, Javad. *The Samanid History: The Golden Era of Iran after Islam*. Tehran: Amir Kabir, 2001.

Heravī, Muhammad b. Ahmad Mustowfī. *Al-Futūh: A 13th-Century Persian Translation*. Edited by Majid Gholāmreda Tabātabā'ī. Tehran: Sherkate Entesharate Elmi va Farhangi, 2001.

Hodgson, Marshall G.S. *The Venture of Islam: Conscience and History in a World Civilization*. Vol. 2: *The Expansion of Islam in the Middle Period*. Chicago: University of Chicago Press, 1974.

Homer. *The Iliad*. Translated by Robert Fitzgerald. New York: Alfred A. Knopf, 1974.

Hosseini, Sā'ed. *Shahnameh: Shahkar-e Andisheh* [The masterpiece of thought]. Shiraz: Entesharat-e Navid, 1995.

Hourani, George F. *Reason and Tradition in Islamic Ethics*. Cambridge: Cambridge University Press, 1985.

Housley, Norman. "Crusades Against Christians: Their Origins and Early Development, c.1000–1216." In Housley, *Crusading and Warfare*, 17–36.

– ed. *Crusading and Warfare in Medieval and Renaissance Europe*. Aldershot: Ashgate Publishing Limited, 2001.

Hovannisian, Richard G., ed. *Ethics in Islam: Ninth Georgia Levi Della Vida Biennial Conference*. Malibu, CA: Undena, 1985.

Hussaynī al-Zurbātī, Al-Sayyid Hussayn. *Aklāq al-harb fi al-Islam, bayna al-naz ariya wa al-tatbīq*. Qum: Entesharat Dar al-Tafsir, 2002.

Ibn A'tham al-Kūfī. *Al-Futūh*. 3rd ed. Edited by Gholamreza Tabataba'i Majd. Translated to Persian by Mohammad b. Ahmad Mostowfī Heravī. Tehran: Sherkat Entesharat Elmi va Farhangi, 2001.

Ibn Athīr, 'Izzaddīn. *Al-Kāmil fi'l Tārīkh* [Persian]. Translated by Hamidreza Āzhīr. Tehran: Asātīr Publications, 2002.

Ibn Bābawayh. *The Dispositions* [*Al-Khisāl*]. 2 vols. Translated by Ya'qūb Ja'farī. Qum: Nashr Kowthar, 2001.

Ibn Eskandar, 'Unsor al-Ma 'ālī Kaykāvūs. *Qabusnameh: A Mirror for Princes*. Edited by Ghulamhosein Yousefi. Tehran: Sherkarte Entesharat-e Elmi va Farhangi, 2003.

Ibn al-Hassan al-Hurr al-'Āmilī, Muhammad. *Wasā'il al-shī'a ilā tahsīl masā'il al-sharī'a, Kitāb jihād al-nafs*. Translated by Ali Afrāsīyābī. Qom: Entesharat-e Nahavandi, 2001.

Ibn Kathīr. *Tārīkh al-Bidāya wa'l-Nahāya*. Edited by Ismā'il al-Basrī. Beirut: Matba'a al-Sa'āda, 1939.

Ibn Khaldūn, 'Abd al-Rahmān. *Al-Muqaddima*. Edited and translated by Mohammad Vahid Gulpayegani. Tehran: Nashr-e Balkh, 1996.

– *Al-Muqaddima*. Vol. 2. Edited by W.M. de Slane. Translated by F. Rosenthal. Paris, 1858.

Ibn Miskawayh, Ahmad Ibn Mohammad. *Javidan Khirad* [The perennial wisdom]. Translated from Arabic to Persian by Taqi al-Din Mohammad Shushtari. Tehran: Institute for Islamic Studies at McGill University, Tehran branch, 1976.

– *The Refinement of Character* (*Tahdhīb al-akhlāq*). Translated by Constantine K. Zurayk. Chicago: Kazi, 2003.

– *Tahdhib al-akhlaq wa tathir al-a'raq*. Isfahan: Entesharat Mahadavi, n.d.

Ibn Mutahhar Hilli, Hasan Ibn Yusuf. *Tadhkiratu'l fuqaha'*. 15 vols. Qom: Alturath, 1998.

Ibn Quddāmah, Abdullah b. Ahmad. *Al-Mughnī*. 15 vols. Beirut: Dar Ihya al-Turath al-Arabi, 1985.

Ibn Rushd, Abi'l Walid Muhammad. *Bidāyat al-mujtahid wa nahayat al-muqtasid*. Beirut: Dar al-Ma'rifà, 1982.

Ibn Taymīya, Taqī al-Dīn. "Qā'ida Mukhtasara fī Qitāl al-Kuffār." In *Majmū 'at Rasālāt*, edited by M. Hamid al-Fiqqī, vol. 8. Cairo: Al-Sunnat al-Muhammadiya, 1949.

Iskandarī, Mohammad Hoseyn. *Qā'edeye moqābele be methl dar hoqūqe bayn al-melal az did-e Islām* [Retaliation rule in international law from Islam's viewpoint]. Qum: Center of Publication, Islamic Seminary of Qum, 1991.

Izutsu, Toshihiko. *Ethico-Religious Concepts in the Qur'ān*. Montreal: McGill University Press, 1966. Reprint 2002.

Jahanbakhsh, Foroug. *Islam, Democracy and Religious Modernism in Iran, 1953–2000: From Bāzargān to Soroush*. Leiden, Boston, Koln: Brill, 2001.

Jahānbegloo, Rāmin. *Introduction to Nonviolence*. New York: Palgrave Macmillan, 2014.

Johnson, James Turner. "Contemporary Just War." In Reichberg, Syse, and Begby, *Ethics of War*, 660–9.

– "Historical Roots and Sources of the Just War Tradition in Western Culture." In Kelsay and Johnson, *Just War and Jihād*, 3–31.

Johnson, James Turner, and John Kelsay, eds. *Cross, Crescent, and Sword: The Justification and Limitation of War in Western and Islamic Tradition*. New York: Greenwood Press, 1990.

Juwaynī, 'Alā' al-Dīn 'Atā Malek. *Tārīkh-e Jahāngushā*. Edited by Muhammad Qazwini. Leiden: Brill, 1911.

Kadivar, Mohsen. "The Religious Intellectualism." *Āftāb* 82 (August/September 2003): 25–40. Published in English as "Human Rights and Intellectual Islam." In *New Directions in Islamic Thought: Exploring Reform and Muslim Tradition*, edited by Kari Vogt, Lena Larsen, and Christian Moe, 47–74. London: I.B. Tauris, 2009.

– Interview with Daryush Sajjadi on "Islam and Modernity." Section five of the interview. 5 March 2006. http://1384.g00ya.com/columnists/archives/045081.php.

Kant, Immanuel. *Foundations of the Metaphysics of Morals*. Translated by L.W. Beck. Indianapolis: Bobbs-Merrill, 1959.

– "The Good Will and the Categorical Imperative." In Beauchamp, *Philosophical Ethics*, 118–21.

Karaki, Ali Ibn Hossein. *Jāmi' al-maqāsid*. 13 vols. Qom: Ālu'l Bayt, 1998.

Katouzian, Homa. "The Short-Term Society: A Study in the Problems of Long-Term Political and Economic Development in Iran." *Middle Eastern Studies* 40, no. 1

(January 2004): 1–22. Reprinted in *Iran, Politics, History and Literature*, 20–34. New York: Routledge, 2013.

Kelsay, John. "Islam and the Distinction between Combatants and Noncombatants." In Johnson and Kelsay, *Cross, Crescent, and Sword*, 197–220.

Kelsay, John, and James T. Johnson, eds. *Just War and Jihād: Historical and Theoretical Perspectives on War and Peace in Western and Islamic Traditions*. New York: Greenwood Press, 1991.

Kennedy, Hugh. *The Prophet and the Age of the Caliphates*. 5th ed. London: Longman, 1992.

Khadduri, Majid. *War and Peace in the Law of Islam*. Baltimore: Johns Hopkins University Press, 1955.

Khanlari, Parviz N. *Shahr-e Samak*. Tehran: Entesharat-e Agah, 1985.

Kho'ī, Abo'lqāsim al-. *Minhāj al-sālihīn, kitab al-jihad*. 3 vols. Qom: Madinatu'l -'Ilm, 1990.

Khomeini, Seyyed Ruhollah (Imam). *Wilāyat-e faqīh*. Tehran: Entesharat Seyyed Jamal Hedayat, n.d.

Koontz, Theodore J. "Christian Nonviolence: An Interpretation." In Nardin, *Ethics of War and Peace*, 169–97.

Kraemer, Joel L. *Humanism in the Renaissance of Islam: The Cultural Revival During the Būyid Age*. Leiden: Brill, 1986.

– "The *Jihād* of the *Falāsifa*." *Jerusalem Studies in Arabic and Islam* 10 (1987): 288–324.

Laiou, Angeliki E., and Roy Parviz Mottahedeh, eds. *The Crusades from the Perspective of Byzantium and the Muslim World*. Washington, DC: Dumbarton Oaks, 2001.

Lambton, Ann K.S. "Justice in the Medieval Theory of Kingship." *Studia Islamica* 17 (1962): 91–119.

Lapidus, Ira M. *A History of Islamic Societies*. 2nd ed. Cambridge: Cambridge University Press, 2002.

Lau, D.C., and Roger T. Ames, trans. and eds. *Sun Bin: The Art of Warfare; A Translation of the Classic Chinese Work of Philosophy and Strategy*. Albany: State University of New York Press, 2003.

Leaman, Oliver. *A Brief Introduction to Islamic Philosophy*. Cambridge: Polity Press, 1999.

Lee, Robert D. *Religion and Politics in the Middle East*. 2nd ed. Boulder, CO: Westview Press, 2014.

Legenhausen, Muhammad. "Islam and Just War Theory." *Journal of Religious Thought: A Quarterly of Shiraz University* 26 (Spring 2008): 3–34.

Levy, R., ed. *A Mirror for Princes: Qābūs Nāma*. London: Cresset Press, 1951.

Louer, Laurence. *Shiism and Politics in the Middle East*. Translated from French by John King. New York: Columbia University Press, 2012.

Machiavelli, Niccolò. *Art of War.* Translated, edited, and commentary by Christopher Lynch. Chicago: University of Chicago Press, 2003.

MacIntyre, Alasdair. *After Virtue: A Study In Moral Theory.* Notre Dame, IN: University of Notre Dame Press, 1981.

Mahjoub, Mohammad Ja'far. *Āyīn-e Javānmardī* (*Fotowwat*). New York: Bibliotheca Persica Press, 2000.

Majlesī, Mullā Mohammad Bāqir. *Bihār al-Anwār.* Vol. 17. Translated and edited by Abdulhossein Reza'ī. Tehran: Islamiyeh Bookstore, 1984

Makdisi, George. "Ethics in Islamic Traditionalist Doctrine." In Hovannisian, *Ethics in Islam*, 47–63.

Malekīān, Mostafā. "Honar va Sulh [Art and peace]." *Andishe-ye Pouya* 4, no. 29 (2015): 27–9.

Mapel, David R. "Realism and the Ethics of War and Peace." In Nardin, *Ethics of War and Peace*, 54–78.

Martin, Richard C. "The Religious Foundations of War, Peace, and Statecraft in Islam." In Kelsay and Johnson, *Just War and Jihād*, 91–119.

Masud, Muhammad Khalid. "The Scope of Pluralism in the Islamic Moral Tradition." In Hashmi, *Islamic Political Ethics*, 135–48.

Maududi, Abū'l-A'lā. *Jihād fī Sabīl Allāh.* Lahore: Idara Tarjumān al-Qur'ān, 1988.

Māwardī, Abū al-Hasan al-. *Kitāb al-Ahkām al-Sultāniyya*. Edited by M. Enger. Bonn, 1853.

Mayer, Ann Elizabeth. *Islam and Human Rights: Tradition and Politics.* Boulder, CO: Westview Press, 2013.

– "War and Peace in the Islamic Tradition and International Law." In Kelsay and Johnson, *Just War and Jihad*, 195–226.

Mayo, Bernard. "Ethics and the Moral Life." In Beauchamp. *Philosophical Ethics*, 151–4.

McDermott, Martin J. *The Theology of al-Shaikh al-Mufid.* Translated to Persian by Ahmad Aram. Tehran: Tehran University Press, 2004.

McMahan, Jeff. "Realism, Morality and War." In Nardin, *Ethics of War and Peace*, 78–95.

Meisami, Julie Scortt. *Persian Historiography to the End of the Twelfth Century.* Edinburgh: Edinburgh University Press, 1999.

Meybodī, Fazel. "The Essence of War and Peace in Islam [interview]." *Safir-e Hayat*, 2 (June and July 2015): 5–13.

Milani, Farzaneh. *Words, Not Swords: Iranian Women Writers and Freedom of Movement*. Syracuse: Syracuse University Press, 2011.

Mill, John Stuart. "The Contest in America" [1862]. Reprinted in *Dissertations and Discussions*. Vol. 3. London: Green, Reader and Dyre, 1867.

Miller, Richard B. "Divine Justice, Evil, and Tradition: Comparative Reflections." In Nardin, *Ethics of War and Peace*, 265–83.

Minqarī, Nasr Ibn Muzāhim al-. *Waq'at Siffin.* Tehran: Sāzmān-e Entishārāt va Āmūzesh-e Enqelāb-e Islāmī, 1987.

Modarressi, Hossein. *An Introduction to Shī'ī Law: A Bibliographical Study.* London: Ithaca Press, 1984.

Mohaqqeq Dāmād, Mostafā. *Protection of Individuals in Times of Armed Conflict under International and Islamic Laws.* New York: Global Scholarly Publications, 2005.

– *Rowshangari Dīnī* [Religious enlightenment]. 2 vols. Tehran: Entesharat Ettela'at, 2006.

Moshīrī, Fereydoon. *Az Dīyār-e Āshtī* [A breeze from the land of reconciliation]. Tehran: Nashr-e Cheshmeh, 1992.

– *Selected Poems: Luck Those Half-Opened Buds.* Translated by Sara Khalili. Tehran: Sokhan, 2007.

Motahharī, Morteza. "Jihad in the Qur'ān." In Abedi and Legenhausen, *Jihad and Shahādat*, 81–125.

Mottahedeh, Roy, and Ridwān al-Sayyid. "The Idea of Jihād in Islam before the Crusades." In Laiou and Mottahedeh, *Crusades from the Perspective*, 23–9.

Mubārakshāh, Muhammad Ibn Mansūr Ibn Sa'īd. *Ādāb al-Harb wa'l Shujā'a*. Edited by Ahmad Soheily. Tehran: Iqbal, 1965.

Muhaqqiq Hillī, Abu'lqasim Najmeddin Ja'far Ibn Hasan. *Sharāye' al-Islam.* 3rd ed. Tehran: Entesharat Esteqlal, 1982.

Mutahharī, Murtadā. *'Adl-e Elāhī* [God's justice]. Tehran: Sepehr, 1984.

– *An Introduction to Islamic Studies.* Vol. 2, *Theology, Mysticism and Practical Wisdom (ashena'ī bā 'ulūm-e Islamī-kalām, 'irfān, h}ikmat-e 'amalī).* Tehran: Entesharat-e Sadra, 1992.

– "Jihād in the Qur'ān." In Abedi and Legenhausen, *Jihād and Shahādat*, 82–107.

Najafī, Mohammad Hasan. *Jawāhir al-kalām fī sharh-i sharāye 'i al-islam.* 3rd ed. Edited by Sheik Abbas Qouchani. 43 vols. Tehran: Dar al-kutub al-Islamiya, 1943.

Nardin, Terry. "The Comparative Ethics of War and Peace." In *Ethics of War and Peace*, 245–65.

– ed. *The Ethics of War and Peace*. Princeton, NJ: Princeton University Press, 1996.

Nasr, Seyyed Hossein. *Islam: Religion, History and Civilization.* New York: Harper Collins, 2003.

– *Islamic Philosophy from Its Origin to the Present.* New York: State University of New York Press, 2006.

– *Traditional Islam in the Modern World.* n.p.: Kegan Paul International, 1990.

Nasr, Vali Reza. *The Shia Revival: How Conflicts within Islam Will Shape the Future.* New York: Norton, 2007.

Natel-Khanlari, Parviz. "Āyin-e 'Ayyārī." In Corbin, *Āyīn-e Javānmardī*, 169–77.

– *Shahr-e Samak.* Tehran: Agah, 1985.

Navabi, Yahya Mahyar. *Yadegar-e Zariran: The Pahlavi Text with the Persian Translation and Comparison with Shahnameh.* Tehran: Asātir, 1995.

The New American Bible. New York: Catholic Book Publishing Co., 1991.

Nicolle, David. *Medieval Warfare: Source Book, Christian Europe and Its Neighbors*. London: Brockhampton Press, 1998.

– *Medieval Warfare: Source Book, Warfare in Western Christendom.* London: Arms and Armor Press, 1995.

Niebuhr, Gustav. *Beyond Tolerance: Searching for Interfaith Understanding in America*. New York: Viking, 2008.

Nielsen, Kai. "God and the Basis of Morality." *Journal of Religious Ethics* 10 (1982): 335–50.

Ong, Walter J. *Orality and Literacy: The Technology of Word*. 2nd ed. New York: Routledge, 2002.

Orooj, Ahmad Ali. *Al-Qur'ān: A Contemporary Translation.* Princeton, NJ: Princeton University Press, 1993.

Owhadī, Ramzi and Mohammad Reda. *One Thousand and One Stories about Imam 'Ali*. Tehran: Said Novin, 1998.

Paul, Jurgen. *The State and the Military: The Samanid Case*. Papers on Inner Asia 26. Bloomington, IN: Indiana University Press, 1994.

Philpott, D., and G. Powers. *Strategies of Peace: Transforming Conflict in a Violent World.* Oxford: Oxford University Press, 2010.

Pickthall, Marmaduke. *The Meaning of the Glorious Qur'ān*. Tehran: Entesharat Salehi, n.d.

Plato. *Laws*. 16th ed. Edited by Edith Hamilton and Huntington Cairns. Princeton, NJ: Princeton University Press, 1989.

– *The Republic.* Edited and translated by Francis MacDonald Conford. New York: Oxford University Press, 1965.

Pourshariati, Parvaneh. *Decline and the Fall of the Sasanian Empire.* London: I.B. Tauris, 2008.

Procopius. *History of the Wars: The Persian Wars* [Persian]. 4th ed. Edited by Mohammad Sa'idi. Tehran: Sherkat-e Enteshārāt-e Elmī, 2003.

Qara'i, Ali Quli. *The Qur'an with a Phrase-by-Phrase English Translation*. London: ICAS Press, 2004.

Qāshānī, Abd al-Razzāq al-. *Ta'wilāt al-Qur'ān.* Beirut: Dār al-Baydah al-'Arabiyya, 1968.

The Qur'ān. Translated and commentary by Saheeh International. London: Abulqasim Publishing House, 1997.

Radī, Sharīf, ed. *Nhjul-Balāgha*. Potomac, MD: Ahlul-Bayt Assembly of America, 1996.

Raghib, Abī al-Qāsim al-Husayn Ibn Muhammad al-. *Al-Mufradāt fī Gharīb al-Qur'ān*. Tehran: al-Maktab al-Murtazaviyya, n.d.

Rahman, Fazlur. *Islam.* New York: Doubleday, 1968.

– "Law and Ethics in Islam." In Hovannisian, *Ethics in Islam*, 3–16.

Rāwandī, Muhammad Ibn 'Alī Ibn Sulaymān al-. *Rāhat-us-Sudūr wa Āyat-us-Surūr*. Edited by Muhammad Iqbal. Leiden: Brill, 1921.

Rawls, John. *Theory of Justice*. Cambridge, MA: Harvard University Press, 1971.

Rāzī, Abū al-Futūh al-. *Rawh al-Jinān wa Rūh al-Janān*. Vol. 2. Qum: Mar'ashī Library, 1983.

Rāzī, Ahmad Ibn Muḥammad Ibn Ya'qūb Miskawayh al-. *Tahdhīb al-akhlāq wa tathīr al-a'rāq*. Isfahan: Entesharat Mahadavi, n.d.

Rāzī, Fakhr al-Dīn al-. *Mafātīh al-Ghaib*. Vol. 11. Beirut: Dār al-Ihyā' al-Turāth al-'Arabī, n.d.

Reichberg, Gregory, Henrik Syse, and Endre Begby, eds. *The Ethics of War: Classic and Contemporary Readings*. Malden, MA: Blackwell, 2006.

Reinhart, A. Kevin. *Before Revelation: The Boundaries of Muslim Moral Thought*. New York: State University of New York Press, 1995.

Richards, D.S. *The Rare and Excellent History of Saladin*. Aldershot: Ashgate, 2001.

Ridgeon, Lloyd. *Jawanmardi: A Sufi Code of Honor.* Edinburg: Edinburg University Press, 2011.

– *Morals and Mysticism in Persian Sufism: A History of Sufi-futuwwat in Iran.* New York: Routlege Sufi Series, 2010.

Riley-Smith, Jonathan. *History, Crusades, the Latin East, 1095–1204*. Cambridge: Cambridge University Press, 1997.

Roushan, Mohammad, ed. *Tārīkhnāme-ye Tabarī*. Vol. 3. Tehran: Soroush, 2001.

Rousseau, Jean-Jacques. *The Social Contract.* Translated by Maurice Cranston. New York: Penguin Books, 1968.

Rumi, Jalāl al-Dīn Mohammad Balkhī. *Mathnavī-e Ma'navī*. 3rd ed. Edited by Toufiq Sobhani. Tehran: Entesharat-e Rowzaneh, 2003.

– *The Mathnavi, Book One*. Trans. Jawid Mojaddedi. Oxford: Oxford University Press, 2004.

– *Mathnavī-e Ma'navī*. Edited by Abdulkarim Soroush. Tehran: Sherkate Entesharate Elmi va Farhangi, 1998.

– *The Mathnawī of Jalal al-Din Rumi.* Translated, edited, and commentary by Reynold A. Nicholson. Konya, Turkey: Konya Metropolitan Municipality, 2008.

Runciman, Steven. *The History of Crusades*. Translated by Manouchehr Kashef. 3 vols. Tehran: Bongah-e Tarjomeh va Nashr-e Ketab, 1980.

Sachedina, Abdulaziz A. "The Development of Jihād in Islamic Revelation and History." In Johnson and Kelsay, *Cross, Crescent, and Sword*, 35–50.

– *Islamic Messianism: The Idea of the Mahdi in Twelver Shi'ism.* Albany: State University of New York Press, 1981.

Sadeqi, Jafar M., ed. *Tārikh-e Sīstān*. Tehran: Nashr-e Markaz, 1994.

Sa'di, Sheykh Musleh –iddin, *Gulestan and Bustan*. Tehran: Hermes Publishers, 2008.

Salami, Ismā'īl. *The Divan of Hafez.* Tehran: Forouq-e Danesh, 2007.

Sālehī-Najafābādī, Ne'matollāh. *Jahād dar Eslām* [Jihād in Islam]. Tehran: Nashre Ney, 2003.

– *Jihad in Islam.* Trans. Hamid Mavani. Montreal: OAIKHS, 2012.

– *Shahīd-e Jāvīd.* 13th ed. Tehran: Rasa, 1985.

Sane'i, Grand Ayatollah. "Selective Interviews of Ayatollah with Foreign Media." *Safir-e Hayat* (Qom) 2 (June/July 2015): 42–9.

Sapolsky, Robert M. "A Natural History of Peace." *Foreign Affairs* 85, no.1 (January/February 2006): 109.

Saqafī, Seyyed Mohammad. "Invitation to Islam: Through What Means? War or Peace?" *Safir-e Hayat* 2 (June/July 2015): 35–41.

Sarāmī, Qadamali. *Az Rang-e Gol tā Ranj-e Khār.* Tehran: Sherkate Entesharate Elmi va Farhangi, 1990.

Sarraf, Murtreza. *Traités des compagnons-chevaliers.* Tehran: Département d'iranologie de l'Institut franco-iranien de recherche; Paris: Librairie d'Amérique et d'Orient, 1973.

Shabestarī, Mohammad Mojtahed. "Hermeneutics and the Religious Interpretation of the World." Interview by Soroush Dabbagh and Jalal Tavakolian. *Madreseh* 6 (2008).

– *Imān va Āzādī* [Faith and freedom]. 5th ed. Tehran: Tarh-e Now, 2004.

– *Jihad in Islam.* Hanover, Germany: AMSH, 1969.

Shāfī'ī, Abu Abd Allah Muhammad Ibn Idris al-. *Al-Umm.* 2nd ed. Edited by Mohammad Zuhari al-Najjār. 7 vols. Beirut: Dar al-Marifa, 1973.

Shafī'ī-Kadkani, Mohammad-Reza. "Hamāse'ī Shī'ī az Qarn-e Panjom." *Journal of the Faculty of Literature and Human Sciences* (Ferdowsī University Press, Mashhad) 3–4 (Autumn/Winter 2001): 425–95.

Shah-Kazemi, Reza. "Nasr's Universalism vs. Hick's Pluralism." In *The Other in the Light of the One: The Universality of the Quran and Interfaith Dialogue*, 249–66. Cambridge: Islamic Texts Society, 2006.

Shahrūr, Muhammad and Reas Christmann. *The Quran, Morality and Critical Reason.* Leiden: Brill, 2009.

Shambyati, Daryoush. *Glossary of Terms and Phrases in Shahnameh.* Tehran: Aran, 1996.

Shaybānī, Muhammad Ibn al-Hasan al-. *The Islamic Law of Nations: Shaybānī's Siyar*. Translated by Majid Khadduri. Baltimore: Johns Hopkins Press, 1966.

Sherif, Mohammad Ahmad. *Ghazālī's Theory of Virtue*. Albany: State University of New York Press, 1975.

Shikhlī, Said al-. "Guilds and Futūwa." In Corbin, *Āyīn-e Javānmardī*, 211–18.

Shirazi, Seyyed Mohammad. *Aqsāmu 'l-jihad.* Beirut: Mu'assisah al-Mujtaba, 2001.

Shoar, Ja'far and Hasan Anvari. *Razmnāme-ye Rostam va Esfandiyār* (The Epics of Rostam and Esfandiyār). 2nd ed. Tehran: Nashre Qatreh, 2003.

Shriver, Donald W. *Forgiveness in Politics, an Ethic for Enemies*. New York and Oxford: Oxford University Press, 1995.

Sobhani, Jafar. *Doctrines of Shi'i Islam.* Translated and edited by Reza Shah-Kazemi. Qom: Imam Sadeq Institute, 2003.

Soodmandī, Abdolmajid. *War and Peace in Islam: A Critical Review of Shi'i Jurist Perspectives in the Mirror of the Qur'ān and Tradition.* Tehran: Enteshrat Kavir, 2014.

Sorabji, Richard and David Rodin, eds. *The Ethics of War: Shared Problems in Different Traditions.* New York: Ashgate, 2006.

Soroush, Abdolkarim. *Akhlāq-e Khodāyān* [Gods' ethics]. Tehran: Entesharat-e Tarh-e Now, 2001.

– *Farbehtar az Ideology* [More robust than ideology; Persian]. Tehran: Serat, 1996.

– "More Robust Than Ideology [*Farbehtar az ideology*]." *Discourse: An Iranian Quarterly* 2, no.1 (Summer 2000): 81–126.

Tabarī, Abū Ja 'far Muhammad Ibn Jarīr al-. *The History of Al-Tabarī: The Crisis of the 'Abbāsid Caliphate*. Translated by George Saliba. Vol. 35. Albany: State University of New York Press, 1985.

– *The History of Al-Tabarī: The Empire in Transition*. Translated by David Stephan Powers. Albany: State University of New York Press, 1989.

– *The History of Al-Tabarī: Storm and Stress Along the Northern Frontiers of the 'Abāsid Caliphate*. Translated by C.E. Bosworth. Albany: State University of New York Press, 1991.

– *The History of Al-Tabarī: The Zenith of the Marwānid House*. Translated by Martin Hinds. Albany: State University of New York Press, 1990.

– *Jāmi' al-Bayān 'an Ta'wīl āyāt al-Qur'ān*. Cairo: Dār al-Mu'ārif, n.d.

– *Tārīkh al-Umam va'l Mulūk* [Persian]. 2nd ed. Translated by Abu 'Ali Muhammad Ibn Muhammad Ibn Bal'amī. Tehran: Zavvar, 2004.

Tabarsī, Fadl Ibn Hasan al-. *Majma' al-Bayān li 'Ulūm al-Qur'ān*. Vol. 2. Qom: Mar'ashī Library, 1982.

Tabātabā'ī, Mohammad Husayn. *Al-Mīzān: An Exegesis of the Qur'ān.* Translated by Sayyid Saeed Akhtar Rizvi. Vol. 3. Tehran: World Organization for Islamic Services, 1973.

– *Shī'ah: Les entretiens et les correspondances de professeur Henry Corbin avec 'Allāmah Tabātabā'ī* [Persian]. 4th ed. Tehran: Mu'assese Pazhuheshi Hekmat wa Falsafeh Iran, 1984.

– *Shi'ite Islam.* Translated by Seyyed Hossein Nasr. Albany: State University of New York Press, 1975.

– *Tafsīr al-Mīzān* [Persian]. 20 vols. Tehran: Markaze Nashr-e Raja, 1980.

Tafazzolī, Ahmad, trans. *Menog-ī Xrad*. Edited by Jaleh Amoozegar. Tehran: Nashre Tus, 2000.

Richard Tapper, ed., *New Iranian Cinema: Politics, Representation and Identity*. London: I.B. Tauris, 2002.

Tha'ālibī, Abdulmalik. *Tārīkh-e Tha'ālibī: Ghurar Akhbār Mulūk al-Furs wa Siyarihim*. Translated by Mohammad Fazaeli. Tehran: Nashr-e Noqreh, 1990.

Tibi, Bassam. "War and Peace in Islam." In Nardin, *Ethics of War and Peace*, 128–46.

Tor, D. G. *Violent Order: Religious Warfare, Chivalry, and the 'Ayyar Phenomenon in the Medieval Islamic World*. Istanbul: Orient-Institut, 2007.

Toynbee, Arnold J. *Jang va Tamaddon*. Translated by Khosrow Reza'i. Tehran: Entesharat Elmi va Fargangi, 1993. Originally published as *Guerre Civilization: Arnold J. Toynbee's Views on War and Civilization*, edited by Albert V. Fowler. Paris: Gallimard, 1953).

Tūsī, Abū 'Alī Hasan Nasīr al-Dīn al-. *Siyar al-Mulūk*. Edited by Hubert Darek. Tehran: Sherkat-e Enteshārāt-e Elmī, 1999.

– *Akhlāq-e Nāserī*. Edited by Ali Asqar. Tabriz: Dār as-Saltaneh, 1941.

– *The Nasirean Ethics*. Translated from Persian by G.M. Wickens. Liverpool, London, and Prescot: Co. Tinling and Co. Ltd, 1964.

Tūsī, Mohammad Ibn al-Hasan. *Al-mabsūt fī fiqh al-imamīya*. Ed. Seyyed Mohammad Taqi Kashfi. 8 vols. Qom: al-Maktaba al-Murtadiwiyya li Ihya' Athar al-Ja'fariya, 1959.

Tūsī, Muhammad Hassan al-. *Tahdhīb al-ahkām*. 10 vols. Tehran: Dar al-Kutub al-Islamiyya, 1987.

Ury, William L. *The Third Side: Why We Fight and How We Can Stop*. 2nd ed. New York: Penguin Books, 2000.

Vacek, Edward Collins, SJ. "Divine-Command, Natural-Law, and Mutual-Love Ethics." *Theological Studies* 57 (1996): 633–53.

Walzer, Michael. *Interpretation and Social Criticism*. Cambridge, MA: Harvard University Press, 1987.

– *Just and Unjust Wars: A Moral Argument with Historical Illustrations*. New York: Basicbooks, 1977.

Walzer, Richard. *Greek into Arabic: Essays on Islamic Philosophy*. Oxford: B. Cassirer, 1962.

Wāqidī, Muhammad b. 'Umar al-. *Tārikh-e Janghāy-e Payāmbar*. 2nd ed. Translated by Mahmūd Mahdavī Dāmghānī. 3 vols. Tehran: Markaze Nashre Daneshgahi, 1990.

Watt, William Montgomery. *Islamic Philosophy and Theology*. Translated by Abu'lfadl Ezzatī. Annotated by Jafar Shahidī. Tehran: Sherkat Entesharat Elmi, 2001.

Ya'qūb, Ahmad Ibn Abī. *Tārikh-e Ya'qūbī*. Beirut: Dar Sader, 1939.

Zakeri, Muhsen. *Sasanid Soldiers in Early Muslim Society: The Origins of 'Ayyārān and Futūwa*. Weisbaden: Harrasspwitz Verlag, 1995.

Zamakhsharī, Abū al-Qāsim Mahmūd al-. *Al-Kashshāf 'an Haqā'iqi Ghawāmid al-Tanzīl*. Beirut: Dār al-Kutub al- 'Arabī, n.d.

Zanjani, Masoud Roughani. "Based on the Edict of Imam Khomeini, the Headquarter of War Used to Overlook the Government." Interview by Ali Malihi. *Andishey-e Pouya* 4, no. 29 (September 2015): 69–71.

Zarinkoob, Abdolhossein. *Two Centuries of Silence*. 9th ed. Tehran: Entesharat-e Sokhan, 1999.

– "Ahl-e Malāmat wa Fityān." In Corbin, *Āyīn-e Javānmardī*, 196–204.

Zurbāttī, al-Sayyid Hussay Hussaynī al-. *Aklāq al-harb fi al-Islam, bayna'l nazarīyya wa'l tatbīq*. Qom: Entesharat Dar al-Tafsir, 2002.

Zurayk, Constantine K. Translation from Arabic. *The Refinement of Character* (*Tahdhib al-akhlaq*). Chicago: Kazi Publications, 2003.

Index